DISCARDED

THE CRADLE
OF THE EAST

THE CRADLE OF THE EAST

An Inquiry into the Indigenous Origins of Techniques and Ideas of Neolithic and Early Historic China, 5000–1000 B.C.

PING-TI HO

THE CHINESE UNIVERSITY OF HONG KONG
THE UNIVERSITY OF CHICAGO PRESS

The Chinese University Publications Office, Hong Kong
The University of Chicago Press, Chicago 60637
The University of Chicago Press, Ltd., London

© 1975 by The Chinese University of Hong Kong
All rights reserved. Published 1975

No part of this publication may be reproduced, stored in a retrieval system, or transmitted, in any form or by any means, electronic, mechanical, photocopying, recording or otherwise, without the prior permission of The Chinese University of Hong Kong.

Parts of chapter 1 (the section on paleoenvironment) and of chapter 2 have been taken freely from the author's article "The Loess and the Origin of Chinese Agriculture," *American Historical Review*, LXXV, No. 1 (October 1969).

International Standard Book Number: 0-226-34524-6
Library of Congress Catalog Card Number: 73-92407

Printed by Libra Press Limited
56 Wong Chuk Hang Road 5D, Hong Kong

This book is dedicated to
the leaders and scholars whose concern for new frontiers
of knowledge has made the University of Chicago
a very special place

Contents

Foreword, by William H. McNeill		xi
Preface		xvii
I.	Chronology and Paleoenvironment	1
II.	Field Agriculture	43
III.	Animal Husbandry	91
IV.	Pottery	121
V.	Bronze Metallurgy	177
VI.	Numerals, Ordinals, Script, Language	223
VII.	Society, Religion, Thought	269
VIII.	The Birth of China: A Résumé	341
Appendix I.	China and Southeast Asian "Agriculture" and Bronze	371
Appendix II.	The Puzzle of the Chinese Sorghum	380
Appendix III.	A Note on Ancient Chinese Astronomy	385
Appendix IV.	A Further Note on Ancient Chinese Script and Language	393
Appendix V.	The Goat and the Early East-West Trade Route	406
Chinese Characters for Archaeological Sites Mentioned in the Text		409
List of Abbreviations Used in Notes and Bibliography		410
Bibliography		411
Index		435

TABLES

1. Available carbon-14 dates for China's Prehistory — 16
2. Analysis of the pollen of the loess profile of Wu-ch'eng — 28
3. Post-Han records on wild species of rice — 67
4. Animal remains from Yang-shao cultural sites — 93
5. Animal remains from Lungshanoid and Lung-shan sites — 96
6. Animal remains from prehistoric and early historic sites in Inner Mongolia and Kansu — 101
7. Copper deposits near early metallurgical centers — 184
8. Tin deposits near early metallurgical centers — 185
9. Early Chinese numerals — 229
10. Notations for numerals higher than 10 in Shang oracle inscriptions — 234
11. Ancient Chinese ordinals — 237
12. The sexagenary cycle of day-count and the six ten-day sacrificial cycles — 239
13. Hsia rulers with ordinals for ceremonial names — 241
14. A comparison of Sumerian words with Chinese oracle-bone characters — 247
15. Classification of oracle-bone characters according to the six logographic principles — 256
16. A genealogical list of Shang kings — 290

MAPS

1. The distribution of loess in China — 24
2. The spread of bronze in China, circa 1500–221 B.C. — 178
3. Trade routes in the Eurasian steppe — 216
4. The distribution of Yang-shao sites in the Wei River Basin — 270

PLATES

1. Painted pottery bowl from Pan-p'o, Sian, Shensi
2. Painted bowl from Jui-ch'eng, Shansi, with typical Miao-ti-kou I motif
3. Pottery *kuei* water pitcher from Wei-fang, Shantung, showing multimold casting
4. Bronze *chia* wine vessel from Erh-li-kang, Cheng-chou, Honan, showing multimold casting

FIGURES

1. Common shapes of jars of Hassuna – – – 129
2. Common shapes of Yang-shao pottery vessels – 130
3. Typically Sinitic pottery vessels – – – 132
4. Designs of Halafian wares – – – 137
5. Northern Ubaid pottery designs – – – 138
6. Southern Ubaid pottery designs – – 139
7. Jamdat Nasr pottery designs – – – 140
8. Early Iranian pottery designs – – – 142
9. The Pan-p'o human face design and fish design – 154
10. Geometric designs of Pan-p'o – – – 156
11. Evolutionary stages of major Pan-p'o designs – – 161
12. A Miao-ti-kou I basin with five-petal motif – 164
13. Miao-ti-kou I spiral floral patterns – – – 165
14. A Miao-ti-kou I deep bowl – – – 166
15. Counterclockwise spiral designs of Tripolje and Kansu 170
16. Stylistic evolution of the zoomorphic bird of Miao-ti-kou I pottery – – – – 171
17. Stylistic evolution from the zoomorphic bird to the counterclockwise spiral in Ma-chia-yao pottery – 172

18. The Jih-chao Lungshanoid counterclockwise spiral and its influence on Shang decorative art — — 173
19. Painted Tripolje pottery — — — — 173
20. Typical Andronovo decorated jars — — 174
21. Two Yang-shao kiln types of Pan-p'o — — 194
22. Shang and ancient Iranian kilns — — 196
23. Shang bronze vessels and their pottery prototypes — 197
24. Multi-mold for the casting of a four-legged container 202
25. Shang bronze weapons with Seima motifs — — 213
26. Word-signs on Pan-p'o potsherds — — 224
27. A late-Shang bronze vessel bearing the inscription of a compound pictographic character "Black-Bird-Wife," with a symbol of bird on each of its two "ears" — 319
28. An early-Chou grave containing horse chariots — 356
29. The Fei-i monster on Shang wood-carving — — 358
30. Ancient Chinese adaptation of the "hero and beast" motif — — — — — 360
31. A peculiar Shang and ancient Western pottery form — 361
32. Ancient Chinese clan insignias chosen from Shang-Chou bronze inscriptions — — — — 395
33. Pictographic ancient clan insignias chosen from Shang-Chou bronze inscriptions — — — 396

Foreword

FROM TIME to time a field of study, whether scientific or historical, undergoes relatively abrupt transformation. During such critical periods, new organizing principles, new angles of vision, new methods of inquiry come to bear, and rapidly generate new data to fill out details of the emergent intellectual pattern or (to use Thomas Kuhn's term) paradigm. Such fundamental changes come infrequently, for by definition, if the new paradigm is adequate to organize the new data, it is likely to endure so as to channel and direct the thought and sensibilities of subsequent generations indefinitely, until new concepts and data demand some further refinement or correction.

This book belongs among the select company of works that bid fair to achieve a successful reformulation of prevailing understandings in this sort of fundamental way. The author has brought new methods to bear and has synthesized the work of hundreds of others who have been doing the same across the past twenty years. The result is a new, persuasive picture of the origins of Chinese civilization which makes older views obsolete. Future discoveries may modify some details and fill in many others; but it seems unlikely that the basic theses of this book can ever be overthrown, since the evidence on which they rest is logically incontrovertible.

Archaeological study of Chinese origins began only in the 1920s, and the first Westerners who interested themselves in Chinese Neolithic sites were not professional archaeologists. When painted pots turned up from Chinese soil, it was natural to compare them with painted pottery coming from western Asia and the western steppelands; Chinese bronze looked like bronze from the ancient

Near East too; and chariots and horses that appeared at Anyang, the last Shang capital, seemed to confirm connections westward. Moreover, the first students of Chinese archaeology were disposed to view civilization as unitary, and were eager to fit Chinese evidences into the larger picture of human cultural evolution—progressing from stone to bronze and iron ages—which had been elaborated on the basis of Near Eastern and European archaeological studies. Local peculiarities, in other words, seemed less significant than traits shared with the rest of civilized and proto-civilized mankind. The result was to make the beginnings of Chinese civilization appear as one of several peripheral variants of a theme elaborated initially in the ancient Near East, simply because the Chinese shared such basic culture traits as field agriculture, oven-baked pottery, and, at a later stage, bronze metallurgy, with peoples of western Asia.

During the past thirty years or so, a series of remarkably sensitive scientific techniques have been brought to bear on archaeological remains. Dating through measurement of carbon-14 decay rates is the best known of these methods, but by no means the only one. Analysis of pollen grains preserved in peat allows marvelously accurate reconstruction of the floral ecology of past ages, wherever suitable cores, cut from bogs, can be studied. Or again, chemical analysis of trace elements in mineral and metal objects can sometimes show which body of ore or mother lode the substance came from. When enough such assays have been made, it ought, in fact, to become possible to trace ancient dispersion patterns of semiprecious items such as obsidian, tin, and jade from their places of origin with exactitude. Finally, careful statistical analysis of bone fragments and other debris from early archaeological sites can supplement and modify relationships ascribed on the basis of an earlier generation's reliance on sherds of pottery as the only usable or important indicator of cultural affinities.

To be sure, these and other refinements of scientific archaeological analysis have been applied only sporadically to Chinese sites. But enough has been done to alter drastically the picture created by the first students of Chinese origins. Moreover, completely traditional methods of philological scholarship, as applied by a generation of Chinese experts to the inscriptions on the so-called oracle bones, discovered by the thousands at Anyang in this century, have reaped a rich harvest. Many of the Shang royal names, as recorded in Chinese classical literature, have been found on the oracle bones, thus confirming the historicity of later tradition in truly remarkable fashion. In addition, a considerable variety of information about social and religious practices has been teased out of these texts, in large part through ingenious and learned comparison of what the bones have to say with passages scattered through the corpus of Chinese classics.

In the nature of things, archaeological field reports and discussion of the meanings and implications of ancient logography is confusing to a beginner, and engages experts in debate over details which can easily become so intense that they, too, lose any clear sense of the state of knowledge as a whole even within the relatively narrow fields of their specialization. Indeed, during a period when new ideas and new data flood in with great rapidity, as is here the case, old interpretations and synoptic views are bound to break down, and it becomes necessary for some fresh mind to attempt a general reordering of the field.

To this task the author of this book boldly addressed himself. Being master of traditional Chinese learning as well as of the scholarly and scientific learning of the West, he was not deterred by the formidable task of acquainting himself with the technicalities of contemporary archaeology. Indeed, the critically important contributions this book makes to the study of Chinese origins result very largely from the application of new methods and scientific concepts to the data accumulated by recent Chinese archaeological enterprises. For example: the results of recent, chemically precise soil science when applied to the conditions of farming on the loess of ancient China explain very well the practicability of a three-year rotation of sown and fallow for the cultivation of millet as described in some ancient texts. It thus becomes clear how the exceptional geographical and technical conditions of the loess permitted early farmers to establish permanent agriculture without having to move their fields to new sites from time to time as was true for most Near Eastern Neolithic farming. More than that, the exactitude with which the ancient loess cultivators adjusted their practices to local circumstances makes it hard to doubt that domestication of millet and the development of communities dependent on the seeds of that plant for their main food source took place on the Chinese soil independently of agricultural developments elsewhere.

Similarly, careful study of Chinese methods of bronze casting shows that molds were made differently from the way bronze founders of the ancient Near East made theirs. Indeed, the difference between the cire perdue method of western Asia and the ceramic molds of China is so fundamental that, again, it becomes almost impossible to doubt that the invention of bronze metallurgy occurred in China independently from developments in the Near East.

The general thrust of these and other data is to emphasize the autochthony of Chinese skills. The argument seems conclusive: it is hard to imagine what kind of evidence could upset or seriously modify the general conclusion of this work. I am unable to assess the force of parallel arguments based on early occurrences of Chinese numerical terms and usages and on the interpretation of other ancient Chinese writings. But, a priori, it seems entirely credible that intellectual traditions and peculiar forms of the Chinese written language might descend from remote antiquity, inasmuch as, from the time when proto-Chinese farmers developed a self-sufficient, permanent type of cultivation on the loess of the Yellow River valley, they established a society that was superior in wealth, numbers, and stability to any other lying within contact range. Under such circumstances, those enjoying superior skills are unlikely to want to change their ways very fundamentally, and by the time the then fully civilized Chinese did have occasion to encounter peoples influenced by the civilizations of western Asia, that is, about the 13th century B.C., the patterns and style of Sinitic society and culture were so well consolidated that only marginal changes seemed necessary or desirable.

No doubt such a view flatters contemporary Chinese national and cultural consciousness. It also requires Westerners to abandon their older opinion that all mankind followed essentially the same paths to civilization—a view, incidentally, enshrined in Marxian teachings about the universal stages of social development from primitive communism to capitalist exploitation, and beyond. Just how necessary adjustments will be made remains to be seen, whether in China or among Western scholars and ideologists. But the fact that the argument of this book requires men to rethink such basic elements in their view of themselves and of the course of human history is an indication of the seminal importance of *The Cradle of the East*.

WILLIAM H. MCNEILL

Preface

ABOUT THIS book I should like to make a confession and three apologies. I was born two years before the inception in 1919 of the so-called Chinese Renaissance. The intellectual tide unleashed by the Renaissance consisted of two complementary streams, namely, a nearly unqualified admiration for things Western and an almost exuberant iconoclasm toward China's past. The much more sober academic atmosphere of my college years in the mid-1930s was not conducive to systematic rejection of China's cultural heritage, but it certainly did nothing to dampen my unbounded enthusiasm for the West. In fact, prior to the sleepless night of 8 February 1968, when I stumbled on archaeological evidence of the much later beginnings of rice culture in India than in China, I had taken for granted that China must have owed some of her vital cultural elements to the ancient West. Should this book appear to some to smack somewhat of Chinese chauvinism, it can only be accounted for by the fact that for decades I was an unknowing victim of certain forms of Western intellectual chauvinism, of which, as I now look back, the most subtle and effective was the theory of the monogenesis of Old World civilizations. Actually, there is nothing about my specific conclusions on the indigenous origins of each of the major Chinese cultural elements and my overall conclusion of the independent birth of the Chinese civilization that is not based on a faithful analysis of the massive data at my disposal. After making this intellectual confession, I should turn to my apologies.

First, I am not an archaeologist or an anthropologist by training. While trying to keep myself abreast of significant contributions to various periods of Chinese history during the first fifteen of my postdoctoral years, I confined my research largely to the last two dynasties of Ming and Ch'ing. Not until four and a half years ago, when I decided to work on a preliminary synthesis of Chinese history, did I begin to peep into the formidable field of prehistoric archaeology, which, at its current best, employs a variety of scientific disciplines. This field was all the more forbidding to a victim of the world's most bookish tradition, dating all the way back to Confucius, "whose four limbs know no toil, nor can he distinguish the five cereal grains." Although I have had to acquire the minimum of scientific knowledge necessary for a proper understanding of the origins of Chinese civilization, I am still only too aware of my own limitations.

Second, ideally, a study of the origins of Chinese civilization should include a fairly systematic comparison of the Chinese and other major ancient civilizations of the Old World. But I could do little more than make a minimal, and often spotty, comparison of cultural elements of early China with those of the ancient Near East, mainly Mesopotamia. This arbitrary choice seemed justified because the Near East is undoubtedly the cradle of the West; as such, it offers a primary-level comparison with China, which the aggregate evidence of this book establishes as the cradle of the East. In my search for evidence of prehistoric and early historic cultural exchange between China and the West, the two areas which I found no less important than the Near East were southern Siberia and Soviet Central Asia. A language barrier compelled me to rely on the Russian archaeological literature available in English translation, although with help I did manage to examine some comprehensive Russian studies dealing with the pottery and metallurgy of Soviet Asia. Although I will discuss certain aspects of Chinese civilization in the context of Eurasian history, limited time and tools make it inevitable that this book be written almost exclusively from the Chinese point of view.

Third, up to the completion of the first draft of this book in February 1971, not a single radiocarbon dating was available for

China's long prehistory. The total lack of firm chronology for China's prehistory made it necessary for me to plan the book so as to avoid the likelihood of its being made obsolete once comprehensive series of radiocarbon datings should become available. Consequently, much of the book consists of a systematic analysis of the distinctively Sinitic character of the major cultural elements that eventually coalesced in the Shang civilization—an approach which does not have to depend so much on absolute dates. Although from January 1972 onward the Institute of Archaeology of the Academia Sinica in Peking began to release some carbon-14 dates including the vital ones for the Yang-shao culture—the earliest full-fledged Neolithic culture so far discovered in China—it will be many years before a firm, comprehensive chronology for the various phases of China's prehistory is established. Having invested five years in what was originally planned as the prelude to a larger project, I must conclude this study without further delay. It is inevitable that some technical details discussed in the present work will have to be verified and, possibly, rectified by carbon-14 determinations not yet available at the time of my final revision of the manuscript at the end of 1973.

It is not possible for me to mention by name all those to whom I owe thanks. But I should like to express my special gratitude to these colleagues at the University of Chicago: Professor William H. McNeill, for being the first critic of practically all the draft chapters, and for writing a Foreword for the book which assesses its possible significance to perspectives on world history; Professor Robert J. Braidwood, for giving me initial advice and putting me in safe scientific hands; Professors Robert McCormick Adams and Hans J. Nissen, for rectifying some errors on ancient Near Eastern technology and for suggesting pertinent technical literature on Mesopotamia and Iran; Professors A. Leo Oppenheim and Miguel Civil, for enlightening me on the basic nature of the Sumerian and Akkadian scripts; Professor David E. Pingree, for graciously consenting to contribute to Appendix III after confirming my layman's hunch that there was no Babylonian influence in pre-Han astronomy; Professor Fred Eggan, for commenting on the chapter dealing with society, religion, and thought; Professor Harrie Vanderstappen, for helping me in a preliminary comparison of ancient Near Eastern and Chinese ceramic motifs; and Professor Edward Shils, for his sustained interest and encouragement.

To two scientists whom I met through Professor Braidwood I owe an intellectual debt which is difficult for me to repay: Jack R. Harlan, Professor of Plant Genetics and Director of the Crop Evolution Laboratory, the University of Illinois, Urbana, for contributing to Appendixes I and II and especially for putting at my disposal his vast fund of knowledge on paleobotany, agronomy, and primitive agriculture which enabled me to deepen my studies on the origins and characteristics of Chinese agriculture; and Charles A. Reed, Chairman, Department of Anthropology, the University of Illinois, Chicago Circle Campus, for tutoring me on the fundamentals of osteo-archaeology.

I can never thank the following scholars enough for their invaluable help: Dr. Cheng Te-k'un of Cambridge University, whose profound knowledge of Shang pottery was derived from his pre-1937 field studies in An-yang and, after 1949, research in Academia Sinica in Taiwan, contributed an authoritative discussion of the intimate relation between mold-casting in pottery and bronze-casting in Shang times; Dr. Noel Barnard, Department of Far Eastern History, the Australian National University, who allowed me to make generous use of his meticulous studies on ancient Chinese metallurgy, including a number of illustrations; William A. C. H. Dobson, Professor of Chinese, University of Toronto, whose expert philological advice helped me greatly in the section on the nature of the Chinese language; Kwang-chih Chang, Chairman, Department of Anthropology, Yale University, who virtually served as my counselor on Chinese archaeology; and Dr. John E. Pfeiffer, New Hope, Pennsylvania, who criticized the whole manuscript from a science-writer's point of view.

I am indebted to a former Tsing Hua teacher and to many friends from whose varied erudition I sought much that was generously given. They are Professor Kung-ch'üan Hsiao of the University of Washington; Professor Fang-kuei Li of the University of Hawaii, Professor K'un Chang of the University of California, Berkeley; Professor G. William Skinner of Stanford University, Professor Kan Lao of the University of California, Los Angeles; Mrs. Wilma Fairbank, Cambridge, Massachusetts; Professors Francis W. Cleaves, Lien-sheng Yang and Ying-shih Yü of Harvard University; and two leading paleographers of Southeast Asia, Professor Li Hsiao-ting of Nanyang University, Singapore, and Professor Jao Tsung-i of the University of Singapore.

I am also grateful to Professor Lee Yim of The Chinese University of Hong Kong for checking and preparing the archaic Chinese characters of Chapters VI and VII.

This long list of acknowledgments does not, of course, imply that my findings are fully endorsed by all the scholars I have consulted. In fact, my insatiable intellectual curiosity frequently made me reluctant to stay within the disciplinary boundaries which some of my scholarly friends considered to be safe. The present text incorporates some of their constructive criticism, but I must take full responsibility for any remaining errors and shortcomings.

I also wish to thank the Division of the Social Sciences and the Committee on Far Eastern Studies of the University of Chicago for three annual research grants, which facilitated the completion of this study.

Finally, while it is obvious to all members and friends of the University of Chicago that I owe a key phrase in the dedication to my colleague Professor Milton Friedman, I take this occasion to acknowledge my debt to "a very special place."

Chicago
December 1973

I
Chronology and Paleoenvironment

THIS INTRODUCTORY chapter will discuss tentative and absolute chronologies for China's prehistory and early history, and the paleoenvironment of the area in which the earliest Chinese Neolithic culture occurred.

In discussing chronology, let us begin by working backwards from the earliest absolute date in Chinese history. This is 841 B.C., the year in which King Li 厲王 of Western Chou was deposed and a regency was set up in the Chou royal domain under the Lord Kung 共, named Ho 和. There is no question that the Western Chou came to an end in 771 B.C., but the year of the Chou conquest of the Shang has been a subject of endless controversy. It is beyond the scope of this chapter to review all the modern literature pertaining to the dating of the beginning of the Chou period, for much of it is based not on a careful weighing of ancient sources of vastly unequal values but rather on personal preferences and biases.

Of the various dates in question, two merit only our passing mention while a third deserves detailed scrutiny. The so-called orthodox chronology gives 1122 B.C. as the year of the Chou conquest of Shang. This date is derived from computations by Han scholars based on the post-105 B.C. calendar. Ancient chronology reconstructed with the help of a calendar prepared a thousand years later is obviously questionable. Another traditional date—1111 B.C.—was computed by T'ang astronomers on the basis of the new

T'ang calendar of the early eighth century A.D. This calendar, of equally dubious accuracy, achieved some distinction in recent decades because it was endorsed by the late Tung Tso-pin 董作賓 of Academia Sinica, a leading paleographer but not an expert in astronomy. The traditional date that merits our special attention is the one based on the *Chu-shu chi-nien* 竹書紀年 (Bamboo Annals), a work compiled for the ruler of the Wei 魏 state during the early years of the third century B.C. and found in his grave in A.D. 281. According to this ancient work, which deals mainly with chronology, 1027 B.C. is the year in which the Chou conquered the Shang dynasty.

As will be discussed in chapter 7, ancestor worship, which was prehistoric in origin, accounted at least in part for the historical-mindedness of the ancient Chinese. Of the various records kept by the Shang and Chou royal houses, none was more important than the royal genealogical lists. When the *Bamboo Annals* was compiled, the Chou royal house and the ruling houses of other large states still maintained with great veneration the chronicles based mainly on the specific reigns of their past rulers. The Wei was one of the three successor states to the Chin 晉, which had been created at the beginning of the Western Chou period. In a normally rational intellectual atmosphere, there should be no doubt about the accuracy of the Chou chronology as given in this important late-Chou work. In fact, there is even reason to believe in the authenticity of its chronology of the latter half of the Shang dynasty, because early Chou statesmen testified to the existence of documents and archives in Shang times,[1] and the Shang's legal heir in Chou times—the Sung 宋 state—was not annihilated by a powerful eastern state until 286 B.C.

Modern study of ancient Chinese chronology, however, has been complicated by two historical incidents: the large-scale destruction of literary works and documents shortly after the Ch'in 秦

---

[1] Bernhard Karlgren, tr., *The Book of Documents* (Stockholm, 1950), p. 56.

Courtesy of the Palace Museum of Peking.

PLATE 1. Painted pottery bowl from Pan-p'o, Sian, Shensi.

Courtesy of the Palace Museum of Peking.

PLATE 2. Painted bowl from Jui-ch'eng, Shansi, with typical Miao-ti-kou I motif.

PLATE 3. Pottery *kuei* water pitcher from Wei-fang, Shantung, showing multimold casting.

Courtesy of the Palace Museum of Peking.

PLATE 4. Bronze *chia* wine vessel from Erh-li-kang, Cheng-chou, Honan, showing multimold casting.

Courtesy of the Palace Museum of Peking.

unification of China in 221 B.C., and the eventual loss of the authentic text of the *Bamboo Annals* some time during the latter half of the Sung dynasty (A.D. 960–1279). The destruction of many ancient records has wiped out all but one Chou source that corroborates the Chou chronology in the *Bamboo Annals*. Fortunately, passages from the authentic *Bamboo Annals,* as distinguished from those in the text forged during Ming times, had been cited in a number of pre-Sung and early-Sung works, thus enabling modern scholars to collate fragments of the text of the authentic *Bamboo Annals*.[2] The collated fragments show that the year of the Chou conquest was 1027 B.C., and that the year in which the capital city of the Shang was moved to An-yang was 1300 B.C. Significantly, a quotation from the authentic *Bamboo Annals* found in a work of the fifth century A.D. and another quotation in a work of the eleventh century A.D. concur in giving an inclusive total of 257 years for the Western Chou period; so we can rule out the possibility that this vital date is subject to numerical textual error.[3]

The first systematic effort to test the accuracy of the date 1027 B.C. was made in 1931 by the late Lei Hai-tsung 雷海宗 (1902–62), who, after receiving advanced training in European history, had begun a preliminary synthesis of Chinese history.[4] Lei first computed, with necessary minor adjustments, the duration of

---

[2] For this study, I have consistently used the collated text, Fan Hsiang-jung, *Ku-pen Chu-shu-chi-nien chi-chiao ting-pu* [Collated Text of the Authentic *Bamboo Annals* with Textual Criticism and Annotations] (Shanghai, 1956), which is based substantially on earlier collations by Chu Yu-tseng and Wang Kuo-wei.

[3] *Shih-chi* (Taipei reprint of Ch'ing palace ed.), ch. 4, "The Annals of Chou," pp. 26a–26b, the commentary by P'ei Yin, fifth century A.D.; and also *Tzu-chih t'ung-chien wai-chi* [A Chronological History prior to 403 B.C.] (SPTK ed.), ch. 3, pp. 13a and 24b.

[4] Lei Hai-tsung, "Yin-Chou nien-tai k'ao" [A Study of the Shang and Chou Chronology], *Wen-che chi-k'an* [Quarterly Journal of Liberal Arts, Wu-han University], II, No. 1 (1931), pp. 1–14. Unfortunately, this important article was for decades little known even to Chinese and Western scholars who specialized in ancient Chinese chronology.

each generation of ruler or rulers in Chinese history, including the Chou period subsequent to the restoration in 827 B.C. The average was about twenty-five years. To make a rough reconstruction of Western Chou chronology, Lei did not treat as a full generation the first ruler King Wu 武王 because Wu was already advanced in years at the time of the Chou conquest; and he treated as a single generation two brothers who reigned in succession. Using the generational average of twenty-five years and projecting backwards from both the restoration in 827 B.C. and the end of the Chou dynasty in 256 B.C., the beginning of Western Chou falls within the narrow range of 1020 B.C. and 1030 B.C. Lei also found that his projection agreed remarkably well with some generalized statements on Chou chronology given in such authentic late-Chou works as the *Tso-chuan* (Annals of Feudal States) and the *Works of Mencius*.

Lei's most convincing argument in favor of the *Bamboo Annals* date of 1027 B.C. rests on the specific chronological data given in the chapter on the feudal state of Lu 魯 in the *Shih-chi* 史記 (Historical Records), written by the Grand Historian Ssu-ma Ch'ien 司馬遷 during the late second and early first century B.C. In that chapter the specific number of years for each reign is available for all the lords of Lu except for the very first. As is well known to students of Chinese history, Ssu-ma Ch'ien was so cautious about ancient chronology that he did not give specific figures for the reigns of Chou kings prior to 841 B.C. He testified that during his grand tour of Han China (at the age of twenty) he spent some time studying near Confucius' old residence in the capital city of the ancient Lu state, where Confucius' horse-carriage, costumes, ceremonial utensils, and the records of the specific ages of twenty-two of Confucius' disciples were still reverently kept.[5] The *Shih-chi*'s list of Lu lords and the accompanying specific chronological data must, therefore, have been based on ancient Lu records that had survived the Ch'in proscription. And, since the *Bamboo Annals* was

---

[5] *Shih-chi*, ch. 47, p. 29a, and ch. 130, p. 7a.

unknown to Ssu-ma Ch'ien, his Lu chronology is an extremely important independent source, just as valuable as the *Annals* itself, for our reconstruction of ancient Chinese chronology. The *Shih-chi*'s data show that the second lord of Lu began his reign in 998 B.C., a mere twenty-nine years away from 1027 B.C.[6] We learn from some late-Chou works that King Wu reigned but seven years after the conquest and the first lord of Lu was enfeoffed in the first year of the reign of the second Chou ruler, King Ch'eng 成王. If the first lord of Lu is allowed a reign of twenty-two years, the Lu chronology agrees completely with that of the *Bamboo Annals*.[7]

Since the *Bamboo Annals*, the Lu chronology in the *Shih-chi*, and some generalized statements about Chou chronology in the *Tso-chuan* and the *Works of Mencius* are in substantial agreement, 1027 B.C. should certainly be accepted as the absolute date for the year of the Chou conquest.[8] The unreliability of the two traditional dates of 1122 B.C. and 1111 B.C. is best shown by the *Shih-chi*'s Lu chronological data, for it is hardly possible for the first lord of Lu to have reigned for more than 90 or 100 years. That 1027 B.C. has not yet been unanimously accepted by sinologists in China and the Western world is largely because of Tung Tso-pin's endorsement of 1111 B.C. and his negative criticism of the Chou chronology in the *Bamboo Annals*—criticism which merits a brief discussion.

---

[6] *Shih-chi*, ch. 33.

[7] It is here that the leading Swedish sinologist, Bernhard Karlgren, by culling and cross-checking every fragment of information given in various Chou texts about the reigns of early Chou kings and about the first lord of Lu, has made most of the remaining twenty-nine years between 998 B.C. and 1027 B.C. accountable. See his "Some Weapons and Tools of the Yin Dynasty," *BMFEA*, No. 17 (1945), pp. 101–144, esp. pp. 116–120.

[8] It is interesting to observe that prior to 1945 Karlgren had used the traditional date of 1122 B.C. as the beginning of Chou. In his 1945 article mentioned in note 7, his methods of testing the accuracy of 1027 B.C. are almost exactly the same as those used by Lei Hai-tsung fourteen years earlier. Since 1945 the date 1027 B.C. has been fairly widely accepted in the West and is generally regarded as "Karlgren's date." To be fair, this date should be called "Lei Hai-tsung's date."

There is reason to believe that Tung twisted ancient Chinese chronology in more ways than one in order to justify 1111 B.C. as the year for the inception of the Western Chou dynasty. To begin with, although he accepted as "most reliable" the *Bamboo Annals'* inclusive total of 257 years for the Western Chou period, he defined the Western Chou period in an astoundingly arbitrary way. Instead of counting backwards from the fall of the Western Chou in 771 B.C. as scholars generally do, Tung took the deposing of King Li in 841 B.C. as the "end" of this dynastic period. But even this distortion of chronology took him back only to 1098 B.C., still thirteen years short of 1111 B.C. He therefore argued that the *Bamboo Annals'* inclusive total of 257 years should start from the final pacification of the entire Shang world rather than from the initial Chou conquest of the Shang capital area near An-yang in northern Honan, and thus filled the remaining gap quite arbitrarily.[9] There is nothing about Tung's argument for the year 1111 B.C. that is not forced and distorted.

Tung's negative criticism of the *Bamboo Annals'* date of 1027 B.C. is, on the surface, more impressive. The first reason for his rejection of the date 1027 B.C. is a sentence in the long chapter on calendrical matters in the *Hsin T'ang-shu* (New History of the T'ang Dynasty): "According to the *Bamboo Annals,* in the eleventh year [of King Wu's reign], *keng-yin* 庚寅, the Chou launched its war against the Shang."[10] *Keng-yin* is the designation for the 27th day or year in the typically Chinese sexagenary cycle of day-count or year-count.[11] By modern computation 1027 B.C. should be designated *chia-yin* 甲寅, the 51st in this never-ending sexagenary cycle.

[9] Tung Tso-pin, *Yin-li p'u* [A Chronology for the Shang Period] (Academia Sinica, 1945), Part I, ch. 4, and his "Hsi-Chou nien-li p'u" [A Chronology of the Western Chou Dynasty], *BIHP,* XXIII, Part II (July 1952), pp. 681–760, esp. pp. 681–686.

[10] *Hsin T'ang-shu* (Taipei reprint of Ch'ing palace ed.), ch. 27A, p. 19a.

[11] For details of this sexagenary cycle, its origins, and religious and institutional contexts, see ch. 6 below, section on ordinals.

The difference between *keng-yin* and *chia-yin* within a sexagenary cycle of year-count is 24 years, but it could be 84 years if the two year-designations belong to two successive sexagenary cycles. By adding 84 years to 1027 B.C., we get 1111 B.C.—the date of the Chou conquest computed in T'ang times according to the T'ang calendrical system. But the year-designation *keng-yin* that is alleged to have been cited from the *Bamboo Annals* in the long chapter on calendrical systems from ancient times to the T'ang is spurious for an obvious reason. Although the origins of the sexagenary cycle of day-count can be traced back at least to Shang times, the neverending sixty-year cycle of year-count was not adopted until, roughly, the beginning of the Later Han (A.D. 25–220).

Tung's second reason for rejecting 1027 B.C. is that this year does not fit some dated events in the year of the Chou conquest given in the chapter "The Successful Completion of the War" in *The Book of Documents*.[12] Since such events were designated with sexagenary-cycle terms and further related to the waxing and waning of the moon, these dates are therefore of some use for checking the accuracy of traditional chronologies. Tung found that these dated events agree with the calendar for the year 1111 B.C. which he himself had reconstructed.

It should be noted that Tung's reconstruction is based on the calendar system which, starting in the fifth century B.C., was gradually adopted by various feudal states and is very likely to have been more accurate than the early-Chou calendar. For whereas Western Chou bronze inscriptions not infrequently testify to a thirteenth or even a fourteenth month—an indication of the fairly

---

[12] The original text of the chapter entitled "Wu-ch'eng" [The Successful Completion of the War], in *The Book of Documents,* was lost after Han times. The present version of this chapter was a post-Han forgery. Fragments of the original text which contain such dated events are preserved in the chapter on calendrical matters in the *Han-shu* [History of the Former Han Dynasty] (Taipei reprint of the edition with Wang Hsien-ch'ien's syncretic commentaries), ch. 21B, pp. 60a–61a.

chaotic ad hoc nature of the calendrical adjustments necessitated by errors of computation—the calendar system from the fifth century B.C. onward assumed the solar year to consist of $365\frac{1}{4}$ days and the synodic month to consist of 29.530851 days, which is surprisingly close to the modern figure of 29.530388 days. Although much about the early-Chou calendar remains to be investigated, one can be reasonably sure that an early-Chou calendar reconstructed by Tung could hardly be the same as that actually used by the Chou people shortly before and after their conquest of the Shang.

Methodologically, an absolute requisite for reconstructing an early-Chou calendar is a secure knowledge of the exact ways in which early-Chou calendar experts divided lunar months and adjusted such divisions to the waxing and waning of the moon. Although the majority of modern scholars have, by and large, accepted the theory of the late Wang Kuo-wei 王國維 (1878–1927) that in early-Chou times the lunar month was divided into four quarters, almost everyone working on ancient Chinese chronology has his own reservations and makes his own minor revisions of Wang's theory. According to Wang, *ch'u-chi* 初吉 ("felicitous beginning") should stand for the first 7 or 8 days of the month; *chi-sheng-pa* 既生霸 ("after the birth of the crescent") for the quarter from the 8th or 9th to the 14th or 15th; *chi-wang* 既望 ("after full moon") for the quarter from the 15th or 16th to the 22nd or 23rd; and *chi-ssu-pa* 既死霸 ("after the death of the crescent") for the quarter from the 23rd or 24th to the end of the month. Since it includes 29 or 30 days, no lunar month can be exactly divided by 4 without leaving a residue of one or two days. This provides an ample margin for a modern student to manipulate to suit his preferred long-range chronological reconstruction. As the paleographer Huang Sheng-chang 黃盛璋 has demonstrated with solid evidence from Chou bronze inscriptions and literary records, what Wang and his followers believed to be the first lunar quarter of seven or eight days actually included the first ten days of the month—a proven fact about the early-Chou calendar that challenges the very foundation of Wang's theory.[13]

Unlike the majority of modern scholars, who have more or less accepted Wang's theory, Tung worked out his own "fixed points theory." According to Tung, the first and fourth terms should stand for the first day of the month only, the second for the 15th day only, and the third for the 16th, 17th, and 18th days only. Critical reviews of this theory by Huang Sheng-chang and Yabuuchi Kiyoshi 籔內清, the well-known Japanese historian of Far Eastern sciences, have proved beyond doubt that these strikingly different definitions are actually based on Tung's purposefully distorted interpretation of some key passages in Chou bronze inscriptions.[14]

It is now clear that, in spite of more than half a century of studies by Chinese and Japanese scholars of the early-Chou calendrical system, even the definitions of certain basic early-Chou calendrical terms remain uncertain. It is no exaggeration to say that the accumulated fund of knowledge is too meager to enable anyone to reconstruct a calendar for the year of the Chou conquest; and

[13] For Wang's four quarters theory, see Wang Kuo-wei, *Kuan-t'ang chi-lin* [Selected Works of Wang Kuo-wei] (Taipei reprint), ch. 1, pp. 1a–5b. By far the most effective criticism of Wang's theory is Huang Sheng-chang, "Shih ch'u-chi" [An Interpretation of "Ch'u-chi," as a Method of Calculating Dates], *Li-shih yen-chiu* [Historical Research], 1958, No. 4, pp. 71–86.

[14] Tung's theory is expounded in his "Ssu-fen-i-yüeh-shuo pien-cheng" [A Refutation of the Theory of Quadruple Division of the Lunar Month], *Hua-hsi-Hsieh-ho-ta-hsüeh wen-shih-yen-chiu-so chi-k'an* [Bulletin of the Institute of Chinese Studies of the Western China Union University], II (1941), pp. 1–23, and also in his "Chou chin-wen chung sheng-pa ssu-pa k'ao" [A Study of Sheng-pa and Ssu-pa in the Light of Chou Bronze Inscriptions], in *Fu-ku-hsiao-chang Ssu-nien hsien-sheng chi-nien lun-wen-chi* [Essays Commemorating the Late President Fu Ssu-nien] (Taiwan University, 1952), pp. 139–152. The most telling blow to Tung's theory is dealt by Huang Sheng-chang, "Shih Ch'u-chi" (see n. 13 above), esp. p. 83, and Yabuuchi Kiyoshi, "Kuan-yü Yin-li ti liang-san-ke wen-t'i" [Some Problems Concerning the Shang Calendar], Chinese translation, in *Hsien-Ch'in-shih yen-chiu lun-chi* [Collection of Studies on pre-221 B.C. Chinese History] (*Ta-lu tsa-chih*, Taipei, 1960), I, pp. 131–137, esp. p. 136.

that the few dated events belonging to that year as given in *The Book of Documents* cannot be used. All in all, therefore, there is not a single valid argument against the accuracy of the Chou chronology given in the *Bamboo Annals*.[15] Had the text of the authentic *Bamboo*

[15] Chou Fa-kao, "Certain Dates of the Shang Period," *Harvard Journal of Asiatic Studies,* XXIII (1960–61), first tried to reconcile the *Bamboo Annals* and those few dated events in *The Book of Documents* by suggesting the year 1018 B.C. as the one for the Chou conquest of Shang. This view has been amplified in his recent article, "Chronology of the Western Chou Dynasty," *Hsiang-kang Chung-wen-ta-hsüeh Chung-kuo-wen-hua-yen-chiu-so hsüeh-pao* [Journal of the Institute of Chinese Studies of The Chinese University of Hong Kong], IV, No. 1 (1971), pp. 173–205.

Chou's view does not seem tenable for two reasons. First, the calendar for the year of the Chou conquest which Chou Fa-kao used is the one reconstructed by Tung Tso-pin. Since those dated events, with their sexagenary-cycle designations and with their association with the waxing and waning of the moon, recur every thirty-one years, by using Tung's calendar and by moving Tung's year of 1111 B.C. 93 years downwards, Chou arrived at 1018 B.C. Unlike the highly arbitrary and dogmatic ways in which Tung dealt with early-Chou chronology, Chou is remarkable for his intellectual candor. He says in his latter article, p. 180: "We may raise the question: Is the calendar reconstructed just the same as that of the Western Chou people? Of course not." If "of course not," then Chou's attempt proves nothing. For to have an accurate identification of the few dated events belonging to the year of the Chou conquest, pin-point precision is needed, starting with a calendar reconstructed entirely in accordance with actual early-Chou calendrical practices. As has been discussed in the text, the absolute prerequisites for reconstructing an early-Chou calendar simply do not exist. In fact, because of our complete ignorance of the many likely ad hoc adjustments in the early-Chou calendar, we are not certain whether those dated events in *The Book of Documents* can (or cannot) be fitted into the year 1027 B.C.; nor are we even sure whether the surviving fragments of those dated events are textually beyond reproach in the first place.

Second, in trying to reconcile the *Bamboo Annals* and the dated events in *The Book of Documents,* Chou relies entirely on the vaguest of the three references to the inclusive total of Western Chou chronology. The version Chou Fa-kao relies on is the one paraphrased by Liu Shu in the eleventh century A.D.: "From King Wu to King Yu there were 257 years." But even here Chou Fa-kao has to force his argument by suggesting that "King Wu" should count from his accession to the Chou throne a few years before he launched the war against the Shang. As is well known, the chronology of pre-conquest Chou cannot be lumped together with the post-conquest period to form the Western Chou dynasty. Chou Fa-kao's interpretation can hardly be reconciled with another comment by Liu Shu: "The Western Chou [lasted] 257 years." It certainly clashes head on with by far the earliest and most

Annals not been lost, there would have been probably very little ado about the inception of the Western Chou. The textual problem which involves the vital date of 1027 B.C. should now be regarded as having been solved. In my opinion, the year 1027 B.C. should be accepted as an absolute date.

We will now turn to the chronology of the first verified historical dynasty of Shang. The *Bamboo Annals* contains two broad chronological statements about the Shang dynasty—its total time span of 496 years and an inclusive total of 273 years from the moving of its capital to An-yang to its final downfall. The figure of 273 years for the entire An-yang or late-Shang period has been unanimously accepted by all modern scholars and was used even by the late Tung Tso-pin as the very foundation for his reconstruction of Shang chronology. Using 1111 B.C. as the datum, Tung fixed the beginning of the An-yang period at 1384 B.C., whereas if one takes 1027 B.C. as the date of the Chou conquest, one arrives at 1300 B.C. Since the Shang capital city was never moved after 1300 B.C., and since the Shang chronology handed down to the Chou and kept by Shang's successor state, the Sung, was almost certainly based on Shang documents and genealogical lists, 1300 B.C. may also be considered an absolute date.

We are less sure about the accuracy of the *Bamboo Annals'* figure of 496 years for the entire Shang dynasty. According to various Chou works, the Shang capital had been moved several times before An-yang was chosen as the permanent capital. Frequent

---

specific citation from the *Bamboo Annals* by P'ei Yin of the fifth century A.D., the famous commentator of the *Shih-chi*: "The *Bamboo Annals* says: 'From the annihilation of the Yin [Shang] by King Wu to [the end of] King Yu, there were altogether 257 years.'" (Cf. note 3 above for precise references.)

Chou's persistent and sincere effort to reconcile the *Bamboo Annals* and the dated events in *The Book of Documents* is methodologically instructive in that he understood only too well that, insofar as the dating of the Chou conquest is concerned, no version can hope to receive wide acceptance by the learned world if it conflicts with the *Bamboo Annals*.

moving of the capital might have resulted in serious losses of government documents. Whereas the *Bamboo Annals'* date of the Chou conquest tallies remarkably well with the generalized chronological statements in the *Tso-chuan* and the *Works of Mencius*, the *Annals'* total of 496 years for the Shang dynasty as a whole falls about a century short of those of the *Works of Mencius*. The unearthing and publishing of tens of thousands of oracle-bone inscriptions of the post-1300 B.C. period enables us to make a further check on the *Bamboo Annals'* aggregate Shang figure. In the 273 years of the An-yang period there were twelve kings belonging to eight genealogical generations, giving an average of 34 years each generation. If we accept the *Bamboo Annals'* figure, we would have to crowd into the remaining 223 years nineteen kings belonging to nine generations of the pre-An-yang period, thus averaging only 25 years for each genealogical generation. This is not impossible, but it is very unlikely because the much higher incidence of lateral succession in the pre-1300 B.C. period would suggest a longer average generation.[16] A conservative guess would put the beginning of the Shang dynasty somewhere before 1600 B.C. On the other hand, one can never rule out the inception of the Shang dynasty at 1523 B.C., as the *Bamboo Annals* states. A total of 471 years is given by the same work for the Hsia "dynasty," but this is yet to be archaeologically identified and must be accepted as tentative.

China definitely entered the bronze age during the Shang dynasty. The preceding millennia should, for the time being, be regarded as prehistoric and Neolithic but protoliterate, although evidence of primitive copper metallurgy has been found in a late prehistoric culture of the Kansu area. Before discussing the chronologies of China's prehistoric cultures in the light of recent carbon-14 datings, it is necessary to review the sequence in which various Neolithic cultures took place.

The first well-defined Neolithic culture in China is the Yang-

---

[16] See ch. 7, Table 16.

shao, named after the village in western Honan where, in 1921, the Swedish geologist J. G. Andersson discovered painted pottery and other Neolithic artifacts. In 1928, at the village of Ch'eng-tzu-yai near the capital city Chi-nan, in Shantung province, the Institute of History and Philology of Academia Sinica discovered another Neolithic culture, characterized by black pottery and oracle-bones, which was named after the nearest township of Lung-shan. Although Yang-shao, Lung-shan, and Shang dynasty cultural remains were subsequently found in temporal succession in several northern Honan sites, the time span separating these two Neolithic cultures and their interrelations remained matters of conjecture and debate throughout the 1930s and 1940s. The relative chronologies suggested and revised by Andersson were probably the only ones widely known in the West until 1949, but they were little more than educated—and sometimes self-contradictory—guesswork. Only with the discovery in the 1950s of a number of important local and regional Neolithic cultures throughout China were archaeologists able to reclassify China's major Neolithic cultures with more systematic data. It is now reasonably clear that the newly discovered Neolithic cultures, such as the Miao-ti-kou II culture of western Honan, eastern Shensi, and southern Shansi, the Ta-wen-k'ou culture of Shantung, the Ch'ing-lien-kang culture of the Huai River and the Lower Yangtze region, and the Ch'ü-chia-ling culture of the lower Han River area in Hupei, represent a period of cultural transition from the Yang-shao to the Lung-shan stage.

Using the method of developmental classification, an archaeologist-anthropologist from Yale University, Kwang-chih Chang, has given these newly discovered local and regional Neolithic cultures the generic name of Lungshanoid.

Largely speaking, these phases [that is, the newly discovered Miao-ti-kou II culture, and so forth] are all characterized by painted pottery but differ substantially from the Yang-shao, and the features on which they differ from the Yang-shao are similar to those of the Lung-shan. In time they were without exception demonstrably earlier than the Lung-shan cultures wherever they occurred with these cultures, but at the same time they were later than the Yang-shao within the area in which the latter occurred.[17]

Up to the end of 1971 the only relatively firm date with which to estimate the chronologies of China's major Neolithic cultures was the one concerning the so-called Taiwan Lungshanoid culture discovered at Feng-pi-tou near the southwestern corner of Taiwan by a Yale University expedition in 1964–65. The sites at Feng-pi-tou generally consist of four cultural layers. The lowest is characterized by cord-marked pottery, and the one immediately above it by red fine and sandy pottery. For these two lower layers no shells or carbon-14 dates are available. The upper two layers, which yield many shells and some carbonized materials, give a series of carbon-14 dates ranging from 1400 B.C. to 400 B.C.[18] Based on carbon-14 data of upper layers and other materials of the lower layers, K. C. Chang suggests that this Taiwan Lungshanoid culture "began here around 2500 B.C. at the latest."[19]

After the Institute of Archaeology of Academia Sinica in Peking had resumed, at the beginning of 1972, the publication of its official organ, *K'ao-ku* (Archaeology), the scholarly world belatedly learned that the institute had already carried out its first series of radiocarbon age determinations in 1965–66 and that the announcement of the results had been delayed by the Cultural Revolution. Up to the fall of 1973, thirty-one radiocarbon dates have been made available, of which the twenty-one given in Table 1 deal with China's prehistory.

Radiocarbon dates are calculated on the assumption that the

[17] Kwang-chih Chang, *The Archaeology of Ancient China* (New Haven, Conn., 1968), p. 132.

[18] K. C. Chang and Minze Stuiver, "Recent Advances in the Prehistoric Archaeology of Formosa," *Proceedings of the National Academy of Sciences,* LV (March 1966); K. C. Chang, "The Yale Expedition to Taiwan and the Southeast Asian Horticultural Evolution," *Discovery,* I (Spring 1967); and K. C. Chang, *Fengpitou, Tapenkeng, and the Prehistory of Taiwan* (New Haven, Conn., 1969), pp. 50–51.

[19] Chang, *Fengpitou, Tapenkeng, and the Prehistory of Taiwan,* p. 53.

radiocarbon content of the atmospheric carbon dioxide has remained constant during Pleistocene and recent times. Since 1958, however, it has been proved that this assumption is not completely valid. Various attempts have been made to check radiocarbon dating against other dating methods and to investigate the reasons for discrepancies in the results. One of the recently developed and widely used methods is the one based on a comparison of the radiocarbon dates of very ancient bristlecone pines against the calendar years determined by the growth rings of the same wood samples. "The results of this comparison," as two scientists summarize it, "show an increasing unilateral divergence of precisely dated woods and their radiocarbon dates, beginning with about 800 B.C. and continuing to the present limit of dated tree-ring samples (5150 B.C.)." They suggest that radiocarbon dates (when calculated with the 5,730 year half-life) may be corrected according to the following scale:[20]

Time period represented by radiocarbon dates	Average deviation of radiocarbon dates (+=younger, −=older)	Time period represented by radiocarbon dates	Average deviation of radiocarbon dates (+=younger, −=older)
A.D. 1525–2000	+ 50	1699–1325 B.C.	+250
A.D. 925–1524	0	2099–1700 B.C.	+350
A.D. 450–974	− 50	2499–2100 B.C.	+450
A.D. 1–449	− 50	2949–2500 B.C.	+550
449– 1 B.C.	+ 50	3999–2950 B.C.	+600
924– 450 B.C.	+ 50	4499–4000 B.C.	+750
1324– 925 B.C.	+100		

[20] The quotation and the scale by which radiocarbon dates are converted to bristlecone-pine dates are taken from *Radiocarbon Variations and Absolute Chronology: Proceedings of the Twelfth Nobel Symposium held at the Institute of Physics at Uppsala University*, edited by Ingrid U. Olsson (Stockholm and New York, 1970), pp. 109–111.

Table 1 presents both the available Peking radiocarbon dates and the "corrected" dates based on latest scientific findings. It should be pointed out, however, that all Chinese B.P. dates are reckoned as from 1965, whereas according to international practice B.P. dates are normally reckoned as from 1950.

TABLE 1

AVAILABLE CARBON-14 DATES FOR CHINA'S PREHISTORY

Site	Culture	Carbon-14 Dates (half-life: 5,730 years)	Bristlecone-Pine Dates
1. Huang-shan-hsi 黃鱔溪, Tzu-yang 資陽, Szechwan	not clear	5535±130 B.C.	?
2. Pan-p'o 半坡, Sian 西安, Shensi	Yang-shao 仰韶	4115±110 B.C.	4865±110 B.C.
3. Ta-tun-tzu 大墩子, P'ei-hsien 邳縣, Kiangsu	Ch'ing-lien-kang 青蓮崗	3835±105 B.C.	4435±105 B.C.
4. Pan-p'o	Yang-shao	3955±105 B.C.	4555±105 B.C.
5. Pan-p'o	Yang-shao	3890±105 B.C.	4490±105 B.C.
6. Pan-p'o	Yang-shao	3635±105 B.C.	4235±105 B.C.
7. Hou-kang 后崗, An-yang 安陽, Honan	Yang-shao	3535±105 B.C.	4135±105 B.C.
8. Sung-tse 崧澤, Ch'ing-p'u 青浦, Shanghai	Ch'ing-lien-kang	3395±105 B.C.	3995±105 B.C.
9. Miao-ti-kou 廟底溝, Shan-hsien 陝縣, Honan	Yang-shao	3280±100 B.C.	3880±100 B.C.
10. Ch'ien-shan-yang 錢山漾 Wu-hsing 吳興, Chekiang	Liang-chu 良渚	2750±100 B.C.	3300±100 B.C.

TABLE 1 *(continued)*

	Site	Culture	Carbon-14 Dates (half-life: 5,730 years)	Bristlecone-Pine Dates
11.	Ts'ao-chia-tsui 曹家嘴, Lan-chou 蘭州, Kansu	Ma-chia-yao 馬家窯	2575±100 B.C.	3125±100 B.C.
12.	P'ao-ma-ling 跑馬嶺, Hsiu-shui 修水, Kiangsi	Neolithic	2335±95 B.C.	2785±95 B.C.
13.	Miao-ti-kou	Lungshanoid	2310±95 B.C.	2760±95 B.C.
14.	Huang-lien-shu 黃楝樹, Hsi-ch'uan 淅川, Honan	Ch'ü-chia-ling 屈家嶺	2270±95 B.C.	2720±95 B.C.
15.	Ma-chia-wan-ts'un 馬家灣村, Yung-ching 永靖, Kansu	Ma-chia-yao	2185±100 B.C.	2635±100 B.C.
16.	Ch'ing-kang-ch'a 青崗岔, Lan-chou, Kansu	Pan-shan 半山	2065±100 B.C.	2415±100 B.C.
17.	Shuang-t'o-tzu 雙砣子, Lü-ta 旅大, Liaoning	Lung-shan 龍山	2060±95 B.C.	2410±95 B.C.
18.	Wang-wan 王灣, Lo-yang 洛陽, Honan	Honan Lung-shan 河南龍山	2000±95 B.C.	2350±95 B.C.
19.	T'a-li-t'a-li-ha 搭里他里哈, No-mu-hung 諾木洪, Chinghai	not clear	1825±90 B.C.	2175±90 B.C.
20.	Ta-ho-chuang 大何莊, Yung-ching, Kansu	Ch'i-chia 齊家	1725±95 B.C.	2075±95 B.C.
21.	Ta-ho-chuang	Ch'i-chia	1695±95 B.C.	1945±95 B.C.

SOURCES: The Laboratory of the Institute of Archaeology, "Fang-she-hsing-t'an-su-ts'e-ting nien-tai pao-kao (I)," [Report on Radiocarbon-Determined Dates (I)], *KK*, 1972, No. 1, pp. 52–56; and "Fang-she-hsing-t'an-su-ts'e-ting nien-tai pao-kao (II)," *KK*, 1972, No. 5, pp. 56–58; the third date for the lowest cultural stratum of the Ta-tun-tzu site in P'ei-hsien, Kiangsu, is mentioned in Wu Shan-ching, "Lüeh-lun Ch'ing-lien-kang-wen-hua" [A Brief Discussion of the Ch'ing-lien-kang Culture], *WW*, 1973, No. 6, p. 57.

While a systematic chronology for China's prehistory must await more comprehensive radiocarbon age determinations from Peking, the available data already yield solid information for a fresh review of the chronology and main phases of the Yang-shao culture—the first full-fledged Neolithic culture in China—and for a better understanding of the sequence in which some major regional Lungshanoid cultures emerged.

By far the most comprehensive series of radiocarbon dates is that related to the Pan-p'o phase of the Yang-shao culture. The Pan-p'o phase is of utmost importance for an understanding of the beginnings of Chinese civilization because it is the earliest known phase of field agriculture based largely on millet, animal domestication centered mainly on pigs, settled village communities with well-patterned graveyards, painted pottery, and the archetypal Chinese script and numerals. A series of four radiocarbon dates together with our converted bristlecone-pine dates show that this site was almost continuously occupied for six hundred years during the fifth millennium B.C. As will be discussed in chapter 6 and Appendix IV, the archaic clan insignias and the numerals on Pan-p'o potsherds certainly represent the first serious attempt by man to create a system of writing.

The emergence of the mature Pan-p'o phase, however, cannot be equated with the birth of the Yang-shao culture. As will be explained toward the end of this chapter, the earliest known phase of the Yang-shao culture is that exemplified by the Li-chia-ts'un 李家村 site in Hsi-hsiang 西鄉 county in Shensi, barely south of the natural demarcation of the Ch'in-ling 秦嶺 Mountains. Although no remains of grains have so far been found in this and similar cultural sites north of the Ch'in-ling, the presence of cord-marked pottery and especially of stone spades and millstones would indicate some form of sedentary life and protoagriculture. It is reasonably safe to assume that the Li-chia-ts'un phase of Yang-shao culture must have emerged some time during the sixth millennium B.C.

Culturally almost vying with Pan-p'o in importance is the type of Yang-shao culture represented by the Miao-ti-kou site in western Honan. This type, characterized chiefly by the unique floral motif spirals on its painted pottery, was geographically distributed over westernmost Honan, southern Shansi, and the lower Wei River valley east of Sian. The temporal and historical relation between the Pan-p'o and the Miao-ti-kou types has been a subject of considerable debate since the late 1950s.[21] Only when radiocarbon dates became available did we find that the Miao-ti-kou type emerged considerably later. In fact, it appeared slightly later, even, than the Hou-kang type, which reveals strong Pan-p'o influence but also distinct local characteristics.[22] Recent studies also show that the Pan-p'o type spread more widely than the Miao-ti-kou type. Although the Yang-shao cultures discovered in northern Honan and in southern and western Hopei had local characteristics, they showed unmistakable Pan-p'o influence.[23]

---

[21] At the Hsia-meng-ts'un 下孟村 site in Pin-hsien 邠縣, Shensi, the Pan-p'o cultural stratum was stratigraphically below the Miao-ti-kou layer, but the reverse was the case at the Hsi-wang-ts'un 西王村 site in Jui-ch'eng 芮城 county at the extreme southwestern corner of Shansi. See "Shan-hsi Pin-hsien Hsia-meng-ts'un Yang-shao-wen-hua i-chih hsü-chüeh chien-pao" [A Brief Report on Renewed Excavations at the Yang-shao Cultural Site of Hsia-meng-ts'un, Pin-hsien, Shensi], *KK*, 1962, No. 6, pp. 292–295; and "Shan-hsi-sheng shih-nien-lai ti wen-wu k'ao-ku hsin-shou-huo" [New Cultural and Archaeological Finds of Shansi Province during the Past Ten Years], *WW*, 1972, No. 4, pp. 1–4. These cases can now be regarded as intrusive situations. See also An Chih-min, "Lüeh-lun wo-kuo hsin-shih-ch'i-shih-tai wen-hua ti nien-tai wen-t'i" [A Brief Discussion of the Chronology of Chinese Neolithic Cultures], *KK*, 1972, No. 6, pp. 35–44.

[22] "1972 nien ch'un An-yang Hou-kang fa-chüeh chien-pao" [A Brief Report on Excavations at Hou-kang, An-yang, in the Spring of 1972], *KK*, 1972, No. 5, esp. p. 18.

[23] "1971 nien An-yang Hou-kang fa-chüeh chien-pao" [A Brief Report on Excavations at Hou-kang, An-yang, in 1971], *KK*, 1972, No. 3, esp. p. 17. An Chih-min, "Kuan-yü wo-kuo jo-kan yüan-shih-wen-hua nien-tai ti t'ao-lun" [A Discussion on the Chronologies of Certain Primitive Cultures in China], *KK*, 1972, No. 1, pp. 57–59.

As to the various regional "Lungshanoid" cultures that appeared later than the Yang-shao, recent radiocarbon dating shows that they were chronologically disparate rather than roughly contemporaneous. Long before the Yang-shao culture had run its course, the Ch'ing-lien-kang culture had already emerged in eastern China. On the basis of published reports as well as new data not yet released by the Nanking Museum, Wu Shan-ching 吳山菁 (the last of the three sources for table 1) has arrived at the following generalizations about the Ch'ing-lien-kang culture. First, of some four scores of Ch'ing-lien-kang cultural sites so far discovered, sixty-five are within the boundaries of Kiangsu province. From Kiangsu this culture spread westward to parts of Anhwei, northward to southern and central Shantung, and southward to northern Chekiang, where it later merged with the Liang-chu culture. The total area within the orbit of the Ch'ing-lien-kang culture is 100,000 square kilometers. Second, the Ch'ing-lien-kang culture can be divided into the northern and southern types. The northern type consists of four phases and the southern type consists of three phases. Stratigraphically and culturally the three phases of the southern type can be synchronized with the first three phases of the northern type. Third, the early phase of the northern type, exemplified by the lowest cultural stratum of the Ta-tun-tzu site in P'ei-hsien, northern Kiangsu, has recently been radiocarbon-dated at 3835 ± 105 B.C. (bristlecone-pine date: 4435 ± 105 B.C.). No radiocarbon age determination has yet been carried out for the lowest cultural stratum of the Ma-chia-pin 馬家濱 site in Chia-hsing 嘉興, northeastern Chekiang, which best typifies the early phase of the southern type. The only available radiocarbon date for the likely late stage of the early phase of the southern type, represented by the lowest cultural stratum of the Sung-tse site near Shanghai, is 3395 ± 105 B.C. (bristlecone-pine date: 3995 ± 105 B.C.). In Wu's opinion, a difference of 440 years provided by these two dates is more likely to represent the approximate duration of the early phase of both the northern and southern types than to indicate the earlier emergence of the northern type.

Equally unexpected is the early emergence of the Liang-chu culture in northern Chekiang around 3300 B.C. (bristlecone-pine date), a culture which was generally believed to have appeared considerably later than those more northerly regional Lungshanoid cultures. As will be discussed in chapters 2 and 3, the Ch'ing-lien-kang and Liang-chu dates are important in establishing the beginnings of rice culture and in providing clues for early domestication of cattle and water buffalo in China.

The other regional Lungshanoid and Lung-shan cultures arose between the late fourth and late third millennia B.C., according to bristlecone-pine dendrochronology. The two dates for the Aeneolithic Ch'i-chia culture in Kansu are fairly close to the beginning of the Shang dynasty. We will need many more series of radiocarbon age determinations to date the various phases and types of the Lungshanoid and Lung-shan cultures; still, we can at least begin to study the origins of certain major cultural elements starting from 5000 B.C.

Our discussion will now turn to the paleoenvironment of the nuclear area in which the Yang-shao culture emerged. The proto-Chinese of the Yang-shao period lived in the southwestern part of the loess highlands, which from the geological point of view may be regarded as a "classic" loess area. This area comprises the Wei River valley in central Shensi, southern Shansi, and western Honan. Here, not only are the loess deposits unusually thick, but the fine particles that make up the loessic soil are exceptionally homogeneous in texture. The exceptional textural homogeneity of the soil of this area can be explained only by the high probability that it was wind, rather than any other natural agent, that transported the loess material from far and near and deposited it during the long periods of desiccation that characterized the Pleistocene climate of North

China.[24] Indeed, recent deposition of loess by the wind on various parts of North China is well attested by three thousand years of Chinese historical records.[25]

During the past million years there have been four periods of desiccation interrupted by three periods of relative abundance of rain. It was during the comparatively rainy periods that erosion on a large scale took place; as a result, the loess material was carried by water from higher grounds to the low plains of North China. Although the causes of the formation of the loess of the low plains are highly complex, much of the soil of this area is of alluvial and diluvial origins. In many localities in the low plains the soil contains a mixture of pebbles, gravels, and conglomerates. In contrast, the loess of the highland area, which is largely of aeolian origin, is texturally uniform, friable, and porous, and hence offered much less resistance to primitive wooden digging sticks. This may have been one of the reasons why, in spite of more arid climatic conditions, the loess highland area was the cradle of Chinese Neolithic culture.

The climate of North China is severe, noted for its icy winters, hot summers, and frequent spring sandstorms. The average rainfall of the loess highlands is between 250 and 500 millimeters (slightly less than 10 to 20 inches). The average rainfall of the low plains is between 400 and 750 millimeters. The 750-millimeter rainfall line generally marks the southern and eastern boundary of the redeposited loess. An annual rainfall of between 10 and 20 inches, if evenly distributed over the four seasons, should meet the minimal requirements of ordinary dry-land farming. But in the loess area much of the rain is concentrated in the summer, when the temperature and rate of evaporation are both very high: there is usually inadequate

---

[24] Liu Tung-sheng *et al.*, *Chung-kuo ti huang-t'u tui-chi* [The Loess Deposits of China] (Peking, 1965), probably the most systematic study of the loess in any language, have arrived at this conclusion from various scientific angles.

[25] Wang Chia-yin, "Li-shih shang ti huang-t'u wen-t'i" [The Problem of Loess Deposition in Chinese History], *Chung-kuo ti-ssu-chi yen-chiu* [*Quaternaria Sinica*], IV, No. 1 (1965), pp. 1–8.

moisture in winter and spring. This, together with the fact that much of North China lies on the margins of the two main rain-producing systems of warm-season monsoons and cool-season cyclonic storms, makes the loess area of China a semiarid region.

During the past few decades there has been considerable controversy about the paleoclimate of North China. The latest opinion on the subject, based on scientific investigations of the Chinese loess, is that, despite the alternations between very dry and relatively wet periods during the entire Pleistocene epoch, the long-range climatic tendency was one of periodic and probably progressive desiccation[26]

The arid conditions in which the loess was formed are best reflected in the physical and chemical properties of the soil. As is well known, soils of humid regions are well weathered, leached, and acidic, whereas soils of dry belts are little weathered, unleached, and alkaline. The loess of the highland area of China has undergone little weathering, has retained much of its minerals, and is almost invariably alkaline. After meticulous comparison with the loess of several European countries, Chinese geologists have concluded that the Chinese loess was formed under climatic conditions more arid than those that existed during the process of loessification in Europe.[27]

For the purpose of studying climatic changes in North China during the Pleistocene, Chinese geologists in recent years have paid much attention to the various layers of reddish soil buried in the thick loess deposits. The buried soil is of considerable scientific interest because only under conditions of above-normal warmth and humidity could the loess be weathered into reddish soil. Yet a systematic analysis of various samples of the reddish soil taken

---

[26] J. S. Lee, *The Geology of China* (London, 1939), p. 371. Lee's early views on the Pleistocene climate of North China are now fully upheld by many recent studies, of which Liu *et al.*, *Chung-kuo ti huang-t'u tui-chi,* may be regarded as the best preliminary synthesis.

[27] *Ibid.*, pp. 141–227.

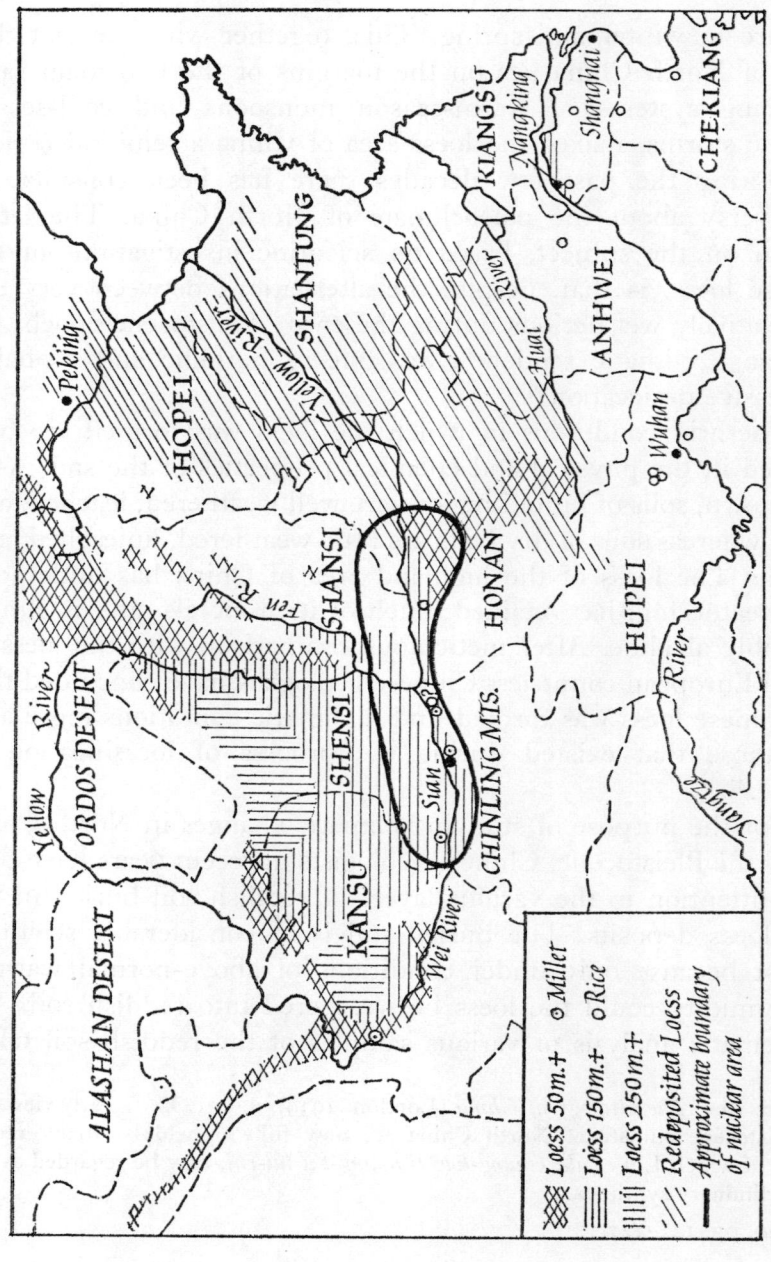

MAP 1. The distribution of loess in China.

from the loess profile of Li-shih 離石 county, Shansi province, shows pH values ranging from 7.5 to 8.8.²⁸ In other words, the buried soil is still moderately or fairly strongly alkaline. What is even more revealing is the composition of the pollen found in the uppermost layer of the buried soil in a loess profile of Wu-ch'eng 午城 county, Shansi province. This particular layer lies between 10.6 and 10.9 meters under the land surface, a stratum that should represent a "humid" subperiod of a rather recent geological age. Of forty-seven grains of pollen found in this stratum, only four are arboreal (*Abies,* 1; *Pinus,* 3): the remaining forty-three are accounted for by the single genus of *Artemisia,*²⁹ one of the best botanical indicators of arid and semiarid environments. As is well known, the most typical and ubiquitous plant in the driest belt of the United States, located between the Rocky Mountains and the Cascades and Sierras, is sagebrush *(Artemisia tridentata).*³⁰ In discussing the paleoclimate of North China, the world "pluvial" must therefore be used with caution and only in a relative sense.

Of all the scientific factors relating to the paleoenvironment of North China, the most puzzling is the faunal assemblage, which runs the whole gamut from animals of tundra and subarctic habitats, such as the two species of haired rhinoceros *(Coelodonta antiquitatis* and *Rhinoceros tichorhinus)* and mammoth *(Mammuths primigenius),* to animals of warm areas, such as the elephant *(Elephas indicus)* and the ordinary rhinoceros (*Rhinoceros* sp.). Some scholars today would still use the elephant and the rhinoceros as evidence to argue that the paleoenvironment of North China must have been warm and humid at certain times in the past. This

---

²⁸ Liu Tung-sheng and Chang Tsung-yu, "Chung-kuo ti huang-t'u" [The Loess of China], *Ti-chih hsüeh-pao* [*Acta Geologica Sinica*], XLII (March 1962), p. 2, table 1.

²⁹ *Ibid.,* p. 6, table 2.

³⁰ For a discussion of the predominance of sagebrush in the dry belt of the United States, see W. R. Chapline and C. K. Cooperrider, "Climate and Grazing," in *Climate and Man* (Washington, D.C., 1941), esp. pp. 364–365.

argument can be offset easily by an equally partial listing of haired rhinoceroses and mammoths, normally of subarctic habitats, and of camels and ostriches, now confined almost exclusively to desert and semidesert areas. Besides, many fossils of elephants and rhinoceroses found in North China during the early decades of this century were not accompanied by detailed stratigraphic reports, with the result that they were wrongly attributed to various strata of loess. A recent systematic reexamination of the relevant verified paleontological data shows that fossils of elephants and rhinoceroses almost always came from lacustrine beds, which were formed during periods of erosion and which are as a rule unconformably overlain by deposits of loess. After considering all aspects of the faunal data, a leading synthesist of the Chinese loess concludes that ever since the mid-Pleistocene epoch the faunal assemblage of the loess area has been dominated by species of rodents, especially *Myosplax* sp., a clear indication of a semiarid steppe environment.[31]

Probably the most remarkable recent advance in the study of the paleoenvironment of the loess region lies in the field of palynology. Of the ten available pollen studies relating to North China,[32]

---

[31] Liu *et al.*, *Chung-kuo ti huang-t'u tui-chi*, pp. 115–132. It should be noted that in ancient times North China, especially the low plains, had marshes where elephants and rhinoceroses lived. Elephants trekked south in Shang times, but rhinoceroses are known to have lingered in marshy areas of North China until rather late in Chou times (1027–256 B.C.). For details, see Ho, *Huang-t'u yü Chung-kuo nung-yeh ti ch'i-yüan* (Hongkong, 1969), p. 24, notes 18, 19. Possibly the puzzle of elephants and rhinoceroses in ancient North China may be accounted for by the animals' remarkable range of mobility and equally remarkable ability to adapt themselves over a certain length of time to environments different from those of their favorite habitats.

[32] These studies are so valuable that a complete listing may be useful to Western scientists: Sung Chih-ch'en, "San-men-hsi chih-wu-hua-shih ho p'ao-tzu-hua-fen-tsu-ho ti yen-chiu" [A Study of the Fossilized Plants and Pollen Spectrum of the San-men Series], *Quaternaria Sinica*, I, No. 1 (1958); Chou K'un-shu *et al.*, "Shan-hsi Li-shih Wang-chia-kou Ch'en-chia-yai lao-huang-t'u mai-ts'ang-t'u-jang chung ti p'ao-fen chi chih-wu-ts'an-t'i" [The Pollen and Paleobotanical Remains of the Buried Soils in the Old Loess Deposits of Ch'en-chia-yai, Wang-chia-kou,

the analysis of the pollen of an entire loess profile of Liu-shu-kou 柳樹溝, Wu-ch'eng county, Shansi province, is for various reasons the most relevant. Few localities can offer a more complete loess profile than Wu-ch'eng, a name that in recent years has been used by Chinese geologists to exemplify all strata of the loess deposited during the early Pleistocene period. Unlike other studies of the pollen of North China, which deal with certain specific periods of the Pleistocene epoch, the Wu-ch'eng study chronologically covers the past million years. The entire Wu-ch'eng profile of 121 meters is divided, for palynological study, into as many as 106 strata, so that vegetational and implied climatic changes can be studied in minute detail. Since my study is more concerned with the vegetation and climate of the geological period nearest to the dawning of Chinese agriculture, I have tabulated separately the pollen of the loess profile of the upper twenty meters.

Li-shih County, Shansi Province], *ibid.*, III, Nos. 1–2 (1960); Hsü Jen, "Chung-kuo-yüan-jen shih-tai ti Pei-ching ch'i-hou-huan-ching" [The Climatic Environment of the Peking Area during the Times of the Chinese Ape Men], *ibid.*, IV, No. 1 (1965); Sun Meng-jung, "Chou-k'ou-tien Chung-kuo-yüan-jen-hua-shih-ts'eng ti p'ao-tzu-hua-fen tsu-ho" [The Pollen Spectrum of the Stratum of the Chinese Ape Men of Chou-k'ou-tien], *ibid.*; Liu Chin-ling *et al.*, "Yen-shan nan-lu ni-t'an ti p'ao-fen tsu-ho" [The Pollen Profile of the Peat Bogs of the Southern Foothill of Yen-shan], *ibid.*; Chou K'un-shu, "Tui Pei-ching-shih fu-chin liang-ke mai-ts'ang-ni-t'an-chao ti tiao-ch'a chi ch'i p'ao-fen fen-hsi" [A Field Survey of Two Peat Bog Marshes Near Peking and an Analysis of Their Pollen Composition], *ibid.*; Liu Mu-ling, "Ho-nan Shan-hsien Hui-hsing-chen Hui-hsing-kou tsao-keng-hsin-shih tui-chi chung ti p'ao-fen-tsu-ho ch'u-pu yen-chiu" [A Preliminary Study of the Pollen Composition of an Early Pleistocene Deposit at Hui-hsing-kou, Hui-hsing-chen, Shan-hsien, Honan], *ibid.*; Ch'en ch'eng-hui *et al.*, "Liao-tung-pan-tao P'u-lan-tien fu-chin han ku-lien-tzu ti ch'üan-hsin-shih ch'en-chi-wu ti p'ao-fen fen-hsi" [An Analysis of the Pollen of the Holocene Deposit of P'u-lan-tien, Liao-tung Peninsula, Which Contains Ancient Lotus Seeds], *ibid.*; Liu and Chang, "Chung-kuo ti huang-t'u," which offers by far the most systematic palynological data of a classic loess area, Wu-ch'eng County, Shansi Province; Chou K'un-shu, "Hsi-an Pan-p'o hsin-shih-ch'i-shih-tai i-chih ti p'ao-fen fen-hsi" [An Analysis of the Pollen Gathered at the Pan-p'o Neolithic Site Near Sian], *K'ao-ku* [*Archaeology*], No. 9 (1963).

TABLE 2
ANALYSIS OF THE POLLEN OF THE LOESS PROFILE OF WU-CH'ENG

Plant	Total Number of Pollen Grains (1–20 m.)	Total Number of Pollen Grains (20–121 m.)	Total Number of Pollen Grains (Entire Profile, 1–121 m.)
A. Arboreal			
Abies	2	0	2
Pinus	15	13	28
Cupressaceae	3	0	3
Juglans	0	3	3
Carpinus	0	3	3
Quercus	2	6	8
Ulmus	0	1	1
Morus	2	0	2
Acer	0	1	1
Ephadra	0	2	2
Salix	7	12	19
Corylus	2	0	2
Total (Arboreal)	33	41	74
B. Nonarboreal			
Typha	1	1	2
Gramineae	56	118	174
Cyperaceae	3	3	6
Humulus	3	16	19
Chenopodiaceae	18	58	76
Caryophyllaceae	1	1	2
Clematis	48	5	53
Convolvulus	14	0	14
Artemisia	722	330	1,052
Compositae	32	45	77
Dicotyledoneae	72	1	73
Total (Nonarboreal)	970	578	1,548
Total (A + B)	1,003	619	1,622

This table is based on Liu and Chang "Chung-kuo ti huang-t'u." In the original table *Filicales* and *Bryales* constitute a small separate category; since the latter has not been counted in the original table, I omit these two species entirely from the summary.

Table 2 reveals several important aspects of the paleoenvironment of the loess highland. First, the fact that trees and shrubs account for merely 74 of the 1,622 grains of pollen testifies that this area was, much as it is today, rather meager in forest resources. The relative significance of *Pinus* (pines) and *Salix* (willows), which account for 47 of a total of 74 arboreal pollen grains, should be briefly discussed. It is well known that with its two air sacks pine pollen can travel a long distance from its mountainous habitat, and willows generally grow along edges of water. In other words, the overall meager forest resources and the likely special habitats of the two numerically significant groups of trees would indicate that the level areas of the semiarid loess highland were little, if at all, forested.

Second, the most striking phenomenon in the pollen profile is the overwhelming predominance of herbaceous plants, which account for 1,548 grains of pollen or 95.4 percent of the total. There can be little doubt that the loess highland area, except for its mountains, hills, slopes, and places near watercourses, has always been a nonwooded steppe. The fact that *Artemisia* alone accounts for as much as 64.8 percent of the pollen emphatically reflects the ecology of a semiarid steppe.

Third, whereas *Artemisia* represents 53.3 percent of the pollen found deeper than twenty meters, it represents 71.8 percent of the pollen found in the upper twenty meters. This sharp increase in the percentage of *Artemisia* indicates that the climate in the late Pleistocene epoch was becoming cooler and drier.

Fourth, next to *Artemisia* the most significant groups of herbaceous plants are the family of Gramineae, which consists of many kinds of weeds later domesticated by men as food crops, and the family of Chenopodiaceae, which consists of a large number of spinach-like wild plants sometimes used as vegetables and often grown by primitive men for their seeds. Gramineae account for 10.7 per cent of the pollen total and are fairly evenly distributed chronologically throughout the past million years. In the light of archaeological and literary evidence concerning the earliest Chinese cereal crops, the prevalence of Gramineae cannot be interpreted as an indication that a wide range of potential food plants has existed since the early Pleistocene epoch; on the contrary, it indicates the existence of rather few kinds of potential cereal plants which, in spite of the prolonged and relentless struggle against such xerophytic plants as *Artemisia* and Chenopodiaceae, had survived in a semiarid area in sufficient quantities to be utilized eventually by the Yang-shao farmers.

The main characteristics of the paleoenvironment revealed by table 2 are corroborated not only by studies of pollen profiles gathered from other localities in North China but also by the botanical records preserved in ancient Chinese literary works. Of all the literary works, *The Book of Odes (Shih-ching)* contains by far the most extensive botanical records. Sinologists the world over agree on the authenticity and textual excellence of this ancient work, which illuminates the life of the Chinese from the late eleventh century to the middle of the sixth century B.C. It is true that this anthology of 305 songs and odes collected from the Chou royal domain and the feudal states[33] mentions less than 150 plants, a number that is infinitesimal as compared with the number of species known to botanists today. But when it is remembered that the total numbers of plants known to and mentioned by the ancient Egyptians,

---

[33] Bernhard Karlgren, after a meticulous study of the strict rhyming system of the odes, concludes that most if not the entire text of *The Book of Odes* seems to have been edited by officials in the court of the Chou kings. In other words, the odes as they now stand were written in the elite language of Chou times rather than in ancient regional and local dialects. Sinologists generally agree on this major conclusion. But Karlgren's other conclusion that the odes are musical airs and do not in any way reflect the life of the Chinese from the late eleventh to the middle of the sixth century B.C. is shared by none except the late Henri Maspéro. For Karlgren's opinion on *The Book of Odes,* see his introductory remarks in "Glosses on *The Book of Documents,*" *BMFEA,* No. 20 (1948). For the more important ancient sources and modern research supporting the view that the odes were collected from, or submitted to the Chou court by, the various feudal states, see Ho, *Huang-t'u yü Chung-kuo nung-yeh ti ch'i-yüan.*

the Bible, Homer, and Herodotus are only 55, 83, 60, and 63, respectively,[34] *The Book of Odes* is really a mine of information for historians and botanists. For a majority of cases, moreover, *The Book of Odes* states the type of topography in which a plant grows— mountain, plain, wet lowland near water, marsh, pond, or river. The geographic areas covered by the 305 songs and odes are Shensi, Shansi, and Honan provinces, the Han River Valley down to the middle Yangtze Valley, western and central Shantung, northwestern Anhwei, and southern Hopei. It is fortunate that the volume's botanical records on the southeastern part of the loess highland are especially comprehensive.

Using archaic Chinese written records to check recent scientific findings on the loess area, I have identified, analyzed, and tabulated all the arboreal and nonarboreal plants in *The Book of Odes* except the aquatic plants and cereals, since my concern is the ancient "natural" vegetation. I have supplemented the botanical data of *The Book of Odes* with information culled from various classics, historical, geographical, and philosophical works written or compiled mostly before and during the Former Han period (206 B.C.–A.D. 8), and from *Wen-hsüan* 文選, the earliest comprehensive literary anthology compiled during the first half of the sixth century A.D. By comparing literary records with modern scientific findings I have reached the following conclusions.[35]

First, there has been little, if any, significant change in the composition of North China's forests since the late Pleistocene

---

[34] F. Kanngiesser, "Die Flora des Herodot," *Archiv für die Geschichte der Naturwissenschaften und der Technik,* III (1912), p. 81.

[35] Much of Part II of Ho, *Huang-t'u yü Chung-kuo nung-yeh ti ch'i-yüan,* deals with the identification and tabulation of fifty-four arboreal and forty-one herbaceous plants, along with bamboos, recorded in *The Book of Odes.* Table 3 (pp. 42–56) provides the Chinese and scientific names of such plants, together with their habitats, described in *The Book of Odes.* The types of trees and shrubs named in *The Book of Odes* and other ancient Chinese literary works are compared in Table 4 (pp. 57–64) with results of recent pollen analyses.

epoch, and deciduous trees have always been numerically more important than conifers.

Second, an examination of the habitats of trees and shrubs mentioned in *The Book of Odes* reveals that they were virtually confined to mountains, hills, slopes, and places near watercourses. In other words, apart from the uneven seasonal distribution of rain and high evaporation in summer, the level loess areas of North China do not seem to have been able to retain enough water for the growth of trees and shrubs. The statements made by the late V. K. Ting, founder of the China Geological Survey, in his famous review of Marcel Granet's *La civilisation chinoise,* which depicts the loess highland as a dense woodland dotted with marshes, are largely valid and still worth citing:

> Now all geologists agree that in the loess there has never been any forestation . . . the water table is so low that even today trees planted in the loess need to be watered in their young stages until the roots become sufficiently deep. . . . It is not denied that forests existed on mountain slopes, but the loess area has always been a semi-steppe. Marshes exist even today in the alluvial plains, but most of Professor Granet's marshes lay in loess-land.[36]

My only revision of Ting's view is that the Wei River Basin in Shensi Province even today has marshes, caused by poor drainage owing to special physiographic factors.[37] In spite of climatic conditions that cannot be regarded as humid, the poorly drained areas in the low plains abounded in marshes and peat bogs, some of which are known to have been formed during late prehistoric and early historic times.

Third, it is by no means coincidental that *The Book of Odes* provides an eloquent testimonial to the predominance of *Artemisia* on the loess plains, which can be gauged from the number of its

[36] V. K. Ting, "Professor Granet's *La civilisation chinoise,*" *Chinese Social and Political Science Review,* XV (1931), pp. 267-269.

[37] Kuan En-wei, "Wei-ho ku-ti ti-mao fa-yü-shih chi ch'i yu-kuan wen-t'i ti t'ao-lun" [A Discussion of the Physiographical History of the Wei River Basin and Other Related Problems], *Quaternaria Sinica,* IV, No. 1 (1965), pp. 195-203.

varietal names and from its frequency of occurrence. The single genus of *Artemisia*, with ten varietal names, leads all the plants recorded in this ancient work, arboreal and nonarboreal, by a wide margin. In terms of the number of times various plants appear in the odes, *Artemisia* is barely exceeded by mulberry by a ratio of nineteen to twenty and followed by the *shu* and *chi* subspecies of millet *(Panicum miliaceum)*, which appear in fifteen and twelve odes, respectively. Since *P. miliaceum* was the most important source of food for the ancient Chinese, and since mulberry was vital to sericulture and was extensively grown in various parts of North China during Shang-Chou times, the fact that weeds of the *Artemisia* genus receive such prominent mention in *The Book of Odes* is an unmistakable indication that the loess area was a semiarid steppe.[38]

Fourth, while *The Book of Odes* mentions Chenopodiaceae only twice, the combined evidence of other ancient works shows their prevalence on the loess plains. Unless weeds of the family of Chenopodiaceae were truly endemic, it would be hard for modern scholars to explain why in Chou times the fallow land was generally called *lai* (Chenopodiaceae) and the virgin soil *ts'ao-lai* (literally grasses and Chenopodiaceae).[39] As is well known to botanists and phytogeographers, although Chenopodiaceae require more water than *Artemisia* for growth and perpetuation, many species of this family can tolerate alkalinity and salinity of the soil better than most plants. Species of Chenopodiaceae are known to have thrived in the sun-baked saline and alkaline desert of south central Iraq where few plants can survive.[40]

The main characteristics of the ancient vegetation of the loess plains revealed in archaic Chinese literature concur, therefore, remarkably well with those of recent palynological studies. Taking

[38] For more details, see Ho, *Huang-t'u yü Chung-kuo nung-yeh ti ch'i-yüan*, pp. 73–79.

[39] *Ibid.*, pp. 80, 85.

[40] Nicholas Polunin, *Introduction to Plant Geography and Some Related Sciences* (London, 1960), p. 386.

into account such major factors as the climatic conditions under which the loess was deposited, the physical and chemical property of the loessic soil, the predominance of typical steppe animals in the faunal assemblage, the relative sparsity of arboreal plants, and the preponderance of such xerophytic and halophytic plants as *Artemisia* and Chenopodiaceae in both geological and early historical times, it is difficult not to arrive at the conclusion that the natural environment of the loess highland, in ancient and modern times, has always been one of a semiarid steppe.

It is important for scholars interested in the origins of Chinese agriculture to keep in mind that, although the natural environment of the loess highland has been unquestionably harsh, it nevertheless has had certain advantages. Precisely because of its aeolian origin and the prolonged arid and semiarid conditions in which the loess was formed, the soil is unusually homogeneous in texture, friable, and porous. There is reason to believe that the grass cover of the loess highland has never been as dense as is usually found in other major steppe and forest-steppe belts of Eurasia. It is significant to observe that while "the most current surface rocks [of the forest-steppe zone of the USSR] are loess and loesslike formations," the characteristic soils of this belt are blackish "meadow chernozem" and those of Russia's "steppe zone" are the classic dark chernozem, an indication of their much denser cover of grass.[41] A leading synthesist of world history is certainly right in pointing out that agriculture in the Old World first appeared, as a rule, on wooded slopes and foothills because "natural grassland offered stubborn resistance to the wooden digging sticks."[42] That in the Old World the only major exception is Yang-shao China is substantially explained by the peculiar property of the loess and its relatively sparse grass cover. Since the loess is little weathered, it has retained

[41] A. A. Rode, *Soil Science* (Washington, D.C., 1962), p. 364; for a detailed description of the soils of these two belts, pp. 363–420.

[42] William H. McNeill, *The Rise of the West: A History of the Human Community* (Chicago, 1963), p. 16.

much of its minerals and is therefore very fertile. In spite of a limited rainfall of less than twenty inches, its concentration in summer enabled the Yang-shao farmers to grow successfully the few kinds of cereal plants that survived the prolonged process of natural selection in a semiarid environment. All in all, therefore, the natural environment of the nuclear area in which agriculture and Neolithic culture first occurred in China definitely imposed certain restrictions on its early inhabitants; but a limited range of opportunities—probably peculiar to China's loess highland—partially compensated for these restrictions.

The remaining section of this introductory chapter will deal with the ethnic and probable geographic origins of the Yang-shao people. Although cumulative research in physical anthropology has established beyond doubt that the first Yang-shao farmers of the Neolithic nuclear area were Mongoloid and ancestors of the modern Chinese, little is as yet known of the origins of the Yang-shao people. So far, two British scholars have explicitly speculated on the geographic origin of the Yang-shao people. They both believe that during the postglacial period this people moved into the southeastern part of the loess highlands from the north. In the millennia immediately preceding the appearance of the Yang-shao people in the loess highlands, they point out, much of the southern half of China was covered by glaciers. The main reason they give for the sudden burst of the Yang-shao culture is that "people moving in from the north were presented with a challenge offered by the loess deposit; they responded to their challenging opportunity by settling and developing a civilization."[43]

---

[43] Ian J. Smalley, "The Loess Deposits and Neolithic Culture of North China," *Man*, III, No. 2 (June 1968), pp. 224–241; quotation from pp. 235–236. While this article has incorporated some new scientific data on the loess of China, its hypothesis of "northern" origins of the Yang-shao people is largely a reiteration of that of P. M. Roxby, "The Terrain of Early Chinese Civilization," *Geography*, XXIII (1938), pp. 225–236.

The hypothesis of northern origins of the Yang-shao people would be partially valid if existing scientific data could prove that glaciation was confined to the southern half of China and that it was of such a "continental" type as to make human habitation in the south extremely difficult. But available scientific data indicate, rather, that glaciation in China was not of the continental type, that it was confined mostly to mountains, and that mountain glaciers occurred in both North and South China.[44] Of the 1,120 localities where glaciers and vestiges of glaciers have been found in China in recent decades, more than 30 percent are located in the upper half of China, north of the Ch'in-ling mountain range.[45]

There are other basic scientific facts which indicate the repeated occurrences of mountain glaciers and the absence of continental ice sheets in China during the Pleistocene. For instance, there exist in many localities in northern and southern China soils that developed from Cretaceous (120,000,000 to 60,000,000 years ago) and Tertiary (60,000,000 to 1,000,000 years ago) parent materials. Since polyglaciation was strictly a recent geological phenomenon confined to the last million years, the existence in many places in China of soils that developed long before the onset of the great ice age is important evidence that glaciers in China were limited largely to mountains and that the country as a whole was never covered by continental ice sheets.[46]

---

[44] Sun Tien-ch'ing and Yang Huai-jen, "Ta-ping-ch'uan shih-ch'i Chung-kuo ti ping-ch'uan i-chih" [The Great Ice Age Glaciation in China], *Ti-chih hsüeh-pao*, XXXXI, Nos. 3-4 (December 1961), pp. 233-244.

[45] By far the most comprehensive listing of glaciers and vestiges of glaciers in China is made by Liu Tung-sheng *et al.*, "Chung-kuo ti-ssu-chi ch'en-chi-wu ch'ü-yü fen-pu t'e-cheng ti t'an-t'ao" [An Investigation of the Characteristics of the Regional Distribution of Deposits in China during the Quaternary], *Ti-ssu-chi ti-chih wen-t'i* [Symposium on Geological Problems of the Quaternary] (Peking, 1964), pp. 1-44, esp. Appendix I and Map 10.

[46] Chou T'ing-ju and Liu P'ei-t'ung, *Chung-kuo ti ti-hsing ho t'u-jang kai-shu* [An Outline of the Physiography and Soils of China] (Peking, 1956), p. 65.

Phytogeographic evidence testifies even more strongly against the view that the southern half of China was several times sealed in ice during the Pleistocene. A Chinese botanist has summarized the main phytogeographic characteristic of the southern half of China thus:

> The extraordinary richness of the ligneous flora of eastern Asia is a well-known fact. In China alone no less than 959 genera of woody plants were reported in 1935. This exceeds in number of genera all the rest of the North Temperate Zone [in the world] and is more than three times the number (313) found in North America, floristically a closely related region. Recent discoveries may possibly bring the total to nearly a thousand.... The richness of the flora of eastern Asia, especially China, is due to its great diversity in topographic, climatic, and ecologic conditions. Historically, the absence of extensive glaciation during the Pleistocene permits the preservation of a large number of genera formerly extensively distributed but which later became extinct in other parts of the world.[47]

Because of the occurrences of continental ice sheets in the temperate zones of other continents in the northern hemisphere and their absence in China, there are a number of so-called relic plants that have survived only in China, having become extinct elsewhere. *Ginko biloba,* the lone survivor of an entire order of gymnosperms, and *Metasequoia,* the unique primeval relic conifer, are but the most famous of the "living fossils" that testify to the absence of continental ice sheets in China.[48]

In view of the above scientific data, there is reason to believe that during the last glacial period the lowlands south of the Ch'in-ling are likely to have been more congenial to early man than were the northerly areas, in terms of climate and especially of available natural resources for human sustenance.

There can be little question that the Yang-shao culture was a product of the loess area. But during the last glacial era the forebears

---

[47] Hui-lin Li, "Endemism in the Ligneous Flora of Eastern Asia," *Proceedings of the Seventh Pacific Science Congress,* V (1953), p. 1.

[48] Hui-lin Li, "Floristic Significance and Problems of Eastern Asia," *Taiwania,* I (1948), pp. 1–12; also "Metasequoia, a Living Fossil," *American Scientist,* LII, No. 1 (March 1964), pp. 93–109.

of the Yang-shao people might have taken refuge barely south of the Ch'in-ling, an ideal windbreak. This speculation is partially supported by evidence of physical anthropology. In recent years a significant number of human skeletons unearthed from Yang-shao cultural sites at Pan-p'o, Pao-chi, and Hua-hsien in the Wei River basin have been studied.[49] As compared with other divisions of the Mongoloids, the Yang-shao people bear the closest physical resemblances to the modern Chinese of the southern half of China and to the modern Indo-Chinese. Their next closest resemblance is to the modern Chinese of North China. They have physical characteristics markedly different from those of the Eskimos of Alaska, the Tungus of Manchuria, the Tibetans, and the Mongoloids of the Lake Baikal area. According to the Soviet anthropological terminology adopted by mainland Chinese scholars, the Yang-shao Chinese are classified under the "Pacific branch of the Mongoloid" or under the "Southern Mongoloid race," and are distinguished from the prehistoric Mongoloid peoples of the Lake Baikal area and the proto-Tungus of Manchuria, who are classified under the "Northern Mongoloid." This basic physical anthropological fact agrees with linguistic evidence that the Chinese language from time immemorial has been fundamentally different from those agglutinative tongues spoken by various "Northern Mongoloid" ethnic groups who belong to the Altaic language family. Both anthropological and linguistic evidence points to the Yang-shao people's "southern" affiliations.

Even stronger evidence of the Yang-shao people's "southern"

---

[49] Yen Yin et al., "Hsi-an Pan-p'o jen-ku ti yen-chiu" [Investigations of the Neolithic Human Skeletons Unearthed from Pan-p'o], *KK*, 1960, No. 9, pp. 36–47; which also appears as Appendix I to *Hsi-an Pan-p'o*, with an English abstract; Yen Yin et al., "Pao-chi hsin-shih-ch'i-shih-tai jen-ku ti yen-chiu pao-kao" [A Report on the Investigations of the Neolithic Human Skeletons Unearthed from Pao-chi], *Ku-chi-ts'ui-tung-wu yü ku-jen-lei* [*Paleovertebrata et Paleoanthropologia*], II, No. 1 (March 1960), pp. 103–111; and Yen Yin, "Hua-hsien hsin-shih-ch'i-shih-tai ti jen-ku yen-chiu" [Investigations of the Neolithic Human Skeletons Unearthed from Hua-hsien], *KKHP*, 1962, No. 2, pp. 85–104.

affiliations is artifactual and cultural. V. Y. Larichev, one of the very few Soviet scholars at home with both Northeast Asian and Chinese archaeology, has discussed the characteristics of Yang-shao artifacts in the context of Asian prehistory:

> The most striking trait of the stone artifacts of the Yangshao culture, apart from their typological uniqueness, is the prevalence of polished tools. The people of this culture did not know the techniques of flaking and chipping. In manufacturing axes, spear points, and arrowheads, and ploughs, sickles, and punch awls, they used the grinding method. This demonstrates the specific cultural traditions and sources of the Yangshao culture, which are not related to the north where the percussion technique was prevalent but to the south and the eastern maritime regions of China.[50]

While crude chipping techniques were in fact known to the Yang-shao Chinese, Larichev's comparative typological statement remains, by and large, true.

By far the most definite evidence of the southern cultural affiliations of the Yang-shao people is the cultural sequence recently established by mainland Chinese archaeologists that the earliest phase of the Yang-shao culture is to be exemplified by the artifactual complex of the Li-chia-ts'un site in Hsi-hsiang county, Shensi, on the southern side of the Ch'in-ling Mountain. Here, at Li-chia-ts'un, many of the pottery shapes are similar to those of other Yang-shao sites, but with two important differences: the prevalence of cord-marked pottery and the absence of painted pottery. In a number of Yang-shao cultural sites in the Wei River basin north of the Ch'in-ling and in western Honan the stratum containing the Li-chia-ts'un type of pottery lies immediately beneath the strata containing the characteristic Yang-shao painted pottery.[51]

Since along the Pacific coast of East and Southeast Asia and in many parts of the southern half of China the earliest pottery is invariably cord-marked, and since Li-chia-ts'un is on the southern

---

[50] V. Y. Larichev, "Ancient Cultures of North China," in Henry N. Michael, ed., *The Archaeology and Geomorphology of Northern Asia: Selected Works* (Toronto, 1964), pp. 233–234.

[51] See Map 4, ch. 4 below.

side of the Ch'in-ling and on the upper Han River which links up Shensi with central Yangtze, a southern cast to the cultural heritage of the Yang-shao people can no longer be seriously doubted. This probable southern cultural heritage does not detract from the fact that the Yang-shao culture as a whole was a product of the loess highlands. Yet it does help to explain why the Yang-shao culture had so little in common with the Microlithic cultures that flourished from Manchuria through the Inner Mongolian steppe to westernmost Kansu and Sinkiang from pre-Yang-shao times to the early historical periods.[52]

Since the vast areas south of the Ch'in-ling have been archaeologically much less extensively surveyed than the loess highlands, the cultural evolution of the Yang-shao people prior to their habitation of the Wei River basin is little known. The artifacts of the Li-chia-ts'un site include cord-marked pottery, stone axes, adzes, spades, chisels, sinkers, and millstones.[53] Stone axes, adzes, and chisels suggest wood cutting and wood dressing; stone sinkers suggest deepwater fishing; spades and millstones suggest some protohorticultural or protoagricultural activities, the exact mode of which is impossible to tell. The use of pottery also suggests that the

[52] So far the only evidence of the spread of the Microlithic culture of China's northern steppe into the eastern-central Shensi area is the cultural remains of the so-called Sha-yüan culture. The absence of pottery and the existence of animal bones in a partially fossilized state suggest that this culture was probably "Mesolithic," and certainly earlier than Yang-shao. Referring to the fifteen spots in a sand-dune area in eastern-central Shensi, where the Sha-yüan artifacts are found but with no recognizable evidence of human habitation, K. C. Chang is of the opinion that they "are really nothing more than fifteen spots where cultural remains happen to have been concentrated" by the strong sand-bearing winds. See K. C. Chang, *The Archaeology of Ancient China*, p. 71.

[53] "Shan-hsi Hsi-hsiang Li-chia-ts'un hsin-shih-ch'i-shih-tai i-chih" [The Neolithic Site at Li-chia-ts'un, Hsi-hsiang, Shensi], *KK*, 1961, No. 7, pp. 352–354; and "Shan-hsi Hsi-hsiang Li-chia-ts'un hsin-shih-ch'i-shih-tai i-chih i-chiu-liu-i-nien fa-chüeh pao-kao" [Report on the 1961 Excavations of a Neolithic Site at Li-chia-ts'un, Hsi-hsiang, Shensi], *KK*, 1962, No. 6, pp. 290–295.

people enjoyed a certain degree of "settled" life. While in recent decades Near Eastern archaeology has directed its attention more and more to the phase of increasingly efficient food collection immediately preceding the appearance of the "settled food-producing level of existence,"[54] similar studies for China must await more intensive archaeological work in areas adjacent to the southern fringe of the Yang-shao nuclear area.

Although we have so little detailed knowledge about the early cultural evolution of the Yang-shao people, we can suggest some basic reasons why the area south of the Ch'in-ling was much less conducive to the rise of field agriculture and of a full-fledged Neolithic settled village community than the loess area immediately to its north. It is true that much richer flora and fauna south of the Ch'in-ling encouraged more intensive food gathering and food collecting. But the vast area south of the Ch'in-ling presented early mankind with two great difficulties: forests that covered hills and mountains, and the heavy, clayey soils of the southern plains that were covered by forests and sometimes by luxuriant grass. While many primitive peoples, including the prehistoric inhabitants of the island of Taiwan, could clear forests by barking and burning, one peculiar trait of prehistoric and early historic Chinese was their inability or unwillingness to destroy the forests by such a simple and wanton method.[55] In the opinion of a leading mainland Chinese archaeologist, the lack of effective means to clear forests on a significant scale accounted, at least in part, for the considerably

---

[54] Robert J. Braidwood and Charles A. Reed, "The Achievement and Early Consequences of Food Production: A Consideration of the Archaeological and Natural-Historical Evidence," *Cold Spring Harbor Symposia on Quantitative Biology*, XXII (1957), p. 19; Halet Cambel and Robert J. Braidwood, "An Early Farming Village in Turkey," *Scientific American*, CCXXII, No. 3 (March 1970), pp. 50–56.

[55] Ho, *Huang-t'u yü Chung-kuo nung-yeh ti ch'i-yüan*, Part II, Ch. 4, "An Outline of the History of Deforestation in China," pp. 85–106.

later occurrences of full-fledged Neolithic cultures in the southern half of China.[56] The clayey soils of various southern plains also offered much greater resistance to primitive agricultural implements as compared with the texturally uniform and friable loess.

[56] Hsia Nai, "Chang-chiang-liu-yü k'ao-ku wen-t'i" [Archaeological Problems of the Yangtze Area], *KK,* 1962, No. 2, p. 1.

II
Field Agriculture

FEW PROBLEMS in human history are more fundamental and challenging than the origins of agriculture. Agriculture, throughout this study, refers to field agriculture based on cereal grains, in contrast to "vegeculture" based on root crops. This conventional and rigid definition for agriculture seems justified for two reasons. First, the word agriculture has in recent decades been so loosely used, especially by scholars specializing on Southeast Asia, as to have become almost synonymous with protohorticulture or horticulture. Second, it was field agriculture based on cereal grains that gave rise to the first civilizations in both the Old World and the New.[1]

---

[1] The relationship between cereal agriculture and the rise of higher culture is systematically discussed in E. D. Merrill, "Plants and Civilizations," *Scientific Monthly,* XLIII (November 1936), pp. 430–439, but it is most effectively stated by Paul C. Mangelsdorf in "Wheat," *Scientific American,* CLXXXIX (July 1953), pp. 50–59: "No civilization worthy of the name has ever been founded on any agricultural basis other than the cereals. . . . It may be primarily a question of nutrition. . . . Cereal grains, like eggs and milk, are foodstuffs designed by nature for the nutrition of the young of the species. They represent a five-in-one food supply which contains carbohydrates, proteins, fats, minerals and vitamins. . . . Perhaps the relationship between cereals and civilization is also a product of the discipline which cereals impose upon their growers. The cereals are grown only from seed and must be planted and harvested in their proper season. In this respect they differ from the root crops, which in mild climates can be planted and harvested at almost any time of the year. . . . The growing of cereals has always been accompanied by a stable mode of life. . . . Cereal agriculture in providing a stable food supply created leisure, and leisure in turn fostered the arts, crafts and sciences. It

The origins of field agriculture in Mesopotamia and Meso-America have been intensively studied by archaeologists and by scientists of many other disciplines. All except a handful of extreme diffusionists have conceded that these areas were the two independent nuclei from which agriculture and early civilizations developed and spread throughout the hemispheres. It is the purpose of this chapter to demonstrate with archaeological, botanical, literary, and philological data that field agriculture occurred in the Neolithic nuclear area of North China independently of Mesopotamia. Insofar as theories of geneses of agriculture are concerned, therefore, China holds as crucial a position as do Mesopotamia and Meso-America.

In the Old World, field agriculture first occurred in southwestern Asia, on the hilly flanks of the "Fertile Crescent," around 7000 B.C.[2] Some time after 5000 B.C. more intensive agriculture took place on the irrigated fields of the great flood plains of the Tigris and Euphrates. The ancient agriculture of Egypt and the Indus River valley also depended on flood plains and primitive irrigation. Among the main characteristics of the earliest Chinese agricultural system, however, was its freedom from the influence of the great flood plain of the lower Yellow River and, as a corollary, the absence of primitive irrigation.

In the early decades of the present century little was known about China's prehistory. Scholars generally believed that the cradle of Chinese civilization was probably the great flood plain of the Yellow River because, among other things, since the turn of the nineteenth century, tens of thousands of oracle bones had been unearthed in An-yang, a locality in northern Honan that lies within the area of the low plains. In the West this view was systematically

---

has been said that 'cereal agriculture, alone among the forms of food production, taxes, recompenses and stimulates labor and ingenuity in an equal degree.' "

[2] Robert J. Braidwood, "The Agricultural Revolution," *Scientific American*, CCIII (September 1960), pp. 130–148.

expounded by the late Henri Maspéro and, through Arnold Toynbee's monumental synthesis of history, has gained currency among Western historians.³ During the past twenty years, so many Neolithic sites have been excavated and so much more about the general sequence of major Chinese Neolithic cultures has become known that there can be little doubt that the cradle of Chinese civilization is the southeastern part of the loess highland, an area that has little in common with the great flood plain of the lower Yellow River.

From generalized and specific descriptions given in massive archaeological reports on northern Chinese sites that belong to the Yang-shao, Lung-shan, and other prehistoric cultures, the following facts have clearly emerged. Most such sites, in the highlands as well as on the low plains, are loess terraces or mounds along various tributaries of the Yellow River rather than along the great river itself. A closer examination of these sites shows that most are clustered along numerous small rivers and streams that often do not appear on detailed general maps of China and are known only locally. This is an important testimonial to the basic fact that the birth of China owed little to the Yellow River itself, although in theory such numerous small rivers and streams are within the drainage of the Yellow River.⁴

There are, to be sure, a few scores of prehistoric sites in Kansu northwestern and southwestern Shansi, and western Honan, which are along the upper and middle course of the Yellow River itself. Topographically, however, these sites are exactly like all the rest:

---

³ Henri Maspéro, *La Chine antique* (Paris, 1927), pp. 20–26; Arnold J. Toynbee, *A Study of History* (10 vols., London, 1934–54), I, pp. 318–321.

⁴ For detailed discussion of the topography of Neolithic sites in North China, see Ho, *Huang-t'u yü Chung-kuo nung-yeh ti ch'i-yüan*, pp. 107–117. Even as late as Chou times the major cities were still along tributaries of the Yellow River or at various foothills. See Tsou Pao-chün, "Chung-kuo wen-hua ch'i-yüan-ti" [The Region Where Early Chinese Culture Occurred], *Ch'ing-hua hsüeh-pao* [Tsing Hua Journal of Chinese Studies], New Series, VI (December 1967), pp. 22–34.

loess terraces or mounds of varying altitudes ranging from fifteen or twenty to hundreds of feet above the riverbeds. All the prehistoric sites of North China are, in other words, close to water, but are also sufficiently high to be safe from floods. The elevated terraces and mounds provide the best argument against the possibility of irrigation before the invention of sophisticated water wheels and water pumps.

Although the generalized descriptions of the environments of over a thousand Neolithic sites already imply the impossibility of irrigation in very early times, I shall present positive evidence that irrigation arrived late in China. It is true that ditches and trenches have been discovered at the Yang-shao site of Pan-p'o near Sian and also at Hsiao-t'un in An-yang, the last Shang capital. But the main trench of the Pan-p'o site is believed by Chinese archaeologists to have existed for the purpose of defense, and the smaller ditches, which all pass through the residential area, cannot possibly have been used for irrigation.[5] The more elaborate network of ditches of Hsiao-t'un, which cuts through much of the ensemble of royal palaces, ancestral halls, residential houses, and workshops, is clearly for the purpose of drainage.[6] Indeed, in an extensive study of relevant inscriptions on Shang oracle-bones, a leading Chinese paleographer is struck by the people's fear of floodwater and general ignorance of diking, water conservancy, and irrigation.[7]

The first account of the construction of ditches in the fields, most probably for the purpose of irrigation, is given in the *Tso-chuan* (Chronicles of Feudal States). It declares that some time after

[5] *Hsi-an Pan-p'o* [Report on the Archaeological Site of Pan-p'o, near Sian] (Peking, 1963), p. 52.

[6] Shih Chang-ju, *Hsiao-t'un,* Vol. I, *Yin-hsü chien-chu i-ts'un* [Architectural Remains of the Last Shang Capital City] (Taipei, 1959), p. 268.

[7] Yü Hsing-wu, "Ts'ung chia-ku-wen k'an Shang-tai she-hui hsing-chih" [The Characteristics of the Shang Society Revealed in Oracle-Bone Inscriptions], *Tung-pei jen-min-ta-hsüeh jen-wen-k'e-hsüeh hsüeh-pao* [Journal of Humanistic Studies of the People's University of the Northeast], Nos. 2-3 (1957), pp. 103-104.

Tzu-ssu's 子駟 appointment as the chief minister of the Cheng 鄭 state in north central Honan in 571 B.C., "in laying out the ditches through the fields, [he] had occasioned the loss of fields" to five aristocratic clans; consequently Tzu-ssu was assassinated in 563 B.C. by a band of "ruffians" instigated by the five clans. While the exact year for constructing these ditches is not given, it is likely to be nearer 563 B.C. than 571 B.C. This abortive irrigation project was resumed some twenty years later by Tzu-ch'an 子產, the most famous statesman of Cheng. In so doing he first incurred the wrath of the people, but three years later won their high praises when the benefits of irrigation became known.[8] Unless irrigation had been novel and little known, these two statesmen would not have encountered such initial resistance. The *Tso-chuan* further states that in 548 B.C. the powerful Ch'u 楚 state of the central Yangtze began "enumerating the boundaries of flooded districts [and] raising small banks on the plains between dykes."[9]

The late beginnings of irrigation are further reflected in the scale of the first famous irrigation network, completed by the Wei state between 424 and 296 B.C., in the Chang River area in northern Honan. From the meticulous description in the *Shui-ching-chu* 水經注 (Commentaries on the Classic of Waterways) of the fifth century A.D., we learn that this whole irrigation system was only twenty li in length, a little over five miles.[10] Not until the third century B.C. did

---

[8] James Legge, tr., *The Chinese Classics*, V, *The Ch'un Ts'ew with the Tso Chuen* (Hongkong, 1872), pp. 447–448, 558.

[9] *Ibid.*, p. 517. It ought to be pointed out that *Hou-Han-shu* [History of the Later Han Dynasty] (Taipei reprint of Ch'ing palace ed.) ch. 76, p. 6b, states that in A.D. 83 Wang Ching, governor of Lu-chiang (south of the Huai River in northern Anhwei), revived and expanded the irrigation network that was said to have been started around 600 B.C. by the Ch'u prime minister, Sun-shu Ngo. But this may well be only a courtesy attribution to a famous ancient man and not authentic.

[10] Yu Yü, "Kuan-tzu tu-ti-p'ien t'an-yüan" [A Study of the Chapter on Hydraulic Engineering in the *Kuan-tzu*], *Nung-shih yen-chiu chi-k'an* [Bulletin of Studies in Agricultural History], I (1959), p. 2.

large-scale irrigation networks appear in the Wei River Basin in Shensi and in the Red Basin of Szechwan.

It is sufficiently clear, therefore, that the rise of Chinese agriculture and civilization bore no direct relation whatever to the flood plain of the Yellow River, and that, of all the ancient peoples who developed higher civilizations in the Old and the New Worlds, the Chinese were the last to know irrigation.[11] Insofar as ancient China is concerned, the theory of the "hydraulic" genesis of culture or of "despotism" is completely groundless.[12]

In our long-range historical perspective, the foundation of the world's most persistently self-sustaining agricultural system, a system which has had so much to do with the enduring character of Chinese civilization, was laid in the Yang-shao nuclear area in Neolithic times. This remarkably self-sustaining agriculture was an outcome of the response of the Yang-shao people to a natural environment which was in some ways restrictive but in one peculiar way uniquely favorable. The environment was restrictive in terms of extremities of climate, light rainfall, relative scarcity of plant resources, and rather dissected land forms. The susceptibility of the loess to erosion and its ability to form vertical walls has accounted for the prevalence in the Wei River basin and elsewhere in the loess highlands of deep and often ramified gullies and ravines, with small flat divides between them. What the natives of this area, at least since early-Chou times, have called the *yüan* 原 (literally "plains") are but small and comparatively level stretches of land bounded by gullies, ravines, and riverside terraces and mounds. It was on such

---

[11] Irrigation began in Meso-America around 800 B.C. See Richard S. MacNeish, "Mesoamerican Archaeology," in *Biennial Review of Anthropology,* ed. Bernard J. Siegel and Alan R. Beals (Stanford, Calif., 1967).

[12] Karl A. Wittfogel, *Oriental Despotism: A Comparative Study of Total Power* (New Haven, Conn., 1957), expounds the theory of "hydraulic" genesis of "oriental despotism." When his theory is applied to China, the most important and most enduring of the "oriental despotisms," it is against all known historical facts.

numerous riverside terraces and mounds that the Yang-shao farmers made their debut. Not only does the topography of the Yang-shao homeland differ from those where other ancient agricultural systems of the Old World arose; the highly dissected land forms were hardly conducive to the practice of the classical type of "slash-and-burn," "swidden," or "shifting" agriculture characteristic of the tropics.

The one most important natural endowment of this area, which on balance more than offsets its natural disadvantages, is the loess. With a rare sense of history among pioneering investigators of the loess, Raphael Pumpelly, an American geologist who led an archaeological expedition to Russian Turkestan in 1904, pointed out the important role played by loess soil in the history of man, with special reference to the loess in China:

Its fertility seems to be inexhaustible, a quality it owes partly, as [Ferdinand von] Richthofen remarks, to its depth and texture, partly to the salts brought to the surface after rains by capillary attraction acting through the tubular channels left after the decay of successive generations of the grass stems inclosed during its accumulation, and partly to the increment of fresh dust that is still brought by winds from the interior. Its self-fertilizing ability is shown by the fact that crops have been raised continuously, through several thousand years, on its immense areas in China, and practically without fertilizing additions. It is on these lands that dense populations accumulate and grow up to the limit of its great life-supporting capacity.[13]

Since the slash-and-burn system of the tropics is dictated primarily by the inability of the soil to restore its fertility without long fallow, and since the loess of China is famous for its self-fertilizing capacity, it is fairly evident from the standpoint of agronomy that the Yang-shao agricultural system, even during its initial stage, was not slash-and-burn in the conventional sense.

In all likelihood, Yang-shao farmers first cleared the grass by burning. Using stone hoes and spades, they broke up the virgin sods, and very probably they also had wooden digging sticks.[14]

---

[13] Raphael Pumpelly, ed., *Explorations in Turkestan: Prehistoric Civilizations of Anau* (2 vols., Washington, D.C., 1908), I, p. 7.

[14] *Hsi-an Pan-p'o*, pp. 59–75.

Without previous experience in field agriculture, they would almost certainly plant millet soon after the sods were turned over. It should not have taken them long to learn that the yield of the first year was meager but the yields of the second and third years were much better. During the first year the nitrogen in the soil is mostly consumed by the various microorganisms which are the main agent in decomposing plant residues. By the second year, when the plant residues have already been decomposed, the various microorganisms, instead of continually tying up the nitrogen in the soil, release it to nourish the seedplants. This phenomenon of different yields would naturally lead the Yang-shao farmers to the formulation of the simple rule that fresh-broken lands be rested for a year and millet be grown from the second year onward.

It may also be presumed that without previous experience the Yang-shao farmers initially might have tried to grow millet on the same plots of land continually. For those types of loess soil which have superior moisture-holding capacity, consecutive planting of millet for a number of years might not be difficult. But for types of loess which do not hold moisture very well, consecutive planting would result in diminishing returns or even crop failure, especially in years of subnormal rainfall or serious drought, not because of the deterioration of soil fertility but because of insufficient moisture. Plots of land which showed signs of diminishing returns or failed to yield a crop would naturally be rested temporarily. Yang-shao farmers could not fail to realize that, if they did not keep the surface of the temporarily resting land clear of weeds, all their previously invested labor would be lost. Depending on the type of the loess soil, such cleared and resting land would have conserved enough moisture in a year or two to make planting again feasible. There is nothing about the necessity of periodically resting the land that Yang-shao farmers could not have learned empirically. Thus came into being their primitive fallow system.

Unlike the classical slash-and-burn system, which requires a very long fallow for the land to restore its fertility, the Yang-shao system seems to have required only a short one for the land to conserve moisture. The Yang-shao system of short fallow which we have reconstructed out of basic principles of agronomy accords almost exactly with the fallow system in the Shensi area described in *The Book of Odes* and *The Book of Documents*.[15] The three key terms for agricultural land in early Chou works are: *tzu* 菑, *hsin* 新, and *yü* 畬. The character *tzu* consists of three components—the upper part is the radical for grass, the middle part is an archaic form of the character which means "to bring calamity to" or "to kill," and the lower part means the field. From various ancient Chinese etymologists' commentaries we learn that *tzu* has two essential meanings: first, the process by which the "grass [residues] is returned to the soil" after the sods have been turned, and second, the first-year land that is not yet ready for planting. *Tzu* is obviously the newly broken sods which have to wait for a year for actual planting because of the time interval necessary for plant residues in the soil to decompose. Since the term *tzu* appears in two authentic chapters in *The Book of Documents* composed at the beginning of

[15] I did not, as one might suspect, project the early-Chou fallow system backwards to Yang-shao times. As a precaution against any possibly naïve correlating of a few scientific facts for a conjectural reconstruction of Yang-shao agricultural practices, I asked Dr. Jack R. Harlan of the Department of Agronomy of the University of Illinois, without first telling him anything about the early-Chou fallow system, what he would think, in the perspective of agronomy and comparative primitive agriculture, to have been the Yang-shao practices. It was a happy moment for me when he said without hesitation that the Yang-shao practices would be different from those of the slash-and-burn system, which would require at least eight times as much land as was actually cultivated each year to make a long fallow feasible; that Yang-shao farmers would probably need no more than three times as much land as was actually cultivated each year; that much of the land cultivated by Yang-shao farmers would require a short fallow; and that the loess soil of superior moisture-holding capacity could grow millet consecutively without great difficulty. Finally, he enlightened me by explaining that the crucial problem in the slash-and-burn system is fertility, but the crucial problem in Yang-shao agriculture is not fertility but moisture.

the Chou dynasty, this system of initial land preparation is undoubtedly of much greater antiquity than 1000 B.C.[16]

The term *hsin* means the land in its second year of preparedness, ready for planting. That the character *hsin* literally means new is because it is the new land to be actually planted. The term *yü* means the well-treated land in its third year of preparedness, ideal for actual planting. Concerning these two terms there was no disagreement among traditional Chinese etymologists. Ode 275—definitely one of the earliest in *The Book of Odes*—which describes land cultivation in the Chou royal domain in the Wei River basin in Shensi, says:

> Ah! Ah! ministers and officers,
> Reverendly attend to your public duties.
> The king has given you perfect rules;—
> Consult about them and consider them.
> Ah! Ah! ye assistants,
> It is now the end of spring;
> And what have ye to seek for?
> [Only] how to manage the new fields [*hsin*] and those of the third year [*yü*].
> How beautiful are the wheat and barley,
> Whose bright produce we shall receive![17]

The fact that in this ode crops are grown only on the second-year and third-year lands further proves that ancient Chinese etymologists' explanation of *tzu*—the first-year land not yet ready for actual planting—is correct.

The three-year cycle within which lands were rested and cultivated is reflected in the generalized description of the system of land allotment in the *Chou-li* 周禮 (Rituals of Chou). Owing to its inclusion of valuable authentic information as well as Han interpolations of Chou institutions and administrative rituals, the various chapters

---

[16] Legge, tr., *The Chinese Classics*, III, *The Shoo King*, pp. 372–373, 417. The terms *tzu* also appears in ode 178 in *The Book of Odes*. The best modern study of the etymology of these three land terms is Yang K'uan, *Ku-shih hsin-t'an* [New Investigations into Ancient History] (Peking, 1965), pp. 10–14.

[17] Legge, tr., *The Chinese Classics*, IV, *The She King*, p. 582.

and passages in the *Chou-li* are of uneven value as sources of historical information. Each passage must therefore be evaluated separately against relevant information that can be culled from other Chou sources. Concerning the principle of land allotment in Chou times, the *Chou-li* states: "In case of the nonchanging land, each [peasant] household be allotted 100 *mou*; in case of the once-changing land, each household be allotted 200 *mou*; and in case of the twice-changing land, each household be allotted 300 *mou*."[18]

This general principle is very likely to have been true for Chou times because other Chou works often testify to the unit of 100 *mou* as the standard allotment for a peasant household and the fallow system implied in this *Chou-li* passage accords well with the three-year cycle of land use described in *The Book of Odes*. Even the *Chou-li*'s reference to the "nonchanging land," that is, land that was planted continually without fallow, should not surprise agronomists familiar with the nature of the loess soil; nor should it strike the orientalists as exceptional, for some of the best-quality land in the prehistoric Near East could also grow crops consecutively.

Since the *Chou-li* was a work compiled by many hands over a period of centuries, it sometimes contains varied versions of essentially similar rituals and customs. A case in point is its two slightly different statements of the general principle of land allotment. In addition to the version cited above, another version mentions the system by which certain amounts of *lai* 萊, fallow land, are attached to the land allotted to farmers. "In case of the upper-grade land, each male adult be allotted 100 *mou*, together with 50 *mou* of *lai*; any extra male adult [of the household] be allotted the same amount. In case of the medium-grade land, each male adult be allotted 100 *mou*, together with 100 *mou* of *lai*; any extra male adult be allotted the same amount. In case of the inferior-grade land, each male adult be allotted 100 *mou*, together with 200 *mou* of *lai*; any extra male adult be allotted the same

---

[18] *Chou-li chu-shu* (SPPY ed.), ch. 10, p. 9a.

amount."[19] Regarding the medium and inferior grades of land, this principle works out in exactly the same way as does the preceding principle—both enabled the farmer to cultivate 100 *mou* each year while resting either 100 or 200 *mou*.

But this latter principle differs from the former in the amount of the allotment of the upper-grade land. According to the former principle, the total amount of the nonchanging best-quality land allotted was 100 *mou;* according to the latter principle, there were to be 50 extra *mou* of fallow land attached to the allotment of 100 *mou* of upper-grade land. So far this seemingly minor discrepancy has never been satisfactorily explained by classical commentators and historians. It seems that the latter principle may have referred to the low plains of north China, where the soils are somewhat less fertile than those of the highlands but the rainfall is generally adequate. From the standpoint of agronomy, the main problem in land use in the low plains is not so much the accumulation of moisture as the restoration of soil fertility by regular fallow. This would explain why even in the case of the upper-grade land there had to be an extra 50 *mou* of fallow land, in order to enable 50 *mou* of land to be rested each year to regain its fertility.

Historically, the first village communities of farmers appeared in the low plains of North China during Lungshanoid times. Like the Yang-shao farmers, Lungshanoid farmers also preferred terraces, mounds, and isles near small rivers and streams, places where the alluvium was sufficiently fertile to enable them to practice self-sustaining agriculture as they had learned it from Yang-shao farmers. The difficulty of continuing the Yang-shao system of self-sustaining agriculture in a generally less fertile area may have been somewhat mitigated by ampler rainfall and by the availability of richer plant resources. Since the aggregate Chou works yield no vestige whatsoever of a true slash-and-burn and shifting agricultural system, there is reason to believe that the early agricultural system of North

---

[19] *Ibid.*, ch. 15, p. 9a.

China, both in the loess highlands and the low plains, was, by and large, self-sustaining.

During the Lungshanoid period agriculture occurred also in the region south of the Huai River, in the lower Han River valley just north of the modern Wu-han tri-cities in central Yangtze, and in the lower Yangtze delta. In these three more southerly areas the main crop since Lungshanoid times has been rice, which, judging from evidence presented later in this chapter, was of native origin and morphologically similar to modern varieties found in the temperate zone of eastern Asia. In these warmer areas of high rainfall and leached soils the main problem of early agriculture was fertility. The regular deposition of fresh silt by rivers and streams in the swamps, which are rice's favorite habitat, made primitive rice cultivation feasible, but the yields must have been low without fertilizers and irrigation. Lungshanoid farmers might have been able to extend rice cultivation from natural swamps to man-made swamps, but large-scale transformation of alluvial plains into rice paddies had to await the arrival of intricate irrigation networks and the systematic use of manure. According to the first-hand impressions of the Grand Historian Ssu-ma Ch'ien some time before 100 B.C., the population of central and lower Yangtze was sparse and the method of rice cultivation primitive, and the people were able to sustain themselves partly because of the natural abundance of this area.[20] During prehistoric and early historic periods, therefore, the agriculture of the southern half of China was very much less self-sustaining than that of the north.

It was only through incessant human effort during the past two thousand years that the southern half of China has been transformed into China's leading food-producing area. Witness the invention of growing rice-shoots in nursery beds before their transplantation to the paddies, the ever-increasing number of irrigation projects, the

---

[20] For translation of this *Shih-chi* description of the agriculture and economy of the Yangtze region, see Appendix I.

use of various irrigation implements and of human and animal manure, the large-scale migrations of northern farmers to the south during the fourth and twelfth centuries, the introduction and dissemination of early-ripening and relatively drought-resistant varieties of tropical rice from A.D. 1000 onward and the continual breeding of superior strains of rice, the systematic terracing of relatively well-watered hills, the increasingly ingenious crop rotation system and the double and sometimes multiple cropping system—all this, and much else, finally made the agricultural system of the southern half of China even more self-sustaining and productive than that of the north.

In sum, it was largely nature, more specifically the loess, that from the very beginning shaped the basic self-sustaining character of the northern agricultural system. But it is mainly through human effort and ingenuity exerted for two thousand years that the southern agricultural system has become self-perpetuating and highly productive. In our long-range historical perspective, the most striking and important characteristic of Chinese agriculture has been its endurance, and the roots of this enduring agriculture are found in the Yang-shao period.

Now we turn our attention to the prehistoric and early historic cropping system of China. The origins of cultivated plants have been favorite topics of botanical scientists and geographers. There is considerable Western literature on the subject, but it usually does not treat systematically those cereal plants that are indigenous to China and were first extensively cultivated by the Chinese. The language and disciplinary barriers are so great that the vast body of Chinese literature concerning food plants has been little known to Western scientists and has seldom been utilized in an organized manner, even by Chinese botanists. Because of the relative abundance of recent archaeological finds concerning ancient cereal grains, coupled with the rich archaic Chinese literature, we can now discuss the origin of each of the major indigenous and introduced food plants, and suggest possibilities for revising certain views held by Western scientists where they do not seem to stand the test of the aggregate Chinese evidence. These plants—millet, rice, wheat and barley, soybean, hemp, and mulberry—will be discussed in turn.

Chinese millets consist of plants, domesticated and wild, that belong to the two different genera of *Setaria* and *Panicum*. The former is chiefly represented by the species *Setaria italica,* which the Chinese call *su* 粟, and the latter by the two subspecies of *P. miliaceum,* which the Chinese call *shu* 黍 and *chi* 稷. This taxonomic division was, of course, not always understood by ancient or even later Chinese etymologists and herbalists. There is reason to believe that some confusion in the nomenclature of the Chinese millets has persisted from the beginning of China's recorded history. Neolithic millet is reported to have been largely *S. italica,* but Shang oracle-bone inscriptions and *The Book of Odes* both indicate an overwhelming importance of *shu* and *chi* as a source of food. Yet in the works written and compiled during the fourth and third centuries B.C., *Setaria* regains its dominant position.[21] These apparent changes in the relative importance of *Setaria* and *Panicum* can be accounted for only by confusion in nomenclature.

We do know without question that *S. italica* was grown extensively in the loess highlands during Yang-shao times. The most important archaeological evidence is the fact that at the typical early Yang-shao site of Pan-p'o, jars filled with husks of *S. italica* have been found in several storage places. The quantity of the stored millet, along with the abundance of agricultural implements and the whole complex layout of the village, established beyond a doubt that *S. italica* was a crop cultivated and harvested by men.[22] Husks of *Setaria* millet have been found in three more Yang-shao sites in Shensi and southern Shansi and in a site at

---

[21] For detailed discussion on the nomenclature and history of millets in China, see Ho, *Huang-t'u yü Chung-kuo nung-yeh ti ch'i-yüan,* pp. 121–133.

[22] *Hsi-an Pan-p'o,* p. 223.

Ta-ho-chuang 大何莊, Lin-hsia county 臨夏, Kansu province, which belongs to a later Neolithic culture called Ch'i-chia. While most of the millet is *Setaria,* that found at Ching-ts'un, southern Shansi, is reported to contain *P. miliaceum.*[23] According to recent carbon-14 determinations—converted to bristlecone-pine dates—millet began to be cultivated by the proto-Chinese shortly after 5000 B.C., if not earlier.

Two independent experiments carried out by American botanists show that among common cereal plants *S. italica* has the highest "efficiency of transpiration," that is, is best suited to dry conditions.[24] While no similar field experiment has ever been done for *P. miliaceum,* its ability to resist drought is well known. *The Book of Odes* mentions the existence of black, red, white, early-ripening, late-ripening, nonsticky, and glutinous millets, an indication of their varietal richness. Even today wild species of millet can be found in the loess area. All this, together with the extreme antiquity of their cultivation, should establish *Setaria* and *Panicum* millets as indigenous plants.

Although two pioneering investigators of the origins of cultivated plants, Alphonse de Candolle and N. I. Vavilov, both regarded *Setaria* and *Panicum* as native Chinese plants, there is still considerable confusion about their original habitats. The 1936 edition of the famous *A. Engler's Syllabus der Pflanzenfamilien,* for example, attributes the original home of *P. miliaceum* to India. A leading Indian expert on millet thinks that millet in general is native to tropical and subtropical areas rather than to China.[25] Hermann von Wissmann, a geographer known for his studies of the dry belts,

---

[23] Carl W. Bishop, "The Neolithic Age in Northern China," *Antiquity,* VII (December 1938), p. 369.

[24] Lawrence J. King, *Weeds of the World: Biology and Control* (London, 1966), Table 4, p. 180.

[25] N. Krishnaswamy, "Origin and Distribution of Cultivated Plants of South Asia: Millets," *Indian Journal of Genetics and Plant Breeding,* XI (June 1951), pp. 67–74.

states, without giving any evidence, that millet originated in northwestern India.[26] All this, and much else, calls for a reexamination of millet in the context of world history.

In the Old World, *P. miliaceum* has been found in a prehistoric Near Eastern site at Argissa, which is dated between 6000 and 5000 B.C.[27] In the New World, *Setaria* of the foxtail variety "was eaten in quantity" in Tamanlipas, Mexico, between 4000 and 3500 B.C. before maize was introduced into the area.[28] But in these areas millet was soon abandoned in favor of superior crops. Millet in the Near East and in Meso-America never played an important role in prehistoric times as it did in Yang-shao China.

Indeed, as N. I. Vavilov suggested, there are millets other than *Setaria* and *Panicum* that are likely to have originated in Abyssinia. These species are *Eleusine coracana* and *Pennisetum spicatum*.[29] Recent archaeological research on Africa suggests that these African millets may have been cultivated by the people of the "Stone Bowl" culture sometime during the second millennium B.C.[30] This suggested chronology, if fully substantiated by future archaeological work in Africa, would still be too recent to challenge the primacy of the Chinese in the history of the domestication and propagation of millet.

The view that *Panicum* is indigenous to India will not stand

[26] Hermann von Wissmann, "On the Role of Nature and Man in Changing the Face of the Dry Belt of Asia," in *Man's Role in Changing the Face of the Earth*, ed. William L. Thomas, Jr. (Chicago, 1956), p. 285.

[27] J. M. Renfrew, "The Archaeological Evidence for the Domestication of Plants: Methods and Problems," in *The Domestication and Exploitation of Plants and Animals*, ed. Peter J. Ucko and G. W. Dimbleby (Chicago, 1969), table on p. 168.

[28] E. O. Callen, "The First New World Cereal," *American Antiquity*, XXXII, No. 4 (1967), pp. 535–538.

[29] N. I. Vavilov, *The Origin, Variation, Immunity and Breeding of Cultivated Plants* (*Chronica Botanica*, XIII, Nos. 1–6, 1949–50), p. 38.

[30] J. Desmond Clark, "Africa South of the Sahara," and "Conclusions and Afterthoughts," in *Courses Toward Urban Life*, ed. Robert J. Braidwood and G. R. Willey (Chicago, 1962), pp. 19–21.

close scrutiny. For one thing, Indian botanists admit that no wild species are known to exist in the Indian subcontinent. For another, no *Panicum* has ever been discovered in Indian cultural strata that contain India's most ancient cereal grains, wheat and barley. What is more, the philological evidence is overwhelmingly against India as a country of origin. The Sanskrit name for *P. miliaceum* is *cīnaka*, which means "Chinese."[31] The Hindi names of *chena* and *cheen,* the Bengali name of *cheena,* and the Gujarati name of *chino* all sound suspiciously close to "China."[32] A variant Bengali name of *bhutta* clearly indicates Bhutan, the Himalayan foothill country, as a stepping-stone in the long route of its introduction from China.[33] It is also known that the Sanskrit names for a number of cultivated plants introduced from China faithfully reflect their origin, for example, *cīnanī* ("Chinese fruit") for peach and *cīnarajaputra* ("crown prince of China") for pear.[34] The Persian name of *šušu* for *P. miliaceum,* which is undoubtedly from the Chinese *shu-shu* 秫黍 *(P. miliaceum glutinosa),* is additional philological evidence that this food plant was introduced into Western Asia from China in early historical times.[35]

In the study of the origins of cultivated plants, philological evidence alone is seldom decisive. But our evidence is at once archaeological, botanical, historical, and philological; there is also geological and palynological evidence. In the light of the various types of evidence presented in the preceding chapter, the significant position held by the family of Gramineae in the pollen profile of Wu-ch'eng, Shansi, which chronologically covers the past million

---

[31] Berthold Laufer, *Sino-Iranica: Chinese Contributions to the History of Civilization in Ancient Iran with Special Reference to the History of Cultivated Plants and Products* (Chicago, 1919), p. 595.

[32] *The Wealth of India: A Dictionary of Indian Raw Materials and Industrial Products* (New Delhi, 1966), VII, *s. v.* "Panicum."

[33] I owe this valuable information to my colleague, Professor Edward C. Dimock.

[34] Laufer, *Sino-Iranica,* p. 540, p. 567.

[35] *Ibid.,* p. 565.

years, can be substantially accounted for only by *Setaria* and *Panicum*. Indeed, ever since the beginning of agriculture the life of the inhabitants of the loess highlands had been so dependent on millet that even the name of Hou Chi 后稷, the legendary ancestor of the Chou tribe, literally means the "Lord of Millet."

Of the various Neolithic artifacts discovered in 1921 at the Yang-shao village and brought back to Sweden by J. G. Andersson for further study, no single finding could be more significant than what was identified by two Swedish botanists as the imprints of cultivated rice *(Oryza sativa)* on fragments of a pottery jar.[36] "The discovery was," in the words of Andersson, "in a high degree sensational not only because it sets back the history of rice an immense distance in time, but also because it points, not to dry Central Asia, but to the rainy Southern Asia, which is the homeland of rice."[37] Although the name for the first full-fledged Neolithic culture in China is derived from the village of Yang-shao, the whole cultural assemblage discovered at this village is now generally believed to be of a much later type than that of Pan-p'o.

Finds of prehistoric rice in China made after 1949 are exceptionally plentiful. While the rice discovered in 1921 at the Yang-shao village in western Honan has remained the only verified case of rice culture within the southeastern portion of the loess highlands, prehistoric rice has been found in more than ten localities in the area south of the Huai River and in the lower and central Yangtze regions, which lie outside the Neolithic nuclear area. As is shown in chapter 1, table 1, the Ch'ing-lien-kang cultural site at Sung-tse, Ch'ing-p'u county, now within the enlarged municipality of Shanghai, where rice remains were found, is radiocarbon-dated at 3395 ± 105 B.C.—approximately 4000 B.C. when converted to

---

[36] G. Edman and E. Söderberg, "Auffindung von Reis in einer Tonscherte aus einer etwa fünftausendjährigen chinesischen Siedlung," *Bulletin of the Geological Society of China,* VIII, No. 4 (1929), pp. 363–368.

[37] J. G. Andersson, *Children of the Yellow Earth* (London, 1934), p. 336.

bristlecone-pine dendrochronology. The Sung-tse rice has been morphologically identified as the *hsien* 秈 *(Oryza sativa indica)* subspecies—the early-ripening "tropical" subspecies with long grains. The carbonized rice remains from the Liang-chu cultural site of Ch'ien-shan-yang, Wu-hsing county, on the southern fringe of the T'ai-hu 太湖 Lake in northern Chekiang, are radiocarbon-dated at 2750±100 B.C. (bristlecone-pine date: 3300±100 B.C.). Not only do these two rice finds chronologically strengthen each other; the latter finds are extremely important scientifically and historically in that they contain both the *hsien* and the *keng* 秔、稉 (late-ripening rice with round grains) subspecies. The combined evidence further confirms the conclusion of an early study of my own, based exclusively on literary and local-history records, that, although most of the rice varieties grown in China up to about A.D. 1000 were of the heavy-yielding and late-ripening *keng* subspecies, a number of *hsien* varieties had been native to the southern half of China.[38]

It should be further noted that, in the lower Yangtze delta, rice remains have been found from the lowest cultural stratum of the Ts'ao-hsieh-shan 草鞋山 site in Wu-hsien 吳縣 and of the Hsien-li-tun 仙蠡墩 site in Wu-hsi 無錫 which stratigraphically corresponds to the Ma-chia-pin phase—the earliest phase of the southern type of the Ch'ing-lien-kang culture.[39] Since, as has been pointed out in our introductory discussion on chronology in chapter 1, the two available radiocarbon dates for the Ch'ing-lien-kang

---

[38] Ping-ti Ho, "Early-Ripening Rice in Chinese History," *Economic History Review*, 2d Series, IX, No. 2 (December 1956), pp. 200–218, esp. pp. 201–215. For listing of the places where prehistoric Chinese rice remains have been found, see Ho, *Huang-t'u yü Chung-kuo nung-yeh ti ch'i-yüan*, pp. 140–145.

[39] Wu Shan-ching, "A Brief Discussion of the Ch'ing-lien-kang Culture," *WW*, 1973, No. 6, pp. 45–61; and Yin Huan-chang and Chang Cheng-hsiang, "Tui Chiang-su T'ai-hu-ti-ch'ü hsin-shih-ch'i-wen-hua ti i-hsieh jen-shih" [Toward an Understanding of the Neolithic Cultures in the T'ai-hu Lake Area of Kiangsu], *KK*, 1962, No. 3, pp. 147–157.

culture (3835 ± 105 B.C. and 3395 ± 105 B.C.) probably represent the approximate upper and lower chronological boundaries of its early phase, there is reason to expect that future radiocarbon age determinations of prehistoric rice finds of the lower Yangtze area may yield dates a few centuries earlier than that of the rice remains of Sung-tse. The beginnings of rice culture in the lower Yangtze area may well fall within the latter half of the fifth millennium B.C., according to bristlecone-pine dendrochronology.

Outside of the lower Yangtze, unusually large quantities of rice husks which belonged to the Ch'ü-chia-ling culture and which morphologically were of the *keng* subspecies have been found in the baked red clay of several Hupei sites along the Han River. The quantities of rice husks would indicate rice cultivation on a considerable scale, but chronologically these sites can only be dated back to the early half of the third millennium B.C., according to bristlecone-pine dendrochronology.

These rich archaeological finds raise serious doubts about the general view held by botanical scientists that rice is indigenous only to southern and southeastern Asia and that rice was introduced from India to China. The opinion of Vavilov, which has been widely accepted, is worth citing:

Even though tropical India may stand second to China in the number of species of cultivated plants, its *rice,* which was introduced into China, where it has been the staple food plant for the past thousand years, makes tropical India even more important in world agriculture. That India is the native home of rice is borne out by the presence there of a number of wild rice species, as well as common rice, growing wild, as weeds, and possessing a character common to wild grasses, namely, shedding of the grain at maturity, which insures self-sowing. Here are also found intermediate forms connecting wild and cultivated rice. The varietal diversity of the cultivated rice of India is the richest in the world, the coarse-grained primitive varieties being especially typical. India differs from China and other secondary regions of cultivation in Asia by the prevalence of dominant genes in its rice varieties.[40]

---

[40] Vavilov, *The Origin, Variation, Immunity, and Breeding of Cultivated Plants,* p. 29; his view is upheld fully in the long article on "Oryza" in *The Wealth of India,* VII, esp. pp. 115–116.

The scientific reasons given by so eminent and pioneering an investigator as Vavilov for regarding tropical India as the original home of rice merit respect. But historians must further investigate whether rice was indeed introduced into China from India; whether China, at least the area south of the natural geographic demarcation of Ch'inling and the Huai River, may not have been one of the original homes of rice; and whether there is sufficiently strong botanical and historical evidence for the ancient existence of wild species of rice in China.

Studying the problem in the context of world history, one finds, most surprisingly, that existing Indian archaeological and written records all indicate a much later beginning of rice culture. Sir Mortimer Wheeler a few years ago reported on the findings of rice in some Harappan sites which are radiocarbon-dated at 1700 B.C. and slightly later. More recent radiocarbon dating shows the existence of rice in eastern India around 3000 B.C., but it is impossible to ascertain whether the rice was truly domesticated or wild.[41] Our comparative archaeological data show that rice culture in China anticipated rice culture in India by a very wide margin.

It is also significant that the *Rig-Veda,* the earliest sacred book in Sanskrit compiled probably around 1000 B.C. or slightly earlier, never mentions rice but often alludes to wheat and barley. The Sanskrit name for rice, *vrihi,* appears only in the *Antharva-Veda* and other works written after 1000 B.C.[42] In contrast, the oracle records of the Shang and the various works of the Chou period all

[41] Sir Mortimer Wheeler, *Civilizations of the Indus Valley and Beyond* (London, 1966), p. 90; other Harappan rice finds are mentioned in Bridget and Raymond Allchin, *The Birth of Indian Civilization* (Baltimore, 1968). The most recent rice finds in eastern India are discussed in Vishnu-Mittre, "Changing Economy in Ancient India," a paper prepared for the Conference on the Origins of Agriculture, IXth International Congress of Anthropological and Ethnological Sciences, Chicago, 1973.

[42] A. A. MacDonell and A. B. Keith, *Vedix Index of Names and Subjects* (London, 1912); Sir Monier Monier-Williams, *A Sanskrit-English Dictionary* (London, 1956).

testify to rice culture and the brewing of rice wine, although throughout ancient times rice remained an "aristocrat" among cereal grains consumed mainly by the ruling class on ceremonial occasions.

Twenty-three species of the swampy grasses of *Oryza* have been recognized taxonomically by scientists, and only two of the twenty-three have been domesticated. Of the domesticated species, *Oryza glaberrima* is strictly a regional crop confined to Western Africa, and only *O. sativa* has worldwide significance. The regions known to Western scientists where wild species of rice have been discovered are India, Indochina, Indonesia, Taiwan, Western Africa, Madagascar, Central and South America, and Australia.[43] Since the geographic distribution of wild species of rice is truly worldwide, and since climatically and phytogeographically the southern half of China, the world's largest single rice-producing area, has much in common with the rest of monsoon Asia, no generalization about the original homelands of rice is convincing without a thorough search of the historical and modern records of wild species of rice in China.

Not only is the nomenclature of Chinese rice highly complex, but Chinese historical records on rice are the richest in the world. In addition to references to cultivated rice, records of Shang oracles significantly mention a wild species called *ni* 秜.[44] *Shuo-wen-chieh-tzu* 說文解字, the earliest systematic Chinese lexicon compiled shortly after A.D. 100, explains: "The kind of rice that ripens this year and will grow all by itself again next year is called *ni*." *Ni* is almost certainly the common *Oryza perennis*, which is believed by an increasing number of experts on rice to have been the probable progenitor of cultivated rice.[45]

The Chinese vocabulary was rapidly expanding from Shang to

---

[43] *The Wealth of India*, VII, s. v. "Oryza."

[44] Yü Hsing-wu, "Shang-tai ti ku-lei-tso-wu" [The Cereal Crops of Shang Times], *Tung-pei jen-min-ta-hsüeh jen-wen-k'e-hsüeh hsüeh-pao*, 1957, No. 1, p. 101.

[45] *The Wealth of India*, VII, pp. 114–116.

Han times. Because of different pronunciations in different regional dialects and because of the inevitable process of corruption of the original usage, by Han times four homonyms of *lü* 穭, 秐 and a character *li* 離 had been derived from the original character *ni*. *Huai-nan-tzu* 淮南子, an eclectic work of the second century B.C. compiled by scholars employed by the Prince of Huai-nan, contains an important entry about the *li* wild rice: "*Li* ripens somewhat earlier than [cultivated] rice, but farmers treat it as a weed for fear that whatever small crop it might yield would be more than offset by the harm it might do to the main harvest [of cultivated rice]."[46] Kao Yu 高誘, who made systematic commentaries on this work around A.D. 205, explains that "the *li* [wild rice] usually grows alongside the [cultivated] rice." This passage from *Huai-nan-tzu* provides not only the rationale for destroying the wild perennial rice but also the best explanation as to why through conscious elimination the species of wild rice in ancient China had been reduced.

In all likelihood, the term *li* in ancient times might have been peculiar only to the dialect of the area immediately south of the Huai. From Han times onward the common term for wild rice is *lü* in four variant forms. Though used at first as a noun to mean wild rice exclusively, *lü* acquired so many new meanings that it was soon employed as a general term for all kinds of wild cereal plants and also as an adjective or adverb describing the naturally wild state of any food plant. Because of the ever-broadening meaning of *lü*, I have excluded some fifteen entries culled from various dynastic histories in which the character *lü* was used in a general sense without a specific association with rice. It should be noted, however,

---

[46] *Huai-nan-tzu* [Works Compiled under the Auspices of the Prince of Huai-nan] (SPPY ed.), ch. 20, p. 18b. For the identification of the *li* wild rice, see Tuan Yü-ts'ai, *Shuo-wen chien-tzu chu* [Commentaries on the Lexicon *Shuo-wen chieh-tzu*] (Commercial Press ed.), ch. 7A, pp. 87–88. The most systematic treatise on the etymology and evolution of the terminology of the wild rice is Liu Pao-nan, "Shih-ku" [Etymological Studies of Cereal Grains], in *Huang-Ch'ing ching-chieh hsü-pien* [Imperially Compiled Commentaries on Ancient Classics, 2d Series].

that among these excluded entries some might well have actually referred to the occurrence of wild rice, especially when the recorded habitats of such *lü-sheng* 稆生 (wildly grown) grains were found around edges of rivers and lakes south of the Huai River. For prudence I eliminated all entries that are not precisely phrased, and I checked through various post-Han dynastic histories so that none of the entries presented in Table 3 can be construed as escapes from cultivation as a result of temporary abandonment of fields caused by wars or natural calamities.

TABLE 3

POST-HAN RECORDS ON WILD SPECIES OF RICE

Year (A.D.)	Place (Modern Names)	Essential Description
231	Chia-hsing (Chekiang)	Wild rice ripened naturally.
446	Chia-hsing	"Wild rices ripened naturally, being of more than thirty varieties."
537	Kiangsu (south of Huai)	In the ninth lunar month "wild rices had grown over an area of 200,000 *mou* (about 30,000 acres)."
537	Wu-hsing (Chekiang)	Wild rice ripened, much to the benefit of the local poor and hungry.
731	Yang-chou (Kiangsu)	In early spring wild rice ripened in an area of 21,000 *mou*, and perennial wild rices ripened in an area of 180,000 *mou*.
852	Kao-yu and T'ai-hsien (Kiangsu)	Poor people of the two counties procured "strange rice" by straining its grains in public rivers; they called it "divine rice."
874	Ts'ang-chou (Hopei)	Wild rice ripened in an area of more than 200,000 *mou*, much to the benefit of the poor of local and neighboring counties.

TABLE 3 *(continued)*

Year (A.D.)	Place (Modern Names)	Essential Description
979	Su-hsien (Anhwei)	In the eighth lunar month wild rice ripened in lakes; harvest was gathered by the poor who called it "divine rice."
1010	Kung-an (Hupei)	In the second lunar month wild rice ripened, and people procured a harvest of four hundred bushels.
1013	4 counties of T'ai-chou (Kiangsu)	In the second lunar month "divine rice" ripened in various places in the four counties.
1023	Soochow (Kiangsu) and Chia-hsing (Chekiang)	"Divine rice" ripened in the sixth month in the lakes of these areas; harvests were gathered by the poor.

SOURCES: *Chin-shu* [History of the Chin Dynasty] (Taipei reprint of Ch'ing palace ed.), ch. 43, p. 31b, ch. 99, p. 10b; *Sung-shu* [History of the Sung Dynasty (A.D. 420–478)] (Taipei reprint), ch. 29, p. 3a and p. 8a; *Liang-shu* [History of the Liang Dynasty] (Taipei reprint), ch. 3, p. 16a; *T'ang hui-yao* [Compendium of T'ang Institutes] (Taipei, Shih-chieh-shu-chü reprint), ch. 28, p. 534; *Hsin T'ang-shu* (Taipei reprint), ch. 39, p. 17b; and Ma Tuan-lin, *Wen-hsien t'ung-k'ao* [Historical Investigation on Government Institutions and Culture] (Commercial Press ed.), ch. 299, pp. 2367–2368.

The entries in the table represent only a very small fraction of the reports submitted to the imperial government by various provincial and local authorities. Concerning the frequency of reports on the appearance of wild rice in early Sung times, Ma Tuan-lin, the great encyclopedist of the late thirteenth century, said that they were so numerous that he could choose only a few for inclusion in his encyclopedia in the chapter on unusual plants.[47] The founder of the Ming dynasty, who reigned from 1368 to 1398, ordered that natural calamities, but not auspicious natural phenomena, be

[47] Ma Tuan-lin, *Wen-hsien t'ung-k'ao*, ch. 299, p. 2367.

regularly reported to the throne.⁴⁸ This regulation, which was observed by later rulers of the Ming and Ch'ing periods, caused the virtual disappearance of the mention of wild rice from all the central government's records. The continual dissemination of early-ripening and relatively drought-resistant rice since the beginning of the eleventh century, the endless process of breeding better strains of rice, and an increasingly labor-intensive system of rice culture during the past millennium have all contributed to a drastic decline in the incidence of wild rice in China.⁴⁹ Despite all this, the late E. D. Merrill found in the 1910s some wild species of rice in Kwangtung, and Chinese botanists have recently discovered more in Kwangtung, Kwangsi, Yunnan, and the lower Yangtze.⁵⁰

The entries of wild rice tabulated above deserve further analysis. The areas in which wild rice grew and ripened were so extensive as to rule out the possibility of accidental escape from cultivation. The places in which wild rice appeared—public and unnamed lakes, rivers, and marshes—further show that the rice must truly have grown wild. Those kinds of wild rice that ripened in early spring were obviously different from cultivated rice that usually ripened in late summer and early fall. It is most interesting that the vulgar name of "divine rice" suggests not only its wild origin but also the likelihood that it might be *Oryza fatua,* a weed that some rice experts believe to have been the progenitor of cultivated rice. I. H. Burkill, an authority on the flora of southern and southeastern Asia, describes the peculiarities of *O. fatua*:

In the fields of south-western and western India, it [*O. fatua*] is exactly like the annual *O. sativa* in every respect except that it shatters at maturity. In the Gangetic plains it is seen in a different form, but still is just like *O. sativa* except for shattering.

---

⁴⁸ *Ta-Ming hui-tien* [Collected Statutes of the Ming Dynasty] (1587 ed., Taipei photostat reproduction), ch. 103, pp. 3b–4a.

⁴⁹ Ho, "Early-Ripening Rice in Chinese History" (see note 39 above).

⁵⁰ Recent reports of discoveries of wild species of rice in southern China are not available; a brief mention of these discoveries is given in Hsia Nai, "Ch'ang-chiang-liu-yü k'ao-ku wen-t'i," *KK,* 1960, No. 2. Also Dr. Hsia's oral communication, July 1974.

The poor do not ignore it, but tying the awns together before maturity save the grain for themselves, or they collect the fallen grain, which is made an easier process by the length of the awns.[51]

Had it not been for the fact that the "divine rice" shattered at maturity, the poor would not have had to collect the grains by straining through river and lake water. The records on wild species of rice in three thousand years of Chinese literature are impressive.

In spite of the existence of some *hsien* or "tropical" rice strains in the southern half of China since 3300±100 B.C., most of the varieties of rice recorded in Chinese literature prior to A.D. 1000 are of the *keng* subspecies, or *Oryza sativa japonica*.[52] The *keng* varieties are, in other words, usually confined to the temperate zone of eastern Asia and characterized by their shorter and more rounded grains, as compared with grains of the tropical *Oryza sativa indica*. It is well known to geneticists that "the two groups differ in morphological and several physiological features including response to temperature and day length."[53] A preliminary morphological study of the prehistoric and ancient rice husks found in North China and the middle Yangtze Valley shows that they are of the *keng* subspecies. A leading Chinese expert on rice is of the opinion that "the *keng* varieties of [Neolithic] Hupei may have a certain pedigree relationship with those found in the Han tombs of Lo-yang and the Yellow River Valley, as well as with those discovered at the Yang-shao sites."[54]

In any case, our combined archaeological and historical data

---

[51] I. H. Burkill, *A Dictionary of the Economic Products of the Malay Peninsula* (2 vols., London, 1935), II, p. 1593.

[52] Ho, "Early-Ripening Rice in Chinese History."

[53] *The Wealth of India*, VII, p. 116.

[54] Ting Ying, "Chiang-Han-p'ing-yüan hsin-shih-ch'i-shih-tai hung-shao-t'u chung ti tao-ku-k'e k'ao-ch'a" [Notes on the Neolithic Rice Husks Unearthed in Hupei], *KKHP*, 1959, No. 4, pp. 31–34. Also *Ching-shan Ch'ü-chia-ling* [Report on the Archaeological Site of Ch'ü-chia-ling, Ching-shan County] (Peking, 1965), Appendix, pp. 78–80.

seem reasonably to have established China as one of the original homes of rice and probably as the first area in the world where rice was cultivated. Bearing in mind that rice is the main food for more than half of humanity and that the temperate zone of eastern Asia accounts for more than 60 percent of the world's output, with China as the largest single producer, we become aware that China's contribution to world agriculture has been much greater than Vavilov and other botanical scientists realized. Whereas wheat has assumed an eminent position in the agriculture of the Western world only during the past 150 years, rice has been supporting the larger portion of the human race for a millennium. China's contribution to world agriculture is therefore greater than that of Mesopotamia, which first supplied the world with wheat and barley.

Two more points about rice remain to be involved in the discussion on the origin of Chinese agriculture. First, while rice is generally a tropical and subtropical plant, archaeological evidence shows that it was cultivated in the semiarid loess highlands. As has been pointed out, there have been marshes in both the highlands and the low plains of North China, largely for physiographical reasons. Besides water, the rice plant requires a fairly high range of temperature and long exposure to sunlight for growth and maturation. Because of the continental type of climate, the loess provinces have average temperatures of 24° to 26° C., or 75° to 79° F., in July and August—an average is actually considerably higher than the minimum average temperature of 20.5° C. required to bear a normal crop of rice in the temperate zone of eastern Asia. Solar radiation is considerably stronger in North China than in the areas south of the Yangtze. Experiments in recent years show that the highest yield of rice per acre in China is not found in the southern provinces but in Shensi, the nuclear area.[55] Our knowledge of the

---

[55] Chu K'e-chen, "Lun wo-kuo ch'i-hou ti chi-ke t'e-tien chi ch'i yü liang-shih-tso-wu sheng-ch'an ti kuan-hsi" [Some Characteristics of the Climate of China and Their Relationship to Agricultural Production], *Ti-li hsüeh-pao* [Acta Geographica Sinica], XXX, No. 1 (1964).

summer climatic conditions of North China shows that there is actually nothing strange about the growing of rice in the marshes of North China in prehistoric and ancient times.

The second point is whether rice culture in prehistoric times does not necessarily imply some form of irrigation. Indeed, some Chinese paleographers are so sure of the absence of irrigation before the sixth century B.C., and of the dependence of rice on irrigation, that they are reluctant to identify the character for rice in the inscriptions on Shang oracles. The truth is that primitive rice culture does not depend on irrigation, as two Western experts testify concerning southeastern Asia:

> A dry-land crop like wheat requires some sort of tool for working the ground, though it be only a digging stick. For lowland rice no such tool is required. Even today there are localities [in southeastern Asia] where the rice field is neither plowed, spaded, nor hoed. The soil may be thoroughly puddled and all the weeds destroyed merely by driving a carabao around in the flooded field, or the farmer and his family may accomplish the same purpose by splashing around in bare feet.[56]

Chou Ch'ü-fei 周去非, a twelfth-century official, described primitive rice culture in southernmost China:

> Of all the boundless land that lies beyond what human eyes can reach, not 1 percent of such land has been brought under cultivation. In preparing the fields for rice planting, the peasants choose only the kind of land that is evenly submerged under water all year round. If the land is a bit too high [to be submerged constantly], they would reject it. Even when they do cultivate, they would barely break up the ground without deep plowing or hoeing. They simply broadcast the [rice] seeds, never transplant the shoots. After the seeds are broadcast, they do not water the fields during drought; nor do they drain off [the surplus] water after excessive rain. Caring nothing about manuring, deep plowing, and weeding, they leave everything to heaven.[57]

Chou's description of primitive rice culture in the backward southernmost part of China in the twelfth century A.D. must have been

---

[56] V. D. Wichizer and M. K. Bennet, *The Rice Economy of Monsoon Asia* (Stanford, Calif., 1941), pp. 14–15.

[57] Chou Ch'ü-fei, *Ling-wai tai-ta* [Answers to Queries on Southernmost China] (Ts'ung-shu chi-ch'eng ed.), p. 36.

true for the prehistoric method of growing rice. That rice seeds were simply broadcast in prehistoric times is almost certain, for not until after the time of Christ did the Chinese character *yang* 秧 (young rice shoot) begin to appear in the *Shuo-wen,* and not until the second century A.D. was the method of transplanting young rice shoots from nursery beds to the main paddies described in a short agricultural treatise.[58] The technique of transplantation, which contributes so much to the increase of yield per acre, was undoubtedly a Chinese invention, for even today in many parts of India transplantation of rice shoots is not practiced.

The addition of rice to the cropping system accentuated the Sinitic character of prehistoric and ancient Chinese agriculture.

After millet and rice, the next crops in chronological order are wheat and barley. Shang oracle-bone inscriptions contain two names for wheat but none for barley. In view of the fact that wheat was considered an "aristocratic" cereal while barley was not, the absence of the character for barley in oracle-bone inscription is not a sure indication that barley was not known to the poor commoners of late Shang times. Beside paleographic evidence, there has not been a single verified prehistoric find of wheat and barley in China. It is true that nearly a kilogram of carbonized wheat grains is reported to have been found in a Lung-shan cultural site in northern Anhwei along the Huai River, but the fact that the grains are contained in a Chou-type pottery jar makes the preliminary dating of wheat highly suspect.[59]

The number and quality of Western scientific and archaeological studies of wheat and barley make it unnecessary for historians of Chinese agriculture to examine the question of the original habitats

---

[58] The best edition of this agricultural treatise of the Later Han period is *Ssu-min yüeh-ling chiao-chu* [Modern Annotations on Monthly Ordinances for Four Groups of Commoners], ed. Shih Sheng-han (Peking, 1965).

[59] For details, see Ho, *Huang-t'u yü Chung-kuo nung-yeh ti ch'i-yüan,* pp. 160–161.

of these two food plants.⁶⁰ North China must be excluded from the possible homelands of wheat and barley because they are indigenous to areas of winter rain in southwestern Asia, and North China offers a climate and rainfall pattern that is the exact opposite of that of southwestern Asia and the eastern Mediterranean. Even today, wheat growing in many localities of North China is difficult without irrigation because of the uneven distribution of rainfall and especially because of frequent spring droughts.⁶¹

In sharp contrast to the Chinese characters for other cereal plants which invariably have the radical *ho* 禾 (cereal plant), the characters for wheat, *lai* 來 and *mai* 麥, and barley, *mou* 麰, are all derived philologically from the character *lai*, which literally means "come" and which is used as a radical. Whereas the native origins of millet are vividly reflected in many ancient odes, those few odes that mention wheat and barley never fail to point out that they were bestowed on the people by God on High. Knowing that they were not native to North China but not knowing exactly where they had come from, the men of genius who created new characters could only regard these food plants as coming from God, hence the radical "come." Since the characters for wheat are already found in the Shang oracle-bone inscriptions of the post-1300 B.C. period, and since barley is very likely to have been introduced into North China along with wheat, they came to China probably during the second, or late in the third, millennium B.C.⁶²

For over a millennium after their introduction, wheat and barley do not seem to have made rapid progress in North China. Various late Chou and Han works testify to their better adaptability to the low plains, where the rainfall is considerably heavier than it

---

⁶⁰ We need mention only the best literature: Jack R. Harlan and Daniel Zohary, "Distribution of Wild Wheats and Barleys," *Science*, CLIII (1966), pp. 1074–1078.

⁶¹ See note 55.

⁶² For further discussion of the etymology of wheat in Chinese, see ch. 6 below, pp. 250–251.

is in the loess highlands. The difficulty with which wheat and barley were adapted to the semiarid loess highlands is fully reflected in a memorial by Tung Chung-shu 董仲舒, a leading scholar and philosopher of the second century B.C., who, in addition to urging the emperor to exhort the people of the loess highlands to grow more wheat, testified that the people of the metropolitan Shensi area had been generally reluctant to grow wheat.[63]

It is worth noting that, until the time of Christ, wheat and barley had always been grown as dry-land crops in North China. The dry-land culture had been made possible only by the discovery, through trial and error, of certain special ways of saving soil moisture. Fragments of *Fan-Sheng-chih shu* 氾勝之書, a famous agricultural treatise of the first century B.C., give interesting information on the peculiarly Sinitic method of growing wheat and barley:

> If at the time of wheat planting the weather has been rainless and dry for some time, one is advised first to soak the wheat seeds in a thin starchy congee, which, being slightly acidic [through fermentation], should be mixed with discharges of silkworms. [Wheat seeds] should be soaked at midnight and must be sown shortly before dawn, so that the congee and the ground dew will all go down into the soil.
>
> Amidst the autumn drought, [wheat] should be watered by hand at the time when the mulberry sheds its leaves.
>
> In winter after the snow comes to an end, one should use a tool to press the snow into the ground and then have it duly covered, so that the snow will not be blown away by the wind. This process should be repeated after each snow.[64]

This work mentions for the first time the existence of spring wheat. Since spring wheat had been grown in the cooler foothill country of ancient Greece,[65] if not earlier elsewhere in southwestern Asia, and since the Former Han Empire did have diplomatic and military contacts with the Greco-Bactrian states in central Asia, spring

---

[63] *Han-shu*, ch. 24A, p. 16a.

[64] The best modern edition is *Fan-Sheng-chih-shu chin-shih* [Modern Commentaries on the Agricultural Treatise by Fan Sheng-chih], ed. Shih Sheng-han (Peking 1956); the quotations are on p. 20.

[65] Naum Jasny, *The Wheat of Classical Antiquity* (Baltimore, 1944), pp. 70–71.

wheat was almost certainly introduced into China not much earlier than the time of Christ.

Like rice, wheat was a luxury food in ancient China, consumed mainly by members of the ruling class on ceremonial occasions. What is really significant about wheat and barley in ancient China is that, despite their southwestern Asian origin, they were not grown in China on irrigated fields but were adapted to the typically northern Sinitic system of dry-land farming. This fact helps to sharpen our perception of the peculiar regional traits and characteristics of ancient Chinese agriculture, developed independently from those of Mesopotamia.

An additional significant difference between the earliest Chinese and the other ancient agricultural systems of the Old World is the conspicuous absence in the former of leguminous plants rich in protein. No trace of legumes has been found in any Neolithic site in North China or in the records of Shang oracles. Not until Chou times did the soybean appear in bronze inscriptions and *The Book of Odes*.

There is little doubt, however, that the soybean (*Glycine max* L. Merrill) is indigenous to China, for many varieties of its wild ancestor (*Glycine ussuriensis* Regel et Maack) exist in China even today.[66] The typical habitats of wild soybeans are wet lowlands and the edges of rivers and lakes where soybeans grow together with reeds. While wild varieties of soybeans, according to extensive field observations by two Chinese botanists, are found in many parts of China including the loess highlands, they are concentrated mostly

---

[66] B. V. Skvortzow, "The Soybean—Wild and Cultivated in Eastern Asia," *Manchurian Research Society Publications,* Natural History Section, Series A, No. 2 (1927), names some semiwild species of soybeans *Glycine gracilis* Skvortzow, which are now considered taxonomically incorrect. For a detailed taxonomic study of soybeans and related plants, see F. J. Hermann, *A Revision of the Genus Glycine and Its Immediate Allies,* U.S. Department of Agriculture, Technical Bulletin, No. 1268 (1962).

in the eastern provinces north of the Yangtze.[67] Despite the existence of wild soybeans in the loess highlands in modern times, it is not definitely known whether they have been native to that area since prehistoric times. Modern experiments do show that the soybean requires three times as much water as does *Setaria italica* to produce the same amount of solid matter (excluding root), and that its "efficiency of transpiration" is the lowest among common food plants.[68] Botanists know that the soybean can adapt itself only to a comparatively narrow range of environmental conditions and usually requires a long growing season with a plentiful water supply. The natural environment of the loess highlands apparently does not seem to have been congenial to this plant, at least not before suitable strains were developed by men. The absence of Luguminosae in the pollen profiles gathered from Wu-ch'eng and Li-shih in Shansi and from the Yang-shao site at Pan-p'o near Sian, though significant, may not be conclusive evidence that wild soybeans did not exist in the loess highlands in prehistoric times. On the other hand, pollen profiles gathered near Peking, whether of the middle and late Pleistocene or of late prehistoric and early historic times, invariably contain Leguminosae.[69]

Since soybean was domesticated in early historic times, Chou literary works are extremely valuable in enabling us to pin down almost exactly the area where it was first domesticated. The *I Chou-shu* 逸周書 (Lost History of Chou), a late-Chou compilation, which was not rediscovered until A.D. 281 along with the *Bamboo Annals,* contains a chapter describing the tributes brought to the Chou royal court by various peoples shortly after the Chou conquest of Shang. It mentions that the Shan-Jung 山戎 (Mountain

---

[67] Sun Hsing-tung and Keng Ch'ing-han, "Ta-tou p'in-chung ti fen-lei" [A Taxonomic Study of Soybeans], *Chih-wu-fen-lei hsüeh-pao* [Acta Phytotaxonomica Sinica], II, No. 1 (1959).

[68] King, *Weeds of the World,* p. 180.

[69] For full listing of these pollen analyses, see note 32 of chapter 1.

Jung), a proto-Tungusic people who by the eighth and seventh centuries B.C. at the latest had expanded toward northeastern Hopei, offered *Jung-shu* 戎菽 (literally "the beans of the Jung," but actually soybeans) as their special tribute.[70] In some songs and odes in *The Book of Odes,* soybeans are referred to either as *shu* or as *jen-shu* 荏菽; and Han classical commentators were certainly right in interpreting *jen* as a phonetic variation of *Jung,* the name of the above-mentioned proto-Tungusic tribe. The special significance of the *I Chou-shu* account is its precision about the geographic and ethnic origin of the domesticated soybean. The account, moreover, is well corroborated by other, independent late-Chou works. The *Kuo-yü* 國語 (Discourses of the Feudal States) contains a saying of Confucius to the effect that shortly after the Chou conquest of Shang, various peoples including the Su-shen 肅慎, also a proto-Tungusic people and a northern neighbor of the Mountain Jung, came to the court of the Chou king to pay tribute.[71] The *Kuan-tzu* 管子, an eclectic work of political and economic philosophy attributed to the statesman Kuan Chung 管仲 of the Ch'i state in Shantung of the seventh century B.C., which contains valuable Chou records although its compilation was not completed until Han times, states that Lord Huan 桓公 of Ch'i led an army to punish the Mountain Jung and brought back "winter onions and soybeans *(Jung-shu)* for dissemination throughout the various states."[72] By checking with other late-Chou works, we can date this event as having taken place in 664 B.C. The Ku-liang 穀梁 commentaries of the *Ch'un-ch'iu* 春秋 (Spring and Autumn Annals) contain an entry for the year 663 B.C., in which the lord of Ch'i sent some newly acquired soybeans to the lord of Lu as a personal present.[73] These

---

[70] *I Chou-shu* (SPPY ed.), ch. 7, p. 10b.

[71] *Kuo-yü* (SPPY ed.), ch. 5, p. 11b.

[72] *Kuan-tzu* (SPPY ed.), ch. 10, p. 4a.

[73] Cited in Li Ch'ang-nien, ed., *Tou-lei* [Selected Historical Sources on the Legumes] (Shanghai, 1958), p. 33.

additional accounts are valuable in showing that, although soybean was known to the Chou royal court shortly before 1000 B.C., it did not become widely disseminated in North China until after 664 B.C. These facts explain satisfactorily why, in various works of the fourth and third centuries B.C., soybean and millet were almost unanimously regarded as the two most important food crops.

From these remarkable Chou records it is fairly certain that the plains of Manchuria must have been the area of greatest concentration of wild varieties of soybean. The area inhabited by the Mountain Jung was hilly and on the fringe of the area of concentration. It was probably because the land of the Mountain Jung was not ideal for the natural propagation of wild soybean that the people had to resort to domestication in which they succeeded after prolonged trial and error. Despite the association in Chou works of the Mountain Jung with the soybean, one cannot rule out the possibility that the soybean may have been domesticated by other proto-Tungusic tribes in the Manchurian plains centuries before the Chou conquest of Shang.[74] In any case, that the soybean was an important contribution to Sinitic agriculture made by proto-Tungusic peoples is beyond doubt.

Once the soybean was known to the Chou people, the peculiar nitrogen-bearing nodules of the root of this plant apparently were carefully observed both by peasants and by those learned men who enlarged the Chinese vocabulary. Unlike the early Chinese logographs for other cereal plants, which emphasize the stem and leaves, the emphasis of the new character *shu* for the soybean was on the nodules of its root. Since the numeral three symbolizes the concept

---

[74] Theodore Hymowitz, "On the Domestication of the Soybean," *Economic Botany*, XXIV, No. 4 (October-December 1970), has made an interesting observation that "the areas of greatest soybean production of both China and the U.S. are located within the 35 to 45 degree north latitudes." The various Chou accounts on the soybean presented above, together with the general remark made in some Chou works that the soybean was a typical plant of the north, seem to indicate its concentration within the 40 to 45 degree north latitude.

of "many," the three elongated dots at the lower left half of the character pictographically represent the root's bulging nodules caused by rhizobium.[75]

The effect of the domestication and dissemination of the soybean on Chinese agriculture and on the nutrition of the ancient Chinese cannot be exaggerated. At long last, the Chou Chinese had found a food plant that, instead of causing soil exhaustion, actually helped to preserve and enhance the fertility of the soil. Soybean supplied all classes of the population with cheaper and more abundant protein and also, in time, with an important source for oil, although the art of extracting the oil was as yet unknown. Not until soybean was domesticated and widely distributed did the ancient Chinese cropping system become well balanced. Within three centuries of the beginnings of wider dissemination in the seventh century B.C., soybean and millet reigned supreme in areas north of the Huai River. The unusually long time-interval between the first domestication of millet and that of the soybean is yet another indication that the maturation of the ancient Chinese agricultural system was an outcome of prolonged trial and error not only by the proto-Sinitic people themselves but also by other

---

[75] Hu Tao-ching, "Shih-shu p'ien" [Discourse on the Character *Shu* (Soybean)], in *Chung-hua wen-shih lun-ts'ung* [Essays on Chinese Literature and History], 3d Series (Shanghai, 1963), pp. 111–115.

ancient peoples who lived in a region which in later centuries of Sinitic expansion would also be called China.

Hemp and mulberry are the final plants to be discussed. Imprints of textiles on Yang-shao pottery have been discovered repeatedly, but scientific identification of the fiber of such textiles cannot be made easily from such imprints. J. G. Andersson suggests, probably quite rightly, that the fiber may be hemp (*Cannabis sativa* L.).[76] With his broad knowledge of phytogeography, Vavilov thought that North China might have been one of hemp's original homes.[77] Modern research indicates that no fiber plant other than hemp could have been grown in North China in Yang-shao times, for the cotton shrub was introduced into China late in the thirteenth century A.D., and ramie is native to more southerly parts of China. The character for hemp is missing from both Shang oracle-bone and Chou bronze inscriptions, but in *The Book of Odes* hemp appears seven times. It is well known that the ancient Chinese not only used hemp as a fiber but also consumed its seeds as auxiliary food.

Much more is known about mulberry *(Morus alba)* and several kinds of "wild mountain mulberries," one of which has been identified as *Broussonetia papyrifera* Vent.[78] Several pollen profiles gathered from the loess highlands and the low plains contain mulberry. In 1927 a Chinese archaeologist made a sensational find at the Yang-shao site of Hsi-yin-ts'un, in southern Shansi, of one-half of a silk cocoon that had been artificially cut.[79] Remnants

---

[76] J. G. Andersson, "An Early Chinese Culture," *Bulletin of the Geological Survey of China*, No. 5, Part I (1923), p. 26.

[77] Vavilov, *Origin, Variation, Immunity, and Breeding of Cultivated Plants*, p. 26.

[78] Ho, *Huang-t'u yü Chung-kuo nung-yeh ti ch'i-yüan*, Table 3, pp. 42–55.

[79] Li Chi, *Hsi-yin-ts'un shih-ch'ien ti i-ts'un* [Prehistoric Remains of Hsi-yin Village] (Peking, 1927). Hsia Nai, "Wo-kuo ku-tai ts'an-sang ssu-ch'ou ti li-shih" [History of Sericulture and Silk Fabrics in Ancient China], *KK*, 1972, No. 2, pp. 12–27, regards the silk cocoon discovered at Hsi-yin-ts'un as a later intrusion.

of textiles on some Shang bronzes have also been identified as fine silk.[80] Shang oracle-bone inscriptions contain characters for mulberry, silk, and kinds of silk fabrics. If the two subspecies of *Panicum miliaceum, shu* and *chi,* are counted separately, mulberry leads all the plants in *The Book of Odes* with twenty occurrences. The areas represented by the odes in which mulberry is mentioned show that mulberry was much more widely distributed in North China in ancient times than it is now. Unlike hemp, which was essentially the fiber of the common people, mulberry was grown extensively for the production of silk for the ruling class.

From our detailed discussion of the origins and early history of the major food and fiber crops, it is obvious that the early Chinese crops were botanically different from those of the ancient West. Wheat and barley, the two important ancient Western food plants, neither of which was probably introduced into North China earlier than 2000 B.C., had to be adapted to the typically Sinitic system of dry-land farming. Crops were but one of the trait complexes that indicate the indigenous origins of Chinese agriculture.

To understand better the effect of the initial phase of field agriculture on subsequent population growth and cultural development, an attempt should be made to estimate the agricultural productivity from Yang-shao to early historic times. The agricultural productivity of the Yang-shao and Lungshanoid periods can be roughly gauged from the estimates of per-acre yields of millet grown on various grades of land that were made around 400 B.C. by Li K'uei 李悝, a famous reforming statesman of the Wei state. Although the time interval between Yang-shao and Li K'uei's lifetime is more than three millennia, there are various reasons to believe that there had been no basic changes in agricultural techniques in this time span. For one thing, the improvements in agricultural implements during this long period were relatively minor.

---

[80] Vivi Sylwan, "Silk from the Yin Dynasty," *BMFEA*, No. 9 (1937), pp. 119–126.

Even down to Chou times the implements were made of stone, shells, wood, and sometimes bones; they were still so comparatively primitive as "to make deep plowing and intensive cultivation impossible."[81] It is true that cast iron can be traced back to 513 B.C. in the southern Shansi area.[82] But the major archaeological finds of recent decades clearly show that the dissemination of iron agricultural implements on a significant scale did not begin until the fourth century B.C.[83] In the context of agricultural implements, therefore, Li K'uei's lifetime was a true watershed. It is almost certain that the average farmer Li K'uei referred to still used nonmetallic implements not fundamentally different from those of the Yang-shao farmers.

Also, between Yang-shao times and 400 B.C. there is no verified evidence that Chinese agriculture had made important innovations in the use of manure or in terms of crop rotation. The subjective interpretation of a rare character in Shang oracle texts as evidence for the use of manure is very probably wrong.[84] Verified evidence of the use of human, animal, and green manure is all of the post-400 B.C. period.[85] The first clear reference to crop rotation is found in

---

[81] *Hsin-Chung-kuo ti k'ao-ku shou-huo* [New China's Archaeological Accomplishments] (Peking, 1962), pp. 60–61.

[82] Legge, tr., *The Chinese Classics*, V, *The Ch'un Ts'ew with the Tso Chuen*, p. 732.

[83] *Hsin Chung-kuo ti k'ao-ku shou-huo*, pp. 60–61.

[84] Hu Hou-hsüan, "Yin-tai nung-tso shih-fei shuo" [On the Use of Manure in Shang Times], *Li-shih yen-chiu* [Historical Research], 1955, No. 1. His argument hinges on his subjective identification of the character 屎 in oracle-bone inscriptions as *shih* 屎, which in later contexts means human discharge. He cites ode 254 of *The Book of Odes* as evidence for the antiquity of using manure for agricultural purpose. The character *shih* in this ode, however, does not mean human discharge; and the whole line in which this character appears means: "Though the people are now groaning." Bernhard Karlgren, tr., *The Book of Odes* (Stockholm, 1950), p. 213.

[85] P'an Hung-sheng and Yang Ch'ao-po, "Chan-kuo-shih-tai ti liu-kuo nung-yeh sheng-ch'an" [The Agricultural Production of the Six Major Eastern States during the Period of Contending States], *Nung-shih yen-chiu chi-k'an*, II (Peking, 1960), esp. pp. 59–60.

Lü-shih ch'un-ch'iu 呂氏春秋, an eclectic work compiled for the Ch'in premier Lü Pu-wei 呂不韋 in 239 B.C.[86] The first definite reference to double-cropping as a result of exceptionally intensive cultivation appears in the *Hsün-tzu* 荀子, the collected works of a famous philosopher of the third century B.C.[87]

Furthermore, with the exception of small parts of the central Honan lowlands and parts of central Yangtze, the vast agricultural lands of the rapidly expanding Sinitic world of 400 B.C. were unaffected by irrigation. As we pointed out at the beginning of this chapter, large-scale irrigation in the Wei River valley and in the Red Basin of Szechwan did not begin until the third century B.C. The small enclaves that had known irrigation since the first half of the sixth century B.C. certainly had nothing to do with millet cultivation.

After relevant factors have been taken into account, there is reason to believe that the state of dry-land millet farming as of 400 B.C. had more in common with that of prehistoric times than with later more intensive and diversified farming. While one cannot rule out the possibility that some of the significant changes in agricultural technology that became verifiable after 400 B.C. could have taken place considerably earlier in some specially enterprising localities, one can be reasonably sure that during Li K'uei's lifetime the "average" farmer who grew millet on dry land is not likely to have been much affected by such changes.

Li K'uei's estimates of agricultural productivity are based on the yields of unhusked millet in Chou *shih* (roughly 20 liters) per 100 Chou *mou* (4.474 acres), the amount of land that a male adult could cultivate effectively in a year. He testified on the average yield: "If a man supporting a family of five persons cultivates 100

---

[86] Hsü Wei-yü, *Lü-shih-ch'un-ch'iu chi-shih* [Annotations of Lü-shih-ch'un-ch'iu] (Peiping, 1935), ch. 26, p. 11a. Also Hsia Wei-ying, *Lü-shih-ch'un-ch'iu shang-nung teng ssu-p'ien chiao-shih* [The Four Chapters on Agriculture in the *Lü-shih-ch'un-ch'iu*: Textual Criticism with Annotative Notes] (Shanghai, 1956).

[87] *Hsün-tzu* (SPPY ed.), ch. 6, p. 5b.

mou of land, each year he will harvest from each 100 *mou* a total of 150 *shih* of unhusked millet."[88] But, according to him, there were years of bumper harvests, when the output could double, triple, or even quadruple the average yield of 150 *shih* each 100 *mou*.[89] There were also years of subnormal yields and of partial and serious crop failure, when the yield per 100 *mou* could drop as low as 100, 70, or even 30 *shih*.

When converted to modern Western units, the average per-acre yield would be roughly 632 liters or 17.9 U.S. bushels of unhusked millet.[90] Since a U.S. bushel of husked millet weighs about 50

---

[88] Li K'uei's estimates of agricultural productivity, food consumption for a family of five persons, the average farmer's tax payments, and other family expenses are preserved in *Han-shu*, ch. 24A, pp. 7a–8b.

[89] The ancient Chinese measures are very complex and have confused many Chinese and Western scholars. Wu Ch'eng-lo, *Chung-kuo tu-liang-heng shih* [A History of Lineal-Areal, Volume, and Weight Measures of China] (Shanghai, 1937), which was once a standard reference, has now been shown to contain some errors. Up to the present, the standard reference in English on ancient Chinese measures consists of some long footnotes on pp. 138–140 in Nancy Lee Swann, *Food and Money in Ancient China* (Princeton, N.J., 1950). While her conversion of the Chou *mou* into the English acre is correct, her conversions of volume and weight measures are wrong. My conversions are based on Wang Ta, "Shih-p'ing *Chung-kuo tu-liang-heng shih* chung Chou Ch'in Han liang-heng mou-chih chih k'ao-cheng," in *Nung-shih yen-chiu chi-k'an*, I, pp. 137–145; and also on Wan Kuo-ting, *Fan-Sheng-chih shu chi-shih* [Critical Annotations on *Fan-Sheng-chih shu*] (Shanghai, 1957), various long footnotes. Wang Ta's article is a review of the errors in Wu's book.

[90] Our conversion rates and calculations are as follows:

A. Area measures:
   1 Chou *mou*—0.2882 modern standard *mou*;
   1 acre—6.0702 modern standard *mou*;
   1 Chou *mou*—0.04746 acre;
   1 acre—21.062 Chou *mou*.

B. Volume measures:
   1 Chou or Han *sheng* (1/100 *shih*)—0.1996875 modern standard *sheng* (or liter);
   1 Chou or Han *shih*—roughly 20 liters;
   1 U.S. bushel—35.2383 liters.

pounds, the per-acre yield in gross weight of unhusked millet would be 895 pounds. Assuming a 25 percent weight loss incurred by husking, the average per-acre yield would amount to 671 pounds of husked millet.

Crop yields at about 2400 B.C. in southern Mesopotamia have been calculated by two scholars of the Oriental Institute of the University of Chicago. The per-hectare yields of barley, emmer, and wheat were respectively 2,537, 3,672, and 1,900 liters.[91] In the United States a bushel of barley usually weighs 48 pounds and a bushel of wheat 60 pounds. Since emmer is presumably in the glume and therefore about 75 percent as heavy as wheat, it should weigh approximately 45 pounds a bushel. In ancient Mesopotamia the per-acre yield of barley was therefore 1,440 pounds, that of emmer 1,894 pounds, and that of wheat 1,309 pounds. The striking difference in yields between ancient Mesopotamia and ancient China was no doubt accounted for by the difference between irrigation and dry-land farming. By about 2100 B.C., however, the Mesopotamian yields had sharply declined, probably because of increasing salinization. Wheat had virtually disappeared as a crop; and the yield of the more salt-tolerant barley had declined to 1,460 liters per hectare, or roughly 804 pounds per acre. Compared with the declined yield of barley in southern Mesopotamia, the per-acre yield of millet in ancient China appears respectable. It looks even better when compared with the present-day yields of millet and sorghum in the

---

C. Weight measures and per-acre productivity:
   1 U.S. bushel—50 lbs. of husked millet;
   25% weight loss in husking;
   Average yield of 100 Chou *mou* (4.4746 acres) of unhusked millet—3,000 liters;
   Average yield per acre—17.9 U.S. bushels of unhusked millet, or 895 lbs.;
   Average yield per acre—671 lbs. of husked millet.

[91] Thorkild Jacobson and Robert M. Adams, "Salt and Silt in Ancient Mesopotamian Agriculture," *Science,* CXXVIII, No. 3334 (21 November 1958), pp. 1251–1258.

Harappan area in West Pakistan, where the ancient Indus civilization flourished. Near Harappa the modern yield of *jowār* (sorghum) is 445 pounds per acre and the yield of *bājrā* (pearl millet) 245 pounds per acre.[92]

For reasons already given, the average yield in Yang-shao times is not likely to have been much less than that in 400 B.C. Besides, the Yang-shao homeland was exceptionally fertile, and the vicinity of Sian today enjoys an annual rainfall of about 25 inches. Possibly, Li K'uei's estimates were based on his observations in areas east of the loess highlands. Whatever the possible margin of error in accepting Li Kuei's estimates of average yields in Yang-shao times, they are a safer guide than modern conjectures.

In estimating the per-capita food consumption in Yang-shao times, we will use a simple arbitrary principle—allowing each Yang-shao person 2,000 calories a day derived exclusively from millet. Food scientists have estimated that an adult working man needs a daily minimum of 2,300 calories to sustain himself. We are reasonably sure that hunting, fishing, gathering, and the incipient pig husbandry were all secondary sources of food for the Yang-shao people.[93] In all likelihood, the degree of dependence on cereal for sustenance in Yang-shao times may have been somewhat less than during the historical periods. But if we err, we want to err on the conservative side.[94]

---

[92] Walter A. Fairservis, Jr., *The Origin, Character, and Decline of an Early Civilization* (American Museum Novitates, No. 2302, 20 October 1967), p. 36.

[93] *Hsi-an Pan-p'o,* plates 56 and 57, confirms that among the food gathered by the Yang-shao people were hazelnuts, celtis seeds, pine seeds, and chestnuts. The keeping of seeds of *Brassica* in pottery jars indicates vegetable growing. Appendix II gives a complete list of wild animals hunted by the Yang-shao people at Pan-p'o. From my analysis of the plants recorded in *The Book of Odes,* the Wei River area in Shensi seems to have abounded in jujube, peaches, and plums, and also hemp. Hemp seeds may have been consumed by Yang-shao people as auxiliary food.

[94] Fairservis, *The Origin, Character, and Decline of an Early Civilization,* p. 34, Table 4, estimates that in the Harappa area in ancient times the average individual would daily consume 477.6 grams of cereal or between 1,500 and 1,600 calories, and

A kilogram (about 2.2 pounds) of most cereals produces about 3,350 calories. Assuming that millet alone provided the average Yang-shao individual with his daily 2,000 calories, he would have consumed 597 grams or roughly 1.3 pounds a day, and his total annual consumption would have been 475 pounds of husked or 584 pounds of unhusked millet. An acre of cultivated land could therefore support 1.4 individuals. The increasingly fruitful application of science to archaeology has taught us that not infrequently land in ancient times had better yields than it does at present:[95] there is, therefore, the possibility that our estimate of the Yang-shao average yield may have been too conservative, especially since the Wei River basin was so well endowed by nature for millet farming and so much of the success of early agriculture depended on nature.

In estimating the number of individuals that one farmer could annually support, we are impressed by the unanimity with which various Chou works testified to the size of 100 Chou *mou* as the ideal allotment that could be gainfully cultivated by a farmer. We are not sure whether the slightly improved implements from Lungshanoid times onward enabled a farmer to cultivate more acreage than could the Yang-shao farmer. It would appear that the advantage of the slightly improved implements from Lungshanoid times onward might have been largely offset by the greater resistance offered by the harder and texturally less homogeneous loess of secondary deposition. If 100 Chou *mou* serves as a rough guide to the amount of friable loess soil that a Yang-shao farmer could annually cultivate, an area of 4.474 acres of cultivated land could then support more than six persons. Even assuming that a Yang-

---

that another 1,000 calories would be derived from vegetables, fruits, oil and fats, meat and fish, and dairy products.

[95] *Ibid.*, p. 35. Fairservis has also estimated that in Harappan times an acre of cultivated land could feed 1.86 persons annually. He further remarks: "This figure compares favorably with figures obtainable for West Pakistan today (Las Bela, 1.19; Larkana District, 2.27; submontane West Pakistan, 1.0)."

shao farmer could cultivate only 3 acres a year, he could still support four or five persons. In any case, there can be little doubt about the ability of Yang-shao agriculture to produce a surplus, thus releasing segments of the population to pursue nonagricultural activities, and hence to give rise to a certain degree of social division of labor. There was also great potential for sustained population growth.

III
Animal Husbandry

FOR SCHOLARS familiar with the archaeology and history of Western agriculture, animal husbandry constitutes as vital a part of agriculture as does grain production. For most Chinese scholars, however, agriculture means essentially if not exclusively field agriculture based on cereal grains. This is because the Chinese agricultural system, as far back as we can trace, has always favored grain production at the expense of animal husbandry. It is the purpose of this chapter to trace the beginnings of animal domestication in China, to analyze the characteristics of animal husbandry in prehistoric and early historic China, to explain why animal husbandry played a subordinate role in Chinese agriculture, and, finally, to recapitulate all the major characteristics of the Chinese agricultural system that warrant the conclusion that its origins were indigenous.

For a study of the origins and early history of animal domestication in China, the existing data leave much to be desired. For one thing, post-1949 Chinese archaeology shares the bias of conventional Near Eastern archaeology of the past in stressing the importance of artifacts and in overlooking natural remains, plant and animal. Most Chinese archaeological reports barely mention the presence in certain cultural sites of animal bones and skeletons, without specifying them. Many mention only bones that are recognized by the fieldworkers, few of whom are zoologists. Some mention only the remains of numerically important animals. So far there have been only five Chinese site reports which contain a detailed zoologist's or paleontologist's appendix, and a few more which, though without such a special appendix, yield the vital information that the osteological remains have been identified by qualified scientists.

But even when the taxonomic identification is meticulously done, it is still very difficult to know whether certain animals were domesticated—a difficulty by no means confined to Chinese archaeology. Besides, while osteoarchaeology concerning the Near East and parts of Europe has shown new vigor and is based on series of carbon dates, only a few radiocarbon dates have been available— and those very recently—for the study of the origins and early history of animal domestication in China.[1] Given the circumstances, the best we can hope for is that a sketchy historical outline may emerge from the following data, which for convenience will be arranged partly chronologically and partly geographically.

Not much about the artifactual assemblages of the Kao-tui and Ch'ih-k'ou-chai sites can be learned from Andersson's article, but, from their geographic locations and that of the Chung-chou-lu site in Lo-yang, it is likely that they fall within the cultural orbit of the Miao-ti-kou type, hence comparatively late. These sites may in fact be later than some early Ch'ing-lien-kang "Lungshanoid" sites. There has not been a full site report on Ching-ts'un in southern Shansi. Of the eight Yang-shao cultural sites, therefore, Pan-p'o and Chiang-chai are the earliest, but Pan-p'o yields by far the most detailed report on osteological remains, carefully prepared by two paleontologists, Li Yu-heng and Han Te-fen.

---

[1] The main problems and difficulties of osteoarchaeology are well discussed in Charles A. Reed, "Animal Domestication in the Prehistoric Near East," *Science,* CXXX, No. 3389 (December 11, 1959), pp. 1629–1639, and also in his "Osteo-Archaeology," in Don Brothwell and Eric Higgs, eds., *Science in Archaeology* (New York, 1963), pp. 204–216. The lack of serious osteoarchaeology in China is partially reflected in Yang Chung-chien, better known to Western paleontologists as C. C. Young, "K'ao-ku-kung-tso ho jen-ku shou-ku teng i-ts'un wen-t'i" [Archaeological Work and the Problems of Human Skeletons and Animal Bones], *WW,* 1956, No. 3, pp. 7–10.

TABLE 4

ANIMAL REMAINS FROM YANG-SHAO CULTURAL SITES

Site	Pig	Dog	Cattle	Sheep	Goat	Horse	Chicken
Pan-p'o, Shensi	x	x	x(w?)	x(w?)		x(w?)	
Chiang-chai 姜寨, Shensi	x	x					
Ching-ts'un 荆村, Shansi	x	x		x			
Kao-tui 高堆, Honan	x		x			x	
Miao-ti-kou I, Honan	x	x					
San-li-ch'iao I, Honan	x	x					
Ch'ih-k'ou-chai 池口寨, Honan	x	x	x				
Chung-chou-lu 中州路, Lo-yang, Honan	x						

(w) = wild

SOURCES: For Pan-p'o, *Hsi-an Pan-p'o,* Appendix II, pp. 255–269; for Chiang-chai in Lin-t'ung 臨潼, which was culturally closely related to Pan-p'o, "1972-nien ch'un Lin-t'ung Chiang-chai i-chih fa-chüeh chien-pao" [A Brief Report on the Excavation of the Chiang-chai Site in Lin-t'ung in the Spring of 1972], *KK,* 1973, No. 3, pp. 134–145; for Ching-ts'un, T'ung Chu-ch'en, "Huang-ho Ch'ang-chiang chung-hsia-yu hsin-shih-ch'i-wen-hua ti fen-pu yü fen-ch'i" [The Distribution and Periodization of the Neolithic Cultures of the Central and Lower Yellow River and Yangtze Regions], *KKHP,* 1957, No. 2, p. 9; for Kao-tui, "Chin-nan wu-hsien ku-tai jen-lei wen-hua-i-chih ch'u-pu tiao-ch'a" [A Preliminary Survey of the Cultural Remains of Early Man in Five Southern Shansi Counties], *WW,* 1956, No. 9, pp. 53–56; for Miao-ti-kou I and San-li-ch'iao I, *Miao-ti-kou yü San-li-ch'iao* (Peking, 1959), p. 63 and p. 92; for Ch'ih-k'ou-chai, J. G. Andersson, "Researches into the Prehistory of the Chinese," *BMFEA,* No. 15 (1943), p. 43; for Chung-chou-lu of Lo-yang, *Lo-yang Chung-chou-lu* (Peking, 1959), p. 18.

In Pan-p'o, the identification of the pig as a domesticate is based mainly on two factors: the prevalence of pig bones in practically every ash pit and the unusually high proportion of yearlings and young adults among the pig population. The pig is believed to have descended from its wild ancestor *Sus scrofa,* native to North China. A fragment of a dog's skull, some broken jaw bones, and whole teeth are all noticeably smaller than and show other marked differences from those of the wolf *(Canis lupus)*—hence the identification of the dog *(Canis familiaris)*.

Only a few fragments of sheep bones (*Ovis* sp.) were found in the entire Pan-p'o site. Some teeth bear a certain resemblance to those of the sheep found at the last Shang capital city near An-yang; the sheep of An-yang (*Ovis shangi* Teilhard and Young—a name which is not taxonomically valid) indicates "a form domesticated during a sufficiently long time."[2] But the extreme scarcity of sheep remains from Pan-p'o makes Li and Han hesitant to say whether the sheep was indeed domesticated. For the same reason they regard cattle and the horse, along with the sheep, as "domesticable" but not necessarily "domesticated." There is further uncertainty whether the cattle was *Bos* or water buffalo *(Bubalus)*. The horse was similar to the wild horse indigenous to North China (*Equus przewalski* Poliakof).

Quantitatively, the bones of water deer *(Hydropotes inermis)* at the Pan-p'o site rank next only to those of pigs; and the aggregate remains of various wild animals, ranging from deer *(Pseudaxis hortularum)*, logomorphs (*Lepus* sp. and *Ochotona* sp.), and gazelle to several kinds of small felines and the fox (*Vulpes* sp.), seem to outnumber those of domesticated and domesticable animals. This fact, together with the prevalence of various types of hunting and fishing tools unearthed from this site, suggests that hunting and fishing at this early Yang-shao stage were probably still more important than incipient animal husbandry based almost exclusively on pigs.

The Yang-shao cultural site of Ching-ts'un in southern Shansi, which was discovered in 1930, is one of unusual interest. It was the

---

[2] P. Teilhard de Chardin and C. C. Young, *On the Mammalian Remains from the Archaeological Site of Anyang* (Paleontologia Sinica), Series C, XII, Fascicle 1 (Nanking, 1936), p. 42.

first Yang-shao site where millets, both *Setaria italica* and *Panicum miliaceum,* were found. Unfortunately, there has been no systematic report on this important site; its artifacts and natural remains have been referred to only briefly in subsequent archaeological articles. The pigs, dogs, and cattle from Ching-ts'un are generally presumed to have been domestic and the chicken regarded as wild; but it is impossible to check on the validity of these identifications. The detailed report on the twin sites of Miao-ti-kou and San-li-ch'iao in Shan-hsien, western Honan, has no appendix on animal remains and merely states that in the Yang-shao strata bones of pigs and dogs are found. The detailed report on the site of Chung-chou-lu, Lo-yang, western Honan, states that in a Yang-shao ash pit as many as 120 bone fragments belonging to three pig yearlings were found and that "domesticated pigs may have supplied a major source of meat" for its dwellers. The Yang-shao site at Ch'ih-kou-chai in Kuang-wu county, north-central Honan, was discovered by Andersson, and its animal remains were subsequently identified by a professional zoologist, Elias Dahr. The pig, the dog, and cattle were all "well represented" and considered to have been "domesticated."

Considering the sparsity of scientific information, there is reason to abide by the cautious generalization of the Institute of Archaeology of the Chinese Academy of Sciences that the proto-Chinese of the Yang-shao period probably domesticated only pigs and dogs, and that hunting and fishing still played an important role when compared with millet farming and incipient animal husbandry based mainly on pigs.[3]

Of the fourteen sites listed in Table 5, only Ch'eng-tzu-yai in Shantung is a typical Lung-shan site. The other sites are all what K. C. Chang call Lungshanoid, which chronologically fall between the Yang-shao and the classical Lung-shan cultures. The full reports

---

[3] *Hsin Chung-kuo ti k'ao-ku shou-huo,* p. 12.

TABLE 5

ANIMAL REMAINS FROM LUNGSHANOID AND LUNG-SHAN SITES

Site	Pig	Dog	Cattle	Sheep	Goat	Horse	Chicken
K'e-hsing-chuang II 客省莊, Shensi	x	x	x[a]	x			
Miao-ti-kou II, Honan	x	x	x		x		x
San-li-ch'iao II, Honan	x	x	x	x			
Pao-t'ou 堡頭, Shantung	x						
Kang-shang 崗上, Shantung	x						
Ch'ü-fu 曲阜, Shantung	x						
Tzu-ching-shan 紫荊山, Shantung	x			x			
Ch'eng-tzu-yai 城子崖, Shantung	x	x	x	x		x	
Ta-ch'eng-shan 大城山, Hopei	x	x	x	x			
Ch'ü-chia-ling 屈家嶺, Hupei	x	x		x			x
Liu-lin 劉林, Kiangsu	x	x	x	x			
Ta-tun-tzu 大墩子, Kiangsu	x	x	x				
Mei-yen 梅堰, Kiangsu			a				
Ma-chia-pin 馬家濱, Chekiang			x[a]				

a = Water buffalo only (*Bubalus* sp.).

x[a]= Both the common cattle (*Bos* sp.) and the water buffalo.

SOURCES: For K'e-hsing-chung II, *Feng-hsi fa-chüeh pao-kao* [Report on the Excavations in the Feng River district in Shensi] (Peking, 1962), Appendix I, pp. 156–159; For Miao-ti-kou II and San-li-ch'iao II, *Miao-ti-kou yü San-li-ch'iao*, p. 82 and pp. 112–113; for Pao-t'ou, Yang Tzu-fan, "Shan-tung Ning-yang-hsien Pao-t'ou i-chih ch'ing-li chien-pao" [A Brief Report on the Archaeological Finds from Pao-t'ou, Ning-yang county, Shantung], *WW*, 1959, No. 10, pp. 61–64; For Kang-shang, "Shan-tung T'eng-hsien Kang-shang-tsun hsin-shih-ch'i-shih-tai mu-tsang shih-chüeh pao-kao" [A Report on the Preliminary Excavations of Neolithic Graves at Kang-shang-ts'un, T'eng-hsien, Shantung], *KK*, 1963, No. 7, pp. 351–361; for Ch'ü-fu, "Shan-tung Ch'ü-fu hsin-shih-ch'i-shih-tai i-chih tiao-cha" [A Survey of Neolithic Sites in Ch'ü-fu county, Shantung], *KK*, 1963, No. 7, pp. 362–368; for Tzu-ching-shan, "Shan-tung P'eng-lai Tzu-ching-shan i-chih shih-chüeh chien-pao", *KK*, 1973, No. 1, pp. 11–15; for Ch'eng-tzu-yai, Li Chi *et al.*, *Ch'eng-tzu-yai* (Academia Sinica, 1934), pp. 90–91; for Ta-ch'eng-shan, "Ho-pei T'ang-shan-shih Ta-ch'eng-shan i-chih fa-chüeh pao-kao" [A Report on the Excavation at Ta-ch'eng-shan, T'ang-shan Municipality, Hopei], *KKHP*, No. 3, p. 33; for Ch'ü-chia-ling, *Ching-shan Ch'ü-chia-ling*, pp. 23, 71 and 74; for Liu-lin, "Chiang-su P'ei-hsien Liu-lin hsin-shih-ch'i-shih-tai i-chih ti-erh-tzu fa-chüeh" [A Report on the Second Excavation at Liu-lin, P'ei-hsien, Kiangsu], *KK*, 1965, No. 2, p. 26; for Ta-tun-tzu, "Chiang-su P'ei-hsien Ssu-hu-chen Ta-tun-tzu i-chih t'an-chüeh pao-kao" [A Report on the Exploratory Excavation at Ta-tung-tzu, Ssu-hu Township, P'ei-hsien, Kiangsu], *KKHP*, 1964, No. 2, p. 18 and p. 49; for Mei-yen in Kiangsu and Ma-chia-pin in Chekiang, Wu Shan-ching, "Lüeh-lun Ch'ing-lien-kang wen-hua" [A Brief Discussion of the Ch'ing-lien-kang Culture], *WW*, 1973, No. 6, p. 57.

on the K'e-hsing-chuang and Ch'eng-tzu-yai sites contain osteological appendixes, which treat all the common animals as domesticates. Animal remains of all four Shantung Lungshanoid sites are yet to be systematically identified. The Tzu-ching-shan site in P'eng-lai 蓬萊 county contains remains of pigs and sheep. The predominance of pigs is consistently striking in Pao-t'ou in Ning-yang 寧陽 county, Kang-shang in T'eng-hsien 滕縣, and Ch'ü-fu 曲阜 county. In nearly every grave unearthed at Pao-t'ou and Kang-shang there are a number of pig teeth and bones that were used as funerary gifts. At the Ch'ü-fu site a clay pig figurine looks so fat, short-legged, and short-tailed that it was unmistakably based on pigs that were domesticated. The animal bones of the Ta-ch'eng-shan site in Hopei were identified by the well-known paleontologist P'ei Wen-chung 斐文中, although there is no detailed report on whether the pigs, dogs, cattle, and sheep were domesticated.

The Ch'ü-chia-ling site in Hupei represents a Lungshanoid phase, which probably began in the early third millennium B.C. The inhabitants were proto-Ching-Man 荆蠻, who until late-Chou or even post-Chou times were still considered by the Chinese of early-developed North China as "southern barbarians." It is there that a large amount of rice husks was found, along with numerous animal bones of which only those of pigs and dogs were identified by fieldworkers. The most interesting finds are artifactual—clay figurines of sheep and chicken, definite evidence of their domestication.⁴ The discovery of wild ancestral forms of domestic fowl in Yunnan in the 1950s⁵ and the presence of predomesticated fowl *(Gallus)* in the faunal assemblage of the "Spirit Cave" in Wan-nien county in Kiangsi indicate that the southern half of China, as well as India and Burma, may have been one of the original homes of wild fowl. But judging from the presence of chicken bones at the early Lungshanoid stratum of the Miao-ti-kou site in western Honan and at an equally early stratum of a Ma-chia-yao cultural site in Lan-chou, Kansu,⁶ in the extreme northwest of China proper, the prehistoric distribution of wild fowl in China may not have been confined strictly to the south. That one of the favorite hunting places of late-Shang kings, on the southern foothill of the T'ai-hang Mountain in western Honan north of the Yellow River, was named Chi 雞 (literally "chicken") is yet another strong piece of evidence of the existence of wild fowl in parts of North China in ancient times.⁷ The accumulated evidence indicates that domestication of the chicken in China preceded that in the Mohenjo-daro area of the Indus River valley by a wide margin.⁸

The twin sites of Ta-tun-tzu and Liu-lin in P'ei-hsien, northern Kiangsu, are typical Ch'ing-lien-kang cultural sites. The lower stratum of the Ta-tun-tze site, which contains numerous pig, some dog, and many cattle bones, has been recently radiocarbon-dated at 3835 ± 105 B.C., or 4435 ± 105 B.C. according to bristlecone-

---

⁴ *Ching-shan Ch'ü-chia-ling*, pp. 23, 71 and 74, and plates 54 and 58.

⁵ Hsia Nai, "Ch'ang-chiang-liu-yü k'ao-ku wen-t'i," *KK,* 1960, No. 2, p. 3.

⁶ "Kan-su Lan-chou Hsi-p'o-wa i-chih fa-chüeh chien-pao" [A Brief Report of the Excavations at Hsi-p'o-wa, Lan-chou, Kansu], *KK,* 1960, No. 9, pp. 1-4.

⁷ Li Hsüeh-ch'in, *Yin-tai ti-li chien-lun* [A Brief Study of the Geography of the Shang Dynasty] (Peking, 1959), p. 21.

⁸ For artifactual evidence of domestic chicken in Mohenjo-daro, see Frederick E. Zeuner, *A History of Domesticated Animals* (New York, 1963), pp. 443-444; for radiocarbon datings of the various strata of the Mohenjo-daro site, which range from 3,900 to 3,600 years ago, see Bridget and Raymond Allchin, *The Birth of Indian Civilization,* p. 337.

pine dendrochronology. The lowest cultural stratum at Liu-lin, which represents the middle phase of the Ch'ing-lien-kang culture, was probably only slightly later than the lowest cultural stratum of the Sung-tse site (radiocarbon date: 3395±105 B.C.; bristlecone-pine date: 3995±105 B.C.). The report on the finds at Liu-lin is quantitatively interesting in that the lowest stratum yields a total of 652 bone fragments (excluding tortoiseshells), of which pigs, dogs, cattle, sheep, and wild deer respectively account for 171, 12, 30, 8, and 59.

The lowest stratum of the Ma-chia-pin site, Chia-hsing county, along the northeastern Chekiang coast, represents the earliest phase of the southern type of the Ch'ing-lien-kang culture. Here, within an excavated area of fifty square meters, hard-shell water chestnuts (*Trapa natans* L.) for which Chia-hsing is still nationally famous, seed grains not yet identified, stone sinkers, wooden oars, millstones, and vestiges of rectilinear houses have been found, along with fishbones, tortoiseshells, mussels, and over a thousand kilograms of animal bone fragments, which weigh more than ten times the total amount potsherds unearthed. Although most of the animal bones are badly preserved, the skulls of wild deer, cattle, and water buffalo have been identified. Especially noticeable is the relative abundance of bones and skulls of water buffalo unearthed here and in a comparable cultural site at Mei-yen, Wu-chiang 吳江 county, on the northern fringe of the T'ai-hu Lake in southern Kiangsu.[9]

In its 1962 synthesis, the Institute of Archaeology regarded the pig, dog, sheep, and water buffalo of these Ch'ing-lien-kang sites as domesticated.[10] Wu Shan-ching, in his recent preliminary synthesis of the Ch'ing-lien-kang culture, further regards the cattle

---

[9] "Che-chiang Chia-hsing Ma-chia-pin hsin-shih-ch'i-shih-tai i-chih ti fa-chüeh" [The Excavation at the Neolithic Site of Ma-chia-pin, Chia-hsing County, Chekiang], *KK*, 1961, No. 7, pp. 245–354, esp. p. 351.

[10] *Hsin-Chung-kuo ti k'ao-ku shou-huo*, p. 32.

as a domesticate.[11] Although careful morphological study of cattle and water buffalo will be needed in order to ascertain whether they were domesticated at such early times, there can be little doubt about the familiarity of the ancient inhabitants of the lower Yangtze area with the use of these bovines as sources of meat. In any case, from available data it seems highly probable that cattle and water buffalo were first domesticated in the lower Yangtze area rather than in the Neolithic nuclear area in the loess highlands.

Although the report on the twin sites of Miao-ti-kou and San-li-ch'iao in western Honan is detailed on artifacts, its brief mention of animal remains without a zoologist's appendix and scientific names presents taxonomic and also, very likely, textual problems. From the Miao-ti-kou II site the report mentions the presence in Lungshanoid ash pits of bones of pigs, dogs, cattle, and goats.[12] In the nearby San-li-ch'iao site, however, the fauna of the Lungshanoid stratum consist of pigs, dogs, cattle, and sheep, but not goats.[13] While the English abstract of the entire site report faithfully includes, in translation, the goat,[14] the final conclusion in Chinese still does not mention the goat, which is replaced by the sheep.[15] Aside from the common difficulty in distinguishing the bones of the goat *(Capra hircus)* from those of the sheep *(Ovis aries)* especially in the absence of horn cores,[16] the lone mention of the goat in the Miao-ti-kou II stratum could conceivably be a typographical error. This typographical error could happen in Chinese more easily than in English because the difference between the sheep (*yang* 羊) and the goat (*shan-yang* 山羊, literally

---

[11] Wu Shan-ching, "A Brief Discussion of the Ch'ing-lien-kang Culture," *WW*, 1973, No. 6, esp. p. 57.

[12] *Miao-ti-kou yü San-li-ch'iao*, p. 82.

[13] *Ibid.*, p. 102.

[14] *Ibid.*, p. 127.

[15] *Ibid.*, p. 113.

[16] Reed, "Animal Domestication in the Prehistoric Near East" (see note 1 above).

"mountain-sheep") is only a prefix. The Miao-ti-kou II goat is therefore highly suspect.

The Miao-ti-kou site report nevertheless throws interesting light on the early history of animal domestication. Although this site contains only 26 ash pits belonging to the Lungshanoid stratum as compared to 168 ash pits belonging to the Yang-shao stratum, the remains of domestic animals from the Lungshanoid stratum far exceeds in quantity those from the Yang-shao ash pits. The aggregate evidence from various Lungshanoid and Lung-shan sites presented above also indicates an increase in the quantity and range of animals domesticated since Yang-shao times.

TABLE 6

ANIMAL REMAINS FROM PREHISTORIC AND EARLY HISTORIC SITES IN INNER MONGOLIA AND KANSU

Site	Pig	Dog	Cattle	Sheep	Goat	Horse	Chicken
A. INNER MONGOLIA							
Sha-wa-tzu 沙窩子	x(w)		x	x		x	
Hung-shan-hou 紅山後	x(w)	x	x	x			
Ta-pei-kou 大北溝			x	x			
Yo-wang-miao 葯王廟	x						
Hsia-chia-tien 夏家店	x						
Chuan-lung-tsang 轉龍藏 western Inner Mongolia	x	x	x	x			
B. KANSU							
Ma-chia-yao	x	x	x(w)				
Hsi-p'o-wa 西坡岋	x	x	x	x			x
Ch'i-chia-p'ing 齊家坪	x	x	x	x	x		
Lo-han-t'ang 羅漢堂	x	x	x	x	x		
Ta-ho-chuang	x		x	x			

(w) = wild

SOURCES: The first five sites of (A) are all in eastern Inner Mongolia, the pre-1949 province of Jehol. For Sha-wo-tzu, Lin-hsi county, Lü Tsun-eh, "Nei-Meng Lin-hsi k'ao-ku tiao-ch'a" [An Archaeological Survey of the Lin-hsi Area in Inner Mongolia], *KKHP,* 1960, No. 1, p. 19; for Hung-shan-hou, Ch'ih-feng county, Hamada Sosaku and Mizuno Seiichi, *Ch'ih-feng: Hung-shan-hou* (Tokyo, 1938), Appendix II of English abstract, p. 11; and also Lü Tsun-eh, "Nei-Meng Ch'ih-feng Hung-shan-hou k'ao-ku tiao-ch'a pao-kao" [A Report on the Archaeological Survey of the Ch'ih-feng Area in Inner Mongolia], *KKHP,* 1958, No. 3, table on p. 39; for Ta-pei-kou, Ch'ih-feng county, T'ung Chu-ch'en, "Chung-kuo yüan-shih-she-hui wan-ch'i-li-shih ti chi-ke t'e-cheng" [Some Characteristics of the Late Prehistoric Society of China], *KK,* 1960, No. 5, p. 27; for Yo-wang-miao and Hsia-chia-tien, both in Ch'ih-feng county, "Nei-Meng-ku Ch'ih-feng Yo-wang-miao Hsia-chia-tien i-chih shih-chüeh chien-pao" [A Brief Report on the Exploratory Excavations at Yo-wang-miao and Hsia-chia-tien, Ch'ih-feng, Inner Mongolia], *KK,* 1961, No. 2, pp. 77–81; for Chuan-lung-tsang, Pao-t'ou Municipality, western Inner Mongolia, *Hsin Chung-kuo ti k'ao-ku shou-huo* (Peking, 1962), p. 38; for the three sites of Ma-chia-yao, Ch'i-chia-p'ing, and Lo-han-t'ang, J. G. Andersson, "Researches into the Prehistory of the Chinese," *BMFEA,* No. 15 (1943), p. 43, and Margit Bylin-Althin, "The Sites of Ch'i Chia P'ing and Lo Han T'ang in Kansu," *BMFEA,* No. 18 (1946), pp. 457–458; for Hsi-p'o-wa, "Kan-su Lan-chou Hsi-p'o-wa i-chih fa-chüeh chien-pao" [A Brief Report on the Exploratory Excavations at Hsi-p'o-wa, Lan-chou, Kansu], *KK,* 1960, No. 9, pp. 1–4; for Ta-ho-chuang, Lin-hsia county, Kansu, "Lin-hsia Ta-ho-chuang Ch'in-Wei-chia liang-ch'u Ch'i-chia-wen-hua i-chih fa-chüeh chien-pao" [A Brief Report on the Excavations of the Two Ch'i-chia Cultural Sites at Ta-ho-chuang and Ch'in-Wei-chia, Lin-hsia County], *KK,* 1960, No. 3, p. 11.

For the study of the possibility of the spread of domesticated animals from ancient hearths in Southwest Asia to North China, two crucial areas are Inner Mongolia and Kansu. Had there been any introduction into North China of animals first domesticated in the Near East, such introduction must have left traces in the areas immediately north and northwest of the loess highlands and the low plains of North China.

Existing knowledge does not enable us to suggest relative chronologies for the prehistoric cultures of Inner Mongolia north of the Great Wall. On this northern steppe, Microlithic cultures based on hunting and fishing, which show Yang-shao and/or Lungshanoid influence, persisted till North China proper had entered well into early dynastic periods. The determination of even approximate dates for the beginnings of animal domestication in Inner Mongolia is therefore extremely difficult.

At the site of Sha-wo-tzu, Lin-hsi county, in northwestern Jehol, formerly the eastern Inner Mongolian province, bones and teeth of cattle, sheep, and horses have been identified. Since these animal remains are found at the bottom of surface sand pits, they probably belong to a period rather close to the beginning of the historic age in North China. The same observation may apply to the remains of Chuan-lung-tsang, near the city of Pao-t'ou, in the former Suiyüan province in western Inner Mongolia.

The most thoroughly explored site in Inner Mongolia is Hung-shan-hou, Ch'ih-feng county, in central Jehol. It was first discovered by a Japanese archaeologist and was successively investigated by Japanese scholars in 1930 and 1935 and by an archaeological team from Peking University in 1956. In the Microlithic-Neolithic stratum of this site only the antlers of wild deer have been found. Bones and teeth of pigs, dogs, cattle, and sheep are present solely in the cultural stratum which is synchronized with the late bronze age in North China, that is, the first half of the first millennium B.C.[17] The Japanese paleontologist Naora Nobuo has identified the dog *(Canis familiaris)* as being domesticated and described the pig as being of small size, the same as the prehistoric pig found at the vicinity of Port Arthur "and clearly not identified with the present Chinese pig, *Sus vittatus.*" "[The pigs] were probably tamed," he concludes, "but under wild conditions."[18] Both the cattle *(Bos taurus)* and the sheep *(Ovis aries)* were regarded as domestic.

It should be noted that both Japanese and Chinese scholars who have investigated this Hung-shan-hou site agree that from its

---

[17] Lü Tsun-eh, "Nei-Meng Ch'ih-feng Hung-shan-hou k'ao-ku tiao-ch'a pao-kao," p. 39.

[18] Hamada and Mizuno, *Ch'ih-feng: Hung-shan-hou,* Appendix II of English abstract, p. 11.

cultural complex the inhabitants must have been primarily farmers but were also engaged in hunting and stockbreeding. The *Setaria* millet reportedly found in the vicinity supports this conclusion.[19] The dates for the cattle and sheep remains from the Ta-pei-kou site, also in Ch'ih-feng, have never been ascertained,[20] but the oracle bones made of pig scapulae unearthed from the Yo-wang-miao and Hsia-chia-tien sites of Ch'ih-feng all come from an upper cultural stratum which chronologically corresponds to the Chou dynasty.[21] The aggregate ascertainable data indicate that animal domestication in Inner Mongolia came later than in North China proper and that the pattern was one of greater reliance on cattle and sheep.

The animal remains at the sites of Ma-chia-yao, Ch'i-chia-p'ing, and Lo-han-t'ang were collected by J. G. Andersson and subsequently identified by the Swedish zoologist Elias Dahr. The stratigraphic conditions at Ch'i-chia-p'ing were so disturbed that "some mandibles of goats and sheep . . . still possess a distinct smell of fat. However, after the elimination of some specimens, the material from Ch'i Chia P'ing shows the same state of conservation as collections from other prehistoric sites."[22] The presence at the Ch'i-chia-p'ing site of a significant number of pig, sheep, goat, and cattle bones is confirmed by the animal remains from the undisturbed site of Lo-han-t'ang. In addition, a pair of goat's horns was found in 1945 by Hsia Nai, Director of the Institute of Archaeology in Peking, from a grave belonging to a later local culture called

---

[19] An Chih-min, "Chung-kuo shih-ch'ien-shih-ch'i chih nung-yeh" [Prehistoric Chinese Agriculture], *Yen-ching she-hui-k'e-hsüeh* [Yenching Journal of Social Sciences], II (1949), p. 33.

[20] T'ung Chu-ch'en, "Chung-kuo yüan-shih-she-hui wan-ch'i-li-shih ti chi-ke t'e-cheng," *KK*, 1960, No. 5, p. 27.

[21] "Nei-meng-ku Ch'ih-feng Yao-wang-miao Hsia-chia-tien i-chih shih-chüeh chien-pao," *KK*, 1961, No. 2, pp. 77–81.

[22] Margit Bylin-Althin, "The Sites of Ch'i Chia P'ing and Lo Han T'ang in Kansu," *BMFEA*, No. 18 (1946), pp. 457–458; also J. G. Andersson, "Researches into the Prehistory of the Chinese," *BMFEA*, No. 15 (1943), p. 43.

Ssu-wa 寺窪, which is generally synchronized with the Chou period in North China proper.[23] It is a problem not of identification but of chronology.

Because of Kansu's crucial geographic position and because of Andersson's persistent opinion that the Ch'i-chia culture, exemplified by the artifacts of the Ch'i-chia-p'ing site, was the earliest Neolithic culture in Kansu, Chinese archaeologists, especially Hsia Nai, have done a great deal of excavation during the past quarter of a century in order to determine the stratigraphical sequence of the Neolithic and early historic cultures of this province.[24] The correct stratigraphical sequence firmly established by Chinese archaeologists is that in the entire loess highlands area the earliest Neolithic culture was the Yang-shao, followed by the Ma-chia-yao and such kindred cultures as Pan-shan and Ma-ch'ang 馬廠, and then followed by the Ch'i-chia culture. All these have been confirmed by recent radiocarbon determinations. The two available carbon-14 dates for Ma-chia-yao (with bristlecone-pine dates in parentheses) are 2575 ± 100 B.C. (3125 ± 100 B.C.) and 2185 ± 100 B.C. (2635 ± 100 B.C.) and the two available dates for Ch'i-chia are 1725 ± 95 B.C. (2075 ± 95 B.C.) and 1695 ± 95 B.C. (1945 ± 95 B.C.).[25]

After presenting data on animal remains chronologically and regionally, a few observations are in order on the origins and early history of animal domestication in China, including the special significance of the Kansu material.

First, a prerequisite for the study of the origins of animal

---

[23] Hsia Nai, "Lin-t'ao Ssu-wa-shan fa-chüeh chi" [A Report on the Excavations at Ssu-wa-shan, Lin-t'ao, Kansu], *Chung-kuo k'ao-ku hsüeh-pao* [Chinese Archaeological Review] (Academia Sinica), No. 4 (December 1949), pp. 104, 135, and Plate Xa. The pair of goat's horns was carefully measured.

[24] The literature on the stratigraphical sequence of prehistoric cultures in Kansu is considerable. A good summary is given in K. C. Chang, *The Archaeology of Ancient China*, p. 171.

[25] See Table 1.

domestication is, obviously, systematic knowledge of the geographic distribution of the wild ancestors of the domestic animals. Let us begin with the wild pig *(Sus scrofa)*. Charles A. Reed's review of the origins of pig domestication, though based on Near Eastern data, is valid for other regions as well:

> In spite of this wide distribution [of *Sus scrofa* in much of Eurasia and parts of North Africa], the ancestor of *all* domestic pig has been singled out as one southeastern Asiatic subspecies, *Sus scrofa vittatis;* if it is true that this subspecies is the common ancestor, domestic pigs must have moved westward, presumably slowly, to reach the Near East and most of Europe in prehistoric times. As yet I have not investigated this problem, but the general pattern seems illogical. I suggest that we at least investigate the possibility that domestication of pigs may have occurred several times, from different wild populations.
>
> Pigs are not difficult to tame as one might imagine; an adult wild boar or sow, it is true, is not an animal one approaches casually, but several people have easily reared the young of wild pigs to adulthood, the females having then produced litters to be reared in captivity. Such pigs are surprisingly docile.[26]

We need to point out once more that in terms of climate, vegetation, and fauna the southern half of China has a great deal more in common with Southeast Asia than is usually believed. Many plants and animals which were supposed to have originated only in Southeast Asia are now known to be indigenous to temperate East Asia as well. Rice and wild fowl are examples that have been discussed in our study. *Sus scrofa vittatis,* which is regarded by some scholars to be of Southeast Asian origin only, existed in a somewhat less primitive form in Pleistocene and post-Pleistocene China.[27] The very fact that pigs are found invariably in every Yang-shao, Lungshanoid, and Lung-shan site listed in tables 4 and 5 and that they are numerically predominant should point to their having China as a native origin.[28] Equally significant is the fact that

[26] Reed, "Animal Domestication in the Prehistoric Near East."

[27] Helga S. Pearson, *Chinese Fossil Suidae* (Paleontologia Sinica), Series C, V, Fascicle 5 (Peking, 1928), p. 75.

[28] Yang Chung-chien and Liu Tung-sheng, "An-yang Yin-hsü chih p'u-ju-tung-wu-ch'ün pu-i" [A Supplement to the Mammalian Assemblage of An-yang], *Chung-kuo k'ao-ku hsüeh-pao,* No. 4 (1949), pp. 145–153.

the semiwild pig from the Hung-shan-hou site in Jehol is definitely different from *Sus scrofa vittatis*. Hence the pigs of East Asia may have descended from more than one subspecies. Recent evidence suggesting very early domestication of pigs in the Crimea, probably a little less than 10,000 years ago,[29] further suggests multiple occurrences of pig domestication in Eurasia. All these lend weight to Reed's well-reasoned view that domestication of pigs may have occurred independently several times in several areas from different subspecies.

The wild prototypes of most other common domestic animals are also known to have existed in prehistoric China. Wild cattle of the species *Bos nomandicus* had already reached China and Siberia in the Holocene from their supposedly original habitats in India.[30] The Chinese water buffalo *(Bubalus mephistopheles)*, far from being solely a southern animal in prehistoric and early historic times, accounted for an astoundingly large portion of the entire osteological remains of An-yang, a fact which has led two well-known Chinese scientists to believe that it was native to both southern China and parts of northern China.[31] The Mongolian wild horse *(Equus przewalski)* is native to North China and the Mongolian steppe.[32] The osteological remains from Pan-p'o prove the existence of the wild horse in Yang-shao times, although its domestication was considerably later than that of pigs and dogs. Some subspecies ancestral to the domesticated sheep *(Ovis aries)* are known to have ranged from Russian and Chinese Turkestan to Mongolia, North China, and the northern Himalayas in prehistoric times.[33] Their prehistoric distribution may have been even wider, since remains

---

[29] E. S. Higgs and M. R. Jarman, "The Origins of Agriculture: A Reconsideration," *Antiquity*, XLIII (1969), pp. 31-32.

[30] Zeuner, *A History of Domesticated Animals*, p. 203.

[31] Yang and Liu, "An-yang Yin-hsü chih p'u-ju-tung-wu-ch'ün pu-i," p. 151.

[32] Zeuner, *A History of Domesticated Animals*, pp. 302-303.

[33] Reed, "The Domestication of Animals in the Prehistoric Near East."

of wild sheep have been recently found in the "Spirit Cave" in Wan-nien county in the lower-central Yangtze province of Kiangsi.[34] Although the wolf *(Canis lupus)* has only recently been established as the ancestor of the dog *(Canis familiaris)*,[35] the dog's wide distribution in the northern hemisphere in prehistoric times has never been questioned, and it is generally believed to have been one of the first animals domesticated by man. While more precise details about the origins of animal domestication in China must await more intensive scientific study, it is at least evident that before the dawning of the Neolithic age all the wild prototypes of the above-mentioned animals existed in China. The only conspicuous absence in prehistoric China was the wild goat *(Capra hircus aegagrus)*, the significance of which will be discussed later.

Second, in reviewing the beginnings of animal domestication in China we find that a general comment by Reed, based mainly on research concerning the prehistoric Near East, also holds remarkably well for China. It is his belief that "a primary requirement for the earliest domestication of the ruminants, and for pigs, is that men settled down to village life." Stockbreeding, according to Reed, "came somewhat later than incipient plant cultivation."[36] The Yang-shao site of Pan-p'o, where the predominance of pig yearlings strongly indicates domestication, yields also a complex village layout and the earliest evidence of cultivation of *Setaria* millet and such vegetables as *Brassica*. Wherever remains of domestic or domesticable animals are found in prehistoric sites in China, they are invariably associated with at least a lithic industry, which reflects incipient farming. Even on the Inner Mongolian steppe,

---

[34] "Chiang-hsi Wan-nien Ta-yüan Hsien-jen-tung tung-hsüeh i-chih shih-chüeh" [Exploratory Excavations at the "Spirit Cave" at Ta-yüan, Wan-nien county, Kiangsi], *KKHP*, 1963, No. 1, Appendix II, p. 14.

[35] Reed, "The Domestication of Animals in the Prehistoric Near East."

[36] *Ibid.*, and also Reed, "The Pattern of Animal Domestication in the Prehistoric Near East," in Ucko and Dimbleby, eds., *The Domestication and Exploitation of Plants and Animals*, p. 367.

where modern scholars would expect to find evidence of early nomadism, incipient stockbreeding occurred in places where the lithic industry indicates sedentary life and marginal field agriculture. Kansu is no exception, for the economy of the Ma-chia-yao culture was based on primitive agriculture and pig husbandry, and that of the Ch'i-chia culture was based as much on millet cultivation as on the breeding of pigs, cattle, and sheep.[37] While a recent study does present some evidence suggesting that not all places in the vast Eurasian land mass followed this pattern,[38] our available evidence shows that in prehistoric China, much as in the ancient Near East, animal domestication followed on the heels of incipient field agriculture.

Third, the sequence in which animals were domesticated in China, as far as can be ascertained, was different from that in the ancient Near East. In the Near East, sheep were the first, then goats, and, after a considerable time interval, pigs and cattle. In Yang-shao and Lungshanoid China, pigs were the first. The scarcity of remains of cattle and sheep from Yang-shao sites makes it impossible to say whether these animals were already domesticated; if they were domesticated, they were certainly quantitatively insignificant. Not until Lungshanoid times do we have substantial reason to think that cattle and sheep were domesticated. The consistent fact that pigs vastly outnumbered other animals in practically all Yang-shao and Lungshanoid sites indicates that animal husbandry in prehistoric China was largely pig husbandry. This contrasts with recent osteological findings in the ancient Near East, where "pigs, prior to the period of Sumerian cities, were found at numerous sites but

---

[37] For the economy of Ma-chia-yao culture, see *Hsin Chung-kuo ti k'ao-ku shou-huo,* pp. 21–22; for the economy of Ch'i-chia culture, see Shih T'ao, "Huang-ho shang-yu ti fu-hsi-shih-tsu-she-hui—Ch'i-chia-wen-hua she-hui ching-chi hsing-t'ai ti t'an-so" [The Patrilineal Society in the Upper Yellow River—An Inquiry into the Social and Economic Characteristics of the Ch'i-chia Culture], *KK,* 1961, No. 1, pp. 3–11.

[38] Higgs and Jarman, "The Origins of Agriculture: A Reconsideration," *passim.*

rarely represented more than 5% of the bones of food animals; they were however more numerous (25%) at Matarrah."[39] In terms of both the sequence and the degree of importance of animal domestication, prehistoric China differed from the Near East.

Fourth, by far the most significant fact is that animal domestication, much like field agriculture, first occurred in the Neolithic nuclear area and then radiated northwestward to Kansu, eastward to the low plains of North China and further south, and northward to Inner Mongolia. Instead of revealing any southwestern Asian influence, the osteological material of the Ma-chia-yao site in Kansu reflects exactly the same pattern of pig husbandry that had characterized earlier Yang-shao sites in North China proper. The even later beginnings of animal domestication in Inner Mongolia argues equally strongly against earlier views held by some Western scholars that animal domestication, like many other major cultural elements, came to China from Mesopotamia.[40]

Finally, the only sure indication of foreign cultural transplant is the presence of the domestic goat in the osteological remains of Ch'i-chia-p'ing and Lo-han-t'ang sites in Kansu. There can be little doubt that the goat was first domesticated in the Near East and that its wild prototype was not native to North China proper.[41] It is in the very area in which modern scholars expect to find a cultural

---

[39] Reed, "The Pattern of Animal Domestication in the Prehistoric Near East," p. 371.

[40] An extreme example was the late Carl W. Bishop, "Beginnings of Civilization in Eastern Asia," *Antiquity*, XIV (1940), pp. 301–316.

[41] Some zoologists, like J. Wolfgang Amschler, are of the opinion that "the primeval center and radiation area for all the forms of domestic goats" might have been in the Siberian Altai. See Shimon Angress and Charles A. Reed, *An Annotated Bibliography on the Origin and Descent of Domestic Mammals, 1900–1955* (Chicago, 1962), p. 21. But Charles A. Reed, in answering my query, wrote: "That area [Siberian Altai] is all *ibex (Capra ibex)* country, and there is no evidence to indicate either that the ibex has ever been domesticated or that the range of the ancestor *(Capra hircus aegagrus)* of the domestic goat extended so far to the northeast [from the prehistoric Near East]."

linkage between China and southwestern Asia that this concrete osteological evidence has been found. The case of the goat, however, has limited significance to our study of the origins of animal domestication in China. For one thing, the Ch'i-chia culture was much later than the Yang-shao, which gave rise to field agriculture and pig husbandry. For another, although the two available radiocarbon dates and our adjusted bristlecone-pine dates for Ch'i-chia indicate the neighborhood of 2000 B.C., the Ch'i-chia cultural stratum in eastern Kansu is usually overlain by the Chou cultural stratum. In other words, the Ch'i-chia goat could be as early as 2000 B.C. or as late as the eleventh century B.C. The reticence of the Institute of Archaeology in Peking with regard to goats in prehistoric Kansu, as well as the fact that goat's horns were very rare and much valued by people belonging to a still later culture called Ssu-wa, lead us to believe that the goat arrived relatively late in the second millennium B.C. In any case, the arrival of the goat was much too late to have affected the beginnings of animal domestication in China. Moreover, although the goat was first domesticated in the Near East by 7000 B.C. at the latest, five thousand years elapsed before it finally reached northwesternmost China, and then only in insignificant numbers. The presence of the goat in some Ch'i-chia sites, incidentally, does not necessarily mean direct cultural contact between the inhabitants of Kansu and Mesopotamia. In view of the extraordinarily long time interval between the goat's first domestication in the Near East and its arrival in Kansu, it is much safer to assume that the goat was brought to northwestern China by one of the many intermediary bands of herdsmen of Central Asia than to assume a direct import from the highly civilized Near East.

Our aggregate data on animal domestication, like those on field agriculture, indicate independent Chinese origins.

The independent origins of animal domestication in China will be better understood when we investigate the reasons why, in sharp contrast to prehistoric and historic Near East and Europe, animal husbandry in China always seems to have played a subordinate role in the agricultural system. Let us begin by examining the peculiar land forms of the Yang-shao nuclear area, which set limits to the growth of animal husbandry. Being dissected by numerous gullies and ravines, this area lacks large open pastures—a requisite for the development of large-scale stock raising. As shown in Map 4, the majority of the known Yang-shao cultural sites are found within a narrow strip of fertile land lying south of the Wei River and north of the Ch'in-ling foothills. Within this narrow strip, where dozens of Yang-shao sites congregate, the various tributary rivers and streams are only between 20 and 50 kilometers in length, and the maximum distances between them vary from 5 to 20 kilometers. Granted that not all of these Yang-shao sites were contemporary, it is still obvious that after deducting the amount of land necessary for dwelling, for annual cultivation, and for fallow, the pasture land available to each village community was limited. This topographic factor substantially accounted for the fact that the numerically predominant domestic animal was always the omnivorous pig, not herbivorous cattle and sheep. Moreover, from what we can learn from the paleoenvironment of this area, the grass cover is not likely to have been dense or ideal for pasturing because of the predominance of *Artemisia* and Chenopodiaceae. Under these circumstances, animal husbandry could not compete effectively against field agriculture for the limited acreage of available land; in addition, long-range population growth also made it necessary for priority to be given to millet farming.

The geographic sphere of agriculture in prehistoric China was greatly expanded from about 4000 B.C. onward, consequent upon the spread of the Yang-shao culture and the rise of a number of regional Lungshanoid cultures both within and without the loess highlands.[42] The Lungshanoid cultures outside the loess highlands

[42] For a systematic discussion of these regional Lungshanoid cultures, see K. C. Chang, *The Archaeology of Ancient China*, pp. 121–160. It should be pointed out

flourished under different and diverse natural environments. The low plains of North China and the Huai River region are a vast expanse of open, flat lands, in contrast to the dissected land forms of the original Yang-shao area. The primeval vegetation of the low plains is likely to have been taller and denser grass, more suitable for large-scale pasturing. The alluvial plains of the central and lower Yangtze, where regional Lungshanoid cultures also occurred, are humid, have rich plant resources, and were forested in prehistoric and early historic times except for the swampy areas, which were probably covered by luxuriant grass. It seems that there was little about the environments of the easterly and southerly Lungshanoid regions that would naturally prevent the agricultural systems from becoming better balanced between grain production and meat production. The importance of animal husbandry relative to grain farming in Lungshanoid and Lung-shan times cannot be gauged without the systematic quantitative data that future archaeological research will have to provide. What we can be reasonably sure of is that throughout China's long historic periods the agricultural system, in spite of increasing regional differences, has always been lopsided in favor of grain production, with animal husbandry playing a subsidiary role.

Throughout the ages the inability or reluctance of Chinese farmers fully to develop animal husbandry may also have been due to the lingering influence of some early cultural traits. Among relevant traits, the most noticeable was the lack of sufficient knowledge to make and utilize dairy products. Since the land forms of the Yang-shao nuclear area were hardly conducive to large-scale

---

that some Lungshanoid cultures occurred within the Yang-shao nuclear area, such as the Miao-ti-kou II culture in western Honan and the K'e-hsing-chuang II culture in the Wei River valley in Shensi. The earliest Neolithic culture in Kansu, generally called the Ma-chia-yao culture or the Kansu Yang-shao culture, was in the loess highlands but outside the original Yang-shao nuclear area. The other regional Lungshanoid cultures were all on the low plains of North China and further south in the eastern part of China.

stock raising, and since we are not even sure whether cattle and sheep were domesticated in China in Yang-shao times, the ignorance of the earliest farmers about dairy products is not to be wondered at. It is not definitely known whether Lungshanoid and Lung-shan farmers knew how to milk cows or ewes, but the Chinese throughout the historic periods certainly regarded as novelties the various dairy products brought in occasionally by tribesmen of the northern steppe and from India.[43] So abiding has been this negative dietary habit that, as the late Berthold Laufer observed in 1914, not only the Chinese but also those East Asian peoples under Chinese cultural influence have generally avoided milk and dairy products. According to Laufer, this curious avoidance of milk and dairy products has culturally set the Chinese, Koreans, Japanese, Indochinese, and Malayans apart from the dairy-using Indo-Europeans, Semites, Scythians, Turks, Mongols, and Tibetans.[44]

As compared with other major ancient civilizations of the Old World, the Chinese had yet another peculiar trait, namely, the unusually late beginnings and persistent underutilization of draft animals for cultivation. The character *li* 犁, which in its late connotation means the plow and consists of the radical *niu* 牛 (ox), appears in late-Shang oracle inscriptions. This has led some unwary modern Chinese paleographers into believing that the cattle-drawn plow already existed in Shang times. The more careful etymologists, however, both ancient and modern, interpret *li* as a bovine with a dappled coat, which has nothing to do with the plow and the use of

---

[43] In the imperial stable of the Ch'in Empire, which unified China in 221 B.C., there were officers whose duty was to milk horses. Accounts of cheese and butter made from cow's and ewe's milk occurred only after North China was conquered by various barbarians from the early fourth century A.D. onward. As one result of the translation of the Indian Buddhist sutra, some members of the Chinese elite learned that cheese and butter were clean and nourishing foods. See Wang Yü-hu, *Chung-kuo hsü-mü-shih tzu-liao* [Selected Sources on the History of Animal Husbandry in China] (Peking, 1958), pp. 107–114.

[44] Berthold Laufer, "Some Fundamental Ideas of Chinese Culture," *Journal of Race Development*, V (1914), esp. pp. 167–170.

cattle for cultivation.⁴⁵ Some traditional and modern Chinese scholars believe that the cattle-drawn plow must have come into existence during Confucius' lifetime (551–479 B.C.) because of the combination of the character *keng* 耕 (cultivation) and *niu* (cattle) in the personal and pen names of two disciples of Confucius.⁴⁶ A leading Ch'ing etymologist, Wang Yin-chih 王引之 (A.D. 1766–1834), however, conclusively proved that the character *keng* in both personal names is actually a synonym and homonym of *k'eng* 牼, which means the shinbone of a bovine.⁴⁷ The negative etymological conclusions on the cattle-drawn plow are no doubt correct, because the combined literary and archaeological evidence all points to very late beginnings for the plow and the cattle-drawn plow.⁴⁸ While one cannot rule out the possibility that the cattle-drawn plow may have first occurred some time before the Ch'in unification of China in

---

⁴⁵ For a comprehensive critical review of various interpretations of the character *li* (plow), see Li Hsiao-ting, *Chia-ku wen-tzu chi-shih* [Cumulative Interpretations of Oracle-Bone Inscriptions] (Academia Sinica, 16 Vols., 1965), II, pp. 337–340.

⁴⁶ Ssu-ma Keng 司馬耕 with the pen-name of Tzu-niu 子牛 and Jan Keng 冉耕 with the pen-name of Po-niu 伯牛.

⁴⁷ Cited in Hsü Chung-shu, "Lei-ssu k'ao" [A Study of Ancient Chinese Agricultural Implements], *BIHP*, II, No. 1 (1930), p. 57.

⁴⁸ A good summary of the recent archaeological finds of Chinese agricultural implements of the Warring States period, roughly from the late fifth century B.C. to 221 B.C., is given in K. C. Chang, *The Archaeology of Ancient China*, p. 316: "The use of cast iron for agricultural implements is undoubtedly a highly significant event in Chinese economic history. The common types of implements during the latter part of the Eastern Chou period included axes, adzes, chisels, spades, sickles, and hoes; the plow was manufactured, but was relatively rare and does not seem to have been effective enough to replace the spade and hoe as a cultivating tool. The earliest iron plows that are well documented archaeologically come from the Warring States tombs at Ku-wei-ts'un, in Hui Hsien, northern Honan. These are flat, V-shaped iron pieces which probably were mounted on wooden blades and handles to serve as working edges. The width of each arm, measured from two complete specimens, averages 18 centimeters. In view of its relatively small size and its mounting device, which could not have been too secure, this primitive plow was probably not capable of turning over the soil to any considerable depth. There is no archaeological evidence that cattle were used to draw the plows."

221 B.C.,[49] the earliest written reference to it can only be dated around the end of the reign of the Han Emperor Wu (140–87 B.C.).[50]

In Mesopotamia the first proof of the use of a rather complex cattle-drawn plow "is probably that found in an archaic Sumerian seal of about 3500 B.C., from the Royal Cemetery at Ur."[51] During the second millennium B.C., possibly considerably earlier, a "seeder" was sometimes attached to the traction plow so that the dropping of seeds into the furrows could be done mechanically.[52] As compared with the ancient Near East, early Chinese agriculture was characterized by its simpler and cruder implements and especially by its lateness in using draft animals, a trait which, along with the lack of full understanding of the value of milk products, reflects the subsidiary role played by animal husbandry in the entire agricultural system.

To summarize this and the preceding two chapters, I shall recapitulate aspects of the origins and abiding characteristic of Chinese agriculture. The southeastern part of the loess highlands is an area of yellow earth par excellence. The manifold scientific findings and ancient Chinese written records concur remarkably well in indicating that the homeland of the Yang-shao Chinese has long been a semiarid steppe, at least since the late Pleistocene. The effect of this semiarid steppe environment surely imposed certain restrictions on its early inhabitants; but it also offered them a narrow range of peculiar opportunities: the classic loess soil of a homogeneous, fine, soft texture, which is not only very fertile but could be worked by primitive agricultural tools; the availability of

---

[49] Hsü Chung-shu, "Lei-ssu k'ao," p. 58.

[50] *Han-shu,* ch. 24A, pp. 17a–18a.

[51] Carl W. Bishop, "Origin and Early Diffusion of the Traction Plow," *The Smithsonian Report for 1937,* p. 535.

[52] A. Leo Oppenheim, *Ancient Mesopotamia: Portrait of a Dead Civilization* (Chicago, 1964), p. 314.

a few types of exceptionally drought-resistant cereal plants which, toughened by a million years of relentless struggle for survival, would be fairly easy for primitive men of ingenuity to domesticate; and the concentration of a limited annual rainfall in the summer, which was practically all the few hardy food plants needed for growth and maturation. The Yang-shao Chinese made full use of these opportunities to lay the foundation of what may justifiably be called a typically Sinitic agricultural system.

During the first four millennia of its history, Sinitic agriculture knew no irrigation and was almost exclusively dry-land farming, except that nature took care of the rice in the marshes and swamps. It was thus fundamentally different from such other major ancient agricultural systems as that of Mesopotamia, Egypt, and the Indus Valley, all of which were based on the common triad of flood plains, primitive irrigation, and a cropping system with wheat and barley as a core.

The autochthonous character of ancient Chinese agriculture becomes even more obvious after our detailed study of the origin of each of its major crops. Going through the list of major food and fiber crops, such as the *Setaria* and *Panicum* millets, rice, soybean, hemp, and mulberry, one cannot fail to be impressed by the fact that it was with these indigenous plants that the Chinese from Yang-shao times created and enriched their agriculture. Major exceptions are, of course, wheat and barley, which are likely to have been introduced into North China in the second or third millennium B.C. But the introduction of these food plants indirectly from southwestern Asia came too late to have an important impact on the already well-established pattern of the Sinitic system of dry-land farming, which by then was two or three thousand years old. No proof of the strength and stubbornness of the Sinitic system of farming can be more eloquent than the fact that the ancient Chinese, instead of slavishly adopting the entire complex of wheat and barley culture of southwestern Asia based on flood plains and irrigation, resolutely grew even these grains as dry-land crops.

This fact further sharpens our perception that ancient Chinese agriculture, with such a distinct and deep-rooted regional trait-complex, can only have been developed independently of Mesopotamia, the ancestral hearth of most of the major ancient agricultural systems of the Old World.

In this chapter we have also discussed the native origins of animal domestication in China and the persistently subordinate role played by animal husbandry in the Chinese agricultural system from ancient times onward. That the Chinese agricultural system leaned so heavily toward grain production at the expense of animal husbandry certainly constituted another fundamental difference from the major agricultural systems of the ancient West.

But if we look beyond Mesopotamia and review the matter in the context of world history, we find that the grain-dependent agricultural system of China is not unique. It does appear unusual, however, to those familiar only with the long tradition of Western agriculture, which can be traced back to the prehistoric Near East and prehistoric Europe and which technologically culminated in the Norfolk system of eighteenth-century England. From the vantage point of the Norfolk system, in which stock raising and grain production reached a perfect equilibrium and became virtually convertible, the Chinese system does appear to have been one-sided. Actually, the early Chinese agricultural system was somewhat less one-sided than the ancient agriculture of the New World, which began almost exclusively with plant domestication and knew of no animals except the dog and the turkey. And even today the agriculture of some African tribes is based totally on grains and plants. Be that as it may, it is pertinent to repeat that the grain-centered agricultural system of China, with its persistent underdevelopment in farming implements and in animal husbandry and with its unusually late beginnings and underutilization of draft animals, further reflects its distinctive regional trait-complex and native origins.

In our long-range historical perspective, the Chinese agricultural system has had its peculiar strength as well as its shortcomings. In spite of its shortcomings when compared with traditional Western agriculture at its best, Chinese agriculture has been singularly successful in terms of its ability to sustain and to rejuvenate itself. By virtue of its capacity to endure, Chinese agriculture, together with certain value systems and institutional factors, has made Chinese civilization the most enduring in the annals of man. Whereas "progressive changes in soil salinity and sedimentation contributed to the breakup of past civilizations" in Mesopotamia,[53] and whereas "the destruction of the local ecological patterns and the consequent failure of food resources" contributed to the decline and fall of the ancient Harappan civilization in the Indus valley,[54] Chinese agriculture today still manages to support more than one-fifth of humanity out of a cultivated area amounting to only 80 percent of that of the United States. Of all the inherent characteristics of the Chinese agricultural system, therefore, none can be more striking than its self-sustaining quality; and this self-sustaining quality has now been traced back to Yang-shao times.

Our overall conclusion of the indigenous origins of Chinese agriculture would have raised the eyebrows of most past-generation archaeologists and historians of the ancient world, who practically took it for granted that anything worthy of the name of agriculture or civilization in the Old World must have originated from the single oldest hearth of southwestern Asia. Even some leading botanical scientists a generation ago, wary of the risks of theoretical speculation and concerned with concrete regional scientific evidence, were inclined to believe that, while agriculture in the New World unquestionably had independent origins, the limits of prehistoric diffusion of agricultural crops and knowledge could only have been

---

[53] Jacobson and Adams, "Salt and Silt in Ancient Mesopotamian Agriculture," *Science,* CXXVIII, No. 3334 (November 21, 1958), abstract.

[54] Fairservis, *The Origin, Character, and Decline of an Early Civilization,* p. 42.

hemispherical.[55] As archaeology has benefited increasingly from the natural sciences, a few archaeologists have lost some faith in the theory of the monogenesis of agriculture in the Old World. What Robert J. Braidwood said in 1960 was prophetic:

> The first successful experiment in food production took place in southwestern Asia, in the hilly flanks of the "fertile crescent." Later experiments in agriculture occurred (possibly independently) in China and (certainly independently) in the New World. The multiple occurrence of the agricultural revolution suggests that it was a highly probable outcome of the prior cultural evolution of mankind and a peculiar combination of environmental circumstances. It is in the record of culture, therefore, that the origin of agriculture must be sought.[56]

While it is obviously beyond the scope of this study, and of my ability, to examine all "the records of culture" of pre-Yang-shao China (chiefly because of the lack of comprehensive archaeological data), I have taken pains to discuss the "peculiar combination of environmental circumstances" as a prelude to more detailed analysis of the main characteristics of ancient Sinitic agriculture.

The outcome of the recent intensive multidisciplinary study of Meso-American archaeology clearly indicates "the multiple origins of agriculture in Mesoamerica," a finding that "may signal a revolution in our thinking about the development of culture and the rise of civilization everywhere."[57] It is at this happy intellectual juncture that our study of the origins of Chinese agriculture may be useful not only to scholars of agricultural origins but to theorists of the geneses of civilizations as well.

[55] E. D. Merrill, "Plants and Civilizations," *Scientific Monthly,* XLIII (November 1936), pp. 430–439.

[56] Braidwood, "The Agricultural Revolution," *Scientific American,* CCIII (September 1960), p. 131.

[57] Richard S. MacNeish, "Mesoamerican Archaeology," in *Biennial Review of Anthropology,* ed. Bernard J. Siegel and Alan R. Beals (Stanford, Calif., 1967), pp. 324–328.

IV
Pottery

UNTIL THE increasingly systematic application of scientific disciplines to archaeology in recent decades, pottery enjoyed a singularly important position in archaeological studies. The ubiquity and easy availability of clay, early man's extensive need for various types of pottery vessels, the relative difficulty with which quantities of pottery can be transported to localities remote from their place of origin, the necessity of replacing broken vessels with new ones, and the nonperishability of potsherds made pottery usually one of the most common artifacts. Since every pottery object represents man's response to the utilitarian and aesthetic needs of a particular milieu at a particular time, pottery was generally regarded as one of the best denominators of a preliterate culture.

The tendency to exaggerate the archaeological importance of

With the employment of an ever-greater variety of scientific disciplines by archaeology, very few, if any, serious scholars nowadays would generalize, as did J. G. Andersson, Gordon Childe, Ludwig Bachhofer, and others about cultural borrowing from a few types of rather simple and common pottery designs. It is, however, an unavoidable chore of China scholars engaging in a study of the origins of Chinese civilization to compare ancient Western and Chinese ceramic designs, for nothing has generated wilder speculation on prehistoric China's cultural borrowing from the West than has painted pottery. To make comparison meaningful, I have accepted the advice of Professors Robert McC. Adams and Hans J. Nissen and made a fairly comprehensive selection from the major groups of ancient Mesopotamian and Iranian ceramic designs, so that virtually all the motifs of the Yang-shao painted wares are illustrated in this chapter. It is hoped that this comparison, while space-consuming and rather unusual for a book dealing with only one culture, may help to direct intercultural speculations into intellectually more profitable channels.

pottery was especially pronounced in the China of the 1920s and 1930s, when very few prehistoric sites had been discovered and little about the cultural complexes of such sites had been systematically studied. Thus the Yang-shao Neolithic culture was generally referred to as the "Painted-Pottery Culture," and the Lung-shan Neolithic culture—exemplified by the artifacts from the Ch'eng-tzu-yai site in Shantung—as the "Black-Pottery Culture." Soon after his discovery in 1921 of painted pottery at Yang-shao-ts'un in western Honan, J. G. Andersson began to talk about the "striking similarities" in design between the Chinese sherds and those of Anau in southern Turkmenia and of Tripolje in the Ukraine.[1] His preliminary report on Chinese Neolithic painted wares provided a renewed incentive for some Western scholars to postulate that Chinese painted pottery, even much of early Chinese culture itself, was of "Western" origin.

There is no need in this chapter either to criticize such wildly speculative writings or to assign pottery to a more appropriate place vis-à-vis other types of artifactual and natural remains unearthed from numerous archaeological sites in post-1949 China. What we need to do is trace the beginnings of Chinese pottery in the light of the latest finds and discuss painted pottery in the context of Old World prehistory. This chapter will, however, have to pay special attention to the problem of painted pottery because it has directly and indirectly generated so much uncontrolled speculation on the origins of Chinese material culture and civilization.

A recent archaeological and scientific finding of fundamental importance to Old World prehistory is the firm evidence of the extremely early beginnings of pottery in the Far East. The "linear relief" pottery that has been unearthed from several sites belonging to the Jomon culture in Honshu, Japan, dates as far back as 10,000 B.C. and thus precedes the first appearance of pottery in the Near

---

[1] J. G. Andersson, "An Early Chinese Culture," *Bulletin of the Geological Survey of China*, No. 5, Part I (October 1923), pp. 1–68.

East by three and a half millennia. When the first series of radiocarbon dating relating to the Jomon culture was made known, it caused considerable stir and skepticism in the world of archaeology. But the concurrence of three series of radiocarbon dates for three different sites of the same culture established beyond doubt the accuracy of the dates.[2] The origins and economic basis of the initial phase of the Jomon culture are not yet clearly understood, but the artifactual and natural remains of the Jomon sites seem to suggest that it was based substantially on extensive exploitation of maritime food resources and that by about 8000 B.C. it had spread over much of the temperate forest and temperate mixed forest zones of western Japan, if not over a considerably larger area.

Recent archaeological research on Taiwan has also shed important new light on pottery. Probably the most significant outcome of the 1964-65 archaeological expedition to Taiwan, sponsored by Yale University, was the discovery and establishment of the cord-marked pottery horizon as the earliest cultural horizon in this subtropical island. Although no direct radiocarbon dates for the cord-marked pottery horizon are available, it is definitely known that it antedated the Taiwan Lungshanoid horizon, which is estimated to have begun around 2500 B.C., by a very considerable period of time because of the marked "depositional disconformity" and "cultural discontinuity" between the two horizons.[3] Other sites outside mainland China where cord-marked pottery has been found are the Bacson district in North Vietnam and the Spirit Cave in northwestern Thailand near the Burmese border. The former, because of its discovery nearly half a century ago, lacks radiocarbon

---

[2] Yoshinobu Kotani, "Upper Pleistocene and Holocene Environmental Conditions in Japan," *Arctic Anthropology,* V, No. 2 (1969), pp. 133-158.

[3] Kwang-chih Chang, *Fengpitou, Tapenkeng, and the Prehistory of Taiwan* (New Haven, Conn., 1969), p. 53. For the implied extreme antiquity of the cord-marked pottery of Taiwan and its possible relation to evidence of very early protohorticultural activities on this island around 9000 B.C., see *ibid.,* Figure 92 on p. 216 and pp. 216-218.

dates.⁴ "Just prior to 6000 B.C.," at the Spirit Cave site where radiocarbon dates are available, "the quadrangular adze, small slate knives and cord-marked pottery appeared as intrusive elements in the continuous local Hoabinhian expression."⁵

On mainland China, large numbers of cord-marked pottery sites have been located in the southernmost coastal province of Kwangtung, in the inland province of Kiangsi in the lower-central Yangtze, in Szechwan province just south of the Neolithic nuclear area of Shensi, and in a number of the earliest Yang-shao cultural sites in Shensi.⁶ Although no radiocarbon dates are available, the finds at Hsien-jen-tung 仙人洞 (Cave of the Spirits) in Wen-nien 萬年 county in northeastern Kiangsu are revealing. Here the cord-marked pottery is associated with other artifacts which indicate fishing, hunting, and collecting as the economic basis of this culture, and with human skulls and shovel-shaped incisors which indicate that its inhabitants were Mongoloid. The description of the potsherds of this site is of technical significance and is therefore cited in full:

Paste: Sandy Red ware. Coarse texture; tempered with quartz grains of various sizes, the largest 1 millimeter in diameter and 0.5 millimeter in thickness; tempering material exhibited very unevenly in the paste. Other tempering materials were used, but are oxidized and occur in grayish-whitish powder form. Firing was low, and the paste is loose and easily breakable; the sherds are difficult to remove from the soil during excavations. The thickness of the sherds varies from 0.7 to 1.4 centimeters; the thickness of a single sherd varies from one portion to another. The color of the

---

⁴ *Ibid.*, pp. 224–225.

⁵ Chester F. Gorman, "Hoabinhian: A Pebble-Tool Complex with Early Plant Associations in Southeast Asia," *Science,* CLXIII, No. 3868 (14 February 1969), pp. 671–673.

⁶ For Kwangtung, see K. C. Chang's excellent summary in his *Fengpitou, Tapenkeng, and the Prehistory of Taiwan,* pp. 223–224; for Szechwan, see Cheng Te-k'un, *Archaeological Studies in Szechwan* (Cambridge, England, 1957), ch. iv, "Pottery," pp. 104–129. Cord-marked pottery of Kiangsi and Shensi will be discussed presently in the text.

core is reddish-brown; one piece exhibits red, gray, and black. The interior surface of the sherds is uneven, indicating that the pottery was handmade.

Shape: Too fragmentary for shape determination. The rims are mostly straight; there are a few that are flaring or inverted. No neck or shoulder sherds. Body sherds show large arc angles. No appendages. No flat base sherds. One restorable pot: lip slightly flaring; upper part of the body vertical; lower part slopes inward to form a possible round base. Thick but uneven. Both exterior and interior impressed with cord-marks. Remaining height 18 cm, the diameter of the mouth 20 cm.

Decoration: All of the sherds are cord-marked. Strands vary in thickness; thick strands 2.5 mm wide, but fine ones only 1 mm. Techniques of decoration include (1) cross-impressed: most common, fine, resembling check patterns; (2) segment-impressed: impressed in units; (3) parallel: fine and regular, thick and fine strands; (4) irregular: often smeared; (5) interior-exterior: impressed on both sides; patterns on the two sides are often not identical.

In addition to cord-marking, there are sherds that were smoothed and exhibit parallel lines. A few rim sherds exhibit one or two rows of circular impressions; a few of these penetrated through the sherds or cracked the walls. On the lips are also found irregular indentations.[7]

It is worth noting that years before cord-marked pottery was discovered in North China, Lauriston Ward had already postulated that the earliest pottery of North China should have been of a type characterized by cord-marking.[8] Recent archaeological finds in Shensi, within and without the Yang-shao nuclear area, have borne out Ward's remarkable prediction. In 1960–61 cord-marked pottery typologically belonging to the Yang-shao culture was discovered at Li-chia-ts'un, Hsi-hsian county, in Shensi, which is barely south of the natural demarcation Ch'in-ling Mountain. Soon afterward similar cord-impressed pottery was found in a number of Yang-shao sites north of the Ch'in-ling in Shensi. Two leading Chinese

---

[7] "Chiang-hsi Wan-nien Ta-yüan Hsien-jen-tung tung-hsüeh i-chih shih-chüeh" [Trial Diggings at the Neolithic Site of Hsien-jen-tung, Ta-yüan, Wan-nien, Kiangsi Province], *KKHP*, 1963, No. 1, pp. 1–16. The description of pottery quoted in the text is drawn from the translation by K. C. Chang, *Fengpitou, Tapenkeng, and the Prehistory of Taiwan*, pp. 222–223.

[8] Lauriston Ward, "The Relative Chronology of China through the Han Period," in Robert Ehrich, ed., *Relative Chronologies in Old World Archaeology* (Chicago, 1954), pp. 130–144, esp. p. 133.

archaeologists took pains to ascertain the stratigraphical sequence, which unmistakably shows that the cord-marked pottery stratum represents the earliest phase of the Yang-shao culture, followed by several phases of the same culture characterized mainly by painted pottery.[9]

It has thus become clear that everywhere in the Far East the earliest ceramics are characterized by cord-marking. Along the southeast coast and in the southern parts of China, which the Yang-shao culture did not reach, the stratum containing cord-marked pottery is invariably overlaid by one which is Lungshanoid or shows Lungshanoid affiliation. In the Yang-shao cultural sphere, the stratum containing cord-marked pottery lies immediately below strata having painted wares. The only problem of fundamental importance to prehistorians and archaeologists which the present state of knowledge cannot settle is whether the cord-marked potsherds discovered in various regions of the Far East were derived from a single place of origin or were of multiple independent occurrences. While the extreme antiquity of the cord-marked pottery of Jomon would seem to favor temperate western Japan as its place of origin, the ceramic and cultural affinities between ancient Japan and Taiwan, let alone the mainland of East and Southeast Asia, are uncertain. In discussing the possible external affinities of the corded wares of Taiwan, K. C. Chang expresses the following opinion:

Aside from the fact that both the Japanese and the Formosan pottery are cord-marked and that occasional incised patterns are common to both, there is very little indication that there was any direct and close cultural relationship between the two areas. The shapes of the Formosan cord-marked pottery and the decorative motifs of

---

[9] "Shan-hsi Hsi-hsiang Li-chia-ts'un hsin-shih-ch'i-shih-tai i-chih" [The Neolithic Site of Li-chia-ts'un, Hsi-hsiang, Shensi], *KK*, 1961, No. 7, pp. 352–354; Hsia Nai, "Wo-kuo chin-wu-nien ti k'ao-ku shou-huo" [Our Country's Archaeological Accomplishments during the Past Five Years], *KK*, 1964, No. 10, esp. p. 486; Su Ping-ch'i, "Kuan-yü Yang-shao-wen-hua ti jo-kan wen-t'i" [Some Problems Concerning the Yang-shao Culture], *KKHP*, 1965, No. 1, esp. pp. 52–56.

the incisions are found but rarely—if at all—in Japan, and the characteristic Jomon shapes and decorations are completely absent from the Taiwan data. Moreover, the associated stone and bone artifacts in Formosa derive evidently from a cultural strain different from their Japanese counterparts.[10]

It seems reasonable, however, to believe that cord-marked pottery is of distinctly Far Eastern origin and that the earliest pottery of the Yang-shao nuclear area was derived from the southern half of China, even though the latter owed much of its mature regional and even local Neolithic culture directly or indirectly to the Yang-shao area.

Our impression of the distinctly Far Eastern origins of Chinese Neolithic pottery will be strengthened by a brief discussion of pottery in the context of Old World prehistory. Although the Near East was the cradle of the world's earliest civilization, it was not the first area in the world to invent pottery. A recent synthesis of world prehistory puts the date of the earliest pottery of the Near East around 6000 B.C.[11] Actually potsherds are present in the upper one-third of the cultural layer of Jarmo, where barley and wheat cultivation is known to have begun shortly after 7000 B.C., and seeds with potsherds are found in a cultural stratum at Ali Kosh, Khuzistan, Iran, which is radiocarbon dated at 6970 B.C.[12] Allowing for the likelihood that the chronology of Near Eastern pottery may be pushed even further back through new finds, it is doubtful that it will ever be anywhere close to 10,000 B.C. Besides, the earliest potsherds unearthed from various Near Eastern sites cannot be categorized as cord-marked.[13] Judging from existing knowledge, a

---

[10] K. C. Chang, *Fengpitou, Tapenkeng, and the Prehistory of Taiwan*, p. 221.

[11] Grahame Clark, *World Prehistory: A New Outline* (Cambridge, England, 1969), p. 86.

[12] I owe this information on Jarmo potsherds to oral communication from my colleague Professor Robert J. Braidwood. By far the earliest Near Eastern sherds with radiocarbon dating is given in Frank Hole, Kent V. Flannery, and James A. Neeley, *Prehistory and Human Ecology of the Deh Luran Plain: An Early Village Sequence from Khuzistan, Iran* (Memoirs of the Museum of Anthropology, University of Michigan, Ann Arbor, 1969, No. 1), p. 336.

[13] Also oral communication from Braidwood.

broader and more fundamental difference in the sequence of cultural development between the ancient Near East and Far East is that, in the former, grain-centered agriculture preceded pottery, whereas, in the latter, pottery preceded field agriculture by a very considerably period of time. The Fertile Crescent and its hilly flanks are more than 4,500 miles from the coast of China and more than 5,000 miles from western Honshu, with most formidable natural barriers in between. Since even a postulation of stimulus diffusion requires material evidence and since it is impossible to establish any real cultural affinity between the pottery groups of the Near East and those of the Far East with existing comparative archaeological data, the ceramic complexes of these two broad regions seem almost certainly to have occurred independently.

Looking back to various theories of cultural origins, the closely reasoned generalization of the late Roland B. Dixon remains a useful antidote to some extreme diffusionist views:

> Inventions based on opportunities which are universal have a greater chance of being duplicated than those arising from opportunities which are more or less local. Thus clay, as affording an opportunity for the invention of pottery, is not only widespread, but caked and dried by the sun or baked by the fire, obtrudes itself in a dozen different ways on man's attention. It invites the genius to take advantage of it.[14]

In this connection, it may not be unreasonable to suggest the possibility of multiple independent occurrences of cord-marked pottery in the vast area of the mainland and archipelagoes of East Asia and Southeast Asia.

That the ceramic complex of Yang-shao and subsequent Chinese Neolithic cultures evolved from origins different from those of prehistoric Near Eastern pottery is evidenced in part by vessel shapes. Even though the shapes of certain simple vessels of daily use, such as bowls, are necessarily more or less similar in practically all ceramic traditions, significant differences in shapes and functions

---

[14] Roland B. Dixon, *The Building of Culture* (New York, 1928), p. 48.

do exist between prehistoric Near Eastern and prehistoric Chinese wares. Take, for example, the great variety of jars which are quantitatively, functionally, and esthetically very important in the Hassuna-Halaf complex. Their bodies are either nearly spherical, or flatbottomed, or on a hollow stand, or oblate; they invariably have a neck, whether low or long and flaring; and they are usually richly decorated with geometric designs (see Figure 1). Jars of these

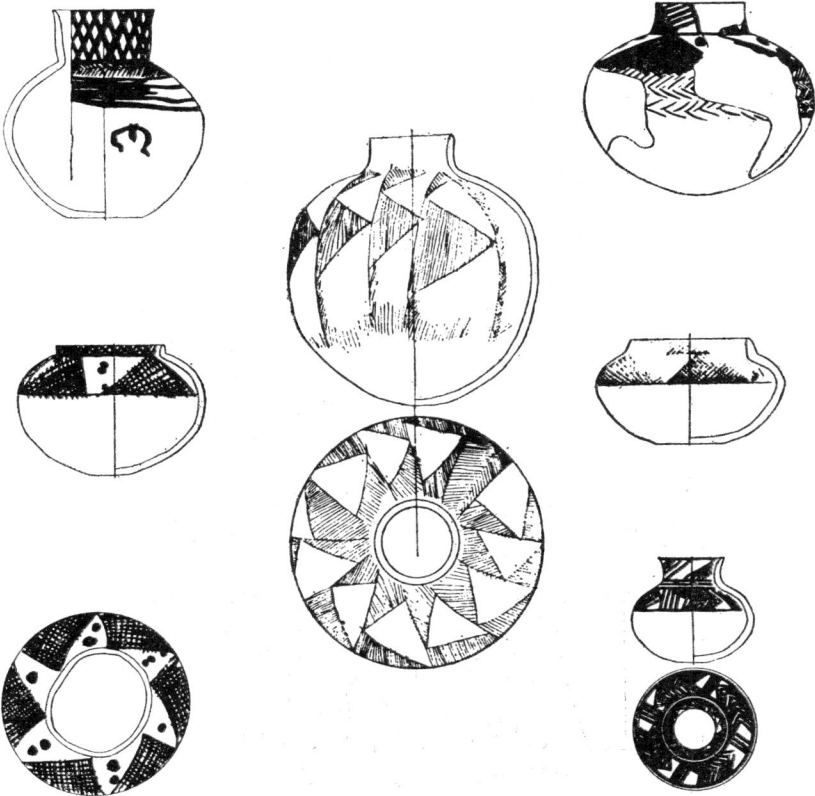

FIGURE 1. Common shapes of jars of Hassuna. All samples are Hassuna standard wares except the lower right, which is the later Samarran ware. Selected from Seton Lloyd and Fuad Safar, "Tell Hassuna," *Journal of Near Eastern Studies,* IV, No. 4 (October 1945), Figures 1-4.

shapes and of comparable designs are totally absent from the ceramic assemblages of Pan-p'o and Miao-ti-kou I (see Figure 2). The only jars of the Yang-shao period are small and undecorated, with lids, and with different body shapes. Dishes and saucers are fairly common among pottery wares of Hassuna and Halaf, but they are also completely missing from the Yang-shao complex. On the

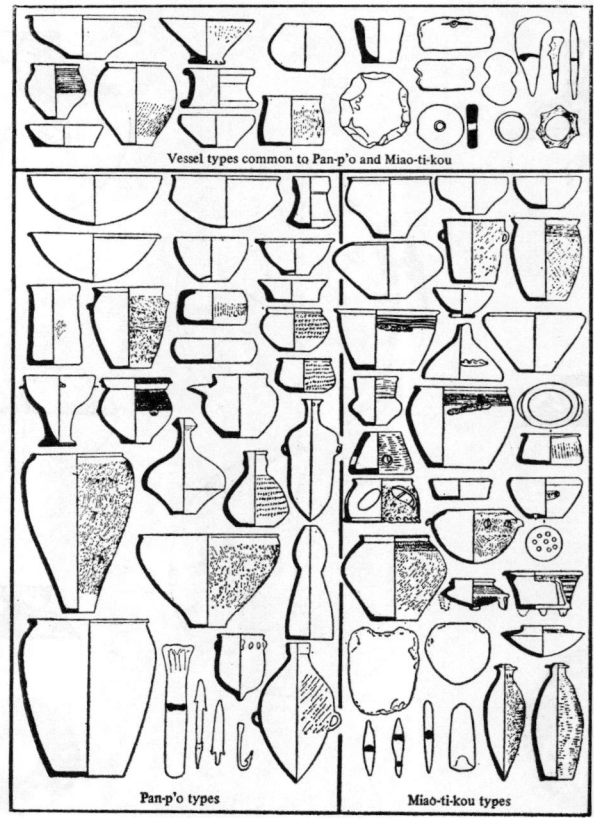

FIGURE 2. Common shapes of Yang-shao pottery vessels (including other common implements). Upper: Vessels common to both Pan-p'o and Miao-ti-kou I. Left: Vessels of Pan-p'o. Right: Vessels of Miao-ti-kou I. From *Hsin-Chung-kuo ti k'ao-ku shou-huo,* Figure 6 on p. 13.

other hand, open pots and urns of the Yang-shao complex, which vary greatly in size and shape, are rarely found in the Hassuna-Halaf assemblage.[15] More significantly, the Yang-shao *tseng*-steamer with holes in the bottom, the *ting*-tripod which began to appear in late Yang-shao period, and an ever-increasing variety of the *ting*-tripod, of the *li*-tripod, and of the three-legged *chia* vessel of the subsequent Lungshanoid and Lung-shan cultures are all unmistakably and uniquely Sinitic (see Figure 3).

Of all types of ceramic wares, painted pottery has the greatest relevance to our study. A reexamination of the erstwhile prevalent Western view that Neolithic China owed much of its culture to borrowings from Southwest Asia—a view based partially or totally on the alleged affinities between Chinese and Western painted wares —is very much overdue. Unlike pottery in general, which undoubtedly first occurred in the Far East, painted pottery calls for a systematic comparative study, at least with regard to design patterns, because prehistoric Near Eastern painted wares are earlier chronologically.

A recent survey of world prehistory dates the beginnings of painted pottery in the Near East at around 5500 B.C.[16] In the Tell Hassuna area in Iraq, painted pottery may have appeared as early as 6000 B.C., although the bulk of the painted wares of Tell Halaf, a most important center, and other localities east of the Euphrates can be dated probably between 5000 and 4500 B.C.[17] This approximate chronology is important because it shows that painted pottery of the Near East was about one thousand years older than that of Yang-shao.

---

[15] This statement is based on my comparison of Figures 2, 3, and 4 in Appendix IV, by Hubert Schmitt, of Max von Oppenheim, *Tell Halaf: A New Culture in Oldest Mesopotamia* (London, 1933).

[16] Clark, *World Prehistory*, p. 99.

[17] This is my summary of oral communications from Professors Braidwood, Robert M. Adams, and Hans J. Nissen.

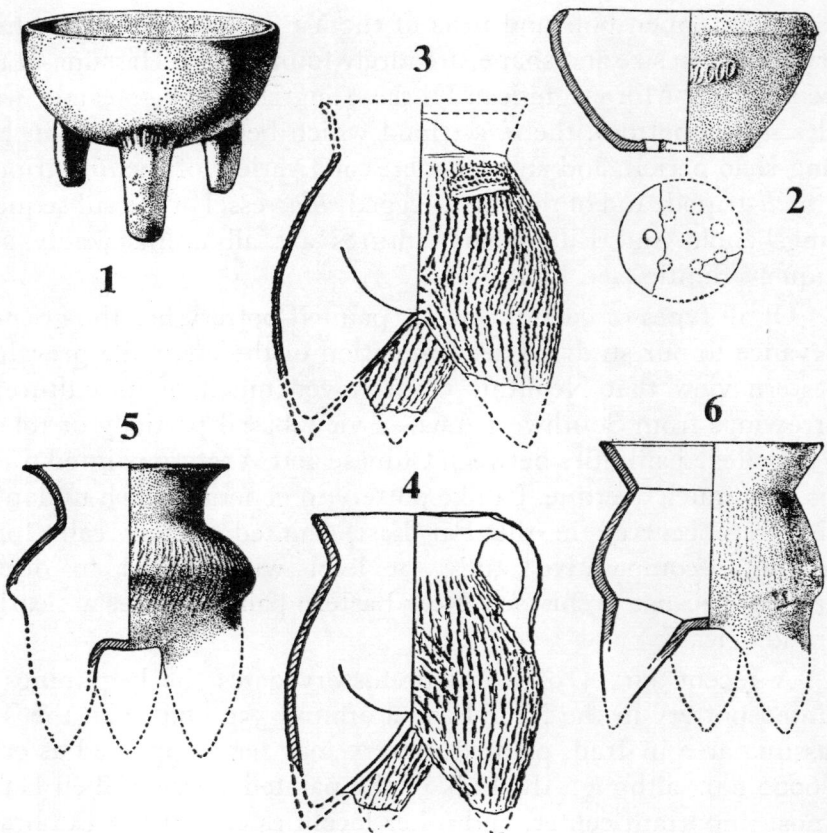

FIGURE 3. Typically Sinitic pottery vessels: (1) The *ting*-tripod, from *Hsi-an Pan-p'o,* Figure 105 on p. 130; (2) The *tseng*-steamer, from the Miao-ti-kou I Yang-shao cultural stratum; (3) and (4) The *li*-tripod, from the Lungshanoid cultural stratum of San-li-ch'iao; (5) and (6) The *chia* vessel, from the Lungshanoid cultural stratum of Miao-ti-kou. Numbers 2–6 are from *Miao-ti-kou yü San-li-ch'iao,* Plate 23 on p. 37, Plate 45 on p. 70, and Plate 62 on p. 94.

Some characteristics of the better Near Eastern painted pottery are summarized by Grahame Clark:

The most brilliant manifestation of early painted pottery in south-west Asia was that named after Tell Halaf. Halafian pottery is outstanding on account of the variety of its forms and above all of its painted decoration and because of its excellent firing;

but it was still hand-made, and there is no reason to think it was necessarily or even probably made by whole-time potters. In addition to dishes and flasks the forms included bowls with sharp-shouldered bodies and flaring necks and bowls and flasks on hollow stands. . . . At the climax of the industry the decoration was polychrome; red, orange, yellow and black paints being used, sometimes highlighted by white spots. The pottery was apparently fired up to 1200°C in great domed kilns with rectangular annexes.[18]

The importance of the maximum firing temperature of prehistoric pottery kilns was not confined to the ceramic industry itself but also had much to do with the beginnings of metallurgy. A number of studies of prehistoric Near Eastern and predynastic Egyptian ceramic sherds show that the firing temperature was between 1000° and 1200°C.[19] For instance, a recent study by a team of scientists of the Massachusetts Institute of Technology indicates that the highest firing temperature of ancient Near Eastern sherds was in the neighborhood of 1000°C, and a technical analysis of the Halafian sherds indicates a firing temperature of about 1000°C.[20] Whatever may be the difference in the estimates of ceramic experts, there is little doubt that prehistoric and early historic Near Eastern pottery kilns of advanced designs could generate temperatures considerably higher than those of prehistoric kilns in other areas of the world.

Up to the present, the only systematic scientific analysis of the technology of early Chinese pottery is in a report by three members of the Institute of Silicate Chemistry and Technology of Academia Sinica, Peking. Although the study is concerned with major types

---

[18] Clark, *World Prehistory*, p. 99.

[19] H. H. Coghlan, *Notes on the Prehistoric Metallurgy of Copper and Bronze in the Old World* (Occasional Paper on Technology, No. 4, Pitt Rivers Museum, Oxford University, 1951), pp. 22–23.

[20] W. D. Kingery, "Progress Report on a Cursory Technical Examination of Some Near-Eastern Ceramic Sherds," with R. J. Brook, R. L. Anderson, S. Prochazka, B. J. Wuensch, R. Shaw and others (manuscript). Also on the Halafian sherds, Van O. Streu, "Zur Technik der altorientalischen Keramik," in Helmuth Scheel, *Zeitschrift der Deutschen Morgenländischen Gesellschaft* (Leipzig, 1943), pp. 359–368.

of early Chinese pottery from Yang-shao to Shang-Chou times, it yields vital information on Yang-shao painted pottery, which is included in what the authors call for convenience Neolithic "red" wares. Since the black "egg-shell" pottery of the late Neolithic Lung-shan culture is unique for its age, we shall include the main findings on this particular type of ware in the following summary so as to enable Western experts of early ceramics to make comparative studies. The salient technological aspects of Neolithic Chinese pottery are as follows:

(1) The chemical composition diagram of sherds, loess, and clays shows that the loess contains a much greater amount of calcium oxide (CaO) than the sherds and is generally poorer in plasticity. In spite of the wide distribution of loess in North China, the ancient potters used natural clays instead in the manufacture of the red, gray, and black wares.

(2) The bulk of Neolithic ... pottery was ring-built but their shapes were often improved on a turn-table.

(3) As early as the Yang-shao stage of the Neolithic Age, the art of the potter had already attained a very high level. The first appearance of pottery can probably be traced back to an even earlier period.

(4) The red, gray, and black wares were fired on the average at between 950–1050°C.

(5) Laboratory experiments and observations conducted on modern parallels have shed much new light on the technology of the black "egg-shell" ware. Its lustre was obtained through polishing with a pebble when the paste was damp. The "smoking" process carried out in the furnace at the end of the firing enabled the carbonaceous soots to penetrate into the pores of the vessel, thus giving a black appearance to it.[21]

---

[21] Chou Jen, Chang Fu-k'ang, and Cheng Yung-p'u, "Wo-kou Huang-ho-liu-yü hsin-shih-ch'i-shih-tai ho Yin-Chou-shih-tai chih-t'ao-kung-i ti k'e-hsüeh tsung-chieh" [Studies on the Technology of Neolithic and Yin and Chou Pottery Unearthed in the Yellow River Basin], *KKHP,* 1964, No. 1, pp. 1–27. The above is cited from its English abstract on pp. 26–27, excluding summary of findings on Shang-Chou wares. The following findings on Shang-Chou wares are certainly of great interest to experts concerned with comparative studies of ancient ceramics: (1) The photograph of sherds of Shang white ware taken from an electronic microscope reveals the presence of kaolinite. (2) Early acquaintance of ancient Chinese potters with china clay, kaolin, and glaze and the use of high-temperature furnaces, especially during later Chou times when some wares were fired at 1230°C, laid the foundation for the subsequent invention of porcelain in China. (3) The glazed pottery of the Shang-Chou period bears a certain resemblance to later celadon.

The finding that even during the Yang-shao period the surface of finer and painted wares was usually smoothed on a turn-table confirms the earlier observations made in the 1930s by G. D. Wu, who was of the opinion that the potter's wheel of late Neolithic China was evolved from the turn-table.[22] It is significant that the standard wares of Hassuna were invariably handmade, and "there is no indication of the use of any kind of wheel or *tournette.*"[23]

The temperature range within which Yang-shao finer and painted wares were fired, between 950° and 1050°C, was lower than the highest firing temperature possible to the most efficient of prehistoric Near Eastern kilns. For making pottery the temperature range 950°–1050° was quite satisfactory,[24] although the lowness of the range may have accounted in part for the late beginnings of metallurgy in China—an aspect which will be discussed in chapter 5. A seemingly minor but culturally highly significant difference in painting technique should be pointed out. Yang-shao potters used, along with some hard, sharp styluses, paint brushes made of animal hair, feather, or soft natural fiber.[25] In the case of Hassuna: "The

---

[22] G. D. Wu, *Prehistoric Pottery in China* (London, 1938).

[23] Seton Lloyd and Fuad Safar, "Tell Hassuna: Excavations by the Iraq Government Directorate General of Antiquities in 1943 and 1944," *Journal of Near Eastern Studies*, IV, No. 4 (October 1945), pp. 255–289, and figures and plates, esp. p. 279.

[24] Anna O. Shepard, *Ceramics for the Archaeologist* (Washington, D.C., 1965), pp. 217–219, thinks that for primitive ceramics a temperature range of "700°–750°C is satisfactory except for the very low-fired wares." The firing temperature of Taiwan cord-marked pottery is estimated between 450° and 550°C and that of Taiwan Lungshanoid wares between 550° and 740°C. See K. C. Chang, *Fengpitou, Tapenkeng, and the Prehistory of Taiwan*, p. 58 and pp. 88–89. It should be noted that while the best of Halafian wares were unusually high-fired, the pottery of Susa in western Iran is very soft and "the experts agree on a very low temperature in the firing." The wares are so soft that the "clay melts in a porcelain furnace." See H. Frankfurt, *Mesopotamia, Syria, and Their Earliest Interrelations* (London, 1924), p. 25, note 3.

[25] G. D. Wu, *Prehistoric Pottery in China*, p. 76; Ma Ch'eng-yüan, *Yang-shao-wen-hua ti ts'ai-t'ao* [The Painted Pottery of the Yang-shao Culture] (Shanghai, 1957), pp. 36–37; *Hsi-an Pan-p'o*, p. 156.

designs were drawn with a fine point, possibly a sharp flint or bone stylus which cut lightly into the clay."[26] To our knowledge, no prehistoric people other than the proto-Chinese ever used the brush first for pottery painting and only later for writing.

While a systematic comparison of the technology of prehistoric Near Eastern and Chinese ceramics must await future scientific studies, the designs and motifs of the painted wares of ancient Mesopotamia, Iran, and Yang-shao China are ample for meaningful comparison. Hubert Schmitt, an authority on the Halafian pottery, has thus summarized the motifs of this group of famous early Mesopotamian wares:

> The designs are geometrical, simple elementary forms being combined into the most manifold figures or variations. The elementary forms consist of horizontal lines—zigzags, curved, waved; strips filled in variously (as with hatching or with latticework); rows of points, rows of triangles, hanging and standing, rows of rhombs variously filled; rows of angles; rows of slant lines. These elementary forms are set one below the other in horizontal belts, or in a vertical arrangement they lead to fields of metopes. Rows of circles are less often found; particularly noticeable are cross-board patterns, clover and the so-called Maltese cross, the so-called spring-oyster (thor-oyster, water-clam), the fiddle motive, together with rings of points and star-like combinations.[27]

The designs of Mesopotamian painted wares later than those of Halaf are shown in Figures 5, 6, 7(a) and 7(b). The designs and motifs of various representative early Iranian painted pottery are shown in Figures 8(a) through 8(l).

Stylistically, though not typologically and technologically, the painted wares of the Yang-shao period fall into two main categories —the Pan-p'o type and the Miao-ti-kou I type. The former, consisting mainly of zoomorphic and geometric designs, should be

---

[26] Lloyd and Safar, "Tell Hassuna," p. 279.

[27] Oppenheim, *Tell Halaf,* Appendix IV, p. 296. Joan L. Lines, "The Al 'Ubaid Period in Mesopotamia and Its Persian Affinities" (Cambridge University dissertation, 1953, unpublished), contains comprehensive illustrations of the pottery motifs of Ubaid. These illustrations have been consulted but not reproduced in this chapter, because this dissertation is available to me only in microfilm.

FIGURE 4. Designs of Halafian wares. From Max von Oppenheim, *Tell Halaf* (London, 1933), Appendix IV, Figure 1, on p. 296.

138 THE CRADLE OF THE EAST

FIGURE 5. Northern Ubaid pottery designs. From Ann L. Perkins, *The Comparative Archaeology of Early Mesopotamia* (Chicago, 1959), Figure 5, on pp. 60–61.

FIGURE 6. Southern Ubaid pottery designs. From Perkins, *The Comparative Archaeology of Early Mesopotamia*, Figure 10, on pp. 82–83.

FIGURE 7(a). "Jamdat Nasr" pottery designs, part I. From Perkins, *The Comparative Archaeology of Early Mesopotamia*, Figure 13, on pp. 108-109.

FIGURE 7(b). "Jamdat Nasr" pottery designs, part II. From Perkins, *The Comparative Archaeology of Early Mesopotamia*, Figure 13, on pp. 108–109.

FIGURE 8(a). Early Iranian pottery designs. This and the following eleven figures, 8(b) through 8(l), are taken from Donald E. McCown, *The Comparative Stratigraphy of Early Iran* (Chicago, 1957), Figures 1–10.

POTTERY 143

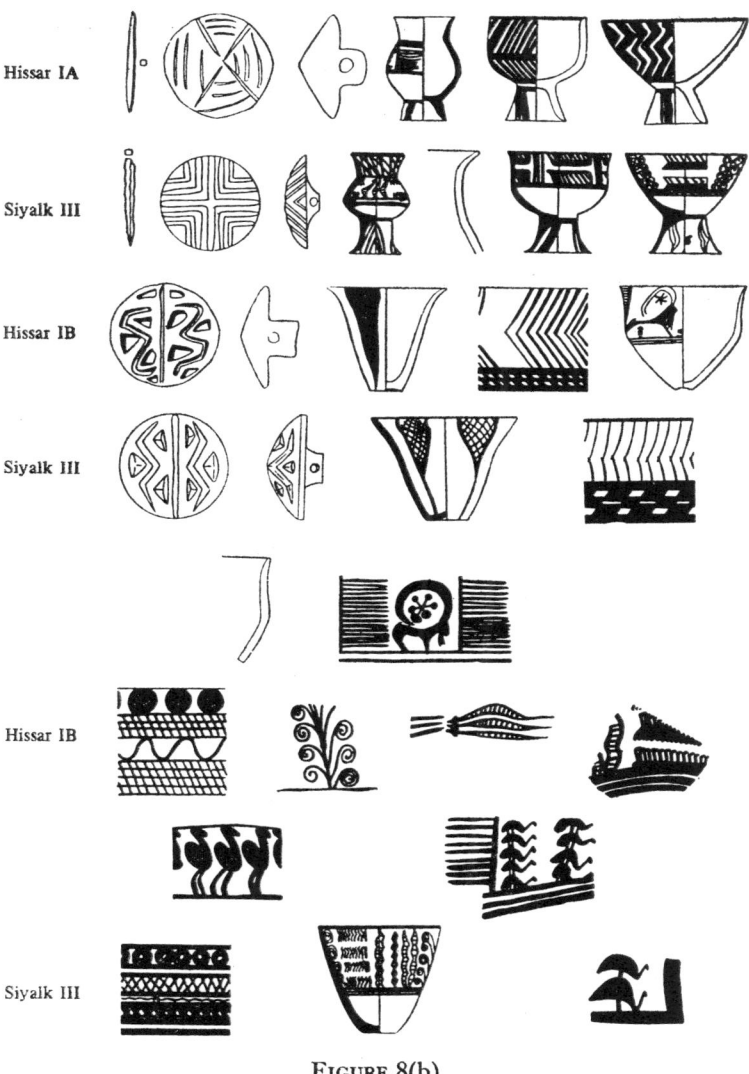

FIGURE 8(b)

144 THE CRADLE OF THE EAST

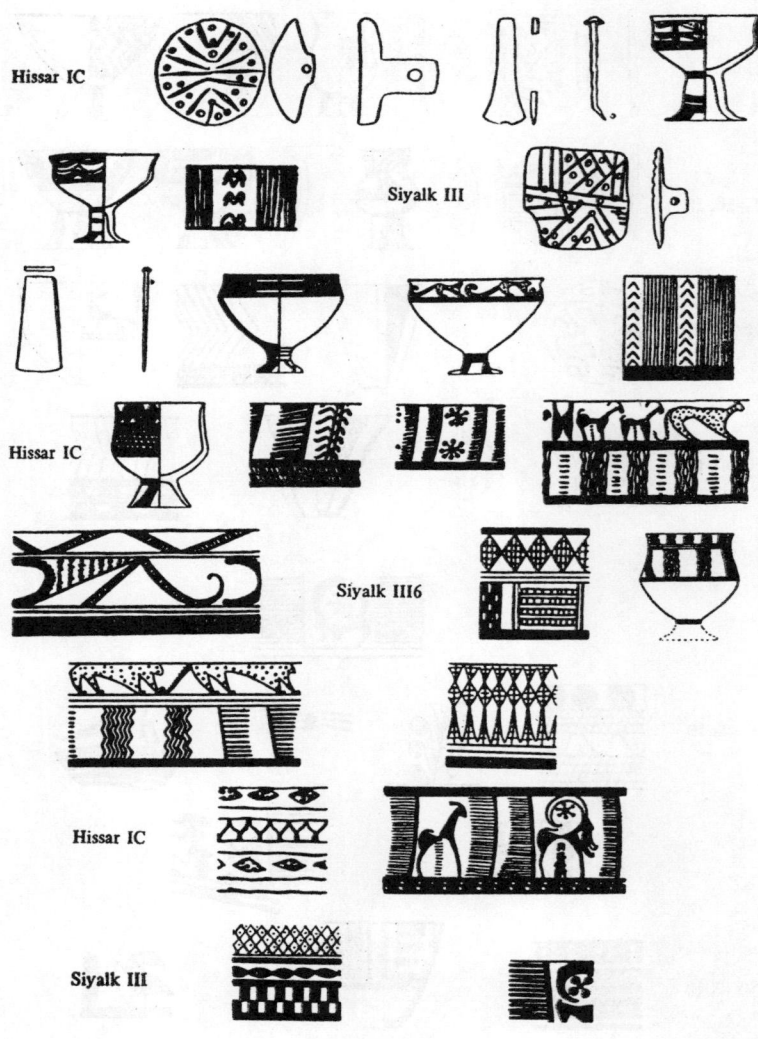

FIGURE 8(c)

POTTERY 145

FIGURE 8(d)

146 THE CRADLE OF THE EAST

FIGURE 8(e)

POTTERY 147

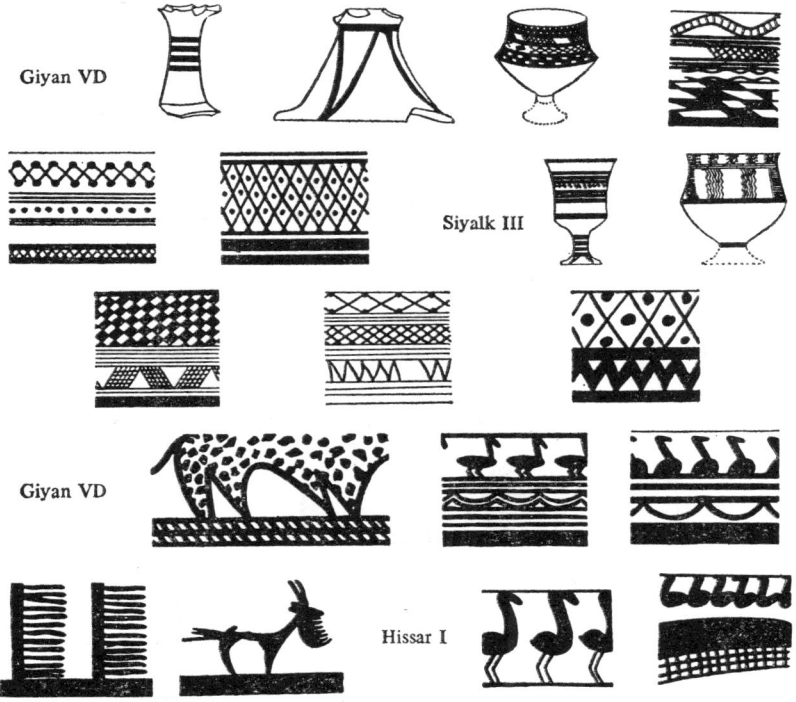

FIGURE 8(f)

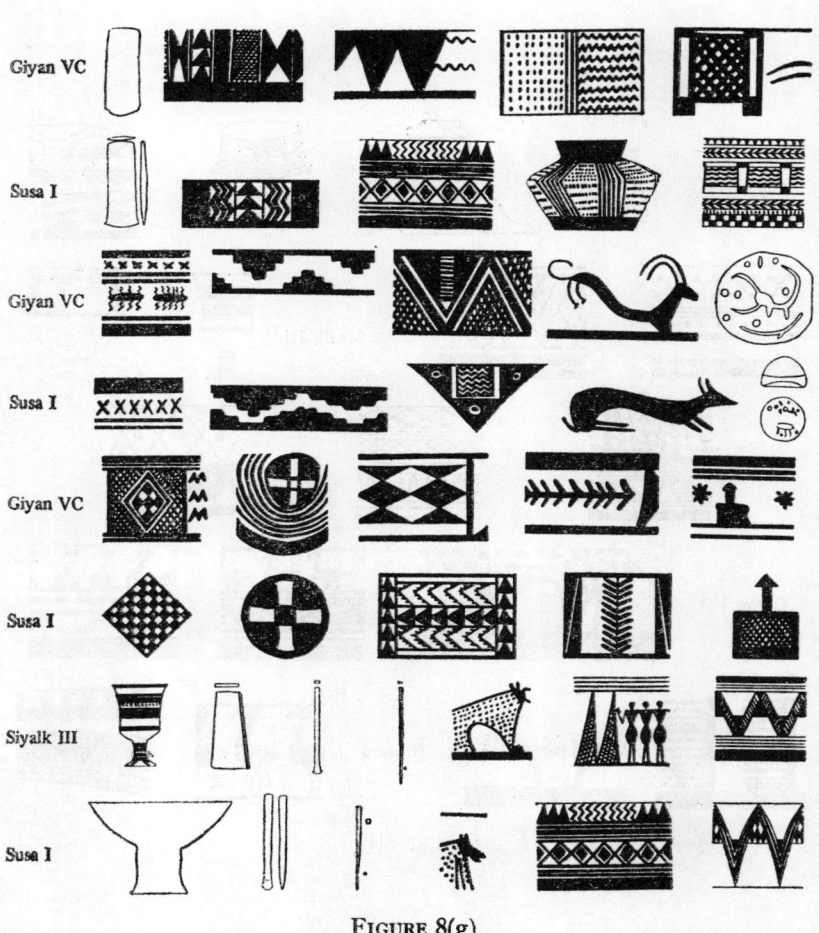

FIGURE 8(g)

POTTERY

FIGURE 8(h)

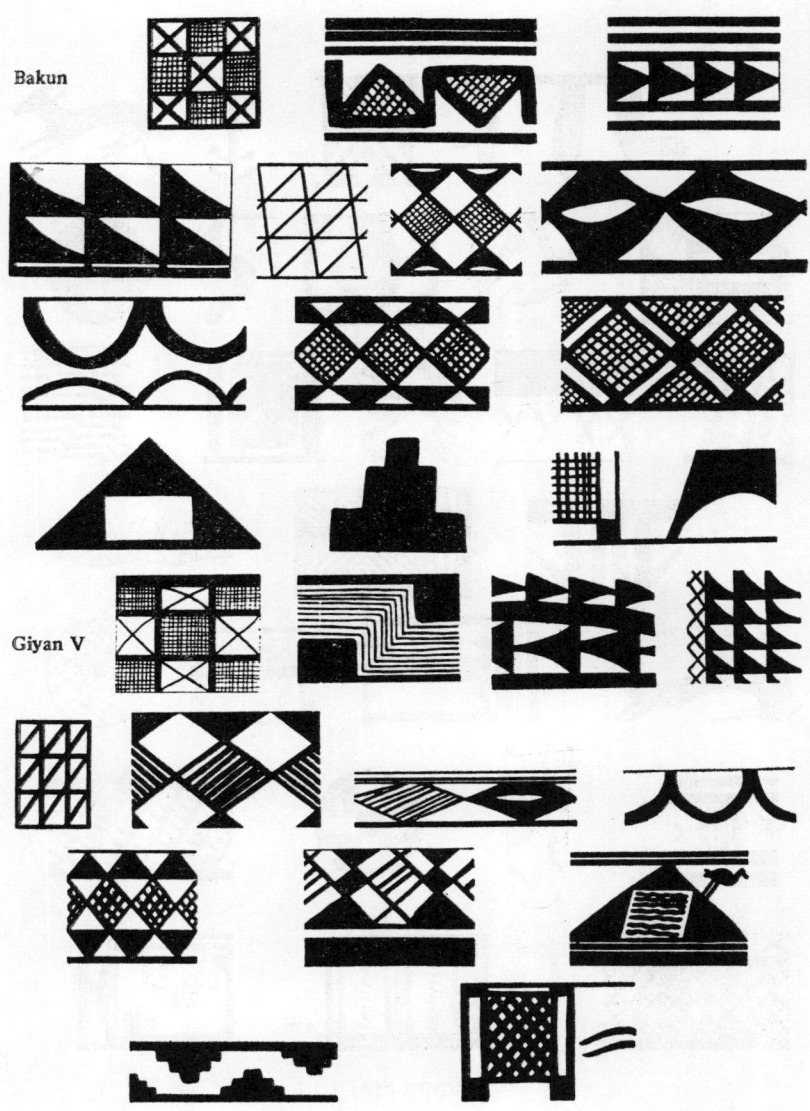

FIGURE 8(i)

POTTERY

Figure 8(j)

FIGURE 8(k)

POTTERY

FIGURE 8(l)

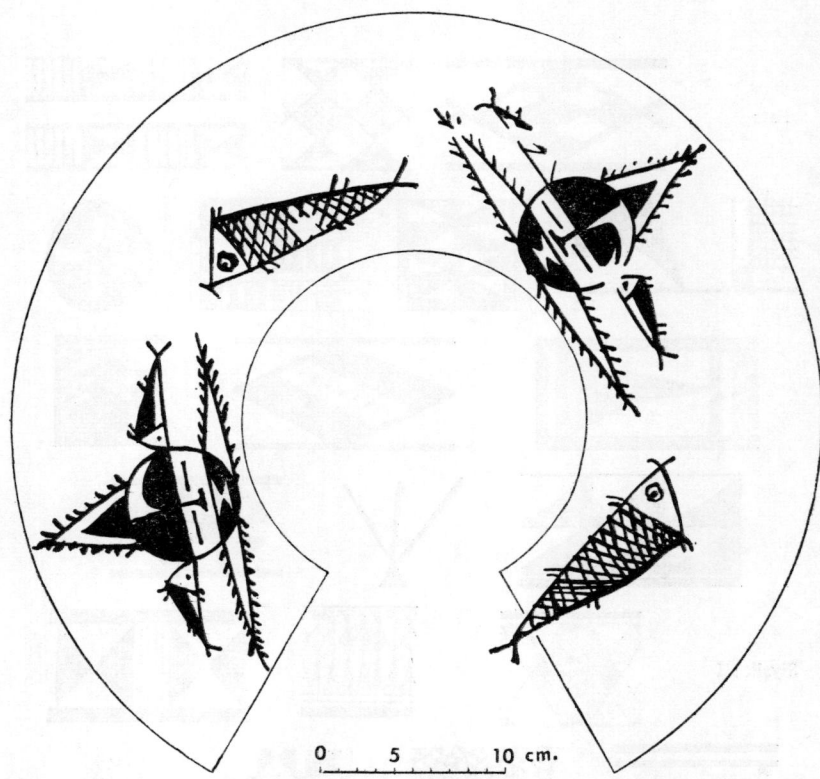

FIGURE 9. The Pan-p'o human face design and fish design. From *Hsi-an Pan-p'o*, Plate 128 on p. 180.

compared first with the designs of various types of early Near Eastern wares. The latter, characterized mainly by its floral patterns, should be compared later with the Halafian four-leaf clover or Maltese cross designs. The English summary of the Pan-p'o site report describes the dominant designs:

The painted decorations found on the Pan-p'o pottery are mostly geometric, with, however, a few conspicuous exceptions which bear striking zoomorphic designs. The color of the paint is usually black though some are decorated with either purple or red paint. The painting is usually applied directly on the paste, with only a few pieces which have a slip of either white or some other color.

POTTERY

Besides the human face, there are zoomorphic designs like the deer and particularly fish. The human designs are all identical and appear on the inner wall of the basin with a curving rim. The fish design appears either singly or in groups but always in a most lively manner. A unique decoration is the composite design of a human face and the head of a fish which might suggest some sort of totem worship [see Figure 9]. . . .

However, the majority of the Pan-p'o painted decorations are geometric and consist of such elements as the band, triangle, vertical and slanted lines, circles, and zigzags. Unlike the painted pottery of the Miao-ti-kou site which is dominated by the spiral pattern, the most conspicuous element here is the vertical lines. By a dexterous combination of these decorative elements the potters of Pan-p'o succeeded in creating a rich variety of geometric designs. . . .

The geometric designs are obtained by combining the various decorative elements in one of the following manners: (1) symmetrical grouping of either patterns consisting of identical motifs or of those consisting of different motifs, (2) asymmetrical grouping of the same, (3) decorating the base of the vessel with bands of identical motifs, and (4) connecting two patterns of different motifs.[28]

The geometric designs and motifs of Pan-p'o pottery, which are reproduced in full in Figures 10(a)–10(d), reveal little, if any, close similarity with those of the early Mesopotamian and early Iranian pottery groups, which are shown in Figures 4–8(l). In general, the Pan-p'o geometric motifs and contexts are much simpler. Of the more complex and dominant Pan-p'o geometric designs, the following ones bear a certain superficial resemblance to those of Northern Ubaid in Mesopotamia and of Siyalk III, Fars, and Giyan V-C in Iran:

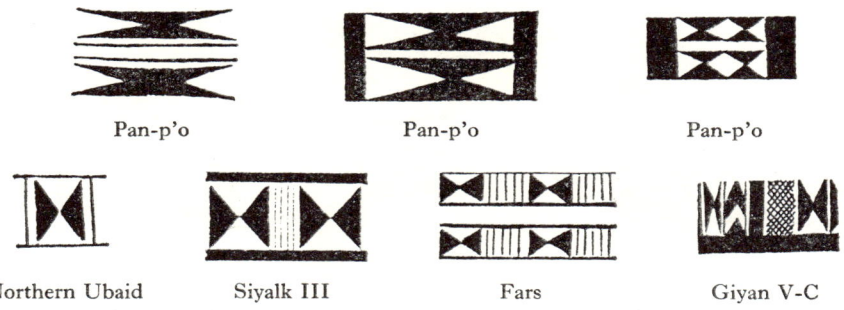

[28] *Hsi-an Pan-p'o*, pp. 312–315 of the English abstract.

156 THE CRADLE OF THE EAST

FIGURE 10(a). Geometric designs of Pan-p'o. This and the following three figures, 10(b), through 10(d), are taken from *Hsi-an Pan-p'o,* Figures 123–126 on pp. 174–177.

POTTERY

Figure 10(b)

158 THE CRADLE OF THE EAST

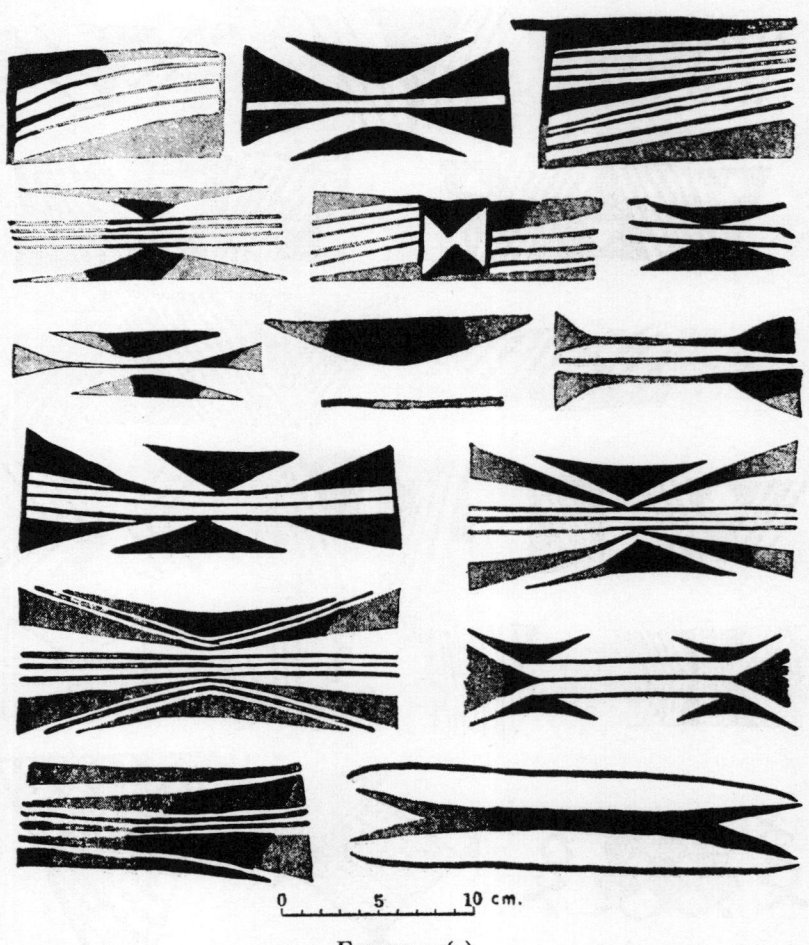

FIGURE 10(c)

POTTERY

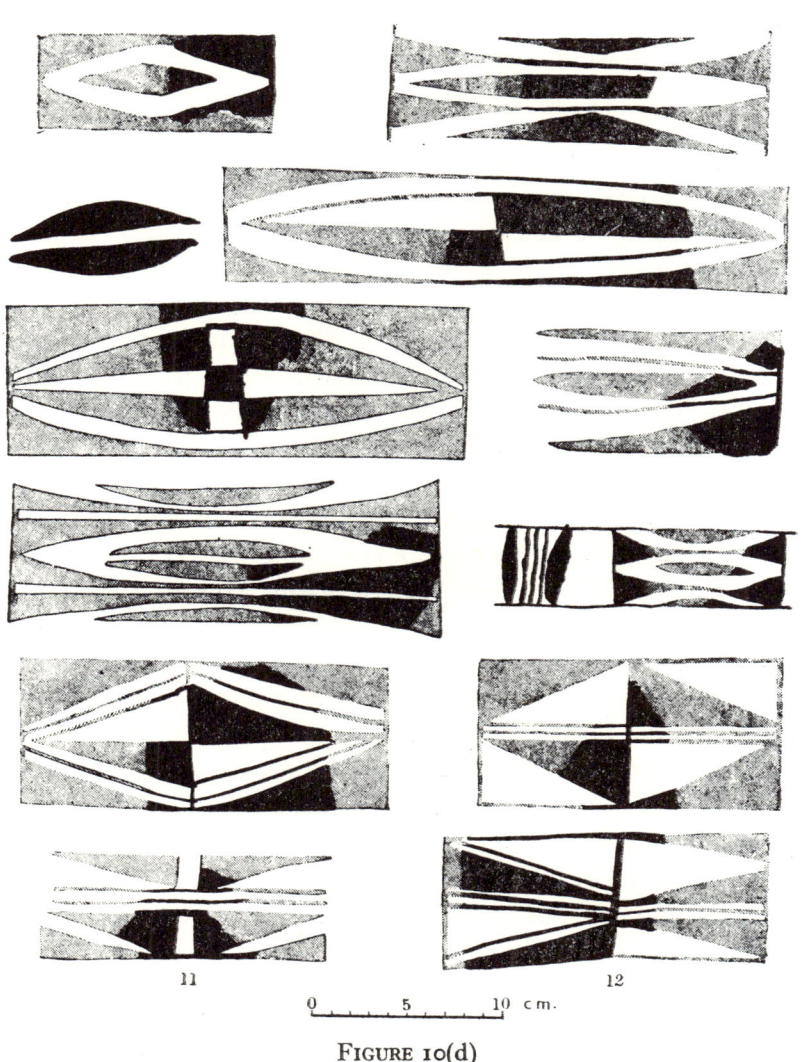

FIGURE 10(d)

Any doubt about the indigenous origins of these Pan-p'o geometric motifs should be dispelled by the fact that they were evolved from the zoomorphic designs of a fish. The processes of this stylistic evolution, most of which are based on actual vessels and sherds and on stratigraphical sequence, are shown in Figures 11(a)–11(c).

The type of Yang-shao culture represented by Miao-ti-kou I, Shan-hsien in western Honan, has been proved by recent radiocarbon datings to be later than the Pan-p'o type. The decorative spiral floral patterns on its painted wares are a major characteristic of this type of culture. Owing to the unearthing at Ch'üan-hu-ts'un 泉護村, a village in Hua-hsien 華縣 in Shensi, of potsherds bearing floral designs which may be regarded as a prototype of those of Miao-ti-kou I, some Chinese archaeologists believe that the Hua-hsien area, with its famous Hua Mountain, may have been the original headquarters of the Miao-ti-kou I type of culture. According to the veteran archaeologist Su Ping-ch'i, however, who had access to artifacts and archaeological data not yet described in published materials, the main sphere of the Miao-ti-kou I type of culture was a strip of fertile land along the Wei River and the southern bend of the Yellow River, stretching from She-hsien in western Honan to the vicinity of Sian in Shensi. In Su's opinion, the sphere of the Pan-p'o type of culture was from Sian westward to Pao-chi in west-central Shensi.[29] Since vessels and sherds bearing the typical Miao-ti-kou I patterns have been found in Ching-ts'un 荊村, a village in Wan-jung 萬榮 county in southwestern Shansi,[30] there is reason to believe that the southern Shansi area may have been more under Miao-ti-kou I influence than under Pan-p'o influence during late Yang-shao times.

[29] Su Ping-ch'i, "Kuan-yü Yang-shao-wen-hua ti jo-kan wen-t'i," esp. pp. 73–75.

[30] The important Yang-shao cultural site of Ching-ts'un in southwestern Shansi, which has been well known for more than thirty years, is yet to have a site report. Superb samples of the Miao-ti-kou I type of painted pottery from Ching-ts'un are given in Ma Ch'eng-yüan, *Yang-shao-wen-hua ti ts'ai-t'ao*, Plate III, 2a and 2b.

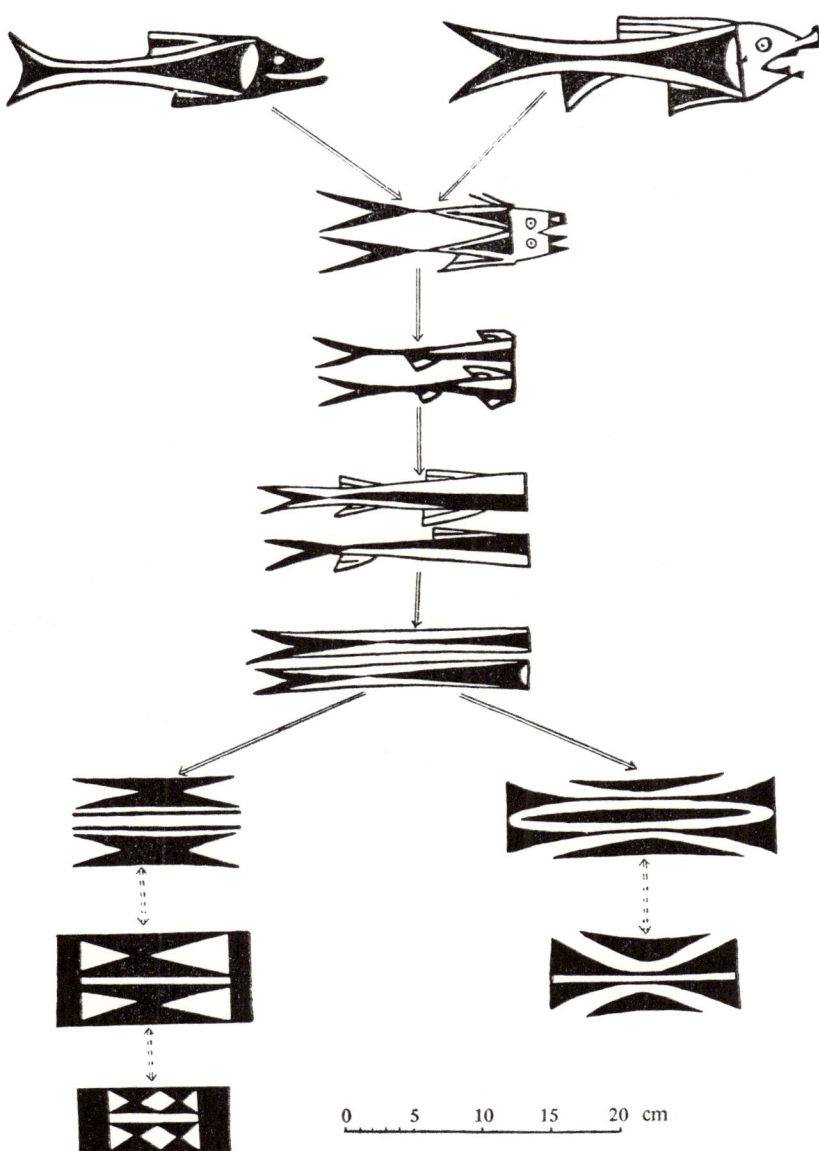

FIGURE 11(a). Evolutionary stages of major Pan-p'o designs. This and the following two figures, 11(b) and 11(c), are taken from *Hsi-an Pan-p'o*, Figures 129–131 on pp. 183–185.

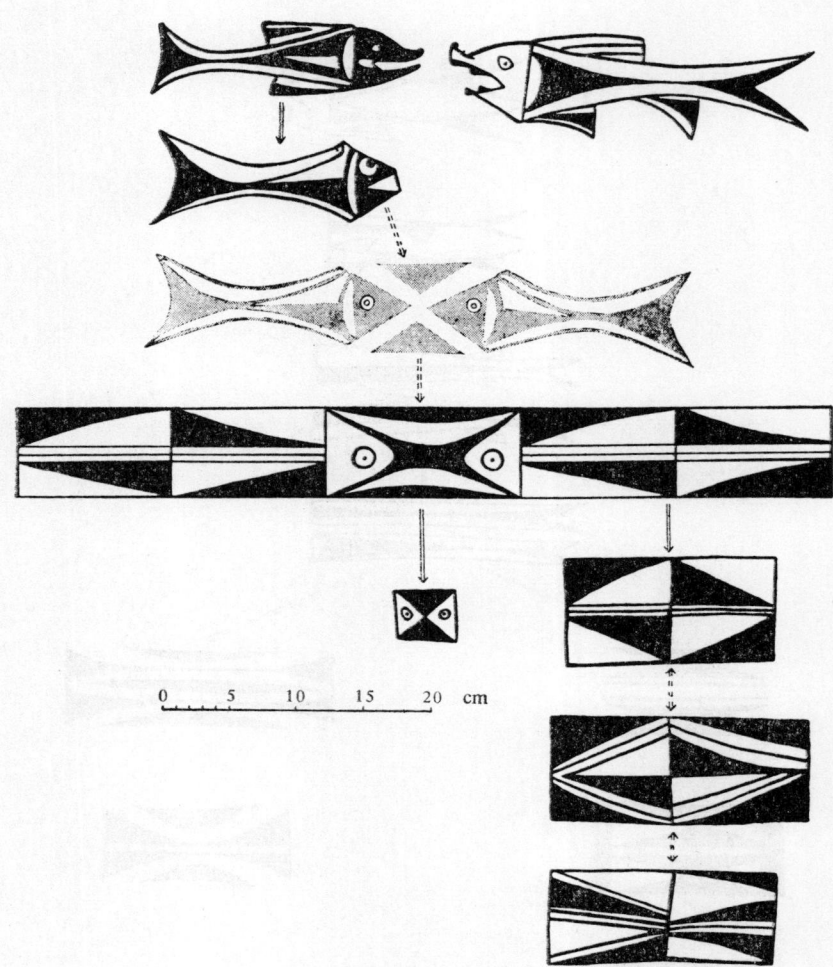

FIGURE 11(b)

POTTERY

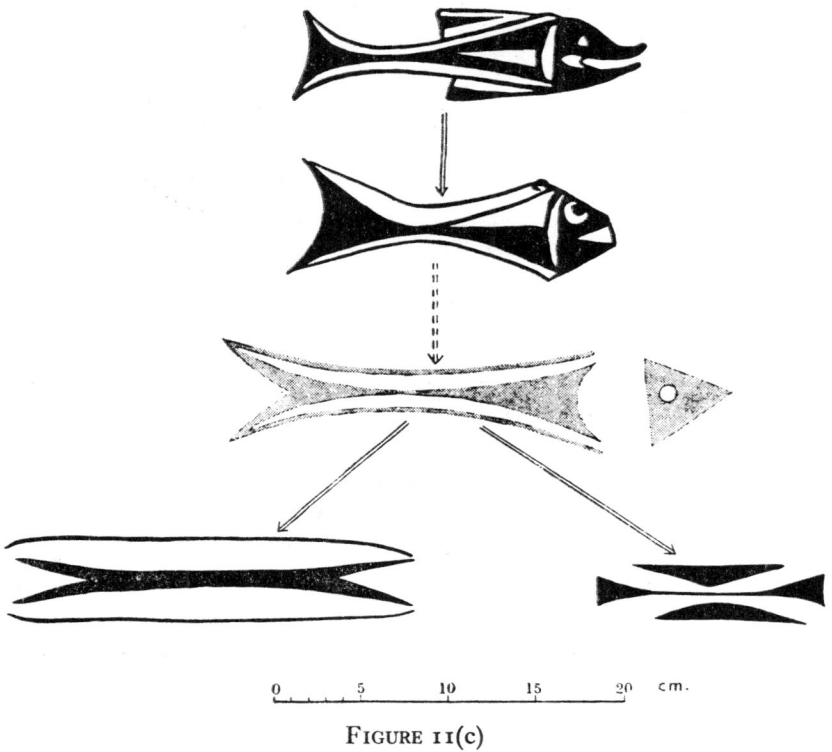

FIGURE 11(c)

Of the various floral motifs of Miao-ti-kou I pottery, the one which bears some resemblance to the Halafian Maltese Cross is that shown in Figure 12. The partial resemblance is, however, superficial and deceptive. For one thing, the motif is not a four-leaf clover but a five-petal flower, probably a rose. For another, the focal point in each unit of design is the stamen, represented by a conspicuous round dot, a focus which never appears in the unit of design of any of a variety of Halafian Maltese Cross patterns. Moreover, the interlocking petals, being superimposed upon one another, give the effect of continuous motion—an effect missing in the neat and static groupings of Halafian clover leaves.[31]

[31] It should be noted that there are interlocking clover leaves in Halafian designs

FIGURE 12. A Miao-ti-kou I basin with five-petal motif. From *Miao-ti-kou yü San-li-ch'iao*, plate following title page.

Though suggesting perpetual motion, the five-petal motif is actually among the most descriptive and representational of Miao-ti-kou I designs. The elementary unit in the majority of designs is a highly stylized form of a component of a flowering plant—stamen, bud, petal, leaf, stem or vine. By arranging some or all of these stylized components helically, the patterns become highly schematized and evoke a feeling of endless rhythmic flow from one unit of design to another. While Halafian decorations achieve balance, harmony, and static beauty, the Miao-ti-kou I spiral floral patterns convey a sense of dynamism rarely if ever seen in prehistoric Near Eastern pottery. Some representative spiral floral patterns are shown in Figure 13.

To be sure, not a few Miao-ti-kou I patterns contain wide vertical lines, bands, and panels which, like those on Halafian wares, disrupt the continuity of movement between units of design. Yet even on Miao-ti-kou I wares that have similar bands and panels, the stylized elementary forms seldom look sedate and static. Although the unavailability of Miao-ti-kou I wares in Western museums

---

too; see Max von Oppenheim, *Tell Halaf*, I, *Die prähistorischen Funde* (Berlin, 1943) Plates LI and LXXXI. But the effect of these interlocking designs is definitely static.

FIGURE 13. Miao-ti-kou I spiral floral patterns. From *Miao-ti-kou yü San-li-ch'iao*, Figures 15 and 16 on pp. 27 and 28.

makes it impossible to ascertain whether on a particular vessel the painting was done with a hard stylus or with a soft brush, the strokes, curves, and arcs on some banded and panelled decorations convey a peculiar strength, power, and controlled freedom reminiscent of the later cursive style of Chinese calligraphy (see Figure 14).

FIGURE 14. A Miao-ti-kou I deep bowl. Courtesy of the Palace Museum of Peking.

After thirty years' research on the archaeology of the Shensi area, Su Ping-ch'i made the following generalization:

One of the important characteristics of the Miao-ti-kou I culture is the spiral floral patterns of its painted pottery, from which the Hua 華 people may have derived their ethnic appellation. Owing to the fact that the Hua Mountain area was the earliest headquarters of the Hua people, the mountain may have derived its name from its inhabitants. Since the spiral floral patterns are absolutely unique among [pottery decorations of] all prehistoric cultures, they are undoubtedly of native origins and growth, as are the Hua people and their culture.[32]

Few scholars would generalize on the native origins of a culture or civilization from the motifs of its painted pottery alone; but existing comparative data on prehistoric painted pottery of the Old World certainly lend support to Su's view of the typically Sinitic character of Miao-ti-kou I painted pottery. The fact that from time immemorial the Chinese have called themselves the people of Hua neither proves nor disproves the validity of Su's hypothesis. But Su's conjectural explanation of the use of Hua as an ethnic identi-

[32] Su Ping-ch'i, "Kuan-yü Yang-shao-wen-hua ti jo-kan wen-t'i," p. 81.

fication by the proto-Chinese appears not only intelligent but reasonable.

The validity of the view that Yang-shao painted wares of the Pan-p'o and Miao-ti-kou I types have native origins can be conveniently checked by a look at their geographical dissemination. If painted pottery had been introduced into North China from the Near East, it should have appeared first in Sinkiang and Kansu, the areas traversed by the historic "silk route." Typological, stratigraphical, and radiocarbon data have established beyond doubt that the painted pottery emanated from the Yang-shao nuclear area in various directions. By integrating the bristlecone-pine dendrochronology of Table 1 and some very recent typological studies, it is possible to trace the main stages by which painted pottery disseminated regionally. Barely four centuries after the debut of painted pottery in the Yang-shao nuclear area, painted wares with simple designs appeared in the Ch'ing-lien-kang cultural sphere, notably in the Ta-tun-tzu site (4435 ± 105 B.C.) in P'ei-hsien, northern Kiangsu. Probably shortly before 4000 B.C. the Ch'ing-lien-kang potters were able to produce polychrome wares of superb beauty, such as those unearthed from the Liu-lin site in P'ei-hsien.[33] From northern Kiangsu, painted pottery spread south to the lower Yangtze and north to Shantung. During approximately the same period the Pan-p'o type of painted pottery spread far and wide, to northernmost Honan and southern and western Hopei. Though having distinctive local characteristics, the painted wares of these

---

[33] The descriptions and color plates of the Liu-lin polychrome wares are given in Chiang Tsuan-ch'u, "Kuan-yü Chiang-su ti yüan-shih wen-hua" [On the Primitive Cultures of Kiangsu], *KKHP*, 1959, No. 4. The dating of the Ta-tun-tzu painted wares is based on a recent radiocarbon date given in Table 1, and the dating of the Liu-lin polychrome wares is based on Wu Shan-ching's comparative stratigraphical generalization. According to him, the early phase of the Liu-lin culture was earlier than the Sung-tze culture near Shanghai (3995 ± 105 B.C.) and the late phase of the Liu-lin culture is roughly synchronized with Sung-tse. See Wu's "Lüeh-lun Ch'ing-lien-kang wen-hua" [A Brief Discussion of the Ch'ing-lien-kang Culture], *WW*, 1973, No. 6, pp. 45–61, esp. pp. 55–57.

northerly localities show unmistakable Pan-p'o influence.[34] From the late fourth millennium B.C. onward, the Miao-ti-kou I type of dynamic spiral designs reached the Ma-chia-yao culture in Kansu, which in turn gave rise to various designs that have made the wares of the later Pan-shan, Ma-ch'ang, and Ch'i-chia cultures of the Kansu area famous. Finally, during the first half of the third millennium B.C., the influence of Yang-shao painted wares reached the lower Han River valley in central Yangtze, the best examples of that influence being the polychrome wares of the Ch'ü-chia-ling culture. It is very clear, therefore, that the pattern of geographic spread of painted pottery, exactly like that of field agriculture and animal domestication, was centrifugal.

Having discussed the origins of Chinese painted pottery, we shall, through ceramics, reexamine evidence of cultural contacts between some prehistoric cultures of the Eurasian steppe and certain very late prehistoric and early historic cultures of the crucial Kansu area. To help readers acquire a sound historical perspective on the problem of painted pottery and its implications, I shall briefly review both the early and the later views of J. G. Andersson, the discoverer of Yang-shao-ts'un and other Neolithic sites in China and a life-long student of Chinese painted pottery.

Within two years of his discovery of painted pottery at Yang-shao-ts'un, Andersson, in a report written in 1923 for the Geological Survey of China, expressed his view that Yang-shao painted wares might have been affiliated with those of Anau and Tripolje. Hubert Schmitt, however, who had conducted the excavation at Anau and whom Andersson had consulted, did not share that view. Schmitt believed, with good reason, that those few elementary geometric forms selected by Andersson for comparison were very simple, and that similarities, if any, were "far from convincing."[35]

---

[34] The spread of the Pan-p'o type of painted pottery to as far northeast as Hopei is discussed in "1971-nien An-yang Hou-kang fa-chüeh chien-pao" [A Brief Report on the 1971 Excavation at Hou-kang, An-yang], *KK*, No. 3, pp. 14–25, esp. p. 17.

[35] J. G. Andersson, "An Early Chinese Culture," p. 39.

Shortly after his retirement as Director of the Museum of Far Eastern Antiquities in Stockholm, Andersson, in 1943, drastically revised his early view on the subject by admitting:

> It would take us much too far to enter into a detailed discussion of the relationship of Tripolje and Anau with the Kansu cultures. But one fundamental feature should not be overlooked here.
>
> When I wrote my first paper on these problems I was only on the outskirts of the fields; I knew only the Yang Shao of Honan.
>
> Today, now that we know the rich successions of painted-pottery stages in Kansu, it is easy to perceive how the closest likeness to the West is not to be found in Yang Shao but in Ma Chang.[36]

By 1943 most of what he firmly believed to be incontrovertible evidence of prehistoric intercultural contacts between Kansu and the Eurasian steppe boiled down to a peculiar counterclockwise spiral design common to the pottery groups of Tripolje and the Ma-ch'ang and Hsin-tien 辛店 cultures of Kansu. The Ma-ch'ang culture, which is somewhat later than the Ma-chia-yao culture of Kansu and the Pan-shan phase, is earlier than the Shang period. The Hsin-tien culture, the first Bronze Age culture in Kansu, is now generally synchronized chronologically with the Chou period. The counterclockwise spiral designs of Tripolje and Kansu are shown in Figure 15.

Superficially, the counterclockwise spiral motifs of Tripolje and of Ma-chang and Hsin-tien appear to be sufficiently peculiar to justify a speculation on their possible stylistic affinity. But the important fact is that similar motifs exist in the painted wares of Ma-chia-yao—the earliest Neolithic culture in Kansu, which was definitely earlier than the Ma-chang culture—and of a Lungshanoid culture in coastal Shantung. The painted wares of Ma-chia-yao demonstrate that stylistically the counterclockwise motif was definitely evolved from the zoomorphic bird; the potsherds of Miao-ti-kou I further suggest that some early stages in such a

---

[36] Andersson, "Researches into the Prehistory of the Chinese," *BMFEA*, No. 15 (1943), p. 287.

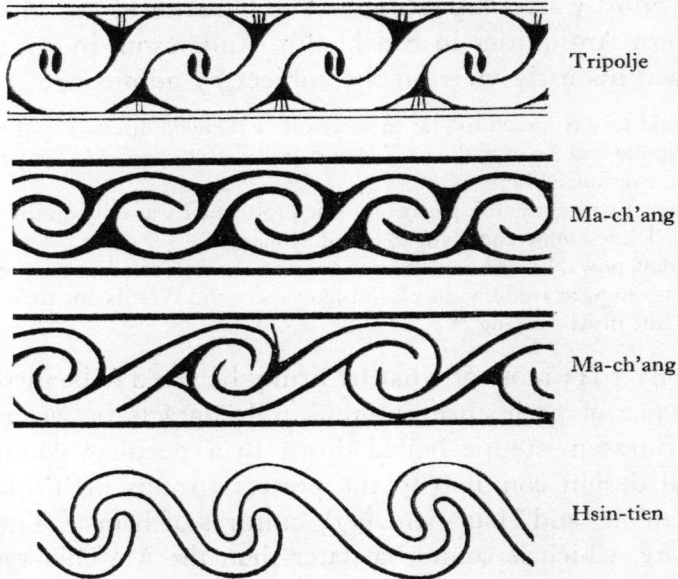

FIGURE 15. Counterclockwise spiral designs of Tripolje and Kansu. From J. G. Andersson, "Researches into the Prehistory of the Chinese," *BMFEA,* No. 15 (1943), Figures 131 and 133 on pp. 288 and 289.

stylistic evolution had already taken place in Yang-shao times. This stylistic evolution and the regional variations of the counterclockwise motif are shown in Figures 14, 15, and 16.

There is no question that the Tripolje culture was much earlier than the late Neolithic cultures of Kansu. Intensive studies of the prehistory of southeast Europe, including a series of carbon-14 dates, indicate that this culture appeared in the Ukraine in the late fifth millennium B.C. and flourished during much of the fourth.[37]

[37] T. Passek, "Relations entre l'Europe Occidentale et l'Europe Orientale à l'époque néolithique," *Atti del VI Congresso Internazionale delle Science Preistoriche e Protostoriche* (Rome, 1962), I, pp. 127–144; Marija Gimbutas, "The Kurgan Culture," *Actes du VIIe Congrès International des Sciences Préhistoriques et Protohistoriques* (Prague, 1966), I, pp. 483–487; and Hans Quitta, "The C14 Chronology of the Central and SE European Neolithic," *Antiquity,* XLI (1967), pp. 263–270.

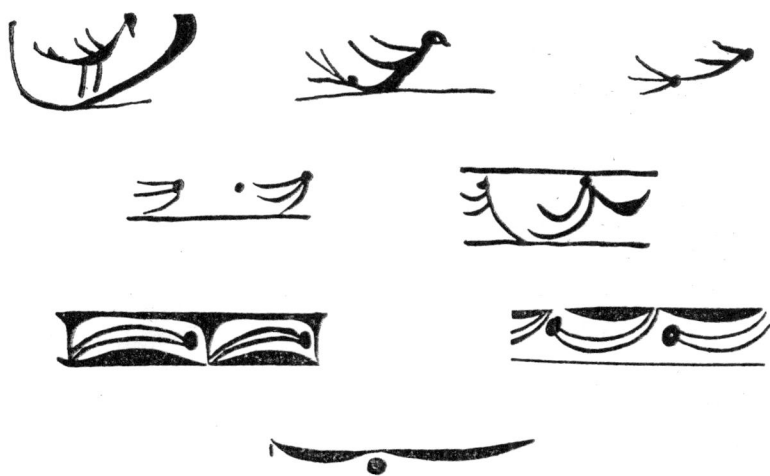

FIGURE 16. Stylistic evolution of the zoomorphic bird of Miao-ti-kou I pottery. From Shih Hsing-pang, "Yu-kuan Ma-chia-yao-wen-hua ti i-hsieh wen-t'i," *KK*, 1962, No. 6, p. 327.

Careful sampling of some available pictures of Tripolje painted pottery jars, sketches of which are given in Figure 19, reveals several points of interest. First, instead of being exclusively counterclockwise as Andersson described, the spirals are both counterclockwise and clockwise. Second, they appear to represent vines, whereas the Chinese spirals are stylistically evolved from the zoomorphic bird of the Miao-ti-kou I wares. Third, the Chinese counterclockwise spirals, whether of the Western Kansu group or of the eastern Jih-chao group, retain the original bird's eye as the focal point for each unit of design, a striking characteristic which is entirely absent from the Tripolje designs. In terms of geometric contexts, therefore, the Tripolje and the Chinese spirals are quite different.

It is further to be noted that if the Tripolje spirals did reach Kansu, they should have left at least some vestige in Soviet Central Asia and in western Siberia. Spreading far and wide in these areas during the second millennium B.C. was the Andronovo culture.

FIGURE 17. Stylistic evolution from the zoomorphic bird to the counterclockwise spiral in Ma-chia-yao pottery. From Shi-Hsing-pang, "Yu-kuan Ma-chia-yao-wen-hua ti i-hsieh wen-t'i," p. 321.

POTTERY 173

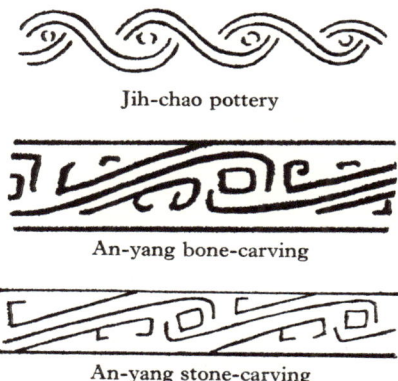

FIGURE 18. The Jih-chao 日照 Lungshanoid counterclockwise spiral and its influence on Shang decorative art. Upper: Jih-chao pottery. Middle: An-yang bone carving. Lower: An-yang stone carving. From Li Chi, "Diverse Backgrounds of the Decorative Art of the Yin Dynasty," *Proceedings of the Fourth Far-Eastern Prehistory and Anthropology Division of the Eighth Pacific Science Congress Combined.* (Quezon City, 1956), Figure 3 on p. 190.

FIGURE 19. Painted Tripolje pottery. A sketch based on the photograph in Alexander Mongait, *Archaeology in the U.S.S.R.* (Moscow, 1959), p. 111.

174 THE CRADLE OF THE EAST

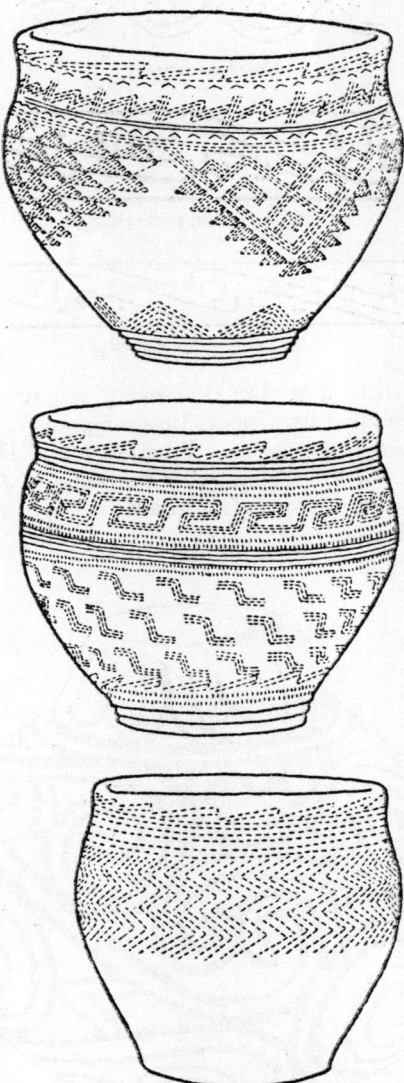

FIGURE 20. Typical Andronovo decorated jars. From A. Mongait, *Archaeology in the U.S.S.R.*, p. 145.

A sampling of the designs of a comprehensive collection of Andronovo decorated pottery in the Hermitage Museum of Leningrad shows no sign of the dominant Tripolje motif. Besides, the various Andronovo designs consist exclusively of incised dots and lines arranged in rather simple and mechanical patterns which bear no resemblance to those of prehistoric Chinese painted pottery.[38]

Andersson expressed his final view on the subject of prehistoric Chinese painted pottery in 1943, when with unusual intellectual candor, he conceded the probability of the "autochthonous" origins of Chinese painted pottery. He also severely criticized some European exponents—specifically Ludwig Bachhofer—of the theory that Chinese culture had "Western" origins: "It is not only unfounded but rather disgraceful when we Europeans, working under a superiority bias that lacks proportion and perspective, speak of 'Herrenvölker' who brought a superior culture to China."[39] Had the recent series of carbon-14 dates of Jomon cord-marked pottery and the rich post-1949 ceramic finds of Pan-p'o and Miao-ti-kou I been known to Andersson, he would have had no hesitation in affirming the indigenous origins of Chinese pottery in general and of Yang-shao painted pottery in particular.

[38] M. N. Komarova, "Otnositelnaya Khronologiya Pamyatnikov Andronovskoi Kultury" [Relative Chronology of Monuments of the Andronovo Culture], *Arkheologicheskiy Sbornik Ermitazha* [Hermitage Archaeological Compendium], 1962, No. 5, esp. map and figures on pp. 52–59.

[39] Andersson, "Researches into the Prehistory of the Chinese," p. 291. It should be noted that in 1943 Andersson still believed in a possible cultural linkage between certain late prehistoric ceramic designs of Kansu and those of Anau. The designs he selected for comparison consist of geometric forms too simple and common to be accepted as valid evidence of transmission from Anau. I have studied the figures and plates of Anau potsherds given fairly exhaustively in Raphael Pumpelly, ed., *Explorations in Turkestan: Prehistoric Civilizations of Anau* (Washington, D.C., 1908), 2 Vols., and have found little that is worth comparing with Kansu ceramic designs given in Nils Palmgren, *Kansu Mortuary Urns of the Pan Shan and Ma Chang Group* (Palaeontologia Sinica, Series D, Vol. III, Fascicle 1, Peiping, 1934).

V
Bronze Metallurgy

PRIOR TO 1949 the earliest attested Chinese bronze articles came from An-yang, which, from 1300 to 1027 B.C., served as the last Shang capital city. Owing chiefly to the lateness of Chinese bronze and partly to the stylistic affinity of a very few types of weapons and tools between An-yang and certain ancient cultures of the northern Eurasian steppe, some Western scholars have postulated that bronze metallurgy was introduced into China from outside. One such Western writer is the art historian Max Loehr, who wrote in 1949:

<blockquote>
Anyang represents, according to our present knowledge, the oldest Chinese metal age site, taking us back to ca. 1300 B.C. It displays no signs of a primitive stage of metal-working but utter refinement. Primitive stages have, in fact, nowhere been discovered in China up to the present moment. Metallurgy seems to have been brought to China from outside. Whence, is an open question; but whatever the sources were, the way led via Siberia, and possibly Eastern Turkestan, so that the northwestern and northern regions of present-day China were in a favored position.[1]
</blockquote>

During the past two decades bronze artifacts and foundry sites have been discovered at Erh-li-t'ou 二里頭 in Yen-shih 偃師 and at Erh-li-kang 二里崗 in Cheng-chou 鄭州, both in the central plain of Honan, which are definitely earlier than those of An-yang and which throw important new light on a more primitive stage of Chinese bronze metallurgy. Yet among Western scholars interested in China but not necessarily familiar with the massive post-1949

---

[1] Max Loehr, "Weapons and Tools from Anyang, and Siberian Analogies," *American Journal of Archaeology*, LIII (1949), pp. 126–144, quotation from p. 129; also his *Chinese Bronze Age Weapons* (Ann Arbor, 1956), esp. pp. 103–105.

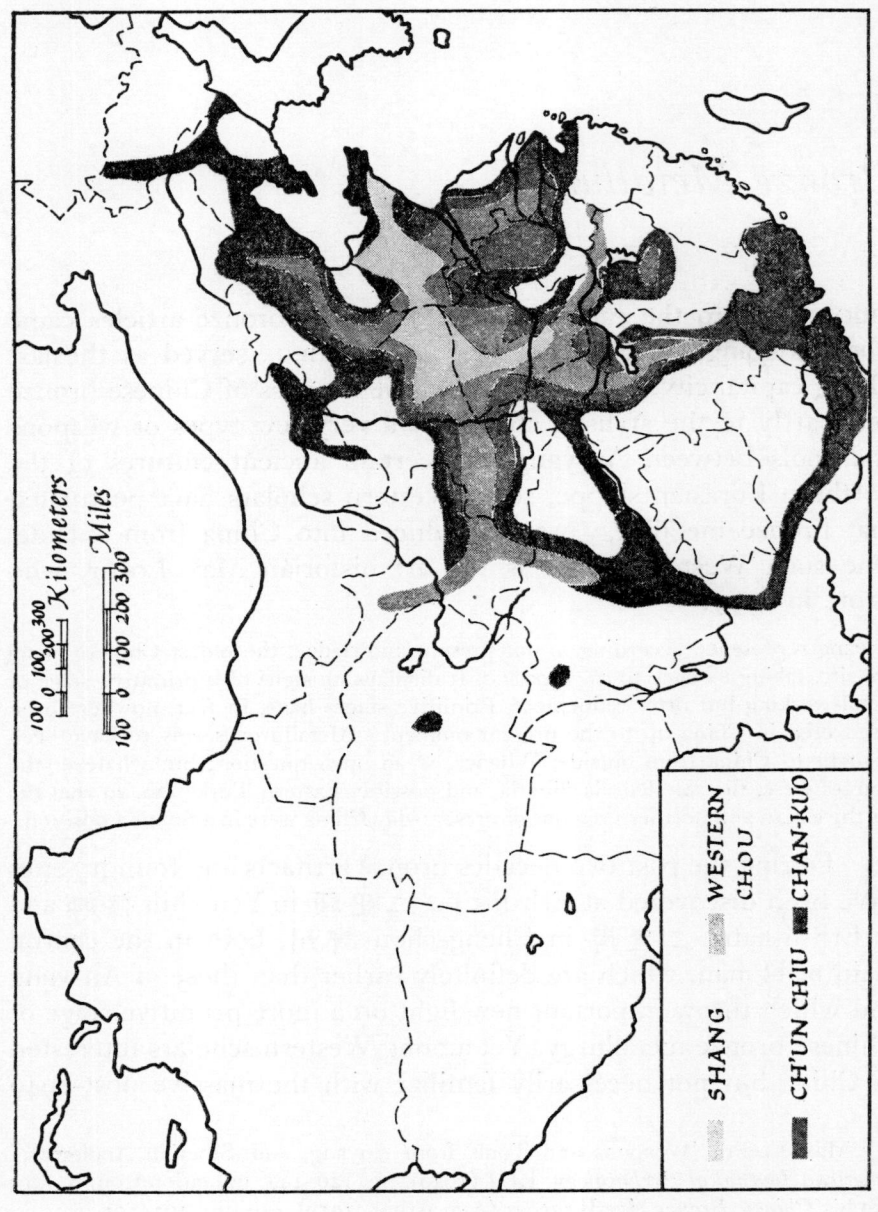

MAP 2. The spread of bronze in China, circa 1500-221 B.C.

mainland Chinese archaeological data, the diffusionist view dies hard. The simplest reason is that chronologically the datable beginnings of the bronze age in China can only be raised from 1300 B.C. to about 1600 B.C.

Methodologically, the fundamental weakness of the diffusionist school—whether in connection with the origins of Chinese bronze metallurgy or with broader problems of the origins of cultures and civilizations—is its unwillingness to examine the aggregate evidence. To make our discussion of the origins and early history of bronze metallurgy in China meaningful, we shall have to examine six correlated problems: (1) whether indeed there was no prior stage of primitive metallurgy before the "sudden" emergence of a mature and technologically unique bronze metallurgy in Shang times; (2) whether copper and tin deposits were available in quantities within or close to the localities where bronze metallurgy made its early appearance; (3) the extent to which Chinese bronze metallurgy developed from certain related aspects of Chinese Neolithic technology; (4) whether early Chinese bronze metallurgy reveals major technological characteristics similar to or different from those of the ancient Near Eastern metallurgy; (5) whether in ancient China the pattern of geographical spread of metallurgy was centripetal or centrifugal; and (6) whether the stylistic affinity of a very few types of bronze weapons and tools between An-yang and the Eurasian steppe warrants an overall conclusion that bronze metallurgy was introduced into Shang China from the ancient West.

1. Recent archaeological data indicate that a primitive stage of metalworking did exist within the area of present-day China proper, even though it occurred outside the territory occupied by the Shang people during predynastic and dynastic periods. In the late 1950s, simple copper articles were found at three Ch'i-chia cultural sites in Kansu, namely, Ta-ho-chuang and Ch'in-wei-chia 秦魏家 in Yung-Ching county and Huang-niang-niang-t'ai 皇娘娘台 in Wu-wei 武威 county. From the more detailed report on

the Huang-niang-niang-t'ai site we learn the following vital facts. First, copper objects were unearthed from the lowest cultural stratum, below which is the thick loess of primary deposition. Second, these objects consist of small knives and bars, which were cast in single molds, and of small drills, chisels, and rings, which were hammered. Third, the site yields ore slags and many funerary gifts made of green stones and semiprecious green stones. Last, chemical analyses of certain specimens by the laboratory of the Kansu Provincial Bureau of Metallurgy show that they contain more than 99 percent copper, some with traces of tin, lead, antimony, and nickel and some with traces of tin and lead only.[2]

Equally interesting, a contemporary geological survey has found that copper deposits exist in at least three localities near the three Ch'i-chia cultural sites where the copper objects were discovered.[3] The aggregate evidence from the Kansu area indicates that copper objects were made with copper smelted from local ores.

---

[2] "Kan-su Wu-wei Huang-niang-niang-t'ai i-chih fa-chüeh pao-kao" [Report on the Excavations at Huang-niang-niang-t'ai, Wu-wei, Kansu], *KKHP*, 1960, No. 2, pp. 53–72; "Lin-hsia Ta-ho-chuang Ch'in-wei-chia Ch'i-chia-wen-hua i-chih fa-chüeh pao-kao" [Report on the Excavations at the Two Ch'i-chia Cultural Sites of Ta-ho-chuang and Ch'in-wei-chia, Lin-hsia, Kansu], *KK*, 1960, No. 3, pp. 9–12. It should be mentioned that at the Ta-ch'eng-shan site in T'ang-shan, coastal Hopei, copper objects have been unearthed from a Lung-shan cultural stratum. See "Ho-pei T'ang-shan-shih Ta-ch'eng-shan i-chih fa-chüeh pao-kao" [Report on the Excavations at the Ta-ch'eng-shan Site, T'ang-shan, Hopei], *KKHP*, 1959, No. 3, pp. 17–36. Some Chinese archaeologists are, however, of the opinion that the copper objects from the Lung-shan cultural stratum might have been later intrusions. See K'ang Chieh, "Kuan-yü T'ang-shan Ta-ch'eng-shan i-chih wen-hua hsing-chih ti t'ao-lun" [An Inquiry into the Nature of the Culture Discovered at Ta-ch'eng-shan, T'ang-shan], *KK*, 1960, No. 6, pp. 21–23; also *Hsin-Chung-kuo ti k'ao-ku shou-huo*, p. 19. For a preliminary discussion of the Kansu stage of copper metallurgy, see Chang Tzu-kao, *Chung-kuo hua-hsüeh-shih kao* [A Draft History of Chemistry in China] (Peking, 1964), pp. 9–10; and also comments by Tseng Chao-yü and Yin-tai in *Chiang-su-sheng ch'u-t'u wen-wu hsüan-chi* [Selected Artifacts Unearthed from Kiangsu] (Peking, 1963), p. 24.

[3] Shih Chang-ju, "Yin-tai ti chu-t'ung kung-i" [The Art of Bronze Casting in Shang Times], *BIHP*, XXVI (1955), pp. 98–99.

The combined facts indicate an initial exploratory stage of copper metallurgy which technologically conforms, by and large, to early metallurgy elsewhere.

Generally speaking, there were two prerequisites for making a beginning in copper metallurgy. The first was the existence of pottery kilns which could reach a temperature range sufficiently high to smelt copper ores. Such kilns existed in many parts of the prehistoric world, including the homeland of the Ch'i-chia culture. The second prerequisite was the early potter's search for and curiosity about some unusually heavy blue or green stones which he used intentionally for decorating ceramics but from which he obtained metallic copper accidentally. For native copper was never of wide geographic distribution, and the common and easily smelted oxide and carbonate ores of copper are blue or green. In many parts of Kansu, including the Wu-wei area where more systematic evidence of copper metallurgy has been found, the most common raw material for the local prehistoric lithic industry was green stones.[4]

Of the three Kansu localities where copper objects have been found, only the Tao-ho-chuang site has been carbon-14 dated. Two laboratory tests yield the dates of 1725 ± 95 B.C. and 1695 ± 95 B.C., which can be revised upward to about 2000 B.C. in bristlecone-pine dating.[5] Since our existing knowledge indicates that the bronze age in China dawned with the inception of the Shang dynasty around 1600 B.C., these Ch'i-chia copper objects are likely to have been made a few centuries earlier than the beginning of the bronze age.

So far no stratigraphical sequence has been established between

---

[4] Shih T'ao, "Huang-ho-shang-yu ti fu-hsi-shih-tsu-she-hui—Ch'i-chia-wen-hua she-hui ching-chi hsing-t'ai ti t'an-t'ao" [The Patrilineal Society of Upper Yellow River—An Inquiry into the Social and Economic Characteristics of the Ch'i-chia Culture], *KK*, 1961, No. 1, pp. 3–11.

[5] Chung-kuo-k'e-hsüeh-yüan k'ao-ku-yen-chiu-so shih-yen-shih [The Institute of Archaeology, Academia Sinica], "Fang-she-hsing-t'an-su ts'e-ting nien-tai pao-kao (I)," *KK*, 1972, No. 1, pp. 52–56.

the Ch'i-chia culture and the Shang culture, and in some localities in eastern Kansu the Ch'i-chia stratum is usually overlain by the Chou cultural stratum. This fact would indicate the probable lack of direct contact between the Ch'i-chia people and the late predynastic Shang people. There is reason, however, to speculate that the first knowledge of metal, if indeed first obtained by the Ch'i-chia people, might have been transmitted to the late predynastic Shang people through the intermediary of the K'e-shen-chuang II culture in the Wei River basin in central Shensi. Close affinity between the Ch'i-chia culture and the K'e-sheng-chung II culture has been established through several types of pottery, the use of animal scapulae for divination, and the existence of clay and stone phallic symbols.[6] There is also ample evidence of intimate contact between the K'e-sheng-chuang II and the Honan Lung-shan culture, which is generally believed to have been one of the precursors of the Shang culture. In fact, archaeologists who excavated at the K'e-sheng-chung II sites did not rule out the distinct possibility that someday evidence of early metallurgy might be found in the Wei River basin.[7] What for the time being makes the Ch'i-chia copper finds theoretically significant is that they show that the basic prerequisites for inventing metallurgy existed in late Neolithic Kansu.

In this introductory section we need only to point out the existence of a prior stage of primitive metallurgy in Kansu. The ultimate question whether knowledge of metal came to the headquarters of the Shang people from the loess highlands or from the ancient West cannot be answered until all the relevant aspects of Shang bronze metallurgy, including the net significance of the stylistic affinity between a few types of An-yang bronzes and those of the Eurasian steppe, have been discussed. For this reason, we shall resume our discussion of the likely ultimate source of information on metal in the concluding section of this chapter.

[6] *Feng-hsi fa-chüeh pao-kao*, pp. 6–9.
[7] *Ibid.*, p. 9.

2. Crucial to the origins of bronze metallurgy in China is the geographic distribution of copper and tin deposits in North China in historic times. Ancient Chinese works as a rule did not give a systematic listing of such deposits, and what modern scholars have been able to trace has been based primarily on general geographic treatises imperially compiled during Ming and Ch'ing times. But since many ancient copper and tin deposits of North China must have been depleted long ago, and their traces progressively obliterated, the fact that Ming-Ch'ing geographic works still testify to the existence of such mines in many localities would indicate a considerably more extensive distribution in pre-Shang and Shang times. The locations of all known historic and existing copper and tin deposits in China were listed by a research fellow of the Institute of History and Philology of Academia Sinica.[8] In view of the state of transportation in Shang times, deposits too remote from Shang metallurgical centers in Honan would not seem to have had any direct bearing on the origins of metallurgy in China. What is most revealing is that many historically recorded copper and tin deposits are located within a radius of 300 kilometers of the three known Shang metallurgical centers of Yen-shih, Cheng-chou, and An-yang.

One vital fact clearly emerges from Tables 7 and 8. The western and eastern foothills of the T'ai-hang 太行 Mountain, which serves as a demarcation between the loess highlands and the low plains, were undoubtedly an area which in historic times abounded in both copper and tin. This area embraces southeastern Shansi to the west, north-central Honan to the south, and northernmost Honan and the southern Hopei panhandle to the east. Another area of extensive distribution of copper and tin deposits is the foothill country of the Chung-t'iao 中條 Mountain, which embraces south-central and southwestern Shansi. Although many of these recorded deposits

---

[8] Shih Chang-ju, "Yin-tai ti chu-t'ung kung-i," tables and text on pp. 96–104 and Map I between pp. 104 and 105. For an English version of this map, see Noel Barnard, *Bronze Casting and Bronze Alloys in Ancient China* (Australian National University, 1961), Map IV, between pp. 50 and 51.

Table 7
Copper Deposits Near Early Metallurgical Centers

Place		Province	Distance from Yen-shih (in km.)	Distance from Cheng-chou (in km.)	Distance from An-yang (in km.)
Teng-feng	登封	Honan	30	76	218
Chi-yüan	濟源	Honan	55	116	195
Yü-hsien	禹縣	Honan	72	72	270
Yang-ch'eng	陽城	Shansi	72	140	180
Lu-shan	魯山	Honan	115	137	291
Yüan-ch'ü	垣曲	Shansi	120	180	260
Chiang-hsien	絳縣	Shansi	146	220	260
I-ch'eng	翼城	Shansi	148	212	265
Ch'ang-chih	長治	Shansi	155	161	100
Hsia-hsien	夏縣	Shansi	161	242	300
P'ing-lu	平陸	Shansi	167	252	(337)
Wen-hsi	聞喜	Shansi	167	258	300
Ch'ü-wo*	曲沃	Shansi	167	222	260
Yün-ch'eng*	運城	Shansi	182	264	(333)
Hsieh-hsien	解縣	Shansi	194	280	(355)
Li-ch'eng	黎城	Shansi	200	185	80
An-yang	安陽	Honan	207	158	—
She-hsien	涉縣	Honan	220	218	80
Sha-ho	沙河	Hopei	290	255	100
Hsing-t'ai	邢台	Hopei	300	273	115
Nei-ch'iu	內邱	Hopei	(323)	294	130
T'ai-yüan	太原	Shansi	(342)	(345)	252
Chi-nan	濟南	Shantung	(446)	(379)	252

Source: Shih Chang-ju, "Yin-tai ti chu-t'ung kung-i," *BIHP*, XXVI (1955), tables and discussions, pp. 96–104. Distances of more than 300 km. are enclosed in parentheses. My conversions of li to kilometers are approximate.

* My addition, based on *KK*, 1962, No. 10, pp. 519–522.

TABLE 8

TIN DEPOSITS NEAR EARLY METALLURGICAL CENTERS

Place		Province	Distance from Yen-shih (in km.)	Distance from Cheng-chou (in km.)	Distance from An-yang (in km.)
Lin-jui	臨汝	Honan	60	102	258
Yang-ch'eng	陽城	Shansi	72	140	180
Sung-hsien	嵩縣	Honan	100	170	300
Ch'in-shui	沁水	Shansi	125	180	190
Ch'i-hsien	淇縣	Honan	160	140	55
Ch'in-yüan	沁源	Shansi	210	242	190
Ch'eng-an	成安	Hopei	255	210	50
Wu-an	武安	Honan	260	228	73
Kuang-p'ing	廣平	Hopei	275	223	85
Chiao-ch'eng	交城	Shansi	(320)	(342)	260
Lai-fu	萊蕪	Shantung	(476)	(430)	300

SOURCE: Shih Chang-ju, "Yin-tai ti chu-t'ung kung-i." Distances of more than 300 km. are enclosed in parentheses.

must have been largely depleted throughout historical times and, in later periods, overshadowed by those of Yunnan and other southern provinces, it should be noted that Ch'ing officials still testified to the lingering economic significance of some of the deposits.[9] Even from the necessarily incomplete information of the distribution of copper and tin ores of the late imperial age, twenty-three copper and eleven tin deposits are known to have existed within a radius of 300 kilometers of at least one of the three Shang metallurgical centers—indicating that North China in ancient times

[9] Cited in Jung Keng and Chang Wei-ch'ih, *Yin-Chou ch'ing-t'ung-ch'i t'ung-lun* [A General Treatise on Shang and Chou Bronze Artifacts] (Peking, 1958), pp. 121–122.

was much more richly endowed with minerals than Mesopotamia, which had to import ores.

For further analysis, we shall divide the mineral-bearing region into three areas by using the T'ai-hang Mountain and the Yellow River as demarcation "lines." South of the Yellow River in Honan there are three recorded copper and two tin deposits, an area which is accessible to Yen-shih and Cheng-chou but relatively remote from An-yang. This area must be regarded as of secondary importance especially since the Shang capital was moved northward to An-yang in 1300 B.C. The two main mineral-bearing areas are, therefore, north of the Yellow River and east and west of the T'ai-hang Mountain. Although the area east of T'ai-hang is reasonably rich in tin deposits which are close to An-yang, the bulk of the copper ores is located west of this mountain. Excluding the three copper deposits in Honan south of the Yellow River, only six such deposits are recorded east of T'ai-hang as compared to fourteen west of it. The availability of tin and the high concentration of copper in the entire southern Shansi area would suggest that it might have been the most important supplier of metals in Shang times.

The ore-rich southern Shansi area lies immediately north of the favorite hunting grounds of the late Shang kings. Southern Shansi is accessible from the favorite royal hunting grounds in the southern T'ai-hang foothills through several small rivers. Oracle texts yield clear records that post-1300 B.C. Shang kings well understood the importance of southern Shansi. Wu-ting 武丁, the fourth king after the moving of the capital to An-yang, whose long reign probably covered much of the latter half of the thirteenth and the early years of the twelfth century B.C., took energetic military action to ensure the control of southern and central Shansi. Although south and central Shansi was invaded by some alien tribes long after Wu-ting's death, from the time of his grandson, King Ling-hsin 廩辛, onward the Shang kingdom regained control of this mineral-rich area. Ti-i 帝乙, the next to the last Shang king, led a long military expedition through the entire southern and central

Shansi area and reached as far as the Wei River valley in Shensi.[10] Although nowhere in the oracle texts is an exact reason given for attaching so much importance to the southern Shansi area, a highly probable one was the necessity of safeguarding the large and constant supply of metals, especially of copper.

Further, in view of the unearthing in recent years of significant quantities of Shang bronze vessels at many sites in at least seven counties in southern and central Shansi (which few scholars expected to find),[11] it seems even more likely that Shang metallurgy relied heavily on this area for metals. It is in west-central Honan at the Erh-li-t'ou site in Yen-shih, which is much closer to southern Shansi than are Cheng-chou and An-yang, that by far the earliest remains of a bronze foundry have been discovered. Since metallic copper and tin are likely to have been discovered near the mines rather than at foundry sites, and since Chou works explicitly point to the southern Shansi area as the headquarters of the Hsia people, one cannot rule out the possibility that the Erh-li-t'ou bronze may have fallen chronologically into the Hsia period, even though most scholars still regard this site as the capital city of the founder of the Shang dynasty, Tai-i 大乙 or T'ang 唐、湯.

For all the prevalence of copper and tin deposits within a radius of 300 kilometers of Shang metallurgical centers, one cannot dismiss the possibility that some mineral might also have been procured from more southerly regions, such as the central Yangtze and the Huai River areas. Oracle texts testify to King Wu-ting's military campaigns toward the lower Han River valley in Hupei and to

---

[10] For the painstaking identifications of place names, the reconstruction of the routes of Shang military campaigns and of royal hunting excursions, see Li Hsüeh-ch'in, *Yin-tai ti-li chien-lun* [A Brief Study of Late-Shang Geography] (Peking, 1959), esp. summary on p. 96; and also Kuo Mo-jo, *Pu-tz'u t'ung-tsuan k'ao-shih* [Textual and Historical Annotations on Selections from Oracle Texts] (Tokyo, 1933), *ts'e* 3 and 4, "Military Campaigns" and "Travels and Hunting Excursions."

[11] "Shan-hsi shih-nien-lai k'ao-ku yü wen-wu kung-tso ti kai-k'uang" [Ten Years' Archaeological Work in Shansi Province], *KK*, 1959, No. 2, pp. 62–64.

repeated late-Shang wars against the Eastern I 東夷 people of Shantung, northern Kiangsu and Anhwei.[12] The unearthing of Shang bronze vessels in Hupei, Anhwei, and Kiangsu,[13] and the discovery at An-yang of quantities of cowrie shells and shells of large tortoises which must have been imported from southerly regions, suggest that the central Yangtze and Huai River regions might have had trading and tributary relations with the kingdom of Shang. Not until Chou times, however, did bronze inscriptions and *The Book of Odes* both explicitly testify that wars against the Ching 荊 "barbarians" (the proto-Ch'u people) of central Yangtze and the I 夷 people of the Huai River area were motivated in part by the desire of the Chou court and some northern feudal states to procure copper and tin. Ode 299 of *The Book of Odes* describes the war booty of Lord Hsi 僖 of the Lu state (reigned 659–627 B.C.):

Far away are the I people of Huai,
They come to present their treasures:
Big tortoises, elephant tusks,
And great contributions of the southern metals.[14]

Vestiges of mines that can be attributed to Shang times have not yet been found because in most cases subsequent mining would have obliterated traces of tools and implements used by Shang miners. Early-Chou works likewise are silent about mining methods. So far the earliest copper mine that can be precisely dated is the one at Tung-kou 洞溝 in Yün-ch'eng 運城 county in southern Shansi,

---

[12] Li Hsüeh-ch'in, *Yin-tai ti-li chien-lun*, pp. 96 and 99; Kuo Mo-jo, *Pu-tz'u t'ung-tsuan k'ao-shih*, ts'e 3, p. 123b.

[13] *Chiang-su-sheng ch'u-t'u wen-wu hsüan-chi*, pp. 23–24.

[14] Kuo Mo-jo, *Liang-Chou chin-wen-tz'u ta-hsi t'u-lu k'ao-shih* [A Comprehensive Selection of Chou Bronze Inscriptions, with Plates, Illustrations, Textual and Historical Annotations] (Peking, 1958), ts'e 6, pp. 54a–54b; ts'e 8, pp. 186a–186b. My translation of this ode is adapted from those of James Legge and Bernhard Karlgren. See James Legge, tr., *The Chinese Classics,* IV, *The She King* (Hongkong, 1862, Taipei reprint), p. 620 and Karlgren, tr., *The Book of Odes* (Stockholm, 1950), pp. 256–257.

and that dating was made possible only because of unusual inscriptions on the rocky walls of the mine pits. The inscriptions bear the dates of A.D. 179, A.D. 184, and the reign period of Kan-lu, A.D. 256–259. There are altogether seven pits, and the ores consist mostly of cuprite (Cu_2O) mixed with a small amount of malachite ($CuCO_3 \cdot CuO \cdot H_2O$). Three aspects of mining at this ancient site are revealing. First, in pit 2 there are quantities of burned charcoal and gangue and unmistakable signs of "fire-setting"—heating up the rocks and then pouring on cold water to cause ore-vein fission. Second, on a piece of level land about 800 meters from the pits there are remains of a receptacle made of burned clay, 2.8 meters wide, 1.5 meters high, and 0.12 meter thick. Heaps of burned charcoal and slugs found nearby indicate that this receptacle was a furnace. Third, the uncovering of a corroded copper ingot measuring 32 cm. in length and between 4 and 5.6 cm. in width, weighing 3.75 kilograms, confirms the smelting of ores near the mine before the metal was shipped to the foundry.[15] There is reason, as will be explained presently, to believe that this mining method and the practice of reducing ores near the mine were essentially the same during Shang times.

In a pioneering study of the technology of Shang bronze metallurgy during the An-yang phase, the late Liu Yü-hsia was of the opinion that the copper ores used were oxides and carbonates rather than sulfides. His tentative conclusion was based on the following: the discovery of a chunk of malachite weighing 18.8 kilograms at the foundry site; the absence of any matte and blister copper, which would have represented the intermediate stages of the complex processes of smelting copper sulfides; and the absence

---

[15] An Chih-min and Ch'en Ts'un-hsi, "Shan-hsi Yün-ch'eng Tung-kou ti Tung-Han t'ung-k'uang ho t'i-chi" [Remains of the Eastern Han Copper Mine and Related Inscriptions at Tung-kou, Yün-ch'eng, Shansi], *KK*, 1962, No. 10, pp. 519–522.

of sulphur in the chemical analysis of Shang bronzes.[16] The fact that only tin ingots were found at the An-yang foundry site led Liu to conclude that metallic tin must have been extracted from cassiterite (tin oxide) near the mines before it was shipped to An-yang for bronze casting. The presence of a chunk of malachite and the absence of copper ingots, however, led him to believe that the copper ore was probably smelted at the foundry—an impression which needs revision in the light of subsequent archaeological finds. For one thing, the amounts of copper ore and slugs uncovered from the foundry sites at Yen-shih, Cheng-chou, and An-yang are negligible.[17] For another, since there was obviously large-scale bronze-casting at Cheng-chou and An-yang, large ore-heaps would certainly have been uncovered if copper ore had been smelted at the foundry. Moreover, the copper mine of the Eastern Han period at Tung-kou in southern Shansi proves beyond doubt that the ore was refined near the mine. Nor is Tung-kou the only such known case. At the Eastern Chou foundry site in Hou-ma county in southern Shansi there are virtually no ore-heaps but many copper ingots, which show some slugs of unsmelted malachite at bottom.[18] The combined evidence seems to uphold Noel Barnard's conclusion that "the Shang founders worked mainly from imported metal already processed."[19]

---

[16] Liu Yü-hsia, "Yin-tai yeh-t'ung-shu chih yen-chiu" [A Study of the Technology of Bronze Casting in Shang Times], *An-yang fa-chüeh pao-kao* [Reports on the Excavations at An-yang] (Academia Sinica), No. 4 (June 1933), pp. 681–696.

[17] For Yen-shih, see Fang Yu-sheng, "Ho-nan Yen-shih Erh-li-tou i-chih fa-chüeh chien-pao" [Report on the Excavations at Erh-li-t'ou, Yen-shih, Honan], *KK*, 1965, No. 5, pp. 215–224; for Cheng-chou, see Hsia Nai, "Workshops at the Dawn of History," *China Reconstructs*, IV, No. 12 (December 1957), pp. 18–21; for Hui-hsien, see *Hui-hsien fa-chüeh pao-kao* (Peking, 1956), pp. 23–27.

[18] "Hou-ma Niu-ts'un ku-ch'eng-nan Tung-Chou i-chih fa-chüeh chien-pao" [Report on the Excavations of an Eastern Chou Site near Niu-ts'un, Hou-ma, Shansi], *KK*, 1962, No. 2, pp. 55–62.

[19] Barnard, *Bronze Casting and Bronze Alloys in Ancient China*, p. 49.

Historians of metallurgy generally agree that, in the ancient Near East, bronze may have been first obtained by smelting a mixture of copper and tin ores.[20] R. J. Forbes is of the opinion that the method of obtaining bronze from smelting two kinds of ore persisted until 1500 B.C., when metallic tin began to appear in the Near East.[21] There is, however, philological and archaeological evidence that metallic tin had been known to Near Eastern founders long before 1500 B.C. and that tin metal had become an important article in interregional and even intercontinental trade in the Near East well before 2000 B.C.[22] The existing evidence would indicate that the use of metallic copper and tin to form bronze began fairly early in culturally advanced Mesopotamia, an area which seems to have depended entirely on the outside for its supply of metals and ores (though the situation in the ore-bearing mountainous areas of the Near East still remains to be studied). Concerning the preliminary step in bronze casting, therefore, the difference between the ancient Near East and Shang China is one of degree, not of kind. All that a student of history can say is that the Shang foundrymen seem to have used metallic copper and tin to form bronze more regularly from the beginning.

[20] H. H. Coghlan, *Notes on the Prehistoric Metallurgy of Copper and Bronze in the Old World* (Occasional Paper on Technology, No. 4, Pitt Rivers Museum, Oxford University, 1951).

[21] R. J. Forbes, *Metallurgy in Antiquity: A Notebook for Archaeologists and Technologists* (Leiden, 1950), pp. 248–252.

[22] The Sumerian words *an.an* and *urudu* and the Akkadian words *annaku* and *eru* mean tin and copper in a metallic state rather than in ore state. See *Chicago Assyrian Dictionary*, 10 volumes not yet completed, edited by Leo Oppenheim (Chicago, 1956—). See also Benno Landsberger, "Tin and Lead: The Adventure of Two Vocables," *Journal of Near Eastern Studies*, XXIV (1965), pp. 285–296. For archaeological evidence of metallic tin and the existence of trade in tin metal in the latter half of the second millennium B.C., see Coghlan, *Notes on the Prehistoric Metallurgy of Copper and Bronze in the Old World*, pp. 24–25. For the trade in metallic tin and copper between Iran, Assur, and Turkey in the nineteenth century B.C., see Mogens T. Larsen, *Old Assyrian Caravan Procedures* (Istanbul, 1967), pp. 173–178.

To complete this section, we should touch on the fuel problem. As had been discussed in chapter 1 and in much greater detail in my recent book in Chinese,[23] the level area of the loess highlands and the North China low plains are not likely to have been forested. But places near water courses and especially hills and mountains were wooded. Neither Yen-shih, Cheng-chou, nor An-yang was far from hills, although no sizable woodland can be expected to have existed in the immediate vicinity of these Shang cities. Since the copper and tin deposits are mostly located in foothills, the supply of wood and charcoal constituted no problem. It stands to reason that the Shang people would have preferred the reduction of ores near the mines where plenty of wood was close at hand. North China is also very rich in coal and the Chinese were the first people in world history to use coal as a fuel. But while coal was definitely known to the Chinese of late-Chou times, the earliest attested archaeological evidence of the use of coal for industrial purposes belongs to the Han period.[24] Charcoal was therefore the fuel used in Shang times. The relative abundance and accessibility of both fuel and metal ores is one of the many carefully assessed factors that have led Noel Barnard, a leading expert on early Chinese metallurgy, to believe in the native origins of metallurgy in China.[25]

3. The third important problem concerning the origins of bronze metallurgy in China is its derivation and evolution from the native Neolithic ceramic industry. The intimate connection between early metallurgy and pottery kilns has long been observed by historians of metallurgy. "Only a civilization," says Forbes, "that made well-baked pottery requiring a high baking temperature would possess the technical equipment that made the reduction of ores

---

[23] Ho Ping-ti, *Huang-t'u yü Chung-kuo nung-yeh ti ch'i-yüan*, pp. 35–85.
[24] *Hsin-Chung-kuo ti k'ao-ku shou-huo*, p. 78.
[25] Barnard, *Bronze Casting and Bronze Alloys in Ancient China*, p. 49.

possible."²⁶ Fortunately, the remains of prehistoric Chinese pottery kilns are sufficient to make a study of kiln types possible.

Even during the Yang-shao period there appear to have been many kiln types, varying in size and efficiency. At the Pan-p'o site near Sian, remains of six pottery kilns have been unearthed which can be classified into four types. The best preserved is a kiln of the late Pan-p'o phase shown in Figure 21(a). It comprises a fire chamber, flue holes, and an oven. The fire chamber measures a little more than 2 meters in length, 0.8 meter in height, and from 0.7 to 1 meter in width. The three main flue holes, each about 10 cm. in width, together with many smaller fire holes, permit an even distribution of heat in the baking oven, which measures about 0.8 meter in diameter.

Another advanced type of kiln uncovered at Pan-p'o is shown in Figure 21(b). Its fire chamber, resembling a pocket-shaped pit, measures about 2 meters in diameter and 1 meter in height. It is connected with the oven through two large flue holes.

Remains of kilns of the Yang-shao period unearthed from the San-li-ch'iao 三里橋 site in Shan-hsien in western Honan show ovens measuring more than 1 meter in diameter. The kilns of the subsequent Lungshanoid period at San-li-ch'iao and at its twin site Miao-ti-kou show somewhat better-designed fire passages and flue holes.²⁷

From a study of Yang-shao pottery and some Yang-shao pottery kilns discovered at the Lin-shan-chai 林山寨 site in Cheng-chou, Yoshida Mitsukuni, a historian of Chinese metallurgy, is of the opinion that certain types of Yang-shao pottery might have been fired at a temperature as high as 1300° or 1400°C.²⁸ As we saw in chapter 4, three members of the Institute of Silicate Chemistry

---

²⁶ Forbes, *Metallurgy in Antiquity*, p. 29.

²⁷ *Miao-ti-kou yü San-li-ch'iao*, Figures 56, 57, and 11, on pp. 86, 87, and 11.

²⁸ Yoshida Mitsukuni, "Chugaku kodai kinzoku gijutsu" [The Metallurgical Technology in Ancient China], *Tohogakuho*, XXXIV (1959), p. 58.

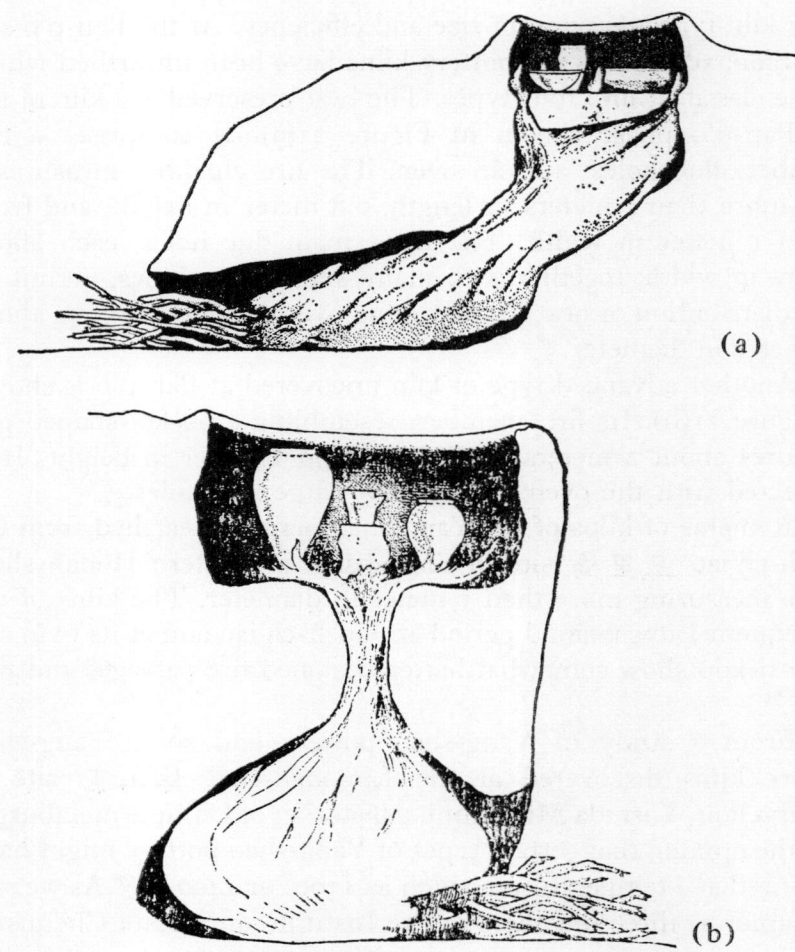

FIGURE 21. Two Yang-shao kiln types of Pan-p'o. From *Hsi-an Pan-p'o*, Figure 118 on p. 160.

and Technology of mainland China believe that the bulk of Yang-shao pottery is likely to have been fired between 950° and 1050°C.[29] Since the latter estimate is based on careful laboratory tests, it is probably the more accurate. If so, the maximum temperature Yang-shao pottery kilns could reach fell just short of 1083° C—the melting point of copper—but was considerably below 1150°C, which is considered the minimum for satisfactory pouring of molten bronze.[30]

Yoshida has sketched a typical early Shang pottery kiln of Pi-sha-kang 碧沙崗 near Cheng-chou and a Tepe Sialk kiln of advanced design of ancient Iran, which are shown in Figure 22. Although he eschews explicit comparison of these two types, it is fairly evident that they bear basic resemblances in design, especially with regard to the regulation of heat through fire passages, except that the Cheng-chou type has a baking oven with a diameter of 1.6 meters as compared to the Tepe Sialk's diameter of about 1 meter. In any case, it was not until ancient Chinese pottery kilns could reach temperatures sufficiently high for melting copper and pouring bronze that the transition from pottery making to bronze casting became feasible. The existing data suggest that this transition had been successfully made some time before the founding of the Shang dynasty, perhaps around 1600 B.C., for Yen-shih in western Honan, probably the capital city of the Shang founder Ta-i, already had a bronze foundry.

The close relation between pottery making in Neolithic China and bronze casting in Shang times is nowhere better revealed than in vessel shapes. Even in 1949, when data on Neolithic Chinese pottery were much more limited, Li Chi was able to trace the evolution of a fairly wide range of vessel shapes from pottery to

---

[29] See note 19 of chapter 4.

[30] Coghlan, *Notes on the Prehistoric Metallurgy of Copper and Bronze in the Old World,* p. 113.

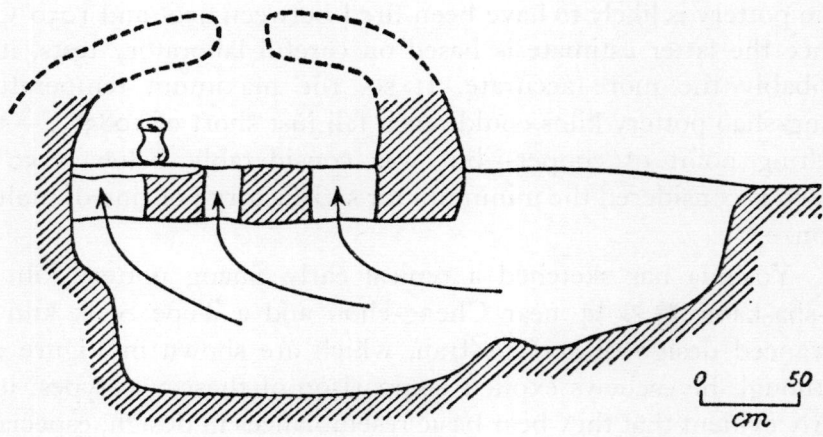

An early Shang kiln at Pi-sha-kang, Cheng-chou.

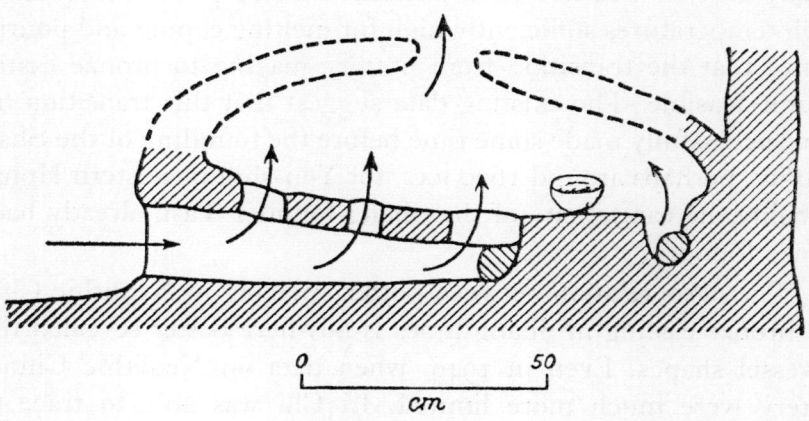

A typical kiln of Tepe Sialk of ancient Iran.

FIGURE 22. Shang and ancient Iranian kilns. From N. Barnard, *Bronze Casting and Bronze Alloys in Ancient China*, Figures 18 and 19 on pp. 63 and 64.

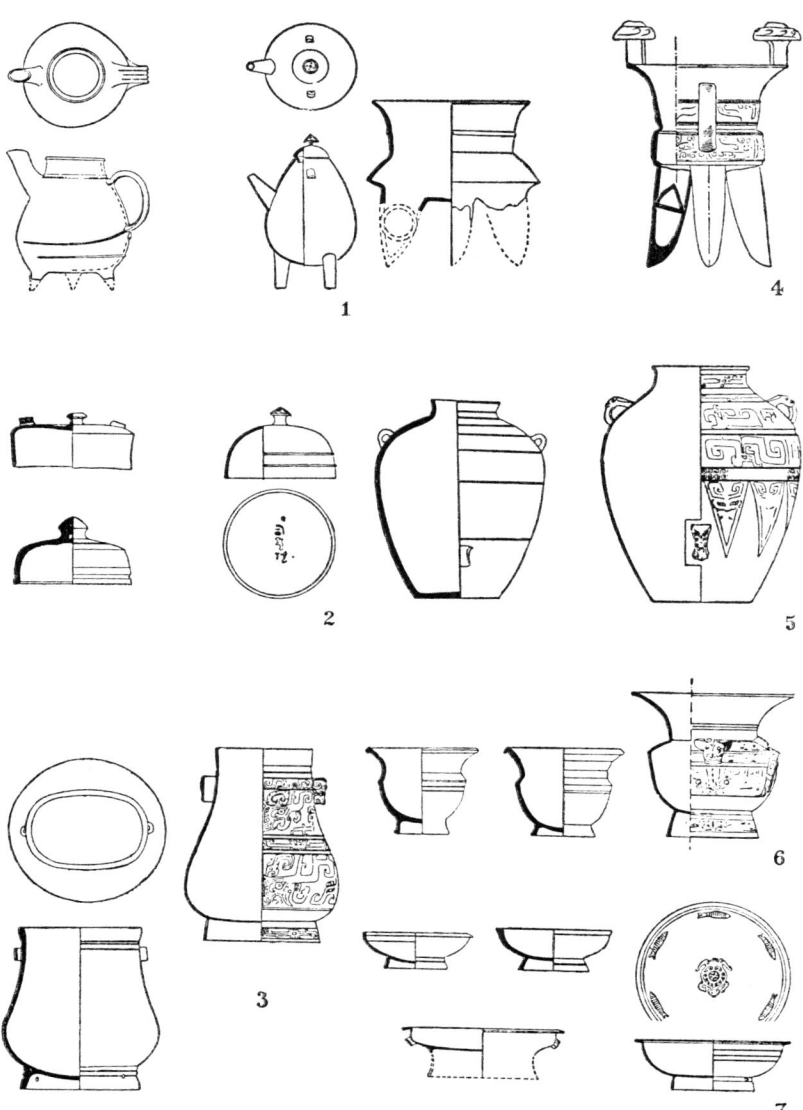

FIGURE 23. Shang bronze vessels and their pottery prototypes. From Barnard, *Bronze Casting and Bronze Alloys in Ancient China,* Figure 16 on p. 60. Within each numbered group the vessels on the left are pottery and those on the right are bronze.

bronze.³¹ Figure 23, which consists of only a few types selected by Noel Barnard from Li Chi's many illustrations, will be self-explanatory. A detailed study of the rich post-1949 pottery finds, if undertaken by an expert, could demonstrate the various stages in the evolution of vessel forms from Yang-shao pottery to Shang bronze. Suffice it to say here that not a few of the Shang bronze vessel types can be traced back to their Yang-shao ceramic archetypes, and that virtually all of the Shang bronze vessel forms have their prototypes in diverse kinds of native Neolithic ceramic.

Wilma Fairbank has made several keen observations on the close connection between ceramic making and bronze casting in ancient China. Of the bronze vessels excavated by the Academia Sinica during nine seasons of field work at An-yang up to 1949, no less than 20 percent are round in cross-section and clearly related to contemporaneous and earlier pottery shapes. "This suggests," she says, "a direct transition from making pottery vessels to producing the same or similar shapes in bronze." She has further pointed out that "the complicated process of bronze casting in Shang China divides properly into two phases, the first of which is essentially *ceramic* (the preparation and successive firing of the elements of the mold assembly, i.e., model, core, and mold) and the second of which is essentially *metallurgical* (the foundry procedures for alloying, melting, and pouring in the metal)." She concludes that little about the complicated piece-mold casting and assembling and the uniquely intricate decoration of Shang bronze is "inconsistent with the application to the metallic medium of ceramic mold form and molding processes long in use in China for reproducing pottery."³²

Dr. Cheng Te-k'un of Cambridge University, who personally

---

[31] Li Chi, "Chi Hsiao-t'un ch'u-t'u chih ch'ing-t'ung-ch'i" [A Description of the Bronze Vessels Unearthed from Hsiao-t'un], *Chung-kuo k'ao-ku hsüeh-pao* [Chinese Archaeological Review], Academia Sinica, No. 3 (1948), pp. 1–99 with 19 plates.

[32] Wilma Fairbank, "Piece-mold Craftsmanship and Shang Bronze Design," *Archives of the Chinese Art Society of America,* XIV (1962), pp. 7–15; quotation from pp. 10–11.

examined a large amount of Shang pottery at An-yang before 1937, at the Academia Sinica in Taiwan after 1949, and at various times in leading Western museums, kindly acceded to my request to discuss the intimate relation between mold casting in pottery and bronze casting in Shang times. I here quote from a long letter that he wrote to me on April 14, 1971:

I must state first of all that mold-casting is one of the many methods employed in pottery construction by the Shang potter. As far as mold-casting is concerned, there are at least three types.

1. Single-mold casting—producing only the lower part of some round-bottomed vessels, the upper part, including the neck and mouth, being constructed with the aid of a turn-table. No mold or fragments of it has been reported and this seems to indicate that it was made of perishable material, presumably wood, bamboo, straw or cord. The vessel could have been fired with the mold on because it would not be easy to remove the vessel from the woven mold. The cord-, basket-, or mat-marks on the finished product are just functional marks. In some cases, the corded material could have been used as a lining in the mold which would facilitate easy removal of the pot from the mold. The lining could then be easily peeled off from the pot before firing.

2. Two-mold casting—producing some globular pots in two spherical halves. They were usually joined together vertically in the middle, and the neck and mouth was constructed at the opening of the upper part of the vessel afterwards.

3. Multi-mold casting—producing some *li* tripods and other three-legged vessels. They were constructed in three identical sections and joined together also vertically with the upper part of the body, the neck and mouth connecting them into one piece. In some cases three pointed projections were added at the bottom of the hollow legs. Sometimes the three-piece mold was made in piece, and so there is no trace of the adjoining parts. Some of the rectangular vessels could have been cast with a four-piece mold, but I have not come across such a specimen so far.

In the mold-casting process, clay was simply pressed to the mold with the fingers and the impressions of the latter are usually visible on the inside of the vessel. In most cases these impressions would hold the fingers comfortably when one runs through the inner surface of the pot. They are quite different from the impressions left by the anvil pressed to the wall when the beater's method was used in the construction. On the outside of the vessel the beater's marks are easily distinguishable from those left by the mold itself. In the latter the cord-marks form a continuous pattern while in the former the decoration is composed of a number of beaten impressions.

The striking similarity of the mold-casting in pottery and in bronze has been previously noted by Dr. Li Chi [of Academia Sinica] too. It seems highly likely that the invention of bronze casting in China owed a great deal to the advanced techniques of the late Neolithic ceramic industry. This can be seen from various angles.

Archaeologically, ruins of the Shang kilns and foundries have been found almost always adjacent to each other in one complex. The equipments of the latter, notably the crucibles and the molds, were the products of the former. The three types of bronze casting in Shang times ([Cheng Te-k'un] *Shang China,* pp. 164–65) are almost replicas of the three types of mold-casting in pottery described above. Moreover, most of the bronze shapes are derived from pottery and the early bronze decorations are invariably similar to those of pottery. I am convinced that the invention of bronze casting in China was actually inspired by the techniques of pottery making. The basic processes and products of the two industries are almost identical.

From Dr. Cheng's authoritative discussion, there can be little doubt about the similarity and continuity between the native ancient Chinese ceramic industry and the art of bronze casting.

4. In this fourth section, we shall compare Chinese bronze casting processes with those of the ancient Near East.

The most basic technological difference in metallurgy between ancient China and the ancient West is the fact that, with the exception of small, simple, and flat objects which were cast in open or bivalve molds, Chinese bronze vessels were invariably products of direct casting in complicated piece-mold assemblies, in sharp contrast to the cire-perdue process of indirect casting of the ancient West. This basic difference in technology is succinctly explained by Wilma Fairbank:

An explanation, however brief, of the alternative to cire-perdue casting by the Shang craftsmen might well begin with the truism that a bronze casting is simply a replica in bronze of a model created in another medium. In the Western tradition this model has typically been made of wax on a clay core, then sheathed in a solid clay outer mold, melted out and replaced with molten bronze. In ancient China, on the contrary, it appears that the model was made of clay . . . around a clay core and that the outer mold was not solid and continuous but segmented. This segmentation (making the outer mold a "piece-mold") was necessitated by the fact that the baked clay model, unlike its wax counterpart, could not be melted out but had to be removed bodily. Thus when the mold segments have received the imprint of the model they are detached from it, the model is broken or scraped away from the core, and the mold segments are reassembled around the core ready to receive the molten bronze in the hollow interstice between the two.

The use and development of piece-molds is *prima-facie* evidence that a wax model was not used since segmented molds are not only unnecessary in cire-perdue casting but also unnecessarily complicate matters for the craftsman, who must, when the casting is finished, file away spicules or fins of bronze which have leaked into the cracks between mold segments. If the cire-perdue process had been known in ancient China, it is difficult to imagine that the more laborious piece-mold system would have been developed there to the point of producing complex vessel forms with intricate decoration at a date when such exploitation and elaboration of this casting process was unknown elsewhere.[33]

As a matter of fact, as early as 1933 the late Liu Yü-hsia of Academia Sinica had already analyzed the concrete evidence of piece-mold casting of the bronze vessels produced at An-yang in late Shang times.[34] In 1935 Orvar Karlbeck, with the help of O. Elmquist, proprietor and manager of the Elmquist Cire Perdue Bronze Foundry in Sweden, gave various reasons why the method of bronze casting in Shang China was one of piece-mold assembly, not one of cire-perdue.[35] In 1955 Shih Chang-ju of Academia Sinica carried on the work left by Liu and confirmed many of Liu's early tentative conclusions.[36] The most systematic and methodical study of the Shang piece-mold system of casting has been made by Noel Barnard.[37]

The findings of all these valuable studies on the technology of Shang bronze metallurgy have been confirmed beyond any doubt by the two recent monographs of Li Chi and Wan Chia-pao, which, though they deal only with the *ku* 觚 wine beakers and the *chüeh* 爵 wine cups, are based on the best attested artifacts excavated by Academia Sinica before 1949. By examining the bronze

---

[33] *Ibid.*, pp. 9–10.

[34] Liu Yü-hsia, "Yin-tai yeh-t'ung-shu chih yen-chiu."

[35] O. Karlbeck, "Anyang Moulds," *BMFEA*, No. 7 (1935), pp. 39–60.

[36] Shih Chang-ju, "Yin-tai ti ch'u-t'ung kung-i."

[37] Barnard, *Bronze Casting and Bronze Alloys in Ancient China*, esp. ch. 5, "Sectional Moulds and the Significance of Sectionalism."

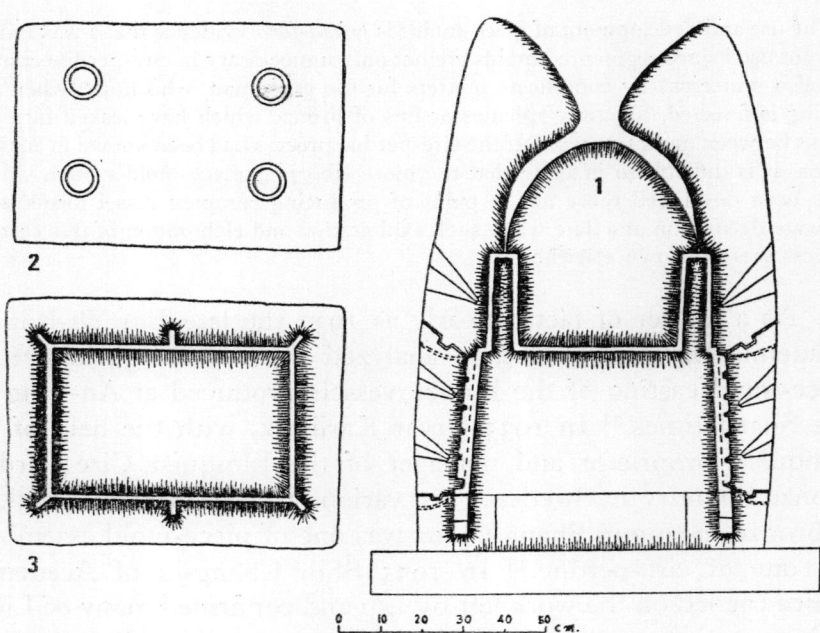

FIGURE 24. Multi-mold for the casting of a four-legged container: (1) cross-section of the mold; (2) cross-section at the legs of the vessel; (3) cross-section at the body of the vessel. From Shih Chang-ju, "Yin-tai ti chu-t'ung kung-i," Figure 8 on p. 117.

vessels and remnants of piece-molds separately and then by cross-checking the peculiarities of vessels and molds, these monographs offer by far the most conclusive evidence that Shang bronze vessels were cast in piece-molds. Although Shang craftsmen filed away mold-joint traces and covered them up with decoration, two to four vertical seams are clearly discernible on many *ku* beakers. While none of these beakers show traces of horizontal seams, "the fact that there were several complete molds with horizontal seams to match adjoining molds means that there must have been horizontal seams which were perhaps completely filed away." Moreover, although certain *ku* beakers resemble each other closely in weight, dimension, inscription and design, no two items are exactly the same and "no two *ku* were cast by the same set of molds."[38]

Dr. Cheng Te-k'un, after examining the question of Shang bronze casting in a broader technological context in his 14 April 1971 letter to me, reached the following conclusion:

A close examination of the Shang bronzes confirms the fact that the bronze manufacturer was a founder who knew only direct casting, even for the elaborate vessels in piece-mold assemblies. Any defect in the form of tiny holes which rarely occurred in casting was mended with drops of the liquid alloy which was pressed into the tiny opening from both sides of the vessel wall. None of the common techniques such as sheet-metal working, riveting, annealing, tracing, engraving, stamp, repoussé, etc. was ever used. The complete absence of smithy methods, cire-perdue, and even so elementary a technique as annealing can only mean that the Shang bronze work had indigenous origins.

Scholarly literature on the unique ancient Chinese method of bronze casting has in recent years been so impressive in quality and quantity that no additional technical discussion is needed for the present study, other than what has been summarized above. As a matter of historical interest, however, I shall discuss in detail the belated awareness of the ancient Chinese of the industrial usefulness of beeswax. Since the cire-perdue process developed in the ancient Near East depended in large measure on beeswax, the absence of any ancient Chinese account of a similar use of beeswax is further proof that ancient Chinese bronze metallurgy was developed independently from the Near East, Western and Central Asia and Siberia.[39]

---

[38] Li Chi and Wan Chia-pao, *Yin-hsü ch'u-t'u ch'ing-t'ung ku-hsing-ch'i chih yen-chiu* [Studies on the Bronze *Ku*-Beakers Unearthed from An-yang] (Academia Sinica, Taiwan, 1964), pp. 119–120. Similar conclusions and observations are given in their *Yin-hsü ch'u-t'u ch'ing-t'ung chüeh-hsing-ch'i chih yen-chiu* [Studies on the Bronze *Chüeh*-Winecups Unearthed from An-yang] (Academia Sinica, Taiwan, 1966).

[39] In Yoshida Mitsukuni's article on ancient Chinese metallurgy published in 1954, he already touched upon the problem of the late appearance of the Chinese character for wax, which problem is summarized in Barnard, *Bronze Casting and Bronze Alloys in Ancient China*. The Japanese journal in which Yoshida's paper

To trace the early history of beeswax in China, it is necessary to study the etymology of three Chinese characters in association— *feng* 蠭、蜂 (bee and wasp), *mi* 蜜 (honey), and *la* 蠟 (beeswax). All these characters are missing from late Shang oracle texts and Western Chou bronze inscriptions. The character for bee or wasp first appears in ode 289 in *The Book of Odes,* which says: "I have been chastened, and I will guard against future calamities; nobody has caused me to be wasp-stung, I have myself drawn upon me this bitter sting."[40] *Tso-chuan* records that in 638 B.C. a statesman of the Lu state in southwestern Shantung warned his lord of the intrigues of some neighboring states with a metaphor that "bees and scorpions carry poison."[41] In the writings of and attributed to the Lord of Shang (d. 338 B.C.) and in the *Hsün-tzu* 荀子 collected works of the great philosopher Hsün K'uang 荀況, (ca. 298–238 B.C.), the sharpness of the iron and steel weapons of the powerful Ch'u state of central Yangtze is likened to the bee's sting.[42]

The ancient Chinese learned the value of honey apparently much later than they knew of the bee's sting. One of the first occurrences of the character for honey is found in *Shan-hai-ching* 山海經 (A Classic on Mountains and Rivers), which, though containing information of the Chou period, was compiled probably after 200 B.C. It says that the Mang Mountain 芒山 north of Lo-yang in western Honan was the place where bees congregated and deposited their honey.[43] The date of *Shan-hai-ching's* passage

appeared is unfortunately not available. I have examined the relevant Chinese literary and historical records reasonably exhaustively, and I shall present the records fully.

[40] B. Karlgren, *The Book of Odes,* p. 249.

[41] Legge, tr., *The Chinese Classics,* V, *The Ch'un Ts'ew with the Tso Chuen,* p. 183.

[42] *Shang-chün shu* (SPPY ed.), ch. 5, p. 6a; *Hsün-tzu* (SPPY ed.), ch. 10, p. 10a.

[43] Hao I-hsing, *Shan-hai-ching chien-shu* (SPPY ed.), ch. 5, p. 13b. The identification of the mountain was made by the Ch'ing scholar Hao I-hsing in his original annotative note. The same work, ch. 12, p. 12b, also mentions a kind of giant bee without its being associated with honey.

being uncertain, the earliest ascertainable reference to honey is in a long poem by Ch'ü Yüan 屈原 (339–278 B.C.), the most famous poet of preimperial China. The association of honey with "jade nectar" in his poetic fantasy suggests that honey must have been very precious.[44] Honey remained precious until at least the early Christian centuries. Emperor Kuang-wu (reigned A.D. 25–57), the founder of Eastern Han dynasty, gave Chu Yu 朱祐 a bushel of honey as a special imperial favor, after recalling the struggling days when he and Chu had used a small amount of honey to concoct medicine.[45] The philosopher Wang Ch'ung 王充 (A.D. 29–109) warned people that honey should be taken only in small doses, lest they be poisoned.[46] Yüan Shu 袁術 (d. A.D. 199), a general from a distinguished aristocratic family, asked for honey on his deathbed.[47] Sun Liang 孫亮, a teen-age prodigy and the second ruler of the Wu kingdom in central and lower Yangtze (reigned A.D. 252–256), kept honey together with other treasures in the royal storehouse.[48] All this reflects the fact that, in the centuries immediately before and after Christ, honey was a comparative rarity, at least in China, consumed primarily by members of the aristocracy.

In the dictionary *Erh-ya* 爾雅, the compilation of which was probably completed in Former Han times, there are two references to bees and wasps.[49] In *Fang-yen* 方言, the dictionary on regional dialects compiled by Yang Hsiung 揚雄 (53 B.C.–A.D. 13), reference

---

[44] *Ch'u-tz'u pu-chu* (SPPY ed.), ch. 9, pp. 10a–10b. For the identification of the authorship of this particular poem, I abide by the opinions of Yu Kuo-en and Kuo Mo-jo, etc.; for the dating of Ch'ü Yüan's birth, I abide by the findings of P'u Chiang-ch'ing. These modern scholars' findings on *Ch'u-tz'u* are all reprinted in *Ch'u-tz'u yen-chiu lun-wen-chi* [Symposium on Ch'u-tz'u] (Peking, 1957).

[45] *Hou-Han shu* (I-wen reprint), ch. 22, p. 2b.

[46] Wang Ch'ung, *Lun-heng* (SPPY ed.), ch. 23, p. 1b.

[47] *San-kuo-chih chi-chieh* (I-wen reprint), ch. 6, p. 78a, note.

[48] *Ibid.*, ch. 48, p. 5b, note.

[49] Hao I-hsing, *Erh-ya i-shu* (SPPY ed.), Book B, ch. 3, p. 10b.

is made to both bee and honey.⁵⁰ In the first comprehensive lexicon, *Shuo-wen chieh-tzu,* completed by Hsü Shen 許慎 in A.D. 100, there are characters for bee and honey, but still none for beeswax.⁵¹

By far the earliest reference to beeswax is found in the year A.D. 268. When the empress dowager née Wang 王 died, her son Emperor Wu of Chin gave orders that an imperial seal be made in replica with beeswax as a part of the funerary gifts.⁵² Be it noted here that the original phrase *"mi-hsi"* 蜜璽 literally means "honey seal," an expression which reflects that no clear differentiation of beeswax from honey had yet been made in general usage. Similar funerary gifts were bestowed on the famous official Shan T'ao 山濤 in A.D. 238 and on the distinguished general T'ao K'an 陶侃 in A.D. 332.⁵³

As far as can be ascertained from historical records, the character *la* 蠟 for beeswax occurs for the first time in A.D. 282. In that year two corrupt and immensely rich officials, Shih Ch'ung 石崇 and Wang K'ai 王愷, were engaged in competitive conspicuous consumption. The former outdid the latter, and among his many acts of extravagance was the use of beeswax in lieu of firewood for cooking.⁵⁴ Juan Fu 阮孚 (A.D. 278–326), a member of a distinguished scholar-official family, was known for his eccentric habit of frequently polishing his wooden sandals with melted beeswax.⁵⁵ When, after a bitter struggle for power, the ambitious general Wang Tun

---

⁵⁰ Yang Hsiung, *Fang-yen* (SPTK ed.), ch. 11, p. 2b.

⁵¹ Ting Fu-pao, *Shuo-wen-chieh-tzu ku-lin* (Shanghai, 1931), ch. 13b, pp. 6036b–6037a.

⁵² *Chin-shu* (I-wen reprint), ch. 20, pp. 24a–24b.

⁵³ *Ibid.,* ch. 43, p. 8b; ch. 66, p. 23b.

⁵⁴ *Ibid.,* ch. 33, p. 29b. The exact year in which this episode took place was determined by the great Sung historian Ssu-ma Kuang (A.D. 1019–1086) in his monumental chronological history, *Tzu-chih t'ung-chien* (Taipei, Chung-hua ts'ung-shu ed.), V, ch. 81, p. 17.

⁵⁵ *Ibid.,* ch. 49, p. 11b.

王敦 died in A.D. 324, his son withheld the news, wrapping the corpse and sealing it with beeswax.[56]

The first written references to the domestication of bees and the gathering of honey and beeswax from "distant mountains" are found in the notes on natural history, *Po-wu chih* 博物志, originally written by the Chin statesman and martyr Chang Hua 張華 (A.D. 232–300).[57] Although this work was subsequently lost and its extant remnants probably contain additions by later scholars, domestication of bees in scattered mountainous localities may well have begun during his lifetime if not earlier because of demands for honey and beeswax by the ruling class. But the extremely limited ways in which beeswax was used even by the Chinese elite up to the fourth century of the Christian era is a striking phenomenon. *Shih-shuo hsin-yü* 世說新語, the famous collection of personal anecdotes of officials and scholars from the Later Han to the end of Chin, written by Liu I-ch'ing 劉義慶, in the early half of the fifth century, mentions the use of *la-chu* 蠟燭 (beeswax candles) as fuel for cooking when he relates the episode involving Shih Ch'ung described above.[58] The *Shih-shuo hsin-yu*'s version may well be accurate in the light of corroborative evidence in the biography of Chou I 周顗 (d. A.D. 322) in the *Chin-shu* 晉書. A man of great moral courage and aspirations, Chou I did not realize that his brother had been living under his shadow for so long. During a drinking fit his brother finally vented his frustration by throwing a lighted beeswax candle at him.[59] To my knowledge, these are the first references to wax candles in Chinese history, for until the late third century A.D. the *chu* 燭 (torch filled with grease) had been used for illumination. Candle-making no doubt increased the demand for beeswax, but the fact still remains that no Chinese

---

[56] *Ibid.*, ch. 98, p. 15b.
[57] Chang Hua, *Po-wu chih* (SPPY ed.), ch. 2, pp. 5a–5b; ch. 10, p. 2b.
[58] Liu I-ch'ing, *Shih-shuo hsin-yü* (SPTK ed.), Book C, Part II, p. 33b.
[59] *Chin-shu*, ch. 69, p. 21b.

historical or literary works of the early Christian era mention the use of beeswax for metallurgical purposes.

Noel Barnard was the first scholar to make an important observation on the earliest available Chinese bronze articles that are likely to have been produced by the cire-perdue process. The 1959 report on the rich finds in a group of tombs belonging to the Former Han period (206 B.C.–A.D. 9) at Shih-chai-shan 石寨山 in Chin-ning 晋寧 county in Yunnan barely reached Barnard in time for him to incorporate this vital observation in his 1961 book, *Bronze Casting and Bronze Alloys in Ancient China*. By studying the plates of some extremely lively bronze figurines of humans and animals fused in groups to weapons and drum-like stands, he reached the tentative conclusion that the method of casting "is decidedly that of cire-perdue."[60] Although mainland Chinese scholars have yet to discuss in print the exact method by which the figurines were cast, these unusual Yunnan bronze artifacts have already attracted so much attention among interested occidental and Chinese scholars in the West that they are now generally considered to have been "quite obviously the products of cire-perdue casting techniques."[61]

Since it was in 109 B.C. that the Chinese ruler of the polyglot Yunnan area ackowledged the sovereignty of the Han emperor and received from the latter the title and seal of "Prince of Tien" (Yunnan) 滇王,[62] and since a golden seal bearing such a title has been unearthed from his grave,[63] these cire-perdue cast bronze articles found in his and other graves should probably be dated

---

[60] Barnard, *Bronze Casting and Bronze Alloys in Ancient China,* pp. 304–305 and plates 48 and 49.

[61] Barnard, "The Special Character of Metallurgy in Ancient China," in *Application of Science in the Examination of Works of Art* (Boston Museum of Art, 1965), p. 204, n. 9.

[62] *Shih-chi* (I-wen reprint), ch. 116, pp. 5a–5b.

[63] *Yün-nan Chin-ning Shih-chai-shan ku-mu-chün fa-chüeh pao-kao* [Report on the Excavations of a Group of Ancient Tombs at Shih-chai-shan, Chin-ning, Yunnan] (Peking, 1959), I, p. 133; II, plate 10(3).

around 100 B.C.—a period of sustained large-scale military and cultural contacts between Han China and Central Asia and India.[64]

While bronze articles cast by cire-perdue method made their debut in this southwesternmost area bordering on Burma shortly before the time of Christ, this method of casting is likely to have been introduced into China proper—perhaps mainly by Indian Buddhists, through the overland "silk route" and by way of the sea—some centuries later. This hypothesis is partially based on our etymological studies of the bee-honey-beeswax complex and indirectly borne out by Japanese data on cire-perdue casting. Because of her insularity, Japan has been better able to preserve old manuscripts and artifacts than China. Yet the earliest Japanese manuscripts testifying to the availability of beeswax in quantities sufficient to suggest its use in cire-perdue casting are dated A.D. 756 and 762, and the earliest extant Buddhist statue cast by cire-perdue in Japan is dated A.D. 630.[65]

In reviewing the cire-perdue casting process in the context of world history, Cyril S. Smith, an authority on metallography, is certainly right in saying that the waste-wax technique "had been devised very early in the Middle East but was slow to diffuse to China."[66] Thus the abundant evidence of the late introduction of the cire-perdue process into China, on the one hand, and the uniquely Chinese system of piece-mold casting, on the other, act like the two halves of a tally stick in establishing the indigenous origins and development of metallurgy in ancient China.

To conclude this section, it should be mentioned that Shang decorative art in general and bronze decoration in particular was

[64] For further discussion of this important chapter of Sino-Western contacts, see Appendix III, "A Note on Ancient Chinese Astronomy."

[65] Yoshida Mitsukuni's findings are summarized in Barnard, *Bronze Casting and Bronze Alloys in Ancient China*, p. 105.

[66] Cyril S. Smith, "Materials and the Development of Civilization and Science," *Science,* CXLVIII (1965), p. 912.

unquestionably developed out of diverse but native Neolithic roots.[67] "The most emphatic aspect of the design," says C. S. Smith, "is the strong symmetry of the flanges, a characteristic of most Shang and Chou bronzes. These flanges did not originate in the artist's fancy but are a direct consequence of the fact that the molds had to be made in several pieces to allow removal of the pattern around which they were shaped and to give access to their inside surfaces for carving the fine details."[68] Thus the peculiarity of the Shang bronze decor was determined by the peculiarly ancient Chinese system of piece-mold casting.[69]

5. We now turn to the historical pattern of the geographic spread of bronze artifacts. It is the good fortune of students of Chinese metallurgy that Noel Barnard, in conjunction with Sato Tamotsu, exhausted all the attested provenance data about ancient Chinese metal artifacts available up to the end of 1964 and has prepared a series of detailed maps showing the various historical stages in the geographic distribution of bronze and iron artifacts and metallurgical centers in ancient China. The purpose and scale of this painstaking work are best explained by Barnard himself:

If the art of metallurgy in ancient China was the result of introduction directly, or indirectly, from an alien cultural sphere evidence of its route of entry would surely be present in some forms or other amongst the many hundreds of sites

---

[67] Li Chi, "Diverse Backgrounds of the Decorative Art of the Yin Dynasty," in *Proceedings of the Fourth Far-Eastern Prehistory Congress and the Anthropology Division of the Eighth Pacific Science Congress Combined* (Quezon City, 1956), pp. 179–194. The indigenous origins of Shang decorative art are more explicitly set forth by Li Chi in his "Chung-kuo shang-ku-shih chih ch'ung-chien-kung-tso chi ch'i wen-t'i" [The Reconstruction of the Ancient History of China and its Problems], *Min-chu p'ing-lun,* V, No. 4 (16 February 1954), pp. 86–89.

[68] Cyril S. Smith, "Materials and the Development of Civilization and Science," p. 912.

[69] For an able discussion of the causal relationship between piece-mold casting and Shang bronze decor, see Wilma Fairbank, "Piece-mold Craftsmanship and Shang Bronze Design."

excavated over the last 30 years or so—particularly over the last 15 years. Approximately 1,000 sites yielding metal artifacts datable from Early Shang (ca. 1500 B.C.) —a few possibly even earlier—and ranging up to the close of Eastern Han (A.D. 220) have been excavated. These comprise more than 13,000 tombs and settlement remains in a total of 400 site-areas which have been reported in varying degrees of detail and of reliability. Plotted on to a map of China this data results in a total of 400 site-areas which are scattered over a sufficiently wide area and in significant geographical pattern—so far as settlement areas and communication routes of antiquity are concerned—to permit us to attempt a survey of distribution patterns.[70]

While all twelve maps he prepared are invaluable to historians of Chinese metallurgy, we need to reproduce here only the one which has pinned down the area in which bronze metallurgy in China first occurred. On Map 2 the four sites of the Shang period which provide the earliest reliable evidence of bronze metallurgy are shown in small white circles within the Shang area. They are, from west to east, Yen-shih, Cheng-chou, Hui-hsien, and An-yang. Aside from the locations given on the map, Shang bronze artifacts and sometimes even traces of foundry sites are reported to have been discovered in Chia-shan 嘉山 and Ch'u-hsien 滁縣 in Anhwei and in Nanking, Chiang-ning 江寧 and Tan-t'u 丹徒 in Kiangsu— places along the Peking-Nanking-Shanghai Railways.[71]

It can be seen from the map that bronze metallurgy in ancient China first emerged in the Honan plain, and within the half millennium of the dynastic Shang period it spread eastward to southernmost Hopei and many parts of Shantung, westward to east-central Shensi, southward to parts of Hupei, and southeastward to a few localities in Anhwei and Kiangsu. Bronze artifacts did not reach eastern Kansu until the Western Chou period (1027–771 B.C.). Even as late as 220 B.C., bronze artifacts did not reach the Kansu Corridor (the path of the historic "silk route"), along which the diffusionists had hoped to find clues to the introduction of bronze metallurgy into China. Only the repeated wars waged by some

---

[70] Barnard, "The Special Character of Metallurgy in Ancient China," p. 186.
[71] *Chiang-su-sheng ch'u-t'u wen-wu hsüan-chi*, pp. 23–24.

northern Chinese states against the proto-Huns during the period of Contending States (453–221 B.C.) brought bronze artifacts to the southern fringe of Inner Mongolia.[72] As to "Eastern Turkestan" and the "northwestern and northern regions of present-day China," the areas in which Max Loehr and other diffusionists expected to find evidence of bronze metallurgy earlier than that of An-yang, it is only from the Han times onward that bronze appeared there. Nothing argues more powerfully against the diffusionists' hypothesis than the distinctly centrifugal nature of the spread of bronze artifacts and metallurgy in ancient China.

6. The one remaining matter requiring clarification is the significance of the few types of bronze weapons and tools of An-yang which bear resemblance to those of several ancient cultures of Siberia and eastern Europe. These artifacts are limited to inward-curving daggers with animal-head terminals, socketed celts, spearheads, and a peculiar bow ornament (see Figure 25).

In a classificatory description of these An-yang artifacts in the collection of the Museum of Far Eastern Antiquities in Stockholm, Bernhard Karlgren expressed the opinion in 1945 that the An-yang weapons and tools were earlier than those of Siberia and beyond.[73] In 1949, Karlgren's conclusion was challenged by Max Loehr, who was of the opinion that the Siberian analogues to these An-yang weapons and tools were earlier and that metallurgy was probably introduced into China from Siberia.[74] In the light of current knowledge, Loehr was right in determining the prototypes, but his suggested chronologies for those ancient Siberian and eastern European cultures show an upward bias.

[72] It should be noted that the so-called "Ordos" style of bronze artifacts in the collections of some Western museums, which chronologically probably correspond to the end of the Shang and Western Chou period, are not included in Barnard's map because of his insistence on precise provenance data.

[73] Bernhard Karlgren, "Some Weapons and Tools of the Yin Dynasty," *BMFEA*, No. 17 (1945), pp. 101–144, with 40 plates.

[74] Max Loehr, "Weapons and Tools of Anyang, and Siberian Analogies."

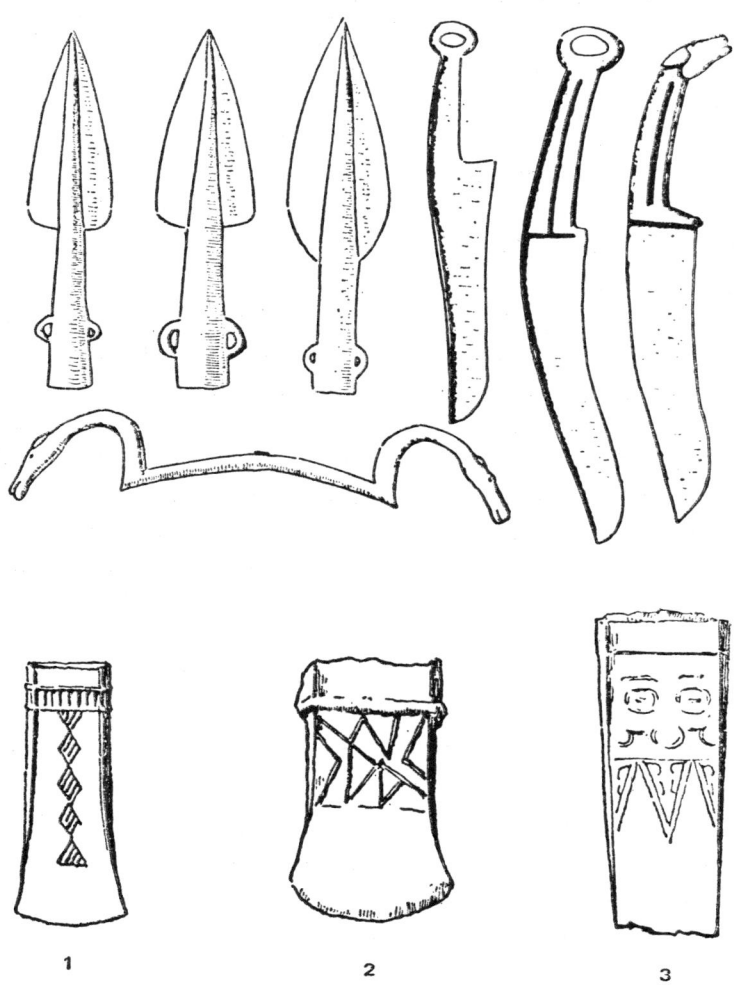

1   2   3

FIGURE 25. Shang bronze weapons with Seima motifs. *(top)* An-yang weapons with Seima motifs. From Marija Gimbutas, "Borodino, Seima and Their Contemporaries: Key Sites for the Bronze Age Chronology of Eastern Europe," *Proceedings of the Prehistoric Society for 1956*, XXII, Figure 14 on p. 158. *(bottom)* Socketed celts: 1—Seima; 2—Ordos; 3—An-yang. From Max Loehr, "Weapons and Tools from Anyang, and Siberian Analogies," Figure 3 on p. 132.

Cumulative research by Soviet archaeologists, which was evaluated and interpreted by S. V. Kissélev in 1960 for the Institute of Archaeology in Peking, has firmly established the following facts. First, these few types of weapons and tools originated in the ancient culture discovered in 1914–22 at Seima, which is located at the confluence of the Volga and Oka Rivers near present-day Gorki. Second, the Seima culture emerged around 1600 B.C. and flourished until about 1300 B.C. During these three centuries it spread eastward to the Lake Baikal region. Third, there can be little doubt that these few peculiar Seima motifs were brought from the Eurasian steppe to the late-Shang metallurgical center at An-yang. Fourth, An-yang was far from being a passive recipient; its bronze artifacts, designs, and motifs exerted unmistakable influence over the various Karasuk cultures (ca. 1300–1000 B.C.) east and west of Lake Baikal, and over the Ordos area of present-day China, which may be regarded to have been a joint Shang-Karasuk cultural sphere. Last, and of utmost importance to students of the origins of bronze metallurgy in China, is the fact that the Seima motifs are totally absent from the rich artifacts discovered at the early Shang center of Cheng-chou.[75] Since bronze metallurgy must have begun in China some time before Cheng-chou became an important center of the early dynastic Shang period, it is obvious that the presence of just a few types of tools and weapons with Seima motifs among the vast An-yang bronze assemblage has no bearing whatever on our study of the origins of bronze metallurgy in China.

The routes along which the Seima motifs diffused have been traced on systematic archaeological data, as shown in Map 3. Since this map does not include the areas south and east of Lake Baikal, we may fairly safely assume that it was more or less by the present-

---

[75] S. V. Kissélev, "Su-lien ching-nei ch'ing-t'ung-wen-hua yü Chung-kuo Shang-wen-hua ti kuan-hsi" [The Relation between the Bronze Age Cultures in the U.S.S.R. and the Chinese Shang Culture], *KK*, 1960, No. 2, pp. 51–53. This is a Chinese summary of his lecture in Russian.

day Lake Baikal-Ulan Bator-Peking route that the Seima motifs eventually reached An-yang.

With Map 3 as a point of departure, we will reexamine the diffusionist postulation in the context of ancient Eurasian metallurgy. What is implied in this map is the high probability that the "Silk Route"—from Sian to the Kansu Corridor and through the narrow pass between the Altai and Tarbargartai Mountains, known as the Dzungarian Gate—was not a thoroughfare for intercultural exchange until well into the historic periods. For one thing, as is clearly shown on Map 3, the ancient east-west trade routes are north of latitude 50° N in the steppe zone, where water supply was not a serious problem. But the area below the 50th parallel, the 2,500-mile stretch from the Caspian Sea to Wu-wei—which roughly represents the eastern end of the Kansu Corridor and where the Ch'i-chia copper has been found—is within one of the world's largest areas of deserts and semideserts. Moreover, the range of high mountains along the present Sino-Soviet and Soviet-Outer Mongolian boundaries, starting from the Pamirs in the southwest to the Altai-Sayan arch in the northeast, form a truly formidable natural barrier. Although this vast dry belt was dotted with more oases in ancient times than it is now, man could not have made the long trips between the oases easily without the help of horses and camels. It is true that the goat's arrival in Kansu from Central Asia was probably close in time to that of the Ch'i-chia copper. But the goat must have been brought in by Central Asian herdsmen, who do not seem very likely agents for the transmission of metallurgical knowledge. The fact that the vast Sinkiang area northwest of the Kansu Corridor was not ushered into the metal age until Han times indicates that, even if the diffusionist postulation were correct, the first knowledge of metal could not have been brought in via the Silk Route.

The remaining area that should be searched for possible evidence of transmission of metallurgical knowledge to ancient China is Siberia. From the aggregate available archaeological data

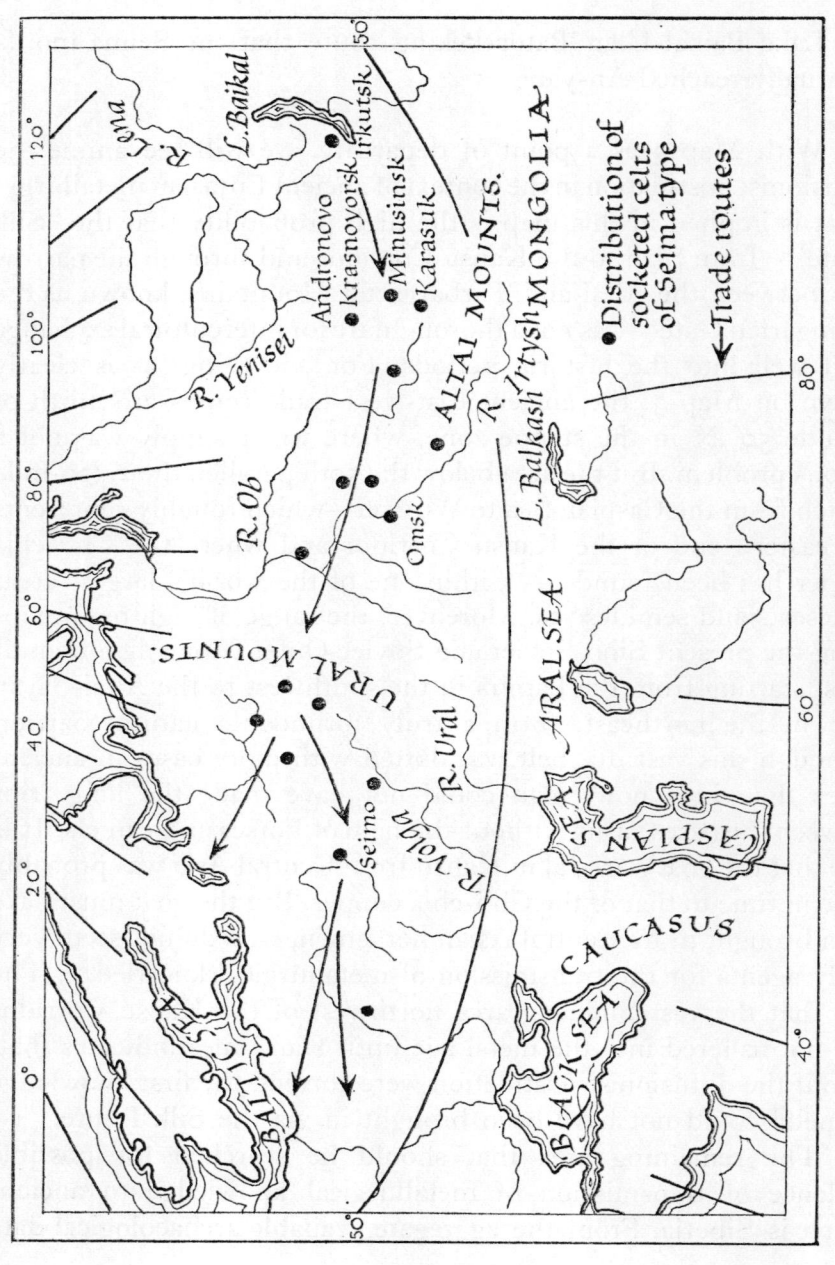

Map 3. Trade routes in the Eurasian steppe.

on metallurgy in Soviet Asia we can distil the following essential facts. First, the earliest and persistently strongest center of metallurgy in the entire Soviet Asia in ancient times was southern Turkmenia, near the Iranian border. Second, from southern Turkmenia, where the first ornaments in gold, copper, and bronze date as far back as ca. 4000 B.C., copper metallurgy spread to various parts of Soviet Central Asia only very gradually; so gradually and sporadically, as a matter of fact, that even down to about 1500 B.C. this area seems to have been probably the only truly significant center.[76] Third, the Afanasievo culture (ca. 2000–1500 B.C.) in the Minusinsk area in upper Yenisei north of the Altai-Sayan arch represents the earliest phase of copper metallurgy so far known in Siberia and is believed to have received its metallurgy and certain other cultural elements from the Aral Sea and the Urals areas.[77] Last but not least, various archaeologists agree in dating the "early bronze age" in both Soviet Central Asia and Siberia from the fifteenth to the thirteenth century B.C.[78]

The combined facts thus indicate that in the vast dry belt and steppe northwest of the present Sino-Soviet border the diffusion of

[76] Grégoire Frumkin, *Archaeology in Soviet Central Asia* (Leiden, 1970), esp. synopsis of metallurgy on p. 132. It is interesting to note that a map showing archaeological monuments in Soviet Asia, in Alexander Mongait, *Archaeology in the U.S.S.R.*, facing p. 387, gives no bronze age sites in the vast dry belt of Central Asia, below the 50th parallel and west of southern Turkmenia. This may partially reflect the likelihood that there were very few, if any, truly significant metallurgical centers in Soviet Central Asia beyond the extreme southwestern corner near Iran, even though copper metallurgy is said to have spread widely up to about 1500 B.C. In Mongait's map, bronze age sites congregate mainly in the upper Yenisei valley north of the Altai-Sayan arch.

[77] A. P. Okladnikov, *Ancient Population of Siberia and Its Cultures* (Russian Translation Series of the Peabody Museum of Archaeology and Ethnology, Harvard University, I, No. 1, Cambridge, Mass., 1959), pp. 22–23; James H. Gaul, "Observations on the Bronze Age in the Yenisei Valley, Siberia," in Carleton S. Coon and James M. Andrews, IV, eds., *Studies in the Anthropology of Oceania and Asia* (Peabody Museum Papers, Vol. XX, Cambridge, Mass., 1943), pp. 152–153, and p. 178.

[78] Notably Okladnikov and Frumkin.

metallurgy was more sporadic and took longer than is usually imagined. The vital fact that the "early bronze age" in all of Soviet Asia does not date beyond 1500 B.C. rules out the possibility of "Siberian" origins for Chinese bronze metallurgy, which was definitely earlier.

The only point of theoretical interest that remains to be investigated is whether China might have received its first knowledge of metal from the Afanasievo culture, whose copper was simultaneous with that of the Ch'i-chia culture.

In spite of the southern Central Asian origins of some of its cultural elements, the Afanasievo culture was distinctly a steppe and woodland culture. "It was still in many ways," as A. P. Okladnikov summarizes, "directly connected with the Stone Age culture."[79] Its economy was just beginning to change from hunting and sheep breeding to more settled cattle raising. A complete inventory of the artifacts of several Afanasievo sites of the Yenisei valley reveals only a very few simple copper objects, which clearly show that copper metallurgy was in a state of infancy.[80] In fact, even the subsequent Andronovo culture that replaced the Afanasievo in the Yenisei valley was characterized by relative poverty in both copper and bronze.[81] The conclusion of Karl Jettmar, an authority on the ancient art of the Eurasian steppe, is truly remarkable because it was made at a time when post-1300 B.C. An-yang represented the earliest known phase of metallurgy in China. In 1951 Jettmar described the Andronovo economy and discussed the implication of its metallurgy as follows: "It shows everywhere a strong tendency to settle. All signs of nomadism or mounted warfare are lacking. The Russian scientists look upon it as a peak point of the complex economy with cattle-raising and agriculture on the steppe.... In any case, we

---

[79] Okladnikov, *Ancient Population of Siberia and Its Cultures,* p. 22.

[80] Gaul, "Observations on the Bronze Age in the Yenisei Valley, Siberia," pp. 149–152.

[81] *Ibid.,* p. 158.

can hardly believe that China got its first knowledge of metallurgy from the Andronovo culture, where metallurgy is very limited and dependent on other centers."[82] East of Lake Baikal, an area which would have been crucial had metallurgy indeed been transmitted from Siberia to China, a culture contemporaneous to the Andronovo is called the Glazkovo, which consisted of "a numerous fishing and hunting population, who, however, had not yet their own metallurgy, and can therefore count as Neolithic."[83]

After all known factors have been analyzed and weighed, there is reason to believe that the predynastic Shang people may have received their first knowledge of metal from the loess highlands of China. While it is conceivable that more clues about the origins of metallurgy may be found in other areas in future, the case for the Ch'i-chia copper seems to be a strong one, in that the two prerequisites for an initial metallurgy were present. For the Ch'i-chia culture had both sufficiently high-firing pottery kilns and a long familiarity with and hence curiosity about green and blue stones. Our existing knowledge would suggest that once the nature of metal was known, the late predynastic Shang people went on to invent a unique system of bronze casting with piece-molds, which owed much to an existing and advanced ceramic technology.

The first bronze that the Shang founders produced may have been "accidental" bronze, that is, bronze with less than 3 percent tin, for it is not unusual for copper ores to be associated with small amounts of tin. The advantages of even accidental bronze, writes a modern expert, "would soon have been noticed; it would have been seen that, compared with the usual soft red copper which could be forged when cold, the new metal was of a more yellow color and gave out a different sound when hammered; it was also much

---

[82] Karl Jettmar, "The Altai Before the Turks," *BMFEA,* No. 23 (1951), pp. 142–143.

[83] *Ibid.,* p. 142.

harder."[84] The fact that chemical analyses of some attested late-Shang bronzes show less than 2 percent tin reflected the coexistence for centuries of accidental and better-quality bronze.[85]

On the other hand, one cannot rule out the possibility that, shortly before the dynastic period, the Shang people may have already discovered bronze through experiments. As a leading authority on Shang artifacts has observed, one of the characteristics of the Shang people in the realm of technology was their insatiable curiosity about things novel.[86] *The Book of Documents* has preserved a saying of a pre-1300 B.C. Shang statesman, Ch'ih Jen 遲任: "In men one seeks such of old standing; in utensils one does not seek old ones, but new."[87] After having obtained the knowledge that metal exists in bluish and greenish stones which are much heavier than ordinary stones, their curiosity would drive them on to a series of tests and experiments with cassisterite, the source of tin, which, if its shining dark color is not quite as appealing esthetically as those of the oxide and carbonate ores of copper, is even more conspicuous by virtue of its exceptional heaviness. Besides, the Shang royal government certainly well understood the importance of bronze and was able to mobilize labor and skill on a large scale for sustained development of bronze metallurgy. In retrospect, it was the piece-mold casting in pottery that led to the system of piece-mold bronze casting, and it was the long tradition of bronze casting that from the sixth century B.C. onward provided the basis

---

[84] Coghlan, *Notes on the Prehistoric Metallurgy of Copper and Bronze in the Old World*, p. 24.

[85] Barnard, *Bronze Casting and Bronze Alloys in Ancient China*, the consolidated table 13, facing p. 193.

[86] Li Chi, "An-yang tsui-chin fa-chüeh pao-kao chi liu-tz'u kung-tso chih tsung-ku-chi" [Report on and Appraisal of the Recent Six Excavations at An-yang], *An-yang fa-chüeh pao-kao*, No. 4 (1933), esp. pp. 576–577; and the reaffirmation of his early impression in his *The Beginnings of Chinese Civilization* (Seattle, 1957), pp. 20–38.

[87] Bernhard Karlgren, tr., *The Book of Documents*, p. 21.

for the rise of a cast-iron metallurgy—a system unique to the Old World and which antedated European cast iron by nearly two thousand years.

The aggregate evidence on early metallurgy within and outside China leads us to the conclusion that the primitive copper metallurgy of the loess highlands of China was of autochthonous local origins; and that the Shang bronze metallurgy, which by all technological criteria must be regarded as an indigenous development, owed its initial knowledge of metal to the loess highlands. While the total lack of evidence of foreign influence on Chinese metallurgy during its formative stage is significant, the indigenousness of Chinese metallurgy is established mainly by a large amount of internal evidence. Our conclusion implies the likelihood that metallurgy originated in several places in the Old World. The validity of this implication seems to have been reinforced by important recent research, based on ample carbon-14 dates and careful stratigraphic sequences, which indicates the high probability of the independent invention of metallurgy also in the Balkans.[88]

[88] Colin Renfrew, "The Autonomy of the South-east European Copper Age," *Proceedings of the Prehistoric Society for 1969* (New Series, XXXV), pp. 12–47.

VI
Numerals, Ordinals, Script, Language

ONE OF the most important recent archaeological finds in China was the discovery at the Yang-shao cultural site of Pan-p'o of one hundred and thirteen pieces of potsherds which bore incised marks of twenty-two different forms (see Figure 26). By comparing these marks with oracle-bone writing and the writing on pre-Chou and Chou pottery, I have become convinced that five of these marks are basic numerals 1, 2, 5, 7, and 8, and that three more are likely to have been archetypal Chinese logographs.[1] Should my identification of the numerals prove to be correct, the beginnings of the Chinese script would have to be pushed back to the fifth millennium B.C. Since the earliest Sumerian cuneiform script dates back to 3100 B.C. or, at most, to 3200 B.C.,[2] the numerals on the Pan-p'o potsherds would have to be regarded as the earliest ever created by man. The extreme antiquity of the Pan-p'o numerals and some archetypal Chinese logographs argue strongly against the possibility of diffusion or stimulus diffusion.

---

[1] See Table 9 and the text immediately following it.

[2] The earliest mature Sumerian cuneiform script is believed to date back to about 3100 B.C. See Ignace J. Gelb, *A Study of Writing* (Chicago, 1963), pp. 60–62; and A. Leo Oppenheim, *Ancient Mesopotamia: Portrait of a Dead Civilization* (Chicago, 1964), pp. 228–249. Glyn Daniel, *The First Civilizations: The Archaeology of Their Origins* (New York, 1968), in illustration 4, shows a small pillow-shaped limestone tablet from Kish, which contains pictograms representing signs for a head, a foot and hand, a threshing sledge and numerals. The tablet is said to date around 3500 B.C., but most orientalists believe that this tablet can probably be dated only about 3200 B.C.

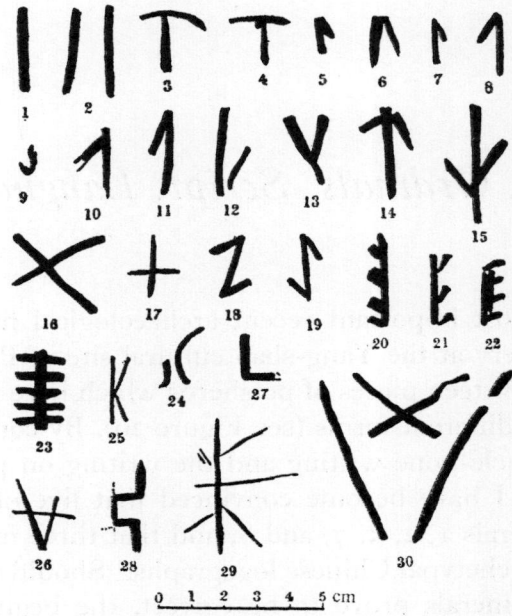

FIGURE 26. Word-signs on Pan-p'o potsherds. From *Hsi-an Pan-p'o*, Figure 141 on p. 197; see also Plates 169–171.

The group of sherds bearing word-signs was found during five consecutive excavations at Pan-p'o carried out by the Institute of Archaeology of Academia Sinica, Peking, between the autumn of 1954 and the summer of 1957, although detailed information was not made available until after the publication of the Pan-p'o site report in 1963.[3] From this site report we learned that the word-signs were invariably incised on the outer rims of the *po* type of bowls, one of the most commonly used vessels in Yang-shao times. The marks were incised on the bowls either before or after firing. Some of the twenty-two word-signs are no doubt potters' marks; but some seem to have served to identify the ownership by clan, families, or individuals. The fact that most of the seventy-two

---

[3] *Hsi-an Pan-p'o*, pp. 196–198; and Plates 169–171.

pieces of potsherds bearing the simplest sign | were unearthed from an area of less than one hundred square meters does seem to relate this particular word-sign to one specific zone of Pan-p'o. If the literary usage of the oracle texts of the post-1300 B.C. period is a reliable guide for interpreting the Pan-p'o word-signs, the sign could mean the first numeral 1 as well as the ordinal "first."

This custom of incising word-signs on pottery does not seem to have been confined to the village of Pan-p'o in Yang-shao times. Potsherds bearing similar signs, sometimes in slightly variant forms, have been discovered at other Yang-shao cultural sites at Ling-t'ai 靈台 near Sian and at Hsin-yeh-ts'un 莘野村 in Ho-yang 邰陽 county in Shensi.[4] Since Hsin-yeh-ts'un is about 150 kilometers northeast of Pan-p'o, there must have been various groups of proto-Chinese in the Wei River basin who, after 5000 B.C., had reached such a stage of cultural development as to feel the need for creating a system of primitive script.

It is well known that in some prehistoric sites outside China simple linear and geometric signs have frequently been found on objects of daily use, such as pots, utensils, weapons, bones, blocks of stone, etc., and that their use extends from the post-Paleolithic period down to modern times.[5] Our task is, therefore, to decipher some of these Pan-p'o signs and to prove that they are part of the earliest Chinese script.

The data available for deciphering the Pan-p'o word-signs are much more limited than those for deciphering other major ancient scripts of the Old World. It has been the good fortune of Western paleographers and epigraphers that of the thousands of cuneiform tablets unearthed in Mesopotamia a considerable number contain multilingual texts. Thus the Sumerian cuneiform script was deciphered through parallel Akkadian texts, which in turn were deciphered through parallel Old Persian texts of the first millennium

---

[4] *Hsi-an Pan-p'o,* p. 198.

[5] Gelb, *A Study of Writing,* p. 37.

B.C.[6] Ancient Egyptian hieroglyphics have similarly been deciphered through the Greek. The linguistic isolation of the prehistoric and early historic Chinese was so great that even as late as 1300 B.C., when abundant oracle texts indicated that the Chinese script had reached a fairly mature stage, the Chinese were still the only literate people east of the Urals and the Indus valley. Clues for the identification of some of the Pan-p'o word-signs must be sought in the late-Shang oracle inscriptions—so far the most archaic Chinese script that has been deciphered.

About one hundred thousand late-Shang oracle bones have been unearthed and the texts of about one-half of them catalogued and reproduced. But so far only two rare groups of pre-1300 B.C. Shang potsherds have been found which bear word-signs and logographs. The fact that prehistoric and early historic Chinese potsherds rarely contain incised word-signs or logographs is not surprising, for pottery was not used as a material for keeping records. Even in the ceremonial precinct at Hsiao-t'un 小屯, An-yang, where tens of thousands of inscribed oracle bones have been found, only 82 out of a quarter of a million Shang potsherds unearthed contain some simple word-signs.[7] What does require a brief discussion is the extreme scarcity of pre-1300 B.C. samples of Chinese writing altogether—a phenomenon which seems to be accounted for by the prolonged lack of suitable and nonperishable writing materials prior to the late-Shang period.

Legends which were still current in Chou times had it that wise men of remote antiquity invented various cord-knots to record major events. Even if these legends contained grains of historical

---

[6] Samuel N. Kramer, *The Sumerians: Their History, Culture, and Character* (Chicago, 1963), ch. 1, esp. p. 6.

[7] Li Hsiao-ting, "Ts'ung chi-chung shih-ch'ien ho yu-shih-tsao-ch'i t'ao-wen ti kuan-ch'a li-ts'e Chung-kuo wen-tzu ti ch'i-yüan" [A Survey of the Origins of Chinese Writing on the Basis of Some Prehistoric and Early Pottery Inscriptions], *Nan-yang-ta-hsüeh hsüeh-pao* [Nanyang University Journal], III (1969), pp. 1–28, esp. p. 9.

truth, cords made of hemp or other natural fibers would have rotted away without leaving any trace. A more precise account of the writing materials used by the ancient Chinese is given in the *Mo-tzu* 墨子, a collection of works by the philosopher Mo Ti 墨翟 (ca. 479–381 B.C.) and his disciples. It mentions several times that ancient sage-kings had their important instructions "written on bamboo and silk, cut in metals and stones, and engraved on bronze vessels."[8] The so-called bamboo tablets, tied together through perforations near one end and thus made into a *ts'e* or volume, were actually in most cases made of wood because of the scarcity of bamboo in North China in ancient times.[9] That most ancient Chinese books and documents were written on wooden tablets is evidenced by the discovery of wooden documents of the Han and post-Han periods in the Kansu corridor, an area of extreme aridity. Without going into a detailed discussion of the types of ancient Chinese writing materials, it suffices to point out that wood, bamboo, and silk all disintegrate quickly except under unusually dry conditions. While there is strong reason to believe that the Shang Chinese had books and documents written on wooden tablets,[10] none has survived in any Shang archaeological site.

Before the rather late invention of bronze metallurgy in China, the Chinese do not seem to have had a practicable material on which to keep records. Neither animal scapulae, nor tortoise shells, nor

---

[8] Sun I-jang, *Mo-tzu chien-ku* [The Works of Mo-tzu, with Textual Emendation] (Taipei, I-wen-shu-chü ed.), p. 284; also pp. 41, 127, and 268. See also Yi-pao Mei, tr., *The Ethical and Political Works of Motse* (London, 1929), p. 147 and p. 167. The most systematic study of ancient Chinese writing materials is T. H. Tsien, *Written on Bamboo and Silk: The Beginnings of Chinese Books and Inscriptions* (Chicago, 1962).

[9] Ho Ping-ti, *Huang-t'u yü Chung-kuo nung-yeh ti ch'i-yüan*, Table 3, "Plants in The Book of Odes," esp. p. 55. For a systematic discussion of the proposition that in ancient China the so-called bamboo tablets were mostly made of wood, see Tung Tso-pin, "Chung-kuo wen-tzu ti ch'i-yüan" [The Origins of Chinese Script], *Ta-lu tsa-chih*, V, No. 10 (1952).

[10] Tung Tso-pin, "Chung-kuo wen-tzu ti ch'i-yüan," p. 29.

stones, nor metals were feasible. It is by no means coincidental that the vast number of oracle bones and shells with inscriptions so far unearthed all belong to the late-Shang period, when North China had entered well into the bronze age. The lateness of the bronze age in China also explains why inscribing on stone began belatedly in the eigth century B.C.[11] The perishability of wood, bamboo, and silk and the difficulty of inscribing on hard surfaces before China had entered into the high bronze age make it understandable why, up to the present, the fragmentary samples of Chinese writing earlier than 1300 B.C. have been found only on potsherds, and then only very rarely.

In the light of the history of other ancient civilizations of the Old World, it is most striking that the Chinese of the pre-Shang period seem never to have learned to use clay as a writing material. It was natural for the Sumerians to make clay into tablets in order to keep records with a simple wooden stylus, because clay is a raw material of virtually unlimited supply and is easy to handle. The Sumerian system of writing on clay was borrowed all over the Near East for more than two thousand years, and yet it was completely unknown to the pre-Shang and Shang Chinese. This basic fact is another reminder that cultural diffusion from the ancient Near East to the ancient Far East cannot be taken for granted and that, insofar as writing material was concerned, the ancient Chinese system seems to have been developed entirely *in situ*.

In our attempt to identify the Pan-p'o numerals and a few other word-signs we have to rely mainly on the late-Shang oracle script because it is the earliest Chinese script that has been deciphered. Some numerals incised on two rare groups of pre-1300 B.C. potsherds unearthed from the Erh-li-t'ou site near Yen-shih, western Honan, and from the Erh-li-kang site near Cheng-chou, central Honan, are used as supplementary data. A fair number of late-Shang

---

[11] Tsien, *Written on Bamboo and Silk*, pp. 64–65.

TABLE 9

EARLY CHINESE NUMERALS

A. Pan-p'o potsherds, after 5000 B.C.
B. Erh-li-t'ou potsherds, before 1500 B.C.
C. Erh-li-kang potsherds, circa. 1500–1300 B.C.
D. Hsiao-t'un potsherds, after 1300 B.C.
E. Oracle inscriptions of An-yang, 1300–1028 B.C.
F. Modern version.

Numerals	A.	B.	C.	D.	E.	F.
1	∣	∣	∣	∣	—	一
2	∥	∥	∥		=	二
3		∣∣∣	∣∣∣	∖∣∖	≡	三
4		∣∣∣∣		∣∣∣∣	≣	四
5	✕	✕	✕	✕ ✕ ✕	✕ ≡ ✕ ✕	五
6					介 ∩ 介 介	六
7	+	+	+		†	七
8	)(*	)(			)(八	八
9					⼎ ⼶ ⼶	九

* *Hsi-an Pan-p'o,* Plate 171, No. 10. The upper part of the left half of this numeral is missing, but it is obviously a curve symmetrical to the right half as reconstructed in this table.

SOURCES: (A) *Hsi-an Pan-p'o,* Plates 169–171; (B) "Ho-nan Yen-shih Erh-li-t'ou i-chih fa-chüeh chien-pao," *KK,* 1965, No. 5, p. 222; (C) *Cheng-chou Erh-li-kang* (Peking, 1959), Plate 31; (D) Li Chi, *Hsiao-t'un,* III, Part I (Academia Sinica, 1966), p. 124, Table 93, and a special appendix (pp. 129–147), in which various numerals and word-signs were identified by Li Hsiao-ting; (E) Kuo Mo-jo, *Pu-tz'u t'ung-ts'uan k'ao-shih* (Tokyo, 1933), *ts'e* 1, Plates 9–36, on numbers; and *ts'e* 2, pp. 4a–14a, explanations of plates.

characters were still unstable in style and had variant forms, and the calligraphic styles of diviners of the royal house probably represented only those used by members of the Shang elite. We therefore have to regard as auxiliary reference the different styles and forms of Chinese script used by ancient Chinese potters.

Among non-numerals, the Pan-p'o symbols ↑ and ⊤ (3 and 4 in Figure 26) resemble the character *shih* ↑ 、 ⊤ in late-Shang oracle inscriptions, meaning *religious sacrifice*.[12] While archaeological evidence indicates that the people at Pan-p'o believed in an afterlife,[13] we are not certain whether the symbols are definitely the archaic form of *shih*. The Pan-p'o symbols ↑ 、 ↑ 、 ↑ 、 ↑ (7, 8, 10, and 11 in Figure 26) are similar to some variant forms of the character *jen* ↑ 、 ↑ 、 ↑ on Chou potsherds, which means men.[14] Another Pan-p'o symbol ↯ looks very similar to one of the common forms of the radical *ts'ao* 草 (grass) in late-Shang oracle texts and in Chou bronze inscriptions, and on Chou potsherds.[15] The prevalence of variant forms in oracle inscriptions and Chou pottery writing makes it difficult to identify some of these Pan-p'o word-signs positively. But there is reason to regard them as archetypal simple Chinese logographs especially because the characters on Shang-Chou potsherds are by no means less crude than those on the Pan-p'o potsherds.

---

[12] Sun Hai-p'o, *Chia-ku-wen pien* (Taipei, 1963 photo-reproduction), ch. 1, pp. 2b–3b. Of a total of 104 samples of the character *shih*, 42 are in form ↑ , the rest in the form ⊤ .

[13] This will be discussed in chapter 7.

[14] Chin Heng-hsiang, *T'ao-wen pien* (Taipei, 1964), p. 59a.

[15] For various samples of "grass" as a radical or component of compound characters, see Sun Hai-p'o, *Chia-ku-wen pien*, ch. 1, pp. 8b–10b; Li Hsiao-ting, *Chia-ku wen-tzu chi-shih*, I, pp. 203, 211, 225, 227, 235, and 241; Li Chi, *Hsiao-t'un*, III, *T'ao-ch'i*, Part I (Academia Sinica, Taiwan, 1956), a special appendix on writing on Shang pottery by Li Hsiao-ting, pp. 139–140; Jung Keng, *Chin-wen pien* (Academia Sinica, 1938), ch. 1, pp. 13a–13b; and Chin Hsiang-heng, *T'ao-wen pien*, ch. 1, pp. 4b–5a.

Epigraphically, the five numerals of Pan-p'o potsherds should be considered to have been positively identified. The striking consistency in form, from Yang-shao to Shang times, of the five numerals in general and especially of the three purely symbolic numerals 5, 7, 8, should rule out any possibility of coincidence. A historical link is thus established between the Pan-p'o numerals and Shang oracle script.

There is yet another valuable source of epigraphic data which suggests that the Yang-shao numerals may have spread fairly widely among clans and tribes of remote antiquity. Writing in 1957, six years before the Pan-p'o numerals were made known, the leading paleographer and epigrapher T'ang Lan 唐蘭 was puzzled by a group of thirteen complex archaic characters appearing in late-Shang and early-Chou bronze inscriptions and on two pieces of inscribed oracle bones unearthed in the Sian area in the winter of 1955–56. All except one of these thirteen unusual archaic characters remain undecipherable and unpronounceable. The inscribed bones from Sian created a sensation among paleographers, because until that time oracle-bone inscribing had been generally believed to be an exclusive practice of the late-Shang court at Hsiao-t'un in An-yang, and no one had expected to find inscribed bones in Sian, the headquarters of the Chou people both before and after their conquest of Shang. The thirteen complex characters culled from various sources including the inscribed bones from Sian reveal one common characteristic: they are formed by piling up three, four, or more archaic numerals together. When these characters appear in late-Shang and early-Chou bronze inscriptions, they invariably stand at the very end of the texts, a position which T'ang Lan believes to indicate that they were insignias of clans or tribes of remote antiquity living mostly in the Wei River basin before Shang-Chou times. T'ang's identification of one of them, 烎, as Wei 隗, a tribe of remote antiquity, would seem to substantiate his view. In his opinion, these characters look so outlandishly archaic, even compared with Shang-Chou script, that they may represent a "lost script" which was definitely older than the Shang-Chou.[16] Since the publication of the Pan-p'o site report, one can, however, be reasonably sure that this so-called lost script was in fact a peculiar form evolved from the Pan-p'o numerals.

Our knowledge about the Pan-p'o word-signs and symbols is secure only insofar as the five numerals, 1, 2, 5, 7, and 8, are concerned. The discovery of these five numerals strongly suggests the existence in Yang-shao times of all the basic numerals from 1 to 9, inscriptions on potsherds being a poor reflection of total vocabulary. Fragmentary as the existing information is, we are indeed fortunate that the available data concern numerals, for "among vocabulary items that can be used in establishing the membership of languages in a family the numerals have always been rated high."[17] An analysis of the Pan-p'o numerals and their comparison with those of other major ancient scripts should therefore be of considerable help in determining whether the Chinese numerals and script are of indigenous origins.

It is true that, in spite of the difference in form, the basic concepts underlying the composition of the numerals from 1 to 4 in the ancient Chinese, Sumeria, Egyptian, and Maya scripts are all iconic. But from the numeral 5 on to 9, the conceptual similarities

---

[16] T'ang Lan, "Ts'ung chia-ku chin-wen chung so-chien ti i-chung i-ching i-shih ti Chung-kuo ku-tai wen-tzu" [A Lost Ancient Chinese Script as Seen from Oracle and Bronze Inscriptions], *KKHP*, 1957, No. 2, pp. 33–36. Similar strange compound characters have been discovered from oracle bones of the An-yang area; see Kuo Pao-chün, "I-chiu-wu-ling-nien ch'un Yin-hsü fa-chüeh pao-kao" [Report on Excavations in An-yang in the Spring of 1950], *Chung-kuo k'ao-ku hsüeh-pao*, V, No. 1–2 (December 1951), p. 56, Plate 41. For similar finds made outside of An-yang and especially from the Sian area, see Li Hsüeh-ch'in, "T'an An-yang Hsiao-t'un i-wai ch'u-t'u ti yu-tzu chia-ku" [On Some Inscribed Oracle Bones Unearthed Outside of the An-yang Area], *WWTKTL*, 1956, No. 11, pp. 16–17; and "Ch'ang-an Chang-chia-p'o-ts'un Hsi-Chou i-chih ti chung-yao fa-hsien" [Important Finds from the Western Chou Site at Chang-chia-p'o-ts'un, Ch'ang-an], *WWTKTL*, 1956, No. 3, plate on p. 40 and text on p. 58.

[17] Murray B. Emeneau, "Numerals in Comparative Linguistics, with Special Reference to Dravidian," *BIHP*, XXIX, Part I (1957), p. 1.

end. Whereas in the Sumerian, Babylonian, Egyptian, and Maya scripts the numerals from 5 upward remain iconic and additive, the Pan-p'o numerals become strictly symbolic and nonadditive.[18] The level of mental abstraction of the Yang-shao Chinese, as revealed by their higher-digit numerals accidentally preserved on potsherds, is truly impressive.

The indigenous origins of Chinese numerals and script can be further studied from the standpoint of mathematical notation. Since the Pan-p'o data is too fragmentary, this discussion has to be based on late-Shang oracle texts. The only noticeable modifications of the Pan-p'o numerals by the late-Shang Chinese are that the numerals from 1 to 4 were normally written horizontally, although in oracle texts they still occasionally stand upright. Generally speaking, by late-Shang times the vertical strokes represented 10, 20, etc., instead of 1, 2, etc. (see Table 10).

Two observations should be made about the archaic Chinese mathematical notations. First, by 1300 B.C. at the latest, the Chinese had developed a place-value principle which is almost as economical and sophisticated as the modern place-value system used the world over. Instead of expressing 114 in the clumsy Roman way, CXIV, which means 100 plus 10 plus 5 and minus 1, the Shang Chinese would simply write down three digits ⊘ | ≡. Because of the place-value indicator ⊘, which means 100, the horizontal stroke ▬ in the first numeral represents 100; and the second and third numerals are respectively 10 and 4 because of their positions. Thus in the ancient Chinese system the magnitude of a numeral is determined by its digital position, just as it is in the worldwide system today,

---

[18] The earliest Sumerian numerals from 1 to 9 are represented by 1 to 9 ᴅ signs; the early Babylonian numerals by 1 to 9 Υ signs; and the ancient Egyptian numerals by 1 to 9 ❘ signs. The Maya numerals are a combination of simple icons with a special symbol for 5; thus numerals from 1 to 4 are represented by 1 to 4 round ● or small circles ○, 5 by a horizontal bar ▬ or ⊂⊃, and 9 by ⁰⁰⁰⁰. See A. Falkenstein, *Archaische Texte aus Uruk* (Berlin, 1936), "Zahlzeichen," pp. 212-214; and Florian Cajori, *A History of Mathematical Notations*, 2 Vols. (Chicago, 1928), I, pp. 1-18 and 43.

TABLE 10
NOTATIONS FOR NUMERALS HIGHER THAN 10 IN SHANG ORACLE INSCRIPTIONS

Numeral	Oracle-bone notation	Numeral	Oracle-bone notation
10		114	
11		148	
13		162	
15*		500	
20		1000	
30		2000	
40		2656	
50		4000	
60		5000	
88		10000	
100			

* In Joseph Needham, *Science and Civilization in China*, III: *Mathematics and the Sciences of the Heavens and the Earth* (Cambridge, Eng., 1959), p. 14, there is a similar table on Chinese mathematical notations, which is excellent except that the notation for 15, prepared by Wu Ch'i-ch'ang, is wrong.

SOURCES: Kuo Mo-jo, *Pu-tz'u t'ung-ts'uan k'ao-shih,* Plates 16–34; Tung Tso-pin, *Yin-hsü wen-tzu chia-pien* (Academia Sinica, 1948), Plates 153, 397, 635, 960, 1077; Tung Tso-pin, *Yin-hsü wen-tzu i-pien* (Academia Sinica, 1949), Plate 2688; Shang Ch'eng-tso, *Yin-ch'i i-ts'un* (Nanking, 1933), Plate 428; Sun Hai-p'o, *Chia-ku-wen lu* (K'ai-feng, 1937), Plate 456.

except for the need of place-value components, which are, however, not themselves numerals. Joseph Needham has compared the ancient Chinese and the ancient Western place-value systems:

The Old Babylonian system, however, was mainly additive or cumulative below 200, like the later Roman; and both employed subtractive devices, writing 19 as 20–1 and 40 as 50–10. But the multiplication process was also introduced, e.g. 10 × 100 representing 1000. Only in the sexagesimal notation of the astronomers, where the principle of place-value applied, was there better consistency, though even then special signs were used for such numbers as 3600, and the subtractive element was not excluded. Moreover, numbers less than 60 were expressed by "piled-up" signs. The ancient Egyptians followed a cumulative system, with some multiplicative usages. It seems therefore that the Shang Chinese were the first to be able to express any desired number, however large, with no more than 9 numerals. The subtractive principle of forming numerals was never used by them.

It is Needham's overall impression "that the Shang numeral system was more advanced and scientific than the contemporary scripts of Old Balylonia and Egypt."[19]

Second, the ancient Chinese numeration was always strictly decimal. Here it was very different from the Sumerian and Babylonian system, which was mainly sexagesimal, though not unmixed with the decimal system. As will be discussed later in this chapter, the ancient Chinese did develop a peculiarly Sinitic sexagenary cycle, but it served only as a system of day-count. The germinal mathematical sophistication based on the Sumerian and Babylonian sexagesimal system was entirely absent in ancient China.

Because of the extreme scarcity of archaeological data on the Chinese written script before 1300 B.C., it is impossible systematically to trace the evolution of the Chinese script from its first appearance in Yang-shao times to its first verified maturation in the late-Shang period. The only major aspect of the evolution of the Chinese script up to 1300 B.C. that one can legitimately trace is the development of the uniquely Sinitic system of ordinal numbers, which by late Shang times was extensively used for a number of purposes.

Indeed, there is a possibility that the basic numerals on Pan-p'o potsherds were used by the Yang-shao people as ordinal numbers. It was pointed out earlier in this chapter that some of the Pan-p'o numerals were related to specific zones of the 250 burials excavated. Our conjecture is not entirely groundless because,

---

[19] Joseph Needham, *Science and Civilization in China*, III, *Mathematics and the Sciences of the Heavens and the Earth* (Cambridge, Eng., 1959), pp. 13–14.

judging from their usage in oracle texts, numerals served both as cardinal and as ordinal numbers. A few examples will suffice. The two characters *i-yüeh* 一月, when translated separately, mean "one" and "month," but the phrase definitely means the "first (lunar) month." The phrase *wang-pa-ssu* 王八祀, consisting of characters which mean respectively "king," "eight," and "sacrificial cycle," means "the king's eighth sacrificial cycle." Since the king in late-Shang times usually counted the year by the longest sacrificial cycle of 360 days, the phrase actually means during "the eighth year of the king's reign." Still another similar usage is found in the system by which late-Shang kings differentiated their ancestors of different generations who were worshiped on days expressed by the same ordinal number in the ten-day cycle called *hsün* 旬. Tsu-Ting 祖丁 (Ancestor Ting), for example, was posthumously so called because he was to be worshiped on the fourth day of a certain ten-day cycle and this particular day was designated *ting*. In the course of time other deceased kings were also worshiped on days designated *ting*, and they were differentiated from Tsu-Ting by prefixes. Although in such titles as "San-Tsu-Ting" and "Ssu-Tsu-Ting" the *san* and *ssu* are literally "three" and "four," the titles as a whole mean the "Third Ancestor Ting" and the "Fourth Ancestor Ting."[20] The use of cardinal numbers as ordinals in a variety of ways has been a peculiar characteristic of the written and spoken Chinese language since at least late-Shang times.

Our main concern here, however, is to trace the origin of two sets of ordinal numbers which are uniquely Chinese. They are given in Table 11 for reference of nonsinologist readers.

In Shang times there were no generic terms for these two series of ordinals. From Han times onward the twelve ordinals of series B began to be used to express the twelve months. By Later Han times the ten characters of series A were called "celestial stems" and the

---

[20] All the above examples of using numerals as ordinals in Shang oracle texts are taken from Shima Kunio, *Inkyo bokuji sōrui* (Tokyo, 1967).

TABLE 11
ANCIENT CHINESE ORDINALS

	Series A			Series B	
1.	chia	甲		tzu	子
2.	i	乙		ch'ou	丑
3.	ping	丙		yin	寅
4.	ting	丁		mao	卯
5.	mou	戊	(modern pronunciation wu)	ch'en	辰
6.	chi	己		ssu	巳
7.	keng	庚		wu	午
8.	hsin	辛		wei	未
9.	jen	壬		shen	申
10.	kuei	癸		yu	酉
11.				hsü	戌
12.				hai	亥

twelve characters of series B "earthly branches." Because of the new generic terms, and especially since these twenty-two characters later became the fundamental symbols of astrological and horoscopic systems, they acquired a certain mystique. What complicates the problem even more is that the written symbols for these twenty-two "ordinals" do not indicate that they had anything to do with numerals; the characters themselves do not convey such meanings as "first," "second," etc. Their use in an ordered series would be very much like the use of *a, b, c,* etc. as ordinals. Strictly speaking, *a, b, c,* etc., cannot be called ordinals except when they serve the specific function of ordinals. Theoretically, so do these twenty-two characters. But as the late Shinjo Shinzo, the well-known Japanese historian of Chinese astronomy, pointed out, the main function of these twenty-two characters of two series was to serve as ordinals.[21]

---

[21] Shinjo Shinzo, *Tōyō temmongaku shi kenkyu* (Tokyo, 1928), pp. 649–658, esp. p. 652. Kuo Mo-jo, an important pioneering researcher on oracle script, made a

In late-Shang times these two series of ordinals were used mainly for denoting days and for forming the shorter ten-day *hsün* cycle and the longer sixty-day cycle. The system of day-count cycles is based on the following rules. First, each day is denoted by two numbers, one from each series, with the one from series A always preceding the one from series B, for example, *chia-tzu* and *i-ch'ou*. Second, all ordinals of the two series must progress sequentially. Third, there is a further restriction that odd numbers of series A can only be combined with odd numbers of series B and that even numbers of series A can only be combined with even numbers of series B. Because of the last restriction, the total number of combinations is reduced from 120 to 60, thus forming the longer sexagenary cycle. Since series A contains ten ordinal numbers and series B contains twelve, within a sexagenary cycle series A numbers complete their progression six times and series B numbers complete their progression five times. Whenever series A numbers complete a progression, there has been a ten-day cycle called *hsün* (see Table 12).

Although the ten-day *hsün* cycle is always included in the longer sexagenary cycle, the two cycles served different purposes. The sexagenary cycle served as an automatic nonending system of day-count which had nothing to do with solar of lunar movements or with seasonal changes. The ten-day *hsün* cycle, while a part of the sexagenary cycle in the system of day-count, however, served as a subdivision of the lunar month and had an important religious significance—an aspect which will be discussed in detail in connection with the origins of these ordinal numbers.

The fact that by late-Shang times these two series of ordinal numbers were already used in such a highly systematic fashion in

---

long study of the etymology of these twenty-two ordinals in his *Chia-ku wen-tzu yen-chiu* [Studies on Oracle Inscriptions] (Shanghai, 1931), Book B, pp. 1a–93b. Much of his etymological discourse is subjective, conjectural, and hence doubtful. Bernhard Karlgren, in his "Grammata Serica: Script and Phonetics in Chinese and Sino-Japanese," *BMFEA*, No. 12 (1940), pp. 1–472, is of the opinion that the etymology of these ordinals is "uncertain."

TABLE 12

THE SEXAGENARY CYCLE OF DAY-COUNT AND THE SIX TEN-DAY SACRIFICIAL CYCLES

I–VI: The six sacrificial cycles
1–60: The never-ending sexagenary cycle of day-count

(I)
1. Chia-tzu	2. I-ch'ou	3. Ping-yin	4. Ting-mao	5. Wu-ch'en
6. Chi-ssu	7. Keng-wu	8. Hsin-wei	9. Jen-shen	10. Kuei-yu

(II)
11. Chia-hsü	12. I-hai	13. Ping-tzu	14. Ting-ch'ou	15. Wu-yin
16. Chi-mao	17. Keng-ch'en	18. Hsin-ssu	19. Jen-wu	20. Kuei-wei

(III)
21. Chia-shen	22. I-yu	23. Ping-hsü	24. Ting-hai	25. Wu-tzu
26. Chi-ch'ou	27. Keng-yin	28. Hsin-mao	29. Jen-ch'en	30. Kuei-ssu

(IV)
31. Chia-wu	32. I-wei	33. Ping-shen	34. Ting-yu	35. Wu-hsü
36. Chi-hai	37. Keng-tzu	38. Hsin-ch'ou	39. Jen-yin	40. Kuei-mao

(V)
41. Chia-ch'en	42. I-ssu	43. Ping-wu	44. Ting-wei	45. Wu-shen
46. Chi-yu	47. Keng-hsü	48. Hsin-hai	49. Jen-tzu	50. Kuei-ch'ou

(VI)
51. Chia-yin	52. I-mao	53. Ping-ch'en	54. Ting-ssu	55. Wu-wu
56. Chi-wei	57. Keng-shen	58. Hsin-yu	59. Jen-hsü	60. Kuei-hai

the day-denotation system and also in forming sacrificial cycles would itself indicate their much earlier origins. In addition, these ordinals are also known to have been used to form a part of the ceremonial names of some "kings" of the so-called Hsia "dynasty," of the ceremonial names of all the kings of the Shang dynasty, and of some of their predynastic ancestors. It is through a study of these ancient royal ceremonial names that the antiquities of these two series of ordinals can best be traced.

For the list of Hsia rulers, the two major sources of information are the *Shih-chi* by the Former Han Grand Historian Ssu-ma Ch'ien and the remnants of the *Bamboo Annals* collated from various pre-Sung works before the text was lost. For the list of Shang kings the sources of information are much more abundant, because aside from the *Shih-chi* and the *Bamboo Annals* there are tens of thousands of oracle bones. Prior to the systematic research on oracle bones undertaken by twentieth-century scholars, much of the history of the Shang period preserved in the *Shih-chi* and other ancient literary works, including the list of Shang kings, was regarded by some hypercritical Chinese historians and paleographers as myths and legends. But two generations of intensive research on Shang oracle texts have proved that the names and sequence of Shang kings given in the *Shih-chi* are essentially correct.[22] The verification of the *Shih-chi*'s list of Shang kings by oracle texts should serve as a reminder that its list of seventeen Hsia rulers may not be summarily dismissed either. The latter list is confirmed by the collated text of *Bamboo Annals,* a source which was unknown to the author of the *Shih-chi*. The *Annals* further mentions that altogether the seventeen Hsia rulers reigned for 471 years, thus averaging 27.8 years per reign.[23] The historicity of the Hsia period will be discussed in chapter 7.

Of the seventeen Hsia rulers given in the *Shih-chi* and the *Bamboo Annals,* the ones included in Table 13 are relevant to our study of the origins and evolution of the two series of ordinal numbers.

---

[22] The modern literature on the names and sequence of Shang kings in the light of oracle texts is considerable. For an excellent summary of modern scholarship on the subject, see Cheng Te-k'un, *Archaeology in China,* II, *Shang China* (Cambridge, Eng., 1960), pp. 218–223.

[23] The restored text of remnants of this ancient work used in the present study is Fan Hsiang-jung, *Ku-pen Chu-shu-chi-nien chi-chiao ting-pu* (Shanghai, 1956), pp. 8–17.

TABLE 13

HSIA RULERS WITH ORDINALS FOR CEREMONIAL NAMES

Sequence in the list	Personal name	Ceremonial name
3d		T'ai-k'ang 太康
4th		Chung-k'ang 仲康
6th		Shao-k'ang 少康
13th	Chin 厪	Yin-chia 胤甲
14th		K'ung-chia 孔甲
17th	Chieh 桀	Lü-kuei 履癸

SOURCES: *Shih-chi*, ch. 2; and Fan Hsiang-jung, *Ku-pen Chu-shu-chi-nien chi-chiao ting-pu*, pp. 8–17.

Chia and *kuei*, as shown in Table 11, are the first and last of the ten ordinals of series A. According to the Han lexicon *Shuo-wen chieh-tzu*, the archaic pronunciation of *keng*, the seventh ordinal of series A, is *k'ang*. Based on archaic pronunciations, on the rhyming system, and also on the archaic forms of the characters *keng* and *k'ang*, a modern study has convincingly shown that these two characters were actually synonyms in ancient times and that the ceremonial names of the third, fourth, and sixth Hsia rulers should therefore be T'ai-keng, Chung-keng, and Shao-keng, which are all based on the seventh ordinal of series A but differentiated from one another by such prefixes as "T'ai" (Great or Elder), "Chung" (Second), and "Shao" (Junior).[24]

More is known about the practice of using ordinals as ceremonial names of the Shang kings and their predynastic ancestors.

---

[24] Yang Chün-shih, "K'ang keng yü Hsia-hui" [On the Characters K'ang and Keng and the Practice of Royal-Name Taboo in Hsia Times], *Ta-lu tsa-chih*, XX (March 1967). It is to be noted that Ch'en Meng-chia, a paleographer in Mainland China, arrived at the same conclusion, though without a systematic discussion. See his *Yin-hsü pu-tz'u tsung-shu* (Peking, 1956), p. 405.

Cumulative research on oracle texts has enabled us to learn the following. First, the ceremonial name of a Shang king does not seem to have had much to do with the date of his birth or death; it merely signified the day in a specific sacrificial cycle on which he was to be worshiped. It was the custom of Shang kings to offer sacrifice not only to their direct ancestors and their legal wives and deceased elder brothers but also to their close collateral seniors, such as deceased uncles and grand-uncles. The sequence of worship had to be determined by generational differences and by the order of seniority within a specific generation. A ceremonial name was therefore mainly a way of finding a berth for a newly deceased king in the normally crowded sacrificial system. It thus differed both from the personal name which a king used during his lifetime and from the canonized titles of emperors of the later imperial age. Since oracle bones were mainly concerned with divination and religious affairs, most oracle texts mention only the ceremonial names of Shang kings. It is only in the various Chou literary works that the personal names of sixteen of the thirty-one Shang kings of the dynastic period have been preserved.[25]

Second, whereas the ceremonial name of each of the thirty-one Shang kings of the dynastic period invariably contains a series A ordinal, the ordinals in those ceremonial names do not follow a sequential progression as they do in forming the sexagenary cycle of day-count. Of the thirty-one ceremonial names, one contains the first ordinal *chia,* five the second ordinal *i,* one the third ordinal *ping,* seven the fourth ordinal *ting,* one the fifth ordinal *mou,* one the sixth ordinal *chi,* four the seventh ordinal *keng,* four the eighth ordinal *hsin,* two the ninth ordinal *jen,* and none contains the tenth and last ordinal *kuei.* The uneven distribution of ordinals among these ceremonial names was accounted for by the progressive elimination of the kings' collateral seniors from the network of

---

[25] For a systematic evaluation of cumulative research on the subject, see Ch'en Meng-chia, *Yin-hsü pu-tz'u tsung-shu,* ch. 12.

worship. Although at any given time during the dynastic period some royal collateral seniors were always included in the network, the emphasis of the worship system was on those who had actually been enthroned as kings. In the course of time, a large number of collateral seniors who had once been worshiped were dropped from the network of ancestor worship. A concrete example will illustrate this complex system at work. Wu-ting 武丁, the twenty-second king of the eleventh generation since the beginning of the dynasty, worshiped twelve members of his father's generation; in other words, during Wu-ting's lifetime his deceased uncles received the same treatment as his father, who had actually served as king. The ceremonial names of the first ten of the twelve take up all the ten ordinals of series A, with the names of the last two repeating the first two ordinals *chia* and *i*. Members of this crowded generation had to be accommodated in two short sacrificial cycles of ten days each. By the time of king Ling-hsin 廩辛, Wu-ting's grandson, only three of the original twelve remained within the sacrificial network.[26]

Third, oracle texts reveal that the last six predynastic ancestors already had ceremonial names made up of series A ordinals. At first glance, this fact might seem to indicate the use of series A ordinals for ceremonial names before the founding of the Shang dynasty. But a close scrutiny of these six ordinals reveals a peculiar feature. Wang Kuo-wei (1877–1927), a leading sinologist and an important pioneering researcher of oracle texts, first noticed that these six predynastic ceremonial names contain respectively the ordinals *chia, i, ping, ting, jen,* and *kuei*—a shortened cycle of sequential progression. Wang thereupon concluded that the six names must have been arbitrarily and belatedly made by the dynastic founder, Ta-i 大乙, commonly known in Chinese historical texts as T'ang 唐、湯.[27] The evidence would suggest that the use of ordinals of series A for royal ceremonial names did not go beyond the founding

[26] *Ibid.,* pp. 404–405.
[27] Wang Kuo-wei, *Kuan-t'ang chi-lin* (Taipei, I-wen-shu-chü photostat reprint), ch. 9, pp. 8b–11a.

of the dynasty some time around 1600 B.C. and that these ordinals must have come into being considerably earlier.

Fourth, by far the firmest evidence of the antiquity of the ordinal numbers of series A and B is found in the case of Hai, the name of a very remote ancestor of the founder of the Shang dynasty, which was first identified by Wang Kuo-wei.[28] It should be noted, however, that Hai was not a ceremonial name but was the personal name of an important leader of the Shang tribe long before the Shang became a dominant power in North China. The special significance of this personal name is that *hai* is the twelfth and last of the ordinals of series B. Although oracle texts seldom mention any predynastic ancestor beyond the sixth generation ascendant of the dynastic founder, they refer to Hai altogether nine times. In oracle texts the personal name of Hai is usually associated with the epithet *Wang* 王, which literally means "king" because of later exaltation, or with the epithet *kao-tsu* 高祖, which literally means "great-great-grandfather" but in the contexts of the oracle script means a very remote illustrious ancestor. All this reflects the very special position held by Hai among the predynastic forebears of Shang kings. What is equally significant is that bits of information about Hai preserved in various Chou literary works all indicate that he was the leader of the predynastic Shang tribe who first successfully domesticated sheep and cattle. In other words, he was portrayed not as a legendary demigod but as a real historical personage who had made important contributions to the welfare of the early Shang tribe.[29]

---

[28] *Ibid.*, ch. 9, pp. 4a–6b.

[29] The most detailed study of Hai after Wang Kuo-wei is Ch'en Meng-chia, *Yin-hsü pu-tz'u tsung-shu,* pp. 338–340. Ch'en is probably right in suggesting that Hai may well be the earliest ancestor within the memories of later Shang kings. He points out that it was never the custom of Shang leaders, either before the founding of the Shang dynasty or later, to use ordinal numbers of series B to form ceremonial names. But Hai is in no way a ceremonial name; it is obviously a personal name given him during his lifetime. He is too remote from the founder of the Shang dynasty to have been given a ceremonial name posthumously.

To sum up, it may be said that series A ordinals were probably used by some Hsia rulers to form ceremonial names; that they were invariably used for the same purpose but with more complex religious connotations in the Shang dynasty since its inception; and that the use of the last ordinal of series B as the personal name by a very remote predynastic ancestor of Shang—which has been archaeologically proved beyond doubt—indicates that the two series of ordinals must have been invented at least a few centuries before the beginning of the Shang dynasty. The fact that, chronologically, Hai falls definitely into the Hsia period indicates that the use of series A ordinals as the ceremonial names of some Hsia rulers described in the *Shih-chi* and the *Bamboo Annals* must have been based on reliable old oral traditions.

From the above discussion of the early history of Chinese ordinals, one may make the following observations. First, the early history of Chinese ordinals suggests that the task of creating a Chinese script, begun by the Yang-shao people at Pan-p'o and other localities in the Wei River valley during the fifth millennium B.C., was carried on in North China by men of genius from more than one ancient tribe during the subsequent three thousand years. Second, the mature script of late-Shang times was certainly evolved from an earlier script, even though archaeological samples of Chinese script before 1300 B.C. are extremely scarce, fragmentary, and mainly confined to basic numerals. Third, the archaic Chinese ordinal-number system has no counterpart in any known major script, ancient or modern. The Sumerian ordinals, the earliest of the Western world, are formed by basic numerals and a special sign pronounced *kam* 𒄬. For example, when the *kam* sign is added to the lower right side of the sign for 1, the compound sign D𒄬 means the ordinal "first."[30] The ancient Chinese ordinals are truly

---

[30] I am grateful to my colleague, Professor A. Leo Oppenheim of the Oriental Institute of the University of Chicago, for this information on the Sumerian ordinal-number system.

unique, for no other civilization has ever developed similarly elaborate sets of ordinals which were used for so many special purposes. Chinese ordinals, like Chinese numerals, reflect their indigenous origins.

To study other aspects of the ancient Chinese script, one has to rely entirely on the post-1300 B.C. oracle inscriptions. Certainly the late-Shang script does not represent Chinese script at its beginning stage. But it does provide the earliest available samples for a comparison with certain basic words in the Sumerian cuneiform script and for an analysis of fundamental Chinese logographic principles. To be sure, no student of philology or history would claim that the comparison of a limited number of words of these two ancient scripts could lead to the firm conclusion that they definitely were—or were not—independently invented, although linguistically, it seems, the agglutinative Sumerian tongue cannot possibly have been related to the monosyllabic Chinese language.[31] The purpose of comparing some basic words of these two ancient scripts is to demonstrate how, despite the similarity of certain simple logographic principles of different groups of early men, their differing cultural traditions made even common words vastly different in form, concept, and context. Such a comparison of basic Sumerian and Chinese words will serve as a useful introduction to a more systematic analysis of archaic Chinese principles of word composition. The eighteen Sumerian words to be used were not chosen at random but were selected by the well-known Sumerologist, Samuel N. Kramer, as truly representative ones.

No. 1 in Sumerian is a picture of a star, which means either heaven or god. In Shang oracle texts heaven and god are two different characters. The character for heaven is represented by a horizontal stroke or rectangle over the head of a grown-up man, suggesting that heaven is high above man. The character for god is

---

[31] Samuel N. Kramer, *The Sumerians*, p. 306.

TABLE 14

A Comparison of Sumerian Words with Chinese Oracle-Bone Characters

	Sumerian	Shang oracle inscription	Modern Chinese
1. a. heaven	an	t'ien	天
b. god	dingir	ti	帝
2. earth	ki	t'u	土
3. man	lu	jen	人
4. woman	munus	nü	女
5. mountain	kur	shan	山
6. slave-girl	geme	pei	婢
7. head	sag	shou	首
8. a. mouth	ka	k'ou	口
b. speak	dug	yüeh	曰
9. food	ninda	shih	食
		ssu	飤
10. eat	ku	shih (same as in no. 9)	食
		hsiang	饗
11. water	a	shui	水
12. drink	nag	yin	飲
13. a. to go	du	chih	之
		wang	往
b. to stand	gub	li	立
14. bird	mushen	chui	佳
		niao	鳥

TABLE 14—cont'd

	Sumerian		Shang oracle inscription		Modern Chinese
15. fish	ha		yü		魚
16. ox	gud		mou		牡
17. cow	ab		p'in		牝
18. barley	she		mou*		牟、麰
wheat**			lai		來
			mai		麥

* The character for "barley" is missing in both Shang oracle texts and the Chou bronze inscriptions.

** The Sumerian word *"she"* may also mean grains including wheat; hence I have added two late-Shang characters for wheat for further comparison.

SOURCES: The eighteen Sumerian words are given in S. N. Kramer, *The Sumerians*, pp. 302–306. The oracle-bone characters are taken from Li Hsiao-ting, *Chia-ku wen-tzu chi-shih* (Academia Sinica, 1955), 16 vols.

believed to have been derived from a homonym *ti* 蒂, which is a picture of a calyx of a plant, symbolizing the source of plant food for the sustenance of man. The Chinese character for god, though itself a picture, is a case of phonetic borrowing.

No. 2 in Sumerian is the word for earth, "although the interpretation of the sign is still uncertain." In Shang oracle texts the character is represented by an earth mound and suggests the worship of the spirit of earth.

No. 3 in Sumerian is a "stylized picture of the upper part of a man's body." In Shang oracle texts it is represented by a much more simplified picture of a man.

No. 4 in Sumerian is "a picture of the pudendum. It represents the word *sal*, 'pudendum.' The same sign is used to represent the word *munus,* 'woman.' " In archaic Chinese it is represented by a simplified picture of a human figure, which, because it is squatting and at work, means woman.

No. 5 in either Sumerian or Chinese is a picture of a mountain, though different in style.

No. 6 in Sumerian "illustrates the ingenious device developed early by the inventors of the Sumerian system of writing whereby they could represent pictorially words for which the ordinary pictographic representation entailed a certain amount of difficulty. The sign for the word *geme,* 'slave girl,' is actually a combination of two signs—that for *munus,* 'woman,' and that for *kur,* 'mountain.' Literally, therefore, this compound sign expresses the idea 'mountain-woman.' But since the Sumerians obtained their slave girls largely from the mountainous regions about them, this compound sign adequately represented the Sumerian word for 'slave girl,' *geme.*" There are a number of archaic Chinese characters for woman of lowly status, which all contain the radical for woman. The nearest to the Sumerian word for slave girl is the character *pei,* the left half of which is the radical for woman and the right half is the homonym *pei* 卑, which means lowly. Oracle texts mention that *pei* and other categories of women of lowly status were sometimes used as human victims.

No. 7 in Sumerian is the word for head, represented by a stylized human head; while the Chinese character is represented by an animal head.

No. 8 in Sumerian "is also a head. The vertical strokes indicate the particular part of the head which is intended—that is, the mouth. The sign therefore represents the Sumerian word *ka,* 'mouth.' The same sign represents the word *dug,* 'to speak.' " In archaic Chinese the words for mouth and speak are two characters. *K'ou* is a conventionalized picture of the mouth and *yüeh* consists of a symbol for mouth with an additional horizontal stroke above it, symbolizing the use of lips.

No. 9 in Sumerian "is probably a picture of a bowl used primarily as a food container." There are several characters in archaic Chinese which mean food and special kinds of food. The word *shih,* which means food in general, is indicated by food placed above a pottery or bronze container. The character *ssu,* which means grain food or solid food, is indicated by a food container but also by a simplified symbol of a man bending over it. It thus means food for human beings.

No. 10 in Sumerian "is a compound sign consisting of the signs for mouth and food. It represents the word *ku,* 'to eat.' " In archaic Chinese there are several characters which mean to eat or to eat in some specific ways. The most common character is *shih,* which can be either a verb or a noun. The character *hsiang* consists of a simplified food container in the middle and two symmetrical simplified symbols for man at each side. It thus means to offer food to some one or for two or more persons to eat together.

No. 11, the word for water, is a picture of currents in both Sumerian and Chinese, though stylistically different.

No. 12 in Sumerian "is a combination of the signs for 'mouth' and 'water.' It represents the word *nag,* 'to drink.' " In archaic Chinese the character *yin* is originally probably pictographic, with the left half representing a wine vessel and the right half representing an armored man arching over the vessel.

No. 13 in Sumerian "is a picture of the lower part of the leg and foot in a walking position. It represents the word *du,* 'to go,' and also the word *gub,* 'to stand.' " In archaic Chinese there are two characters for the verb "to go." The first is *chih,* a symbol of a branch that outgrows, or seems to break away from, the rest of the plant. The second is *wang,* which is derived from *chih.* The simpler form of *wang* consists of the character *chih,* below which is added the symbol of a pair of legs. The complex form further adds the character *ch'üan* 犬, a vertically drawn "dog," to the right of the simpler form of *wang.*

No. 14 in either Sumerian or the two archaic Chinese characters is a picture of a bird, except that the first Chinese character *chui* stresses only the short tail of a bird.

No. 15 in either Sumerian or Chinese is a picture of a fish, though very different in style.

No. 16 in Sumerian "is a picture of the head and horns of an ox." In Chinese the left half of the character *mou* is the character *niu* 牛, "cattle," which is used as a radical; the right half symbolized the genitals of a bull. In spite of the fact that the archaic Chinese vocabulary is much smaller than that of later Chinese, archaic Chinese contains a higher percentage of characters which denote sex genders.

No. 17 in Sumerian "is a picture of the head of a cow." In archaic Chinese the character *p'in* consists of the same radical *niu*, "cattle," but either to the left or right of this radical is a symbol of the genitals of a cow.

No. 18 in Sumerian "is a picture of an ear of barley." The character for barley is missing from oracle texts and Western Chou bronze inscriptions. *Mou,* the character for barley, appears for the first time in *The Book of Odes,* which suggests that barley, being poor man's food, might have been overlooked by Shang-Chou elite centuries before the character *mou* was created. Shang oracle texts contain the character *lai,* "to come," which according to some Chinese paleographers is a simplified picture of an oncoming man, with his arms and legs stretched. Since wheat was introduced into North China from the Eurasian steppe probably during the second millennium B.C., it was at first called *lai,* meaning that it came from abroad. The majority of philologists believe, however, that the character *lai,* "to come," is derived from *lai,* "wheat." This is rather improbable. As is well known, the characters for all cereal plants, except those for wheat and barley, contain the radical *ho* 夂、禾, which indicates a cereal plant. The picture represented by the character *lai* cannot possibly have been that of a plant. From archaeological, literary, and scientific evidence one can be sure that wheat and barley are not indigenous to North China. The earliest character for wheat, *lai,* the alternate name for wheat, *mai,* and the character for barley, *mou,* all contain the radical *lai,* "to come."

After comparing these basic Sumerian and archaic Chinese words, one may make the following observations. First, although the samples are few in number, it is still significant that the pronunciations of these words in the two ancient languages yield no trace of even accidental similarity or closeness. Second, while the earliest scripts are supposed to be largely pictographic, it is obvious that archaic Chinese characters, with the exception of such pure picture-words as "water," "head," "bird," and "fish" are much less faithfully pictographic and much more calligraphic than are the signs in the Sumerian cuneiform system of writing. But even in pure picture-words, archaic Chinese characters invariably show different styles or concepts. Third, such common words as "heaven," "god," "earth," "woman," and "slave girl" reveal not only different logographic concepts but also profound differences in the environmental, cultural, and religious factors that affected the minds of those men of genius who invented the Sumerian and archaic Chinese logographs.

While it is true that in the prealphabet stage the principles by which various logographs are formed are necessarily limited to three—pictographic, ideographic, and phonetic—the Shang script combined these principles much more fully. This was because whereas the Sumerian-Akkadian script soon became fully phoneticized and alphabetized, the Chinese script has remained logographic. To understand the ingenuity with which the ancient Chinese composed various characters, a general knowledge of the Sumerian system of writing is useful as a basis for comparison. S. N. Kramer generalizes thus about the Sumerian script:

The cuneiform script began as a pictographic writing. Each sign was a picture of one or more concrete objects and represented a word whose meaning was identical with, or closely related to, the object pictured. The defects of a system of this type are twofold: the complicated forms of the signs and the great number of signs required render it too unwieldy for practical use. The Sumerian scribes overcame the first difficulty by gradually simplifying and conventionalizing the forms of the signs until their pictographic originals were no longer apparent. As for the second difficulty, they reduced the number of signs and kept them within limits by resorting to various helpful devices. The most significant device was substituting phonetic for ideographic values. . . .

No. 11 is a picture of a water stream. It represents the word *a,* "water." This sign furnishes us with an excellent illustration of the process by which the Sumerian script gradually lost its unwieldy pictographic character and became a phonetic system of writing. Although the Sumerian word *a,* represented by sign No. 11, was used primarily for "water," it also had the meaning "in." The word "in" is a word denoting relationship and stands for a concept which is difficult to express pictographically. The originators of the Sumerian script had the ingenious idea that, instead of trying to invent a complicated picture-sign to represent the world "in," they could use the sign for *a,* "water," since the words sound exactly alike. The early Sumerian scribes came to realize that a sign belonging to a given word could be used for another word with altogether unrelated meaning if the *sounds* of the two words are identical. With the gradual spreading of this practice, the Sumerian script lost its pictographic character and tended more and more to become a purely phonetic script.[32]

To illustrate the fuller exploitation of logographic principles by the Shang, and probably also some pre-Shang, scribes in creating new characters, let us use No. 6, *pei,* "slave girl," as an example. The left half of the character is the radical *nü,* "woman," and the right half is an independent character with exactly the same pronunciation, *pei,* which means "low" or "lowly." Unlike the Sumerian word "in," which is a phonetic loan from the word for "water" and can be differentiated from "water" only syntactically and contextually, the archaic Chinese character for "slave girl" can be easily distinguished from other homonyms *pei* because of its distinct and complete meaning—a woman of lowly status. This character for "slave girl" is representative of numerous Shang and post-Shang characters in which it is often difficult to say which of the pictographic, ideographic, and phonetic principles is most determinative in the composition of a compound character. The radical for woman is pictographic, but this familiar stylized radical does not appear to

[32] *Ibid.,* pp. 302–303.

play a decisive role in suggesting the sense of the character, indicating merely that the compound character has something to do with woman. In other words, it serves as an auxiliary signific of meaning. The character *pei*, "lowly," on the right side of the compound character *pei*, "slave girl," serves both as a signific and a phonetic. From late-Shang times onward the ever-increasing process by which a signific and a phonetic are combined to form new compound characters makes it incorrect to describe the Chinese script as ideographic.[33] Since graphs in Chinese script are associated with semantic-phonetic values and are themselves words *(logos)*, the Chinese script should be regarded as logographic.[34]

In order to understand the evolutionary stage of the Chinese script during Shang times, it is necessary to examine the various principles according to which the characters were composed. The first attempt to classify Chinese characters by logographic principles was made by Hsü Shen 許慎, the famous lexicographer who completed the compilation of *Shuo-wen chien-tzu* in A.D. 100. In his opinion Chinese characters can be classified into *liu-shu* 六書, six categories of script elements:

[33] The Chinese script is regarded as "ideographic" by a number of Western sinologists, notably Herrlee G. Creel, "On the Nature of Chinese Ideography," *T'oung-pao*, 2d Series, XXXII (1936), pp. 85–161.

[34] A brilliant analysis of archaic Chinese, partly as a criticism of Creel's view that the Chinese script is ideographic, is Peter Boodberg, "Some Proleptical Remarks on the Evolution of Archaic Chinese," *Harvard Journal of Asiatic Studies*, II (1937), pp. 329–372. On p. 332 Boodberg says: "The term 'ideograph' which is so widely used by both layman and scholar is, we believe, responsible for most of the misunderstanding of the evolution of writing. The sooner it is abandoned, the better. We should suggest the revival of the old term 'logograph.' Signs used in writing, however ambiguous, stylized, or symbolic, represent *words*. If we associate with a graph several related words, unable to determine which of them it is supposed to represent exactly, this does not mean that the graph *represents* the 'idea' or 'concept' behind those words. Whatever be the significance of these vague terms in psychology, in linguistics they mean absolutely nothing. Linguistic science deals first and last with the word, its only reality. The 'disembodied word' which is what is generally meant by 'idea' or 'concept' does not exist for the linguist. For him, 'les idées ne viennent qu'en parlant.' "

I. *Chih-shih* 指事, indexical symbols, such as 上 *shang*, "up," and 下 *hsia*, "down."

II. *Hsiang-hsing* 象形, pictograms.

III. *Hui-i* 會意, ideographic compounds.

IV. *Chuan-chu* 轉注, characters which already exist but are "used for new notions through extension of meaning." For example, 布 *pu*, "cloth," the meaning of which is extended to represent "money" or "currency."[35]

V. *Chia-chieh* 假借, loan characters; *i.e.*, already existing characters which are used for other words with altogether unrelated meanings owing to sound identity or similarity.

VI. *Hsieh-sheng* 諧聲 or *hsing-sheng* 形聲, phonetic compounds.

From our analysis of the components of the character *pei*, "slave girl," it is evident that it is often difficult to determine which of the above principles is the most decisive factor in the composition of a compound Chinese character. To overcome this classificatory difficulty, a leading Chinese paleographer has devised a more logical method by which a character is counted twice if it employs two principles in its composition. He has classified only those characters in Shang oracle texts whose meanings and archaic pronunciations have been ascertained. The results of his findings are summarized in the following table.

---

[35] This explanation of *chuan-chu* and the example given are Bernhard Karlgren's. See his "Loan Characters in Pre-Han Texts," *BMFEA*, No. 35 (1963), p. 1. It should be pointed out that the original illustration on *chuan-chu* by the Han lexicographer Hsü Shen is so ambiguous that it gave rise to a long series of controversies among post-Han Chinese scholars. In any case, this category of characters is numerically insignificant, no matter how one interprets the meaning of *chuan-chu*.

TABLE 15
CLASSIFICATION OF ORACLE-BONE CHARACTERS ACCORDING TO THE SIX LOGOGRAPHIC PRINCIPLES

Principle	I	II	III	IV	V	VI	Uncertain	Total
Number	20	277	396	0	129	334	70	1226
Percentage	1.63	22.59	32.30	0	10.52	27.24	5.71	100

SOURCE: Li Hsiao-ting, "Ts'ung liu-shu ti kuan-tien k'an chia-ku-wen-tzu" [An Analysis of the Oracle-Bone Script According to the Six Logographic Principles], *Nan-yang-ta-hsüeh hsüeh-pao*, II (1968), pp. 84–106; table on p. 95.

Several aspects of Table 15 deserve comment. First, the total number of oracle-bone characters included in this study is much smaller than the number of characters which actually appear in oracle texts, because to make the study meaningful it had to use only characters whose meanings and pronunciations are both known and understood through cumulative research of at least two generations of Chinese paleographers. Second, since loan characters, which constitute category 5, are almost always based on identity or similarity in sound, this category may be conveniently treated as an extension of category 6—phonetic compounds. Third, by combining categories 5 and 6, one finds that characters which were composed according to phonetic principles constitute the largest single category, accounting for 37.76 percent of the total, as compared with 32.30 percent for ideographic compounds and 22.59 percent for pictograms. The category of indexical symbols was numerically insignificant even during this archaic stage.

The extent to which Chinese characters were already well on their way toward "phoneticization" indicates that the Chinese script of Shang times was not "primitive," as some pioneering researchers of oracle script would have had us believe.³⁶ In the light of our discussion of archaic Chinese numerals and ordinal numbers and their ramified implications, the Shang script must be considered as the outcome of a painfully long period of evolution since Yang-shao times.

Bernhard Karlgren's generalization about the evolution of the Chinese script since about 1000 B.C. can now apply at least a few centuries back to Shang times.

Thus an excellent method had been devised which brilliantly fitted the Chinese language with its numerous homophonous or nearly homophonous short monosyllables. By combining already existing graphs in pairs, one of which functioned as phonetic and the other as signific, new signs could be devised practically without limit. There was a framework, a stock of simple graphs, which, combined in pairs according to this principle, could easily and quickly denote any other word which in itself would be difficult to depict. In rapid sequence hundreds and thousands of such half-ideographic, half-phonetic compounds were created, and in fact nine-tenths of all Chinese characters are constructed according to this principle.³⁷

This generalization largely explains why the Chinese script has remained logographic down to the present day. By exploiting logographic principles more fully than other ancient peoples, the Chinese created a script as adequate as any alphabetic one without resorting to alphabetization. By A.D. 100, of the 9,353 characters listed in Hsü Shen's *Shuo-wen chieh-tzu,* more than 80 percent are phonetic compounds. In the famous chapter 32 of *T'ung-chih* 通志, an encyclopedia compiled by Cheng Ch'iao 鄭樵 (A.D. 1104–1162), the vocabulary had increased to 24,235 characters, of which 90 percent were phonetic compounds, 7 percent ideograms, and only

---

[36] The view that the Shang script is "primitive" was best represented by Kuo Mo-jo, *Chia-ku wen-tzu yen-chiu*. During the thirty-eight intervening years since the publication of this work in 1931, Kuo does not seem to have reassessed the relative maturity of the Shang script, and his current view, if any, may be quite different. In any case, Li Hsiao-ting's view seems to represent that of the majority of Chinese paleographers.

[37] Bernhard Karlgren, *The Chinese Language: An Essay on Its Nature and History* (New York, 1949), p. 13.

3 percent pictograms. As Peter Boodberg has pointed out, had the archaic pronunciations of the 740 "pure" ideograms listed in the *T'ung-chih* been known to its compiler, the majority of these so-called pure ideograms would have had to be reclassified as phonetic compounds.[38] The percentage accounted for by phonetic compounds in the present-day Chinese vocabulary of some 70,000 characters would, if tabulated, be even higher.

While the Shang vocabulary revealed by oracle texts is much smaller than that of modern Chinese, the grammar of Shang oracle writing already shared eight of the nine grammatical characteristics of written Chinese of the subsequent three millennia. The only aspect of the grammar of the post-1000 B.C. period that is missing from Shang oracle texts is the passive voice. Oracle-text grammar agrees with later Chinese grammar on the following eight basic rules:

1. The subject precedes the verb.
2. The object follows the verb.
3. The possessive precedes the possessed.
4. The adjective precedes the modified noun.
5. The adverb precedes the modified verb, adjective, or adverb.
6. Adverbial phrases, such as those with *yü* 於 indicating spatial relation, may only follow the verb.
7. Adverbial phrases, such as those with *i* 以 indicating manner, may either precede or follow the verb.
8. The subordinate clause precedes the main clause.[39]

---

[38] Boodberg, "Some Proleptical Remarks on the Evolution of Archaic Chinese," p. 345.

[39] This outline of grammatical characteristics of literary Chinese since Chou times is based on Wang Li, "Chung-kuo wen-fa-hsüeh ch'u-t'an," *Ch'ing-hua hsüeh-pao*, IX, No. 1 (January 1936), pp. 21–78; a comparison of oracle-text grammar with Wang's conclusions on later Chinese grammar is made by Ch'en Meng-chia, *Yin-hsü pu-tz'u tsung-shu*, p. 133.

Since the literary expressions of oracle texts are necessarily extremely economical and since oracle texts were related mainly to divination, it would not be fair to regard them as representing the whole range of Shang literary writing.[40] We are not even sure that the passive voice was definitely absent from literary writings of Shang times. In any case, the grammar revealed in Shang oracle texts is already a mature one which is essentially similar to that of Chou and post-Chou literature.[41] Necessarily brief as oracle texts are, they still yield examples of rhetorical techniques.[42]

In discussing the origins and evolution of the Chinese script, we should at least touch on its relation to the Chinese language. This relation, of course, can be traced only as far back as literary records will take us. Shang oracle texts and early-Chou literary works reveal that the Chinese language even then was already extremely analytical and isolating; more so, as a matter of fact, than present-day English. This unique character of the Chinese language was best explained for general Western readers by the late anthropologist Alfred L. Kroeber in his broad comparison of Chinese with Indo-European languages:

Chinese a long time ago became an extremely analytical and "isolating" language. That is, it lost all affixes and internal change. Each word element or item became an unalterable unit. Sentences are built up by putting together these atoms. Grammatical relations are expressed by the order of words: the subject precedes the predicate, for instance. Other ideas that in many languages are treated formally, such as the plural or person, are expressed by content elements; that is, by other words: *many* for the plural, separate pronouns instead of affixes for person, and so on. The now uniformly monosyllabic stems of Chinese accentuate this isolating

---

[40] T'ang Lan, "Pu-tz'u shih-tai ti wen-hsüeh ho pu-tz'u-wen-hsüeh" [Oracle-Bone Inscriptions and Early Chinese Literature], *Ch'ing-hua hsüeh-pao*, XI, No. 3 (July 1936), pp. 657–702.

[41] Kuan Hsieh-ch'u, *Yin-hsü chia-ku k'e-tz'u ti yü-fa yen-chiu* [A Study of the Grammar of Late-Shang Oracle Texts] (Peking, 1953), esp. conclusion, pp. 51–52.

[42] T'ang Lan, "Pu-tz'u shih-tai ti wen-hsüeh ho pu-tz'u-wen-hsüeh," esp. pp. 693–700.

character, which however does not depend intrinsically upon monosyllabism. In the Indo-European family, as already mentioned, for over two thousand years there has been a drift toward something of the Chinese type of structure. This drift toward loss of formal mechanisms and toward the expression of grammar by material elements, or by their position only, has been evident in all branches of Indo-European, but has been most marked in English. The chief remnants of the older inflectional processes in spoken English today are four verb endings, *-s*, *-ed*, *-ing*, *-en*; three noun endings, the possessive *-'s* and the plurals *-s* and *-en*, the latter rare; the case ending *-m* in *whom*, *them*; a few vowel changes for plurals, as in *man—men*, *goose—geese*; and perhaps two hundred vowel changes in verbs, such as *sing*, *sang*, *sung*. Compared with Latin, Sanskrit, or even primitive Germanic, this brief list represents a survival of possibly a tenth of the original synthetic inflectional apparatus. That is, English has gone approximately nine-tenths of the way toward attaining a grammar of the Chinese type.[43]

It is very important to understand why Kroeber says that "Chinese a long time ago became an extremely analytical or 'isolating' language." The word "became" implies a prior stage, when the Chinese language was not so analytical or isolating. Kroeber's implication, like the views of other leading Indo-European philologists including Otto Jesperson, is ultimately based on the opinions of the leading Swedish sinologist Bernhard Karlgren:

We have seen that archaic Chinese still possesses typical case inflections in its personal pronouns. . . . Hence, true inflections in the real meaning of the term must have existed in original Chinese, although we are unable to decide, by means of texts from historical times, how far this system of inflections extended in the prehistoric language. Furthermore, we have seen that archaic Chinese presents large word families, the members of which are different aspects of a common word stem, and that these formal variations of a stem sometimes express purely grammatical categories, e.g., a contrast between noun and adjective, between noun and verb, between adjective and verb, between verb and adverb, between transitive and intransitive verb, between active and passive verb, and many others that lack of space has prevented us from illustrating. These interesting features point to the fact that the characters of proto-Chinese was much more like that of our Western languages in essential points. Like the Indo-European tongues, it must have possessed its system of inflections and of word derivation, its formal word classes, in short, a more or less rich morphology. Its character as an isolating language is the result of

---

[43] A. L. Kroeber, *Anthropology: Race, Language, Psychology, Prehistory* (New York, 1948), p. 242.

a development away from those fundamental characteristics which remind us more of the Indo-European languages. In this respect Chinese is analogous to English, although it has proceeded much further along the road towards simplification and ossification than present-day English has as yet gone.[44]

Unfortunately, the above generalization "presents Karlgren's views alone, but leaves the layman with the impression that the views presented are accepted by all scholars."[45] In archaic Chinese there are forms which are both semantically and phonologically related: of two phonologically similar forms, one may be a noun; one may be a verb, the other an adjective; or both may be verbs. Of two phonologically similar verbs, one may be the basic form, the other a causative form. These archaic Chinese alternations of semantically related forms in terms of tones and/or initial consonants cannot, however, be firmly established as regular derivations. They are, in the first place, far too rare. Moreover, a given alternation does not correlate with a given derivation.[46]

---

[44] B. Karlgren, *The Chinese Language*, pp. 98–99.

[45] Robert Schafer's review of Karlgren's *The Chinese Language* in *Journal of the American Oriental Society*, LXX (1950), pp. 139–141.

[46] Paul Demiéville, in his article "Le Chinois," in the *Cent-cinquantenaire de l'école des langues orientales* (Paris, 1948), p. 148, says: "Rares sont les savants qui ont montré assez de fermeté dans le jugement pour maintenir en toute occasion que les parties du discours, comme n'a cessé de le soutenir M. Henri Maspero, sont en chinois un mirage dont il faut nous débarrasser une fois pour toutes. La polyvalence grammaticale des mots est en fait absolue en chinois. Il est vrai que, dans les 'familles de mots' dont je viens de parler, on relève des oppositions entre valeurs substantivales et valeurs verbales, comme *tsuan* 傳 'tradition', vis-à-vis de *tshuan* 傳 'transmettre'; il est vrai encore que certains enclitiques de la langue parlée, notamment ǝr 兒 et tsǝ 子, ont pour effet que les mots auxquels ils s'adjoignent ne peuvent plus, dans la phrase, s'employer en fonction verbale. Mais l'opposition 'tradition-transmettre' est d'ordre lexical, comme toutes les oppositions sémantiques si diverses qui s'observent dans le système des 'familles de mots'; c'est un fait sporadique, n'impliquant pas l'existence de catégories grammaticales pareilles à nos catégories du nom et du verbe." I owe this important technical note to Professor William A. C. H. Dobson, who makes the following comment in a letter to me dated 13 March 1970: "Karlgren's 'word classes' are in fact semantic differences differentiated by phonological means. No phonological laws can be posited by which a word

To assess the validity of Karlgren's contention that proto-Chinese was inflectional, it is necessary to examine his evidence on the so-called case inflections in personal pronouns in Chou literary works. According to him, in archaic Chinese the first-person nominative-genitive was *wu* 吾 and first-person dative-accusative was *wo* 我; the second-person nominative-genitive was *erh* 爾 and second-person dative-accusative was *ju* 汝. The frequency of occurrence in archaic Chinese of *wu* and *wo* in various cases has been tabulated by Karlgren himself:[47]

	Wu	*Wo*
Nominative	540	315
Genitive	285	144
Dative-accusative	7	336

From the above figures it is obvious that the number of occurrences of *wo* (Karlgren's dative-accusative) as nominative is so large as to make any rule of "case inflection" impossible. But there are other factors which weaken his view even more. First, his data are culled exclusively from three late-Chou works only, namely, *The Confucian Analects, The Book of Mencius,* and *The Tso-chuan,* which are too recent to represent truly archaic Chinese. But even within the narrow confines of these three works, the important first-person pronoun *yü* 余, which does not fall into Karlgren's pattern one way or another, is purposely excluded. Second, he has failed to consult the Shang oracle texts, which no doubt provide the earliest extant and most reliable data for the study of archaic Chinese grammar. In oracle texts the first-person pronoun *wo,* which according to

---

or group of words passes from verb to noun or makes any distinction comparable to the Indo-European 'parts of speech.' Phonological differences in a given word are specializations of its meaning, not of grammatical function."

[47] Karlgren, "Le Proto-chinois, langue flexionnelle," *Journal Asiatique,* 2d series, XV (1920), pp. 205–232.

Karlgren should indicate dative-accusative, is used to indicate all four cases. *Wu,* Karlgren's nominative, hardly appears in oracle texts at all. On the other hand, *yü,* which Karlgren excluded from his study, appears in oracle texts and early-Chou works in all four cases.[48]

But the real blow to Karlgren's theory of case inflections in personal pronouns is dealt by Chou Fa-kao of Academia Sinica, Taiwan, who has made an exhaustive study of the usage of second-person pronouns based on a wide range of early- and late-Chou works. The frequency of occurrence of second-person pronouns *erh,* Karlgren's nominative-genitive, and *ju,* Karlgren's dative-accusative, in various cases has been tabulated by Chou:[49]

	Erh	*Ju*
Nominative	190	250
Genitive	252	7(?)
Dative-accusative	106	148
Apposition	80	44

The above statistics dealing with pronoun usage in archaic Chinese clearly indicate the lack of any fixed system which by standards of linguistic science may be justifiably called "case inflections." William A. C. H. Dobson, for example, in his systematic grammatical analysis of early-Chou works, bronze inscriptions, and late-Chou works, never discusses case inflections in pronouns. To him and to a number of Chinese philologists, the Chinese language —insofar as it can be traced—has always been a positional rather than an inflectional language.[50]

---

[48] Ch'en Meng-chia, *Yin-hsü pu-tz'u tsung-shu,* p. 96; Kuan Hsieh-ch'u, *Yin-hsü chia-ku k'e-tz'u ti yü-fa yen-chiu,* pp. 31–33.

[49] Chou Fa-kao, *Chung-kuo yü-wen lun-ts'ung* [Essays on Chinese Language] (Taipei, 1963), Table 1 on p. 79 and Table 2 on p. 80.

[50] W. A. C. H. Dobson, *Early Archaic Chinese: A Descriptive Grammar* (Toronto, 1962), pp. 22–25, 112–114; *Late Archaic Chinese: A Grammatical Study* (Toronto, 1959), pp. 27–28; 137–141.

Since its first appearance in the early 1920s, Karlgren's theory has appealed to Western philologists because it conforms, by and large, to the pattern of historical evolution of Indo-European languages. Yet few Indo-European philologists ever examined the great puzzle created by Karlgren's theory in the light of the vast cumulative fund of knowledge of the history of Indo-European languages. It is well known that it has taken Indo-European languages more than two thousand years gradually to shorten their words (such as the classic example of the change from the Gothic *habaidedeima* to the modern English *had*), to drop many or most of their synthetic grammatical forms, and to become increasingly syntactically analytic, mainly by working out a stricter word order.[51] Present-day English is, of course, the most analytic of all Indo-European languages, but it still retains more than two hundred "remnants of the older inflectional processes." If proto-Chinese had been an inflectional language, as Karlgren would have us believe, why then did the language as far back as thirty-three hundred years ago yield no evidence of what, by the standards of Indo-European languages, may be called inflection? Why was the language already syntactically analytic to an extent that even present-day English has yet to reach? Assuming further the substantial equality of other factors among gifted prehistoric and early historic peoples, why—and how—had prehistoric Chinese people alone accomplished the feat of transforming their "inflectional" language into an extremely analytic and isolating one at a time when, in the opinion of Otto Jesperson, the older Aryan languages had still not reached the level of "*developed* human thought" from which the long linguistic journey toward a stricter word order could be begun?[52]

But this puzzle does not occur if one refrains from drawing analogies between Chinese and European languages and takes full

---

[51] Otto Jesperson, *Language: Its Nature, Development, and Origin* (London, 1922), pp. 361–364.

[52] *Ibid.*, p. 356; italics in original.

cognizance of the fundamental character of Chinese as revealed in the earliest extant Chinese literature. The nature of proto-Chinese is extremely unlikely to have been drastically different from what it was in 1300 B.C., namely, a positional language in which the grammatical functions of words are determined by their positions in a sentence. As to why the Chinese language in remote antiquity had already developed strict rules for word order, only the collective future research of linguistic scientists can enlighten us.

Whatever the reasons why the proto-Chinese and archaic Chinese of Shang-Chou times was already an extremely isolating language, its uniqueness is generally conceded. None of the attempts to connect Chinese with tongues ancestral to the Indo-European languages has been successful. It is obvious also that Chinese is totally unrelated to the agglutinative tongues of the peoples of the Altaic language family and of the Koreans and Japanese, despite the fact that some proto-Turcic and proto-Tungusic peoples were the northern neighbors of the ancient Chinese. Although there has been a tendency for some linguists to regard Chinese and certain languages spoken in northern Vietnam, Thailand, Laos, Burma, Tibet, and the Himalaya region as members of the so-called Sino-Tibetan language family, methodical studies on comparative Sino-Tibetan linguistics seem to indicate that the genetic relation between Chinese and the rest of the group ranges from remote to questionable.[53]

In relating the Chinese language to the Chinese script, one should bear in mind three basic characteristics of the language. First, the language is essentially monosyllabic, and was even more so in ancient than in modern times. Second, the total number of pronounceable monosyllables is fairly limited, although the archaic language had a somewhat richer sound system than modern Chinese. And third, the language is full of homophones, that is, different

---

[53] K'un Chang, "Sino-Tibetan Words for 'Needle,'" *Monumenta Serica*, XXVII (1928).

words having essentially the same pronunciation. The language is therefore intrinsically resistant to the development of a script system which would tend to become fully phoneticized or alphabetized. As a corollary, the language seems to have always encouraged the principle that a separate logograph or character be created for each simple word (in some cases a morpheme) so that different words having the same pronunciation can be differentiated from one another. In this sense, the Chinese script has been "so wonderfully well adapted to the linguistic traditions of China that it is indispensable."[54]

In conclusion, it may be pointed out that everything relating to the Chinese language and script—ancient writing materials, numerals, ordinals and their complex institutional and religious contexts,[55] the ingenious exploitation of various logographic principles by the ancient Chinese to create a script to suit their spoken language, and the extremely isolating character of the language since remote antiquity—all is unmistakably Sinitic. In spite of his attempt to draw broad parallels between Chinese and Indo-European languages, Karlgren has emphatically stated that the Chinese script is "a genuine product of the creative power of the Chinese mind" and is not "like our own writing, a loan from unrelated people."[56]

---

[54] Karlgren, *Sound and Symbol in Chinese* (London, 1923), p. 41.

[55] Professor Fang-kuei Li has recently called my attention to the fact that in some Tai languages, especially in the extinct Ahom language of Assam, there were two series of characters roughly similar in usage to the two series of ancient Chinese ordinals. He writes: "While the second series there seems to have been related to the Chinese, the first series is altogether different." The question of whether these Tai series might have been results of diffusion or stimulus diffusion from North China in ancient times remains to be investigated. For the time being, the uniqueness of the ancient Chinese ordinal system, at least as compared with those of other major ancient languages of the Near and Middle East, remains unquestionable.

[56] Karlgren, *Sound and Symbol in Chinese*, p. 67.

The basic numerals on Pan-p'o potsherds not only preceded those of the Sumerians by more than a millennium but were also the most intelligent ones before the Hindu-Arabic numerals appeared, fairly late in historical times. With the invention of basic numerals and possibly other simple logographs in Yang-shao times, the pre-Shang Chinese may be regarded as having been literate to a certain degree. Only the lack of suitable nonperishable writing materials before the rise of plastromancy after 1300 B.C. has prevented us from ascertaining exactly when the long proto-literate phase in Chinese history ended. In any case, from the invention of numerals during the fifth millennium B.C. to the first available sign of maturation of the Chinese script by 1300 B.C., the Chinese were the only people east of 80° longitude from Greenwich to have created a written language. This fact not only reflects China's prehistoric isolation from the Western world but further supplements important linguistic evidence, uncovered in recent decades, of the uniqueness of the Chinese language and script.

VII
Society, Religion, Thought

SOCIETY, RELIGION, and thought are topics obviously too broad to be covered in a single chapter of a work whose central concern is to ascertain whether the major cultural elements that eventually coalesced in the Shang civilization were of indigenous origins. There are many aspects about the evolution of the societies represented by the various regional prehistoric cultures, from Yang-shao to Shang times, upon which artifacts, because of their silence, shed little or no light. The limited aspects of prehistoric and early historic Chinese society and religion discussed herein are, therefore, *only* those which in my opinion can be meaningfully studied by integrating ancient written records with relevant archaeological data. The study of early Chinese thought is likewise restricted to what can be learned from the earliest extant literary works. Although the aspects covered in this chapter are necessarily highly selective, it is to be hoped that they will be helpful to an understanding of certain characteristics of prehistoric and early historic Chinese society, religion, and thought and of the abiding influence these early characteristics had upon later development.

Before tracing the beginnings and evolution of Chinese social organization and religious beliefs from Yang-shao to Shang times, we should look at the Yang-shao settlement pattern. Starting in the early fifth millennium B.C., possibly even earlier, the Yang-shao people began to settle in the southeastern part of the loess highlands. Archaeologically the best explored part of the Yang-shao nuclear

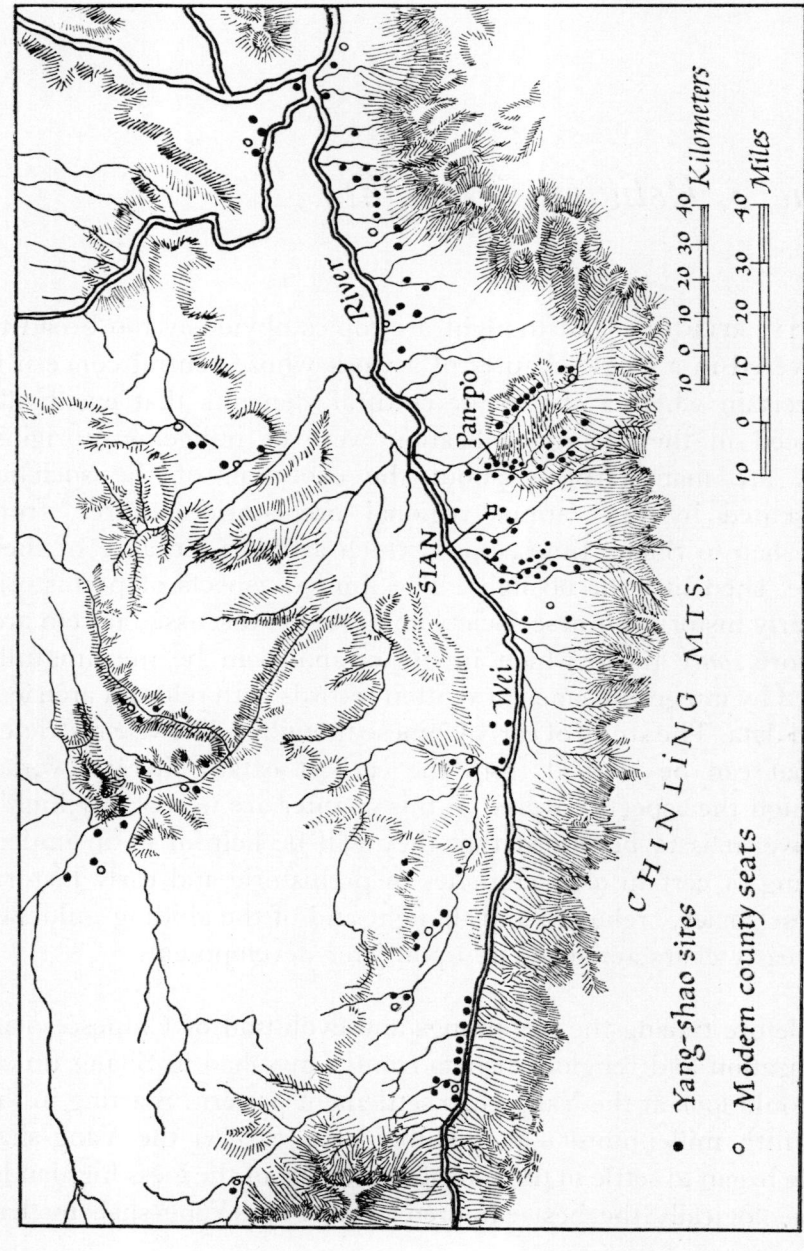

MAP 4. The distribution of Yang-shao sites in the Wei River Basin.

area is the Wei River basin in Shensi, where more than 400 Yang-shao sites have been discovered and preliminarily surveyed. The total land area of the Wei River basin slightly exceeds 21,000 square kilometers, or more than 8,000 square miles. The majority of these sites are located south of the Wei River and north of the Ch'in-ling Mountain, almost invariably along small rivers and streams. Granted that not all the 400 sites were contemporary, Map 4 shows that their distribution was uneven and that the density of sites south of the present provincial capital city of Sian was quite high.[1]

These Yang-shao sites varied greatly in size, from less than an acre to more than two or three hundred acres. The average size of the thirty-three Yang-shao sites within the present boundaries of Ch'ang-an 長安 and Hu-hsien 鄠縣 counties near Sian is 43.43 acres.[2] North of the Wei River and west of Sian, the average size of the twenty-nine discovered and surveyed Yang-shao sites within the boundaries of Feng-hsiang 鳳翔 and Hsing-p'ing 興平 counties is around 30 acres.[3] The unavailability of more specific archaeological data makes it impossible to present demographic, social, and economic details of these Yang-shao settlements, but some features of the Pan-p'o village southeast of Sian, the best-studied of the Yang-shao sites, may serve as a rough gauge. The area of the Yang-shao village settlement at Pan-p'o has been estimated at about 50,000 square meters, or approximately 11.5 acres, and its population at 500 or 600.[4] In comparison, the famous Neolithic

---

[1] *Hsi-an Pan-p'o*, pp. 1–5.

[2] "Shan-hsi Ch'ang-an Hu-hsien tiao-ch'a yü shih-chüeh pao-kao" [A Brief Report on Preliminary Excavations in Ch'ang-an and Hu-hsien, Shensi], *KK*, 1962, No. 6, pp. 305–311. The calculations of the areas of these 33 sites and their conversion to acreage are my own.

[3] "Shan-hsi Feng-hsiang Hsing-p'ing liang-hsien k'ao-ku tiao-ch'a chien-pao" [A Brief Report on the Archaeological Reconnaissance in Feng-hsiang and Hsing-p'ing Counties, Shensi], *KK*, 1960, No. 3, pp. 13–18. The calculations of the areas of the sites and their conversion to acreage are my own.

[4] *Hsi-an Pan-p'o*, pp. 9 and 228.

village at Jarmo in northwestern Iraq, which offers one of the earliest evidences of field agriculture and animal husbandry and is dated about 7000 B.C., comprises an area of 3.2 acres with a population estimated at 150.[5] Taking into account the fact that the Pan-p'o village was considerably smaller than the average in the Wei River basin and that southern Shansi and western Honan were also settled by the Yang-shao people, one gets the impression that the debut of the proto-Sinitic people in the southeastern part of the loess highlands may have been numerically quite significant.

The physical layouts of Yang-shao villages are well summarized by K. C. Chang:

The physical plan of the Yang-shao village is known only where the sites were extensively excavated and the results given in published accounts. An interesting layout is attributed to the Pei-shou-ling site of Pao-chi, in central Shensi, where two rows of houses faced each other across a narrow lane, but detailed descriptions are absent. The best-described village plans are available for the Pan-p'o site. It is on a river terrace about 800 meters east of the River Ch'an, a tributary of the Weishui [Wei River], and about 9 meters above the riverbed. The area of settlement is estimated at about 50,000 square meters, and its shape is an irregular oval with the long axis north-south. The houses (46 of which were excavated) and most of the storage pits and animal pens are clustered at the center of the site in an area of about 30,000 square meters [roughly 7.5 acres] outlined by a ditch 5 or 6 meters deep and wide. The village cemetery is in the northern part of the village, outside the ditched dwelling area, and pottery kilns are concentrated in the village's eastern portion. Within the dwelling area, houses of fairly permanent nature were constructed. The most common kinds were 3 to 5 meters in diameter and were square, oblong, or round, with plastered floors. They were semi-subterranean or at ground level, had wattle-and-daub wall foundations, and upper walls and roofs were supported by large and small wooden posts. During a later occupation, a huge longhouse was constructed (over 20 m long and 12.5 m wide) divided into compartments by partition walls. During this stage the communal house was at the center of the village plaza, with the small houses surrounding the plaza, their doors facing the center. Each house and each compartment of the longhouse were equipped with a hearth

---

[5] The area of Jarmo village and its surroundings is given in Robert J. Braidwood, "The Agricultural Revolution," *Scientific American*, CCIII, No. 3 (September 1960), esp. p. 131; Jarmo's population is reconstructed in R. J. Braidwood and Charles A. Reed, "The Achievement and Early Consequences of Food Production," *Cold Spring Harbor Symposia on Quantitative Biology*, XXII (1957), esp. p. 26.

(a burned surface in the earlier occupations and gourd-shaped pit in the later occupations). The pottery-making center east of the dwelling area had no fewer than six kilns, in one of which were found some unfired pots. North of the dwelling area was the village cemetery, in which were found more than 130 adult burials, single, with the exception of one double and one quadruple—the skeletons lying face upward and stretched out. Infants and children were buried in urns between the dwelling houses.

This Pan-p'o pattern in subdividing a village into a dwelling area, a kiln center, and a cemetery recurs throughout the Yang-shao settlements that have been extensively excavated, such as those near Pao-chi and Hua-hsien in Shensi, and Lin-shan-chai and Miao-ti-kou in Honan. More detailed information on small houses is known from the Miao-ti-kou site; another huge communal building was found at Liu-tzu-chen and the cemetery at Pao-chi has yielded more and richer findings. But the general pattern repeats itself throughout, with such exceptions as that at Liu-tzu-chen where the Yang-shao village did not have its own cemetery but seems to have shared a large one some distance away with neighboring villages. This is a very notable exception nevertheless, since the Liu-tzu-chen site belongs chronologically to a late phase of the Yang-shao stage, for this may indicate a tendency on the part of the farming villages near the end of this stage toward growth and fission. . . . The custom of sharing cemeteries during the later phases of the Yang-shao carries important social implications. It shows that toward the end of this stage the population pressure had caused the fission of residential villages, which probably has important bearing upon the further development of the North China Neolithic culture into the next—Lung-shan—stage. They [the burial areas shared by neighboring villages] also show that a strong lineage consciousness must have been behind the custom of sending the dead to rest in common ancestral ground. This latter inference is substantiated by the community patterns of the Yang-shao farmers. The longhouses at Pan-p'o-ts'un and Liu-tzu-chen, and the planned layout of the Pan-p'o-ts'un, Pao-chi, and Lin-shan-chai villages, as well as the clustered pit houses at Sun-ch'i-t'an, near Lo-yang in Honan, suggest planned and segmented village layouts, and on these grounds and others, lineage and clan types of kinship groupings could be postulated.[6]

Of the various aspects of Yang-shao village layout, the common burial grounds are perhaps most suggestive of the groupings of Yang-shao villagers according to kinship ties. Although some villagers during the late phase of the Yang-shao tended to share burial grounds with members of neighboring villages, during much of the Yang-shao period villages in general maintained their own cemeteries. In spite of the successive disturbances caused by graves

[6] K. C. Chang, *The Archaeology of Ancient China* (1968), pp. 97-103.

of later historic periods, the intact parts of the Yang-shao cemetery at Pan-p'o reveal that the dead were buried close together in neat patterns.[7] The hundreds of skeletons discovered at the common burial grounds of several other Yang-shao sites were also arranged neatly in rows.[8] The social implications of Yang-shao common burial grounds may be gauged from similar ancient customs that still lingered among some North American Indian tribes in the nineteenth century. As an American missionary of the early nineteenth century observed, the reason the Iroquois maintained a common burial ground was that they "reckoned it irreligious to mix the bones of a relative with those of a stranger, as bone of bone and flesh of flesh should always be joined together."[9] In the 1870s Lewis H. Morgan found at the Tuscarora reservation near Lewiston, New York, one common cemetery for the whole tribe, "where individuals of the same gens are buried in a row by themselves."[10]

With Lewis H. Morgan and Frederick Engels as their theoretical guides, mainland Chinese scholars are generally of the opinion that the Yang-shao period represented a stage in which "matrilineal society reached its height of prosperity."[11] Much that has been concluded about the Yang-shao matrilineal society is based on elaborate interpretations of some unusual Yang-shao burial patterns. Among the peculiar burial patterns that have been analyzed are a

---

[7] *Hsi-an Pan-p'o,* pp. 200–216.

[8] Fang Yang, "Yang-shao-wen-hua ho-tsang hsi-su ti chi-tien pu-ch'ung chieh-shih" [Further Comments on the Custom of Collective Burials in the Yang-shao Culture], *KK,* 1962, No. 3, pp. 158–166.

[9] Cyrus Byington, *History of the American Indians* (1827 ed.), cited in Lewis H. Morgan, *Ancient Society* (New York, 1878), p. 83.

[10] Morgan, *Ancient Society,* p. 84.

[11] The literature discussing the nature of Yang-shao matrilineal society is sizable, but we need mention only the most influential synthesis under the nominal editorship of the president of Academia Sinica, Peking. Kuo Mo-jo, ed., *Chung-kuo-shih kang* [An Outline of Chinese History] (Peking, 1962), I, pp. 22–47, especially introductory remark on p. 22.

few large graves discovered at the Pei-shou-ling 北首嶺 site in Pao-chi and at Pan-p'o, in which the bodies of adult males and females were buried separately. According to the interpretation of Chinese archaeologists, the females were sisters; and the males were brothers who had been married off to another matrilineal group during their prime but had to be buried with their own kin after death. These archaeologists have also stressed the phenomena that at other Yang-shao sites there are occasionally cases in which mother and young children were buried together and cases in which mass secondary burials surrounded the body of an adult woman which does not seem to have been reburied. They regard as especially illuminating the grave of a little girl at the Pan-p'o site which yields clear vestiges of a wooden coffin, a rare luxury by Yang-shao standards, and exceptionally rich funerary gifts.[12] Interesting and suggestive as such unusual burial patterns are, they are numerically insignificant as compared to the vast majority of cases in which the dead in Yang-shao times were buried singly in rows in a common village cemetery. Burial patterns alone can seldom determine whether a descent group in a primitive society was matrilineal.

If available archaeological data do not tell much about the nature of the Yang-shao kinship system, the earliest extant Chinese written records do indicate the prevalence of matrilineal descent groups and the rule of exogamy in remote antiquity. One strikingly consistent feature of the legends about the origins of the Shang, Chou, and Ch'in tribes is the "ignorance of paternity," which is regarded as a characteristic of matrilineal kinship in some contemporary primitive societies.[13] Ode 303 of *The Book of Odes,* which is no doubt based on old Shang tribal legends handed down in the ruling clan of the Sung state in Chou times, tells the origin of the

---

[12] For elaborate interpretations of these burial patterns as characteristics of matrilineal society, see *Chung-kuo-shih kang,* I, pp. 26–30.

[13] David M. Schneider and Kathleen Gough, eds., *Matrilineal Kinship* (Berkeley, 1961), p. 13.

Shang tribe: "Heaven bade the dark bird to come down and bear the Shang."¹⁴ Ode 245 tells the beginnings of the Chou tribe:

> She who in the beginning gave birth to the people,
> This was Chiang Yüan.
> How did she give birth to the people?
> Well she sacrificed and prayed
> That she might no longer be childless.
> She trod on the big toe of God's footprint,
> Was accepted and got what she desired.
> Then in reverence, then in awe,
> She gave birth, she nurtured;
> And this was Hou Chi [Prince Millet].¹⁵

The legend about the origin of the Ch'in tribe, which was destined eventually to unify all ancient China in 221 B.C., is almost exactly the same as that of the Shang tribe.¹⁶

The legends about the origins of the Chou tribe are especially illuminating and worthy of further analysis. Verified by detailed Chou works later in date than *The Book of Odes,* we know for sure that the Chiang 姜 clan—which legends traced back to the Lady Yüan, the mother of "Prince Millet"—was actually one of the two powerful clans of the Chou tribe. Another was the Chi 姬 clan, which claimed "Prince Millet" as its male ancestor and was destined to become the Chou royal clan. From their legendary beginnings to late-Chou times these two clans intermarried with each other. The *Kuo-yü* (Sayings of the States), a late-Chou work based on authentic earlier histories and legends, testifies that the Chi clan derived its name from the Chi River and that the Chiang clan derived its name from the Chiang River, both within the Wei River basin in Shensi, the Yang-shao nuclear area.¹⁷

---

¹⁴ Arthur Waley, tr., *The Book of Songs* (New York, 1937), p. 275.

¹⁵ *Ibid.,* p. 241.

¹⁶ *Shih-chi,* ch. 5, p. 1a.

¹⁷ *Kuo-yü* (SPPY ed.), ch. 10, p. 8a. For the identification of the Chi and Chiang Rivers, see Hsü Hsü-sheng, *Chung-kuo ku-shih ti ch'uan-shuo shih-tai* [The Legendary Period in Ancient Chinese History] (Peking, 1962), pp. 40–43.

Another type of evidence suggesting that the earliest Chinese kinship system was generally matrilineal involves the names of those ancient clans which during the Chou period became the ruling clans of various feudal states. The nature of *hsing* 姓, clan names in a Chou context, needs a brief explanation. While generally regarded as a clan, the corporate body under a single *hsing* could be an extremely large conglomerate of common descent groups scattered all over Chou China. The lords of dozens of states were descended from original members of the royal Chi clan. The descendants of members of the original Chiang clan were lords of at least ten states. Such *hsing* groups as the Chi's and the Chiang's were actually larger than what are usually called tribes. For this reason the number of *hsing* recorded in the *Tso-chuan* [The Annals of Feudal States] is rather limited. Of a total of twenty-four recorded *hsing* groups which constituted the ruling clans of various feudal states, the names of sixteen of them contain the radical *nu* 女 (woman). They are: Chi 姬, Chiang 姜, Yin 嬴, Ssu 姒, Chi 姞, Kuei 嬀, Yün 妘, Yao 姚, Chi 己 archaic forms 妀、妃, Feng 風 archaic form 妨, Mi 半 archaic form 嬭, Kuei 隗 archaic form 媿, Ch'i 祁 archaic form 嬯, Ts'ao 曹 archaic form 嫅, Jen 任 archaic form 妊, and Man 曼 archaic form 妟、嫚.[18] Since even by Chou standards these clan names were already very ancient, they further testify to the general ignorance of paternity which must have prevailed during the earliest stage.

By far the best documented evidence of the prevalence of matrilineal groups in remote antiquity was the survival of matrilineal kinship terminology in the essentially patrilineal kinship system of Shang times. "Matrilineal descent groups," according to David M. Schneider's analysis of their distinctive features, "would be more likely to merge lineal and collateral relatives terminologically than

---

[18] The archaic forms of these clan names are culled from Ch'en P'an, *Ch'un-ch'iu-ta-shih-piao lieh-kuo-chüeh-hsing chi ts'un-mieh-piao hsün-i* (Academia Sinica, Taiwan, 1970), 7 *ts'e*.

would patrilineal descent groups."[19] As has been alluded to in our discussion of the institutional and religious contexts of Chinese ordinals in chapter 6 and will be further discussed later in the present chapter, the basic patrilinity of the structure of the Shang royal clan cannot be doubted. Yet the deceased royal father and his brothers were collectively referred to by the king as *chu-fu* 諸父 or *to-fu* 多父 (literally the "many fathers"), and the royal mother and the wives of the king's paternal uncles were collectively referred to by the king as *chu-mu* 諸母 or *to-mu* 多母 (literally the "many mothers"). Likewise, a king's son called his own brothers as well as the sons of his paternal uncles *chu-hsiung* 諸兄 or *to-hsiung* 多兄 (literally the "many brothers").

Also suggestive of the survival of a matrilineal filiation system is the Shang custom of preliminarily naming royal sons according to their biological mothers. A Shang king had many wives, and not all his sons were formally given the status *tzu* (royal sons). Those who attained the *tzu* status were assigned personal names. Those who had yet to attain the *tzu* status were collectively distinguished from one another by the use of their biological mothers' names as prefixes. For example, the sons of King Wu-ting by one of his wives (*fu* 婦), née Hao 好, were collectively referred to as Fu-Hao-tzu 婦好子 (the sons of royal wife Hao).[20] These are clearly cases of reverse teknonymy. Furthermore, unlike the Chou queens and the empresses of post-Chou dynasties who were never posthumously entitled to their own separate temples, two Shang queens did enjoy, posthumously, the privilege of having their own exclusive temples.[21]

Shang-Chou records clearly reflect the prevalence of matrilineal kinship in Neolithic North China. But lack of specific archaeological

---

[19] Schneider and Gough, eds., *Matrilineal Kinship,* p. 27.

[20] For detailed descriptions of Shang royal kinship terminology, see Ch'en Meng-chia, *Yin-hsü pu-tz'u tsung-shu,* chs. 13 and 14.

[21] Chao Lin, *Marriage, Inheritance and Lineage Organization in Shang-Chou China* (Taipei, 1971), pp. 39–40.

data makes it impossible to determine local and regional differences, if any, in the structure and functioning of such matrilineal groups. Nor do we know anything specific about units of social and territorial organizations larger than kinship groups and village communities. We can only infer from the following that larger tribal and territorial organizations probably did exist in Yang-shao times. First, given the high density of Yang-shao settlements along some of the small rivers and streams south of the Wei River and north of the Ch'in-ling Mountain, it is very difficult to see how the population of that area could get along without at least some rudimentary intervillage coordinating authorities. Second, while the life of Yang-shao farmers and their kin centered on their own village, there are definite indications that they maintained contact with and shared the culture of people some distance away. A striking phenomenon is the discovery of the Pan-p'o type of word-signs at the Ling-t'ai site in Ch'ang-an, and also as far away as the Hsin-yeh-ts'un site in Ho-yang county near the Yellow River, more than 150 kilometers northeast of Pan-p'o. And of the raw materials for making various types of tools and ornaments, serpentine is especially significant because it had to be brought to Pan-p'o from hundreds of kilometers away.[22] All this would imply interlocal and intertribal "trade" and barter, which in turn would imply at least limited agreements among the chiefdoms.

Although archaeology has yielded no systematic information on the religious beliefs of the Yang-shao Chinese, there are at least some indications of their belief in a hereafter. The use of pottery wares, spinning wheels, millet, and sometimes ornaments as funerary gifts reflects such a belief. Very significantly, young children were buried in the residential area as if they were to be as dependent on their mothers as they had been during life. Their bodies were usually kept in large pottery urns, with a small hole at the top or middle, as if such a hole would allow their souls to pass through

---

[22] *Hsi-an Pan-p'o,* pp. 228–229.

freely.²³ The composite design of a mysterious human face with four stylized fishes projecting outward from the human ears and mouth (see Figure 9 in chapter 4) looks like a magician or priest. If my interpretation is not too far wrong,²⁴ the word-sign *shih* 示 may indicate some kind of religious worship. Summarizing the results of archaeological reconnaissance in Shansi up to 1959, a Shansi archaeological worker reported the discovery of a piece of scorched divination bone in the Yang-shao cultural stratum at the Ho-ts'un 霍村 site south of Fu-shan 浮山 county in southern Shansi.²⁵ There has been no subsequent detailed report on this particular Yang-shao site, so that we do not know whether that bone came from a true Yang-shao stratum or from an early Lungshanoid stratum. But it is not outside the realm of possibility that scapulimancy in its crudest form might have begun in some late Yang-shao villages.

The aggregate archaeological finds for the Lungshanoid and Lung-shan periods throw some light on the changing kinship structure and tell us much about the rise of the Sinitic religion based on ancestor worship. The most common burial pattern during these periods remained single burials arranged in rows. But here and there in the vastly expanding Sinitic world, graves containing the bodies of an adult male-female pair appeared. In some Ch'i-chia cultural sites in Kansu there were graves which contained the body of a male adult lying in a supine position, sandwiched between bodies of two female adults lying in flexed positions. In various Lungshanoid and Lung-shan sites, clear indications of inequity in funerary gifts reflect an increasing differentiation in social status.

---

[23] *Ibid.*, esp. pp. 218–220.

[24] See chapter 6 above, p. 230.

[25] "Shan-hsi shih-nien-lai k'ao-ku yü wen-wu kung-tso ti kai-k'uang" [A Summary of Archaeological and Cultural Work of Shansi during the Past Ten Years], *KK*, 1959, No. 2, pp. 63–64.

All this, and much else, has been interpreted by mainland Chinese scholars as signs of a budding patrilineal society.[26]

Regardless of whether this interpretation is entirely justified, we know of three major factors which are likely to have facilitated the transition from a matrilineal to a patrilineal kinship system in the post-Yang-shao periods. First, although the matrilineal and patrilineal descent groups are essentially the same in structure, the former is faced with a perennial problem. Whereas in patrilineal descent groups the line of authority and the line of descent both run through men, in matrilineal groups the line of descent runs through women but the line of authority has to run through men. "The lines of authority and group placement," as David M. Schneider puts it, "are thus coordinate in males in patrilineal descent groups but separated between males and females in matrilineal descent groups."[27] This may explain why at the Yang-shao site at Yüan-ch'ün-miao 元君廟, Hua-hsien, Shensi, an old man was buried in an elaborately constructed grave—perhaps a reflection of his fellow Yang-shao villagers' appreciation for the service and leadership he had provided during his lifetime.[28]

Second, historically the Lungshanoid stage was a period in which the proto-Sinitic people expanded far and wide beyond the Yang-shao nuclear area into regions inhabited by different ethnic groups—something which will be discussed in chapter 8. In a period of expansion, migration, and some unavoidable military struggles, the services of adult males as well as firm and able male leadership were badly needed. Furthermore, it is from the Lungshanoid period onward that archaeology proves beyond doubt the rise of the Sinitic religion based on ancestor worship, especially on male-ancestor worship.

[26] Kuo Mo-jo, ed., *Chung-kuo-shih kang*, I, pp. 48–56.

[27] Schneider and Gough, eds., *Matrilineal Kinship*, p. 7.

[28] "Hua-hsien Liu-tzu-chen ti-erh-tz'u fa-chüeh ti chu-yao shou-huo" [Main Findings of the Second Excavation at Liu-tzu-chen, Hua-hsien], *KK*, 1959, No. 11, esp. pp. 589–591.

The rise of the cult in Lungshanoid times is evidenced by ceramic and stone phallic symbols at a number of sites. To be sure, the appearance of the phallic symbol alone may not necessarily be associated with the rise of patrilineal kinship groups. But the significance of the phallic symbol as an artifact in China is greatly enhanced by the etymology of the character for ancestor, *tsu* 且、祖, which is itself a phallic symbol. Ancestor worship was, therefore, essentially male-ancestor worship, a requisite for which must have been patrilineal descent groups.

The ceramic phallic symbols found at Ch'üan-hu-ts'un 泉護村, Hua-hsien, Shensi, are probably the earliest, dating back to the early third millennium B.C., because they come from a cultural stratum corresponding to the Miao-ti-kou II phase—early Lungshanoid. There is not as yet any detailed report on the Ching-ts'un Lungshanoid finds, but the phallic symbol unearthed there is likely to have been roughly contemporary to those of Ch'üan-hu-ts'un. The ones unearthed from the K'e-hsing-chuang II stratum are considerably later, corresponding roughly in date to the classical Lung-shan period.[29] Outside the Yang-shao nuclear area, the earliest phallic symbol yet found was unearthed from the lower cultural stratum at Ch'ü-chia-ling, near the confluence of the Han River and the Yangtze in Hupei. Chronologically it can now be placed in the early half of the third millennium B.C.[30] A stone phallic symbol unearthed from the Ch'i-chia cultural site at Chang-chia-tsui 張家嘴, Lin-hsia 臨夏, Kansu, can probably be dated around 2000 B.C.[31] Still later, and probably corresponding to the Shang dynasty in chronology, is the phallic symbol found at a Hu-shu

---

[29] *Hsin-Chung-kuo ti k'ao-ku shou-huo*, pp. 14–15; *Feng-hsi fa-chüeh pao-kao*, p. 68; and Kuo Mo-jo, ed., *Chung-kuo-shih kang*, I, pp. 52–53.

[30] See the radiocarbon and bristlecone-pine dates of Huang-lien-shu, Hsi-ch'uan, Honan, in Table 1, chapter 1 above.

[31] *Hsin-Chung-kuo ti k'ao-ku shou-huo*, p. 25.

湖熟 cultural site at So-chin-ts'un 鎖金村 near Nanking.³² The locations and comparative chronology both indicate that the Sinitic religion based on ancestor worship, like so many elements of Chinese culture, originated in the southeastern part of the loess highlands. While artifactual reflection of this religion dates back to the period shortly after the Yang-shao culture had run its course, the religious beliefs and rituals implied in the phallic symbol must have been considerably older.

Third, and closely related to the cult of ancestor worship, was scapulimancy—divination from the cracks that develop in scorched shoulder blades of sheep, cattle, pigs, and occasionally deer—and plastromancy, a similar method of divination by the use of tortoiseshells. The former was definitely of Neolithic origin; but the latter, practiced on a large scale in post-1300 B.C. An-yang, may have originated in areas south of the Huai River, where tortoiseshells were plentiful.³³ Scapulimancy in its crude form involved no special treatment of the bone; findings from that stage bear only scorch marks. Gradually, however, the bones were sawn, cut, scraped, polished, and drilled in order to induce more cracking. With Shang China entering into a full-fledged bronze age, the post-1300 B.C. divination method became elaborately standardized. Not only were bones and tortoiseshells expertly treated in advance, but questions were inscribed and the results of divinations were sometimes also recorded. The main recorded subjects of divination were sacrificial

---

³² Chiang Tsuan-ch'u, "Kuan-yü Chiang-su ti yüan-shih wen-hua" [On the Primitive Cultures of Kiangsu], *KKHP,* 1959, No. 4, p. 37.

³³ Shih Chang-ju, "Ku-pu yü kuei-pu t'an-yüan" [An Inquiry into the Origins of Scapulimancy and Plastromancy], *Ta-lu tsa-chih,* VIII, No. 9 (May 1954), pp. 9–13. *Chiang-su-sheng ch'u-t'u wen-wu hsüan-chi,* introduction, p. 4, and pp. 27–28, mentions that the use of large tortoiseshells to protect the genital area was common in the graves belonging to several Lungshanoid and pre-Shang cultures in the Huai River area and further south, although there is not as yet definite evidence of the use of tortoiseshells for divination in these southern Neolithic cultures. It is now generally agreed that most of the tortoiseshells used for divination in the Shang capital were obtained from the Huai River region and further south.

matters, wars and military campaigns, royal hunting excursions, travels, tributes from allied and subdued tribes and states, the weather, harvests, celestial omens, births, deaths, health, and dreams.

So far, seventy-four Neolithic, Shang, and Chou sites containing oracle bones have been discovered. These bones and shells were distributed over twelve provinces: Shensi, Kansu, Honan, Shantung, Hopei, the former Inner Mongolian province of Jehol, Liaoning and Kirin in Manchuria, Szechwan, Hupei, and Kiangsu.[34] In spite of the apparently wide geographic distribution, the area in which the divination method originated is uncertain. Of the seventy-four sites where oracle bones and tortoiseshells have been verified, the bones of the K'e-hsing-chuang II stratum in Shensi and of the classical Lung-shan site at Ch'eng-tzu-yai in Shantung appear to be the earliest, probably dating from shortly before 2000 B.C. It should be noted that all except two of a total of sixteen pieces of oracle bones unearthed from the lower Lung-shan and upper Shang-Chou strata of the Ch'eng-tzu-yai site were cattle scapulae; that eleven pieces had been treated in simple or complex ways before they were scorched; and that five of the eleven treated bones had been scraped, polished, and drilled.[35] On the other hand, none of the six pieces of sheep scapulae used for divination and unearthed from the K'e-hsing-chuang site had been treated before being scorched.[36] Judging from the extremely crude form of the K'e-hsing-chuang oracle bones, there is reason to believe that they may

---

[34] Chang Ping-ch'üan, "Chia-ku-wen ti fa-hsien yü ku-pu hsi-kuan ti k'ao-cheng" [An Account of the Discovery of Oracle-bone Inscriptions with a Study of the Shang Practice of Divination], *BIHP,* XXXVII (1967), Part II, esp. pp. 842–851. It should be noted that the one most important omission in Chang's listing is the divination bones unearthed from the K'e-hsing-chuang II cultural stratum near Ch'ang-an, Shensi, which are probably the earliest verified oracle bones so far found in China.

[35] *Ch'eng-tzu-yai,* translated by Kenneth Starr (New Haven, 1956), p. 147.

[36] *Feng-hsi fa-chüeh pao-kao,* p. 68.

have been earlier than those of Ch'eng-tzu-yai. Besides, divination was no doubt closely related to ancestor worship, and the earliest artifactual evidence of ancestor worship has been found in the southeastern part of the loess highlands. The piece of crude oracle bone reported to have been found in a Yang-shao cultural site at Ho-ts'un, Fu-shan county, in southern Shansi, if verified, will push the chronology of the Sinitic divination system further back and firmly establish the southeastern corner of the loess highlands as the area of its origin.

In the context of world history, not only were scapulimancy and plastromancy uniquely Sinitic, but scapulimancy preceded in time the ancient Western systems of divination. As the late Alfred L. Kroeber pointed out, not until after 2000 B.C. did Babylonian priests work out a system of divination known as hepatoscopy, the pseudo-science of predicting the outcome of events by examination of the liver of animals sacrificed to the gods; and it was only after its spread to Italy that Etruscan priests developed, alongside of it, a new system of divination from the flight or action of birds known as haruspicy.[37] From the Chinese Neolithic nuclear area, scapulimancy spread to many parts of the Old World where sheep were raised and sheep scapulae were therefore available. It spread from North China first to Inner Mongolia and Manchuria, to Japan by the third century A.D., and later to northeasterly Siberia, Tibet, Central Asia, Arabia, westernmost India, all over Europe including Ireland, Islamic North Africa as far as Morocco and, at some unknown time, "to the nonherding hunting tribes living across the Bering Strait in northerly America."[38]

The increasing spread of ancestor worship and of scapulimancy brings us chronologically close to the Hsia period, which was

[37] Alfred L. Kroeber, *Anthropology* (New York, 1948), pp. 476–477.

[38] For the early spread of scapulimancy to Inner Mongolia and Manchuria, see Chang Ping-ch'üan, "Chia-ku-wen ti fa-hsien yü ku-pu hsi-kuan ti k'ao-cheng"; for the spread to other parts of the world, see Kroeber, *Anthropology,* pp. 477–478.

treated in Chou literary works as the "dynasty" immediately preceding the Shang. Although it is only from the Shang period onward that oracle-bone records and archaeology begin to tally, there are various reasons for believing in the historicity of the Hsia period. First, as has been discussed in chapter 6 in connection with Chinese ordinals, the verification by archaeology of the list of Shang kings preserved in ancient Chinese literature has greatly enhanced the confidence of modern students in the value of both Chou works and the *Shih-chi* with regard to the Hsia period—especially the Hsia kings. According to the *Bamboo Annals* and the *Shih-chi,* the seventeen Hsia Kings altogether reigned 471 years, thus averaging 27.8 years per reign.[39] This chronology is fundamentally different from that of the legendary Sumerian kings, in which each reign period covered centuries. Second, there can be little doubt that the Hsia people had their own calendar, which was retained by the Chin 晉 state in southern Shansi during the Chou period (see Appendix III, note 1).

Third, among the ancient states recognized and reinstated by the Chou royal house shortly after its conquest of Shang in 1027 B.C. no fewer than twenty were thought by the Chou government to have been established in Hsia times. Of the lords of these twenty states, seven bore the royal Hsia clan name of Ssu 姒.[40] The early-Chou royal house gave special consideration to the Ch'i 杞 state in Honan, which was consistently referred to as the legitimate heir of the defunct Hsia dynasty, and whose main function was to continue the sacrifices to the spirits of the Hsia kings. Here, the reliability of Chou works is fully proved by Shang oracle records, which repeatedly mention the Ch'i state and some of its women who became royal consorts.[41] When the first lord of the Chin state, T'ang-shu 唐叔,

---

[39] See ch. 6, n. 22.

[40] Ku Tung-kao, *Ch'un-ch'iu ta-shih piao* [Charts and Essays on the Major Events and Institutions of the Ch'un-ch'iu Period] (1748 ed.), Appendix, ch. 5, *passim*.

[41] Chang Ping-ch'üan, "Chia-ku-wen chung so-chien jen ti t'ung-ming k'ao" [On the Identical Personal and Geographical Names in Oracle-Bone Inscriptions],

was given a fief in southern Shansi—part of the territory once belonging to the Hsia state—he was instructed by the second Chou ruler, King Ch'eng 成王, "to commence his government according to the principles of Hsia."[42] In both *The Book of Odes* and the authentic early-Chou chapters of *The Book of Documents*, the Hsia founder, Yü 禹, was treated with reverence, as a historical personage; and in the latter work the licentious last Hsia ruler, Chieh 桀, was repeatedly accused of being the principal reason why the Hsia state lost its mandate of heaven and was replaced by the Shang. There is nothing in all the authentic early-Chou literature to indicate that the historicity of the Hsia period was ever doubted. In addition, the name of Yü and the dynastic title Hsia are found in the inscriptions of at least two Chou bronze vessels.[43]

Lastly, Chinese works that can justly be called literature began only with the Chou period, and in Chou literature the word Hsia was already a broad ethnocultural expression which included everything Sinitic. The well-known phrase "chu-Hsia 諸夏"—that is, all the lands, peoples, and states that shared a common Sinitic institutional, religious, cultural, and linguistic heritage—is almost an exact parallel to such an expression as "all-Hellas" as it would pertain to the ancient Greek world. Some extremely iconoclastic Chinese historians of the twentieth century argue that the phrase "chu-Hsia," which first appears in an entry in the *Tso-chuan* dated 661 B.C., may reflect late-Chou increasing awareness of the expanding Sinitic world and late-Chou idealization of the cultural continuity of the three dynasties of Hsia, Shang, and Chou. However, similar expressions like "yu-Hsia 有夏," "ch'ü-Hsia 區夏," and

---

Ch'ing-chu Li Chi hsien-sheng ch'i-shih-sui lun-wen chi [Symposium in Honor of Dr. Li Chi on His Seventieth Birthday], Part II (Taipei, 1967), esp. pp. 727–728, 769.

[42] Legge, tr., *The Chinese Classics*, V, *The Ch'un Ts'ew with the Tso Chuen*, Chinese text on p. 750, English translation on p. 754.

[43] Wang Kuo-wei, *Wang Kuan-t'ang hsien-sheng ch'üan-chi* [Complete Works of Wang Kuo-wei] (Taipei, Wen-hua reprint), VI, pp. 2079–2080.

"shih-Hsia 時夏" appear frequently in early-Chou literature. As a collective singular, any one of these phrases means the Sinitic world in a very broad sense; as plurals they mean the various lands, peoples, and states once under the leadership of the Hsia but now all belonging to the Chou. Indeed, as will be discussed in Appendix IV, even down to late-Chou times the "standard" spoken language or dialect was still attributed to the Hsia.

Obviously many of the details of the Hsia period remain to be verified. Nonetheless, one cannot ignore the fact that in early-Chou times, when the illustrious Hsia rulers, their deeds and the major events of their reigns, and the Hsia culture as a whole were much better known, it was firmly believed that the ancient state of Hsia had played an important role in the political, social, and cultural evolution of the Sinitic world. In fact, only the lack of suitable and durable writing materials before the dawn of the bronze age in China has accounted for the difficulty in archaeologically identifying the Hsia period with one of a number of predynastic Shang cultures already discovered.[44]

The list of Hsia rulers, most probably based on reliable oral tradition and non-oracle Shang written records, indicates that the royal Hsia clan was patrilineal in structure. Of the seventeen rulers belonging to fourteen generations, lateral succession occurred three times, during the third, tenth, and eleventh generations; the other successions were all lineal. As compared to the Shang, the Hsia period had a considerably lower incidence of lateral royal succession.

---

[44] I should mention in passing that my views on the historicity of the Hsia period are almost exactly the opposite of those of the leading iconoclastic Chinese historian, Ku Chieh-kang. My discussion of the Hsia period is actually a brief refutation of Ku's views, a more systematic refutation being beyond the scope of this book. Suffice it to mention that the general trend in archaeological and historical research in mainland China since 1949 is very much against Ku. For Ku's more important views on the lack of historicity of the Hsia period, see his various essays in *Ku-shih pien* [Discourses on Ancient Chinese History], II, edited by him (Peiping, 1930), which also contains the most effective criticisms of his views by Chang Yin-lin, pp. 271–284.

Not much more can be said about the Hsia society, but from whatever assessment can be made of it from early-Chou accounts, the Hsia state must have reached such a level of social, political, and territorial organization as to have become the dominant power among the various Sinitic and non-Sinitic tribes and states before the inception of the Shang dynasty.

Although there is much more information available for the study of Shang society than for the study of prehistoric Chinese societies, the tens of thousands of oracle texts still do not tell us about all major aspects of Shang life. It is on the structure and the system of succession of the Shang royal clan that the oracle texts supply the most details. For this reason, during the last sixty years one of the favorite subjects of study by Chinese paleographers and ancient historians has been the system of Shang royal succession. Since the problem of royal succession is related only to the very apex of Shang society, we shall discuss it as succinctly as possible, even though the secondary literature on the subject is very rich.

The list of Shang kings during the dynastic period is given in Table 16. The ceremonial names of Shang kings as listed here are based exclusively on the versions given in oracle texts which differ occasionally in prefix from those given in the *Shih-chi*. Altogether there were thirty-one kings (numbered 1–31) belonging to seventeen generations (numbered I–XVII). In the case of lateral succession or successions within a given generation, no solid line or arrow is inserted between the royal brothers because their sequence is already indicated by Arabic numerals. For the same reason, the solid lines and arrows that connect one generation with another do not necessarily indicate sequence but always indicate father-son relationship. Finally, the kings whose ceremonial names are underlined constituted what toward the end of the dynasty was regarded as the "major lineage" (to be discussed later).

Table 16 reveals several things. First, since lineal succession is necessarily intergenerational, there were altogether sixteen lineal

TABLE 16
A Genealogical List of Shang Kings

I. (1) *Ta-i* 大乙
↓
II. (2) *Ta-ting* 大丁 (3) Pu-ping 卜丙 (4) Nan-jen 南壬
III. (5) *Ta-chia* 大甲
↓
IV. (6) Wo-ting 沃丁 (7) *Ta-keng* 大庚
↓
V. (8) Hsiao-chia 小甲 (9) Lü-chi 呂己 (10) *Ta-mou* 大戊
VI. (11) *Chung-ting* 中丁 (12) Pu-jen 卜壬 (13) Chien-chia 戔甲
↓
VII. (14) *Tsu-i* 祖乙
VIII. (15) *Tsu-hsin* 祖辛 (16) Ch'iang-chia 羌甲
↓
IX. (17) *Tsu-ting* 祖丁 (18) Nan-keng 南庚
↓
X. (19) Hu-chia 虎甲 (20) P'an-keng 盤庚 (21) Hsiao-hsin 小辛
    (22) *Hsiao-i* 小乙
XI. (23) *Wu-ting* 武丁
↓
XII. (24) Tsu-keng 祖庚 (25) *Tsu-chia* 祖甲
XIII. (26) Ling-hsin 廩辛 (27) *K'ang-ting* 康丁
XIV. (28) *Wu-i* 武乙
↓
XV. (29) *Wen-wu-ting* 文武丁
↓
XVI. (30) *Ti-i* 帝乙
↓
XVII. (31) Ti-hsin 帝辛

successions during the Shang period. Second, lateral successions occurred during the second, fourth, fifth, sixth, eighth, ninth, tenth, twelfth, and thirteenth generations, altogether fourteen times. In fact, lateral successions occurred only slightly less often than did lineal successions. Third, in generations having lateral succession or successions, the throne passed on from the last king of the generation either to the son of his elder or eldest brother—as between the second and the third, the sixth and the seventh, and the eighth and the ninth generations—or to his own son—as between the fourth and the fifth, the fifth and the sixth, the tenth and the eleventh, the twelfth and the thirteenth, and the thirteenth and the fourteenth generations. In cases where the throne passed from the last king of a generation to his own son, there is likely to have been discontent or protest, for the heirs of the previous kings of the same generation were deprived of their "right" of succession.[45] Fourth, the unhappy consequences of lateral successions and especially of the lack of a fixed rule for intergenerational succession may have accounted for the drastic change in the entire succession system toward the end of the dynasty. It is significant that during the last four generations, from the twenty-seventh to the thirty-first, the old convention of lateral succession was discontinued and each succession was lineal and presumably based on the principle of "primogeniture."[46]

---

[45] *Shih-chi,* ch. 3, has preserved a summarized account of such complaints and protests, which presumably were based on earlier sources no longer extant.

[46] Primogeniture in ancient China had a prerequisite: the heir's mother had to be the legal wife of the king or the lord. This requisite principle is called *ti* 嫡, legitimacy determined by one's mother's legal status. We know that King Wu-ting, for example, had more than sixty consorts and dozens of sons. Yet only three of his consorts were queens and only three of his sons became kings. Apparently the Shang rule of royal succession must have been based first on the principle of legitimacy determined by the legal status of one's mother and then on seniority among those few brothers who were "legitimate" heirs. See Tung Tso-pin, *Chia-ku-hsüeh liu-shih-nien* [Sixty Years' Cumulative Research on Oracle Inscriptions] (Taipei, 1965), p. 78. A concrete case of the application of the rule of legitimacy is given in

Finally, a very important change in the system by which deceased kings were retroactively classified into major and minor lineages took place during the last quarter of the dynasty. To appreciate this change, it is necessary to know the principles of the original system, which were as follows: (1) Each deceased king received a *shih* 示, tablet bearing his ceremonial name, which was kept in the royal ancestral temple. (2) Only a deceased king who had an enthroned son was given the *ta-shih* 大示, great tablet, a privilege which entitled the spirit of his legal wife to receive all five kinds of sacrifice annually offered by the reigning king. (3) Those deceased kings who had no enthroned sons were given the *hsiao-shih* 小示, small tablets, and their legal wives were not entitled to the five kinds of sacrifice. Consequently by late Shang times even the names of the legal wives of those kings who were classified as belonging to the small-tablet group had mostly been forgotten. (4) In its actual working, this system normally would allow only one great tablet for each past generation, even though it might have produced two or more kings. This was because only one son of either the first or the last king of a given generation could be enthroned as the first king of the next generation. The case of the sixteenth king Ch'iang-chia was an exception: although the throne passed on from him to Tsu-ting—son of his elder brother, king Tsu-hsin—his own son Nan-keng succeeded Tsu-ting as the eighteenth king. For the eighth generation, therefore, both Tsu-hsin and Ch'iang-chia were posthumously granted great-tablet status. But from the time of Tsu-chia (twenty-fifth king belonging to the twelfth generation) onward, Ch'iang-chia was relegated to the small-tablet status and the new and uniform principle of granting

---

Shih-chi, ch. 3, p. 10a: "After Ti-i [the 30th king] was enthroned, the Yin dynasty further declined. Ti-i's elder son was Wei-tzu 微子, whose personal name was Ch'i 啓. Because of the humble origin of his mother, Ch'i was not made an heir apparent. [Ti-i's] younger son was Hsin 辛. Hsin's mother was the legal queen, hence Hsin was made the heir."

only one great tablet for each past generation was strictly observed.[47] This more rigid rule of differentiating major and minor lineages, coupled with the uniformly lineal successions during the last four generations, heralded the rule of primogeniture and the system of lineage segmentation of the feudal Chou period.

Each Shang king had many consorts, but there were few queens. The late Shang sacrificial network reveals that the majority of Shang kings had but one queen, who was posthumously referred to as *pi* 妣, a deceased royal mother or a more remote direct female ascendant. Information about royal consorts is especially plentiful for the long reign of Wu-ting, the twenty-third ruler and the sole king of the eleventh generation. He had more than sixty wives, but only three posthumously attained the status of *pi*.[48] In view of his exceptionally long reign (fifty-nine years, according to tradition), his three queens may well have been consecutive rather than contemporaneous. During their lifetime, royal consorts were given the status of *fu* 婦 (royal consorts). A perusal of the pre-marriage clan names of Wu-ting's consorts reveals that some came from tribal states allied to Shang, some from nonroyal but noble Shang clans, and some even from tribal states politically and militarily at odds with the Shang. There is reason to believe that political, diplomatic, and military considerations were significant factors in Wu-ting's marriages. Some of his consorts were charged with palace

---

[47] For complete listing of the "great" and "small" temples, see Shima Kunio, *Inkyo bokuji sōrui,* p. 288; additional data, see Chang Ping-ch'üan, "Wu-ting shih-tai ti i-pan fu-yüan kuei-chia" [The Restoration of One Piece of Inscribed Tortoiseshell of the Wu-ting Period], *Ta-lu tsa-chih,* XXIX (1964), Nos. 10–11, pp. 98–100; for an analysis of the temple system, Chao Lin, *Marriage, Inheritance and Lineage Organization in Shang-Chou China,* pp. 23 and 51.

[48] Hu Hou-hsüan, "Yin-tai hun-yin chia-tsu tsung-fa sheng-yü chih-tu k'ao" [A Study of the Marriage, Family, Lineage System and the Custom of Birth and Childrearing during the Shang period], in his *Chia-ku-hsüeh Shang-shih lun-ts'ung ch'u-chi* [Studies of Shang History Based on Oracle Texts, First Series] (Ch'eng-tu, 1944), I, pp. 8a–8b, which lists the names of 64 consorts of Wu-ting. Tung Tso-pin, *Yin-li p'u,* I, ch. 3, p. 4b, lists Wu-ting's three queens.

and public duties. The two consorts of Wu-ting most frequently mentioned in oracle texts were Fu-hao 婦好 and Fu-ching 婦妌, seasoned amazonian generals rare in Chinese history.

The living king, his full brothers, and their families formed the *wang-tsu* 王族 (the royal lineage). The king's paternal cousins who had attained the status of *tzu* 子 (royal son), together with their families, constituted the *to-tzu-tsu* 多子族 (literally the lineage of the "many royal sons"). Young members of such lineages were educated in special schools.[49] When they reached manhood, they took part in various religious and administrative affairs. A few of the royal sons were given benefices and set up separate households away from the capital.[50] Unlike the majority of imperial clansmen of later dynasties who were more often than not idle and effete, members of the Shang royal lineage and royal sons were frequently sent to war or to garrison duties.

The Shang king was the supreme head of the Shang state, and he reigned and ruled by "divine right." The supremacy of his position can best be indicated by the expression "yü-i-jen" 余一人 (literally "I, the One Man"), which appears in oracle texts as well as in the chapter "P'an-keng" 盤庚 in *The Book of Documents*. He was also the high priest of the realm, a role made even more charismatic by the increasingly elaborate year-round religious rituals at which he presided. He inherited the throne from the deceased king, who according to Shang religious belief ascended to heaven as a *wang-ti* 王帝 (literally "king-god") to serve in the court of the *Shang-ti* 上帝 (God on High), an aspect which will be

---

[49] There are at least three entries in oracle texts that testify to the existence of schools for members of the Shang royal clan. See Ch'en Pang-huai, *Yin-tai she-hui shih-liao cheng-ts'un* [Selected Sources on the Social History of the Shang Period] (Tientsin, 1959), Part II, pp. 9a–10a.

[50] Chao Lin, "The Governmental Institutions of the Shang Dynasty" (a University of Chicago Ph.D. dissertation not yet completed), in ch. 1, "The Kingship," makes a careful analysis of the names of royal sons and reaches a tentative conclusion that only six royal sons seem to have been given benefices.

discussed in the following section on religion. When his tenure as king on earth ended, he was to be worshiped by his living descendants and former subjects as another "king-god."

In the secular sphere, the Shang king can aptly be described as a "patrimonial ruler." "Patrimonialism means," as Max Weber characterized it, "first of all, that the governmental offices originate in the household administration of the ruler." Put another way: "Under patrimonialism the ruler treats all political administration as his personal affairs."[51] Oracle texts seldom show any clear distinction between a king's personal affairs and those of the state.

A vivid reflection of the lack of such distinction is the frequent occurrence in oracle texts of the phrase *"ku-wang-shih"* 古王事, which literally means "to carry out the king's charge" or "to assist in the king's affairs," and the occasional occurrence of the phrase *"ku-chen-shih"* 古朕事, which literally means "to assist in my affairs."[52] An analysis of the texts containing these phrases shows that the nature of the royal assignment was often unspecified. On several occasions the assignment had to do with preparing for certain religious rituals and for royal hunting, but most of the activities in which the tasks were clearly stated were related to wars and military campaigns against alien tribes and states. The assignees could be individuals within or without the royal household or some collective body, such as the lineage of the "many royal sons" or the

---

[51] Reinhard Bendix, *Max Weber: An Intellectual Portrait* (New York, 1960), pp. 334–335. The wording is Bendix's.

[52] There are so many entries of *"ku-wang-shih"* in oracle texts that a comprehensive listing is unnecessary. This phrase on rare occasions is given in a contracted form: *"ku-shih"* 古事 ("to assist in affairs"). An example is found in Lo Chen-yü, *Yin-hsü shu-ch'i ch'ien-pien* (1931 reprint), ch. 7, p. 23a. Examples of *"ku-chen-shih"* are found in *ibid.*, ch. 8, p. 14a, left plate; in Shang Ch'eng-tso, *Yin-ch'i i-ts'un* (Nanking, 1933), plate 14 on p. 2b; and in Kuo Mo-jo, *Yin-ch'i ts'ui-pien* (Peking, 1965; new printing of the 1937 Tokyo ed.), "K'ao-shih" [Transliterations and Annotations], p. 161b.

group of directors of various government departments known as the *to-yin* 多尹.⁵³

Although all authority emanated from him, the Shang king for reasons of self-interest often found it necessary to abide by time-honored conventions and customs, to assure humane treatment of his subjects, and to set certain limits to the exploitation of the masses. Oracle texts repeatedly show the king's concern for the sustenance and welfare of all his subjects, including the *chung* 眾 (literally the "multitude" or the people), who formed the broad social base of the Shang tribal nation. They also occasionally mention the king's wishes personally to "instruct" the mass of the people.⁵⁴ In fact, much about the father-son (or master-servant) relationship between the king and his more remote and lowly subjects which is revealed in the long speech of 1300 B.C. attributed to king P'an-keng and preserved in *The Book of Documents,* is substantiated by oracle texts. That the Shang king took upon himself, at least as a matter of principle, the task of caring for, sustaining, and instructing all his subjects, high and low, sets him apart from the kings of the subsequent feudal Chou period, who restricted their direct political relations almost exclusively to the officials of the royal court and to their vassals—the lords of various feudal states.

Since the main characteristic of the Shang patrimonial administration should already be fairly clear from the above discussion,

---

⁵³ In addition to the works mentioned in the preceding note, two series of oracle texts published by the Academia Sinica are especially useful for an analysis of the nature of royal assignments and assignees. These are: Ch'ü Wan-li, *Yin-hsü wen-tzu chia-pien k'ao-shih* (Academia Sinica, 1961) and Chang Ping-ch'üan, *Yin-hsü wen-tzu ping-pien,* of which five volumes have so far been published by the Academia Sinica in Taiwan between 1957 and 1967. Some long annotations in the latter have culled relevant entries from all published oracle texts so that the careers of particular royal assignees can be conveniently analyzed.

⁵⁴ Chang Ping-ch'üan, *Yin-hsü wen-tzu ping-pien,* I, "K'ao-shih" [Transliterations and Annotations], pp. 44–45.

SOCIETY, RELIGION, THOUGHT

we need only mention the major categories of the functionaries, both civil and military, who constituted the ruling class.[55]

1. A group of heads of government departments were known as *yin* and *to-yin*. The archaic forms of the character for *yin* 尹 、尹 are generally interpreted as pictographic symbols of a man holding a writing brush with his right hand, meaning that he is a decision-making official and not someone's deputy. That there was probably a lack of clear differentiation of functions among the *yin* is reflected in the multifarious assignments given them by the king, ranging from supervision of the large-scale cultivation of new lands and the construction of royal palace chambers, to participation in wars and campaigns as ranking officers and serving as the king's special emissaries to allied or alien states. Western-Chou bronze inscriptions testify that they served as the king's or lord's *shih-pao* 師保 ("instructors and guardians") and that they frequently were assigned the task of compiling document books (*tso-ts'e* 作冊). While these latter functions are not described in oracle texts, we do know that the Shang government kept records and archives and that several Shang statesmen who had served as *yin* were posthumously worshiped by Shang kings. In short, the importance of the *yin* as a group of officials in charge of various government departments is repeatedly reflected in the authentic early-Chou chapters of *The Book of Documents*.

2. Another group of high officials originated from the *shih* 史 (literally the "scribes"). In China, as in the Near East and Egypt, the ability to read, write, record events, and draft royal ordinances and other literary compositions was a great personal asset. Although etymologically the *shih* means the scribe, oracle

---

[55] Much of my description of Shang officials and officers is based on Ch'en Meng-chia, *Yin-hsü pu-tz'u tsung-shu*, ch. 14, "Officials," and ch. 18, "Status Nomenclature," and Shima Kunio, *Inkyo bokuji kenkyu* (Tokyo, 1958), Part II, chs. 3 and 4. For the etymology of various office titles and status terms, I have consulted Li Hsiao-ting, *Chia-ku wen-tzu chi-shih,* 16 volumes.

texts reveal that by late-Shang times various subcategories of *shih* had become important officials whose functions greatly transcended simply recording and drafting. Wang Kuo-wei was the first modern scholar to discover that the *ch'ing-shih* 卿士, chief ministers of the Chou royal house and of the majority of feudal states, were evolved from the late-Shang *ch'ing-shih* 卿史.[56] Though not mentioned in oracle texts, the offices of *ta-shih-yu* 大史友 ("grand recorder") and *nei-shih-yu* 內史友 ("recorder of the interior") definitely existed in the late-Shang period. For in the famous early-Chou "Pronouncement on Drunkenness" in *The Book of Documents*, which was addressed to the Chou people as well as to the subjects of the newly defunct Shang dynasty, these offices are mentioned. Aside from keeping records and assisting in sacrificial rituals, some *shih* were sent on various ad hoc diplomatic and military missions.

3. A numerically rather large group of *ch'en* 臣, with such prefixes as *to* 多 ("many"), *hsiao* 小 ("little"), *wang* 王 ("the king's") and *wo* 我 ("my," i.e., the king's), may generically be regarded as royal stewards. Certain expressions in the oracle texts like "*hsi wo-chiu-ch'en*" 昔我舊臣 ("my former old *ch'en*") and "*wo-chia chiu-lao-ch'en*" 我家舊老臣 ("former old *ch'en* of my household") for deceased royal stewards strongly suggest that these officials evolved from strictly royal household service. Although the transmitting of royal ordinances and the preparation of horse chariots and carriages for the king and his entourage may be construed as royal household chores, in the course of time a number of *ch'en* received ad hoc commissions as army officers and even army commanders during wars and campaigns. There was also a group of royal stewards called *hsiao-chi-ch'en* 小耤臣, whose main function was to supervise the cultivation of royal fields. On the whole, oracle texts reveal rather intimate relationships between the king and his many loyal servants. I suspect that even the prefix "little" was by

---

[56] Wang Kuo-wei, "Shih-shih" [On the Etymology of *Shih*], in his collected works *Kuan-t'ang chi-lin*, ch. 6.

no means derogatory; it might well reflect the king's affection for those who had waited on him for so long. The king was not the only person to have *ch'en*; nonroyal nobles and high officials could have their own *ch'en* as well. Although *ch'en* as revealed in oracle texts had rather high and prominent status, one cannot rule out the possibility that some of the *ch'en* might have been of servile origin, since their original functions seem to have been exclusively domestic. This may explain why in some Western-Chou bronze inscriptions the term *ch'en* was associated with slaves and other servile groups.[57] But to equate the whole category of *ch'en* with slaves, as some modern historians do, is an unjustifiable generalization.

4. Oracle texts show that the choice of generals for a major military campaign was usually made by the king on an ad hoc basis. The general could be a high official, a trusted noble, or even a royal consort (as during Wu-ting's reign). An important category of officers was called *ya* 亞 or *to-ya* 多亞 (the "many *ya*"), but their exact status and functions are not known, despite cumulative research on oracle inscription. It seems that, while the "many *ya*" were merely officers, some holders of the *ya* title enjoyed the confidence of the king and were entrusted with unusually important assignments, such as offering sacrifices to the sun and the Yellow River and commanding an army which even included members of the royal lineage. The generalized descriptions of the Shang government given in early-Chou literature usually associate the term *ya* with those for other high officials and territorial lords.

The titles of all other officers recorded in oracle texts indicate more specific functions. *Ma* 馬 (literally "horse") or *to-ma* 多馬 (the "many horses") were undoubtedly officers of horse chariotry, for there is abundant archaeological evidence of the use of horse

---

[57] See, for example, the term *ch'en* in the text of Ta-Yü-ting 大盂鼎, in Kuo Mo-jo, *Liang-Chou chin-wen-tz'u ta-hsi t'u-lu k'ao-shih* (Peking, 1958), ts'e 6, pp. 33b–35a. But in most cases in Chou bronze inscriptions the term *ch'en* could be more appropriately translated as "retainers."

chariots in the post-1300 Shang domain, and it is well known that cavalry did not begin to replace chariots until late-Chou times. *She* 射 or *to-she* 多射 were officers of special units of archers. *Wei* 衞 were officers of units guarding the outer domain. *Shu* 戍 were officers in charge of the garrison forces stationed on the northern and northwestern frontiers. There were also officers whose main duty was to assist in royal hunting, which often also served the purpose of military exercise or review. Many a late-Shang king had a passion for hunting, and a royal hunting excursion could last months. Since dogs were used for tracking game, the officers in charge of royal hunting dogs were called *ch'üan* 犬 (literally "dogs").

The term for the army or for the largest armed unit is *shih* 𠂤、師, which already appears in the earliest extant oracle texts of the reign period of Wu-ting, the twenty-third king of the eleventh genealogical generation. An oracle text belonging to the period Wu-i and Wen-wu-ting, the twenty-eighth and twenty-ninth kings of the fourteenth and fifteenth generations, testifies to the establishment of three army divisions, "the right, the central, and the left."[58] While some scholars regard this as the beginning of a standing army, the text should probably be interpreted as a step toward regularization of the core of the army organization. Through careful integration of the An-yang archaeological finds and Chou literary records, an archaeologist of Academia Sinica in Taiwan has established that the *shih* consisted of 2,500 men.[59]

5. In addition to civil and military officials, there were also officials in charge of various artisans in the royal capital area. The range of Shang crafts and the high level of Shang craftsmanship have been studied in detail by archaeologists and art historians and so need no special discussion here. The officials supervising various categories of artisans, such as bronzesmiths, carvers of stone, jade,

---

[58] Kuo Mo-jo, *Yin-ch'i ts'ui-pien*, "Transliterations and Annotations," p. 84a.

[59] Shih Chang-ju, *Yin-hsü chien-chu i-ts'un* [Architectural Remains of Hsiao-t'un, An-yang] (Academia Sinica, Taipei, 1959), pp. 8–9.

bone, and ivory, potters, carpenters, masons, tanners, tailors, etc., were called *kung* or *to-kung* 多工 (the "many artisans"). A signifcant term *ssu-wo-kung* 司我工 (literally the "official in charge of our [royal] artisans") is virtually the same as the term *ssu-kung* 司工 in early-Chou bronze inscriptions, which was the precursor of "ministers of public works" (*ssu-k'ung* 司空). When the term *to-kung* is associated with one of the five royal sacrifices which require music, it might mean musicians.[60] One piece of oracle bone yields a clue that some blind people were trained in music,[61] a custom which became common in Chou times.

Any study of the Shang governmental administration, however brief, should not overlook the basic fact that existing data go back only to the reign of Wu-ting, which probably covered the latter part of the thirteenth and the early years of the twelfth century B.C. Oracle records show that the Wu-ting period was one of unusually frequent wars and of territorial expansion. While the main characteristic of the post-1300 B.C. Shang government was patrimonial, this rapid geographic expansion made it necessary for Shang rulers to amplify existing institutional devices, or establish new ones, by which to administer the extrapatrimonial territories. Such institutional devices may have begun before 1300 B.C., but available data take us back only to the last two centuries of the Shang period. Although oracle texts do not explicitly mention the division of territories under Shang jurisdiction into inner and outer domains, such a broad division as described in some early-Chou chapters of *The Book of Documents* did exist because these chapters were addressed to both the Chou and the subjugated Shang people. We learn from these chapters that most of the territories in the outer Shang domain were held by those designated with the *hou* 侯, *tien* 甸 and *nan* 男 titles.

Let us first discuss the meanings of the terms *nan* and *tien*.

---

[60] Ch'en Meng-chia, *Yin-hsü pu-tz'u tsung-shu*, p. 519.
[61] Ch'en Pang-huai, *Yin-tai she-hui shih-liao cheng-ts'un*, pp. 8b–9a.

The archaic forms of the character *nan*, which in Shang oracle inscriptions are [glyphs] and in Chou bronze inscriptions are [glyphs], have two things in common, namely, the symbol for agricultural fields and the symbol for agricultural implements. The character *nan* occurs but rarely in oracle texts, and it is generally regarded by paleographers as a synonym of *t'ien* 田, which simply means "fields." *Tien* in early-Chou bronze inscriptions and literary records is a variant of *t'ien*. These three synonyms originally designated a person holding such a title whose main task was to carry out agricultural colonization in territories newly acquired by the Shang. Since the locality in which he supervised agricultural colonization was relatively remote from the core of the Shang domain, it is likely that he was granted a benefice for his sustenance. If so, it is impossible for modern scholars to know under what terms he held such a benefice. Not until Chou times do we know for sure that the term *nan* meant a baron or barony.

The term *hou* in the feudal Chou period meant a marquis, and the expression *chu-hou* 諸侯 signified the lords or rulers of the various feudal states. But originally the word *hou* did not mean a feudal territorial lord; it meant a person skilled in archery, hence worthy of being entrusted with the vital duty of commanding sentries on the border.[62] Oracle data about the *hou* are less meager than those about the *nan*, but are still not specific enough to enable us to know all the essential technicalities about his status in Shang times. Altogether we find thirty-five different *hou* in the oracle texts of the last two hundred years of the Shang dynasty, which paleographers divide into five subperiods. Of these thirty-five recorded *hou*, eight appear in oracle texts belonging to two or more subperiods, a fact which probably suggests that such *hou* families may have held the title hereditarily, although a generalization is impossible. Those *hou* who were the king's tested loyal servants are

---

[62] Ch'en P'an, "Hou yü she-hou" [On the Etymology of Hou], and Lao Kan's comment, *BIHP*, XXII (1950), pp. 121-128.

likely to have had their titles and benefices in the outer domain royally granted. But some *hou* were originally heads of alien states; as such, they must have had their own domains and are not likely to have received benefices from the Shang king. That they had had the *hou* title conferred on them might have been due to temporary or token submission to the Shang. Conspicuous among these *hou* were Ch'üan 犬, a contraction of Ch'üan-fang 犬方, a state west of the Shang domain, and Chou 周, the future conqueror of the Shang.

In general, the *hou* guarded the outer domain, administered an area which was under his jurisdiction, supervised agricultural production and colonization, regularly shipped part of the locally harvested grain to the royal court, contributed soldiers to and took part in wars and campaigns. The important advantage that set him apart from other royal functionaries was that he held a benefice. A group of oracle texts belonging to the fourth subperiod casts interesting light on one particular *hou* benefice, although it is far from certain whether this was a representative case. The entries focus on two personages, namely, Man 掔, the king's emissary, and the Hsien 先 Hou. The latter seems to have held his benefice and title hereditarily because the title appears also in oracle texts of the first subperiod which date from at least one hundred years earlier. In spite of the fact that this benefice seems to have been held hereditarily for several generations, Man was ordered to carry out royally sponsored agricultural colonization right into Hsien Hou's benefice and further to supervise the cultivation of lands that had long been opened up by the latter and his predecessors.[63] It is clear

---

[63] Yü Hsing-wu, "Ts'ung chia-ku-wen k'an Shang-tai ti nung-t'ien k'en-ch'ih" [The Opening-up of New Agricultural Lands during the Shang Period as Seen from Oracle Texts], *KK*, 1972, No. 4, pp. 40–45, especially p. 41. Hsien Hou appears only in the first subperiod in Shima Kunio, *Inkyo bokuji kenkyu*, pp. 428–429. On the basis of Yü's findings, I have added one to the total number of seven *hou* given in Shima Kunio's work whose names appear in two or more subperiods.

It is interesting to note that Paul Wheatley, in his *The Pivot of the Four Quarters: A Preliminary Inquiry into the Origins and Character of the Ancient Chinese City* (Chicago, 1971), note 187a, pp. 99–100, thinks that the odes of Shang preserved in

that Hsien Hou's benefice did not enjoy the kind of rights and protection that the benefices of the lords of various feudal states during the subsequent Chou period did.

Few expressions in oracle texts are more indicative of patrimonial relationship than the phrase "to assist in the king's affairs." There are several entries in oracle texts about the king's dealings with the *hou* in which this key phrase appears. For example, an augury of the Wu-ting period asked: "Should the lineage of the many royal sons be ordered to follow the Ch'üan Hou to chastise the Chou [Hou], thus assisting in the king's affairs?"[64] It is highly probable that the Shang king still regarded his relationship with the *hou* as largely patrimonial, whatever might have been the significance of the embryonic *hou* system—a significance which is not likely to have been fully perceived by contemporaries.

A term closely related to the *hou* was the *po* 伯, which in the idealized feudal hierarchical system of late-Chou means an earl. Actually the *po* in Shang times meant the head of an alien state which might be allied with or hostile to the Shang. As a rule, the domains held by the various *po* lay outside the Shang borders. Typical of the terminological hodge-podge in Shang times, the titles *hou* and *po* were often interchangeable. In fact, this confusion

---

The Book of Odes contain some remembrance of Shang government, and that the ode 305 "affords no support for the theory that that government was in any way feudal:

> 'Heaven charged the many princes
> To establish the capital where Yü [the Hsia founder] has labored;
> They came [to court] in connection with their yearly service,
> [Saying] Do not punish or reprove us—
> We have not neglected our husbandry.'"

[64] Shima Kunio, *Inkyo bokuji kenkyu*, p. 428, first three entries under item 7. Three similar entries concerning the 🖃 *Hou*, which contain the same key phrase, are cited in Hu Hou-hsüan, *Chia-ku-hsüeh Shang-shih lun-ts'ung ch'u-chi* [A Study of the Feudal System of the Shang Period] (Ch'eng-tu, 1944), p. 24b.

in nomenclature persisted well into Chou times.⁶⁵ The appearance in the Shang period of such titles as *hou, po, tzu*—meaning a royal son in Shang times but a viscount in the Chou feudal hierarchy—and *nan* does not mean that the late-Shang kingdom was feudal. Feudalism, with its well defined rights and obligations between suzerain and vassals, had to wait until after the Chou conquest of the Shang, when the vast territorial expansion by military conquest and diplomacy made it necessary for the early-Chou rulers to delegate political authority on a large scale to their close kin, relatives, and allies.

We can only conjecture about the social base from which the Shang court recruited its officials. The generalized accounts of Shang government and ruling class given in the authentic early-Chou chapters of *The Book of Documents* more than once mention the term *po-hsing* 百姓 (literally the "hundred names"), which in its late-Shang and early-Chou context meant membership in the ruling class. The ancient connotation of this term is therefore very different from its modern meaning—the mass of the population. Most Shang officials were no doubt recruited from the royal clan and the so-called hundred noble clans. But life stories about a few Shang statesmen handed down to Chou times indicate that some of them were originally humble commoners. The most outstanding examples are I-yin 伊尹, the best known of early Shang statesmen, and Fu Yüeh 傅說, one of the ablest of Wu-ting's high ministers.⁶⁶

---

⁶⁵ Of the sizable literature discussing the Chinese feudal noble-rank system, the more important ones are Fu Ssu-nien, "Lun so-wei wu-teng-chüeh" [On the So-called Five Noble Ranks], *BIHP,* II, No. 1 (May 1930); Tung Tso-pin, "Wu-teng-chüeh tsai Yin-Shang" [The Five Titles of the Shang Period], *BIHP,* VI, (1936), pp. 413–430; Ch'en P'an, *Ch'un-ch'iu-ta-shih-piao lieh-kuo-chüeh-hsing chi ts'un-mieh piao hsün-i,* I, second preface, pp. 5b–10a; and Lao Kan's postscript to the above work, VII, esp. pp. 686b–689a.

⁶⁶ For the historicity of I-yin, see Ch'en Meng-chia, *Yin-hsü pu-tz'u tsung-shu,* pp. 361–366; for the historicity of Fu Yüeh, see Li Ya-nung, *Li Ya-nung shih-lun chi* [Historical Studies by Li Ya-nung] (Shanghai, 1962), p. 492.

It appears that in a society as complex as that of the Shang there was at least some room for interclass mobility.

The great majority of the Shang population is collectively referred to in oracle texts as the *chung* 眾 (literally the "multitudes"). The status of *chung* has for decades been a subject of considerable debate—with strong political and ideological overtones—among Chinese paleographers and historians. As early as 1930, Kuo Mo-jo, now president of the Academia Sinica in Peking, then a leading literary figure who had turned to paleography and ancient Chinese history only during his political refuge in Japan, was already expounding the thesis that ancient Chinese society was a slave society and that *hsiao-ch'en* (royal stewards) and *chung* were "slaves."[67] Between 1950 and 1952 he finished additional studies of ancient Chinese society and made a more articulate discussion of the etymology of the character *chung*. According to Kuo, the archaic forms of *chung* 𗥯、𗥰、𗥱 symbolize three men toiling under the sun; and since three symbolize a multitude, these multitudes in Shang times were slaves.[68] Based on the same archaic forms of the character *chung*, Ting Shan 丁山 arrived at an ironically opposite interpretation—that the multitudes under the protection of the sun god must have enjoyed a rather high social status, comparable at least to that of the free citizenry of ancient Rome.[69] It is clear, therefore, since archaic forms of a character can be subjectively interpreted in diametrically opposite ways, that the status of *chung* cannot be defined until the relevant oracle data have been systematically analyzed.

Oracle texts reveal the following characteristics of *chung*: (1) It was *chung* who cultivated royal fields and fields belonging to other

---

[67] Kuo Mo-jo, *Chung-kuo ku-tai she-hui yen-chiu* [Studies in Ancient Chinese Society] (Peking, 1964; reprint of 1930 ed. with some revisions), pp. 211–215.

[68] Kuo Mo-jo, *Nu-li-chih shih-tai* [The Age of Slave Society] (Peking, 1966; reprint of 1952 ed. with minor revisions), pp. 7–8.

[69] Ting Shan, *Chia-ku so-chien shih-tsu chi ch'i chih-tu* [The Clan and Lineage System Revealed in Oracle-bone Inscriptions] (Peking, 1956), p. 38.

lords and officials. (2) *Chung* participated in royal hunting. (3) *Chung* provided an important source for the Shang army. (4) *Chung* could be summoned by the king and by royal sons for war and garrison duties. (5) Shang kings were very concerned about the loss of *chung* in war and about their education, health, and well-being. (6) Most significantly, *chung* were never used by Shang kings or nobles as human victims, as the Ch'iang people and war captives had been.[70] When these characteristics are put together, it is very difficult to see the *chung* as slaves.

The one document that best reflects the status of *chung* is the long chapter of "P'an-keng" in *The Book of Documents*. P'an-keng, the fifteenth Shang king, in A.D. 1300 moved the capital to An-yang. The chapter in question consists of his repeated exhortations, persuasions, and threats to invoke royal ancestral spirits to punish dissidents. Even the most iconoclastic of modern Chinese scholars agree that much of the content of this chapter is authentic, although the text in its present form may well have been polished by early-Chou officials. Parts of P'an-keng's address to the *chung* are as follows:

Formerly, the kings, my predecessors, and your forefathers and fathers, shared together the ease and labours of the States;—how should I dare to lay undeserved inflictions on you? For generations the toils of your families have been approved, and I will not conceal your goodness. Now when I offer the great sacrifices to my predecessors, your forefathers are present to share in them. . . .

The prosperity of the country must come from you all. If it fail in prosperity, that must arise from me, the one man, erring in the application of punishment. All of you be sure to make known this announcement. From this time forward attend respectfully to your business; have the duties of your offices regularly adjusted;

---

[70] By far the most systematic study of the status of *chung* based on oracle data is Chao Hsi-yüan, "Shih-lun Yin-tai chu-yao sheng-ch'an-che 'chung' ho 'chung-jen' ti she-hui shen-fen" [A Preliminary Study of the Social Status of the Main Producers of Shang Times—the "Chung" and "Chung-jen"], *Tung-pei-jen-min-ta-hsüeh jen-wen-k'e-hsüeh hsüeh-pao,* 1956, No. 4. It should be noted that Hu Hou-hsüan's 1944 article, "The Shang Society Was Not a Slave Society," in his *Chia-ku-hsüeh Shang-shih lun-ts'ung ch'u-chi,* is still useful.

bring your mouths under the rule of law:—lest punishment come upon you, when repentance will be of no avail. . . .

Do I force you by my majesty? My object is to support and nourish you all. I think of the toils of my predecessors, who are now the spiritual sovereigns, for your ancestors; I would in the same way greatly nourish you, and cherish you.

Toward the end of his speech, the king exhorted his officials:

Ah! ye chiefs of regions, ye heads of departments, all ye, the hundreds of officers, would that ye were animated by a true sympathy! I will exert myself in the selection and guiding of you;—do ye think reverently of my multitudes.[71]

The chapter "P'an-keng" testifies eloquently to the fact that not only were the *chung* not slaves but they were the very foundation of the Shang state and society. That the *chung's* ancestral spirits were said to share the king's sacrifices with royal ancestral spirits is certainly strong evidence against their enslaved status, for it reveals beyond doubt the then firm belief that the king and his various grades of subjects, including *chung* as a broad social base, were all descended from the same tribal god and were thus inseparable elements of the Shang body politic. This crucial point in "P'an-keng" has now been archaeologically verified: an oracle inscription put it on record that on the eve of a military campaign the general led his *chung* in offering sacrifices to a royal ancestral spirit.[72] From the king's admonition to the *chung* to have "the duties of your offices regularly adjusted," it is fairly clear that, because of the various vital services performed by the *chung* for the state, many of them could climb up the social ladder through individual merit and ability. All in all, this important ancient document reveals that P'an-keng was a patrimonial ruler *par excellence*.

That the Shang society was not a slave society does not mean that slaves did not exist in Shang times. Both oracle texts and archaeological finds confirm the existence of scattered groups of

---

[71] Legge, tr., *The Chinese Classics,* III: *The Shoo King,* pp. 222–247.

[72] Yü Hsing-wu, "Ts'ung chia-ku-wen k'an Shang-tai she-hui hsing-chih" [The Nature of Shang Society Seen from Oracle Texts], *Tung-pei-jen-min-ta-hsüeh jen-wen-k'e-hsüeh hsüeh-pao,* 1957, Nos. 2–3, p. 112.

slaves. It is important to bear in mind two facts about slaves of Shang times: that the oracle-text nomenclature for slaves is rather limited in range; and that, as far as oracle records and archaeological data go, the majority of slaves, both of the royal household and those used for human sacrifice, seem to have been war captives.

Concerning slave nomenclature, there is a surprising lack in oracle texts of a general term for slaves. The character *nu* 奴, which in post-Shang contexts means slaves in general, has not been found in oracle texts. Although the archaic character 㜷 was interpreted by some pioneering scholars of oracle inscriptions to mean "slave," Kuo Mo-jo has convincingly shown that it is actually the word *chia* 妌、嘉 (literally "good," especially in connection with the birth of a male infant), an interpretation which has been widely accepted.[73] The identification of the archaic character 業 as *p'u* 僕 (domestic servant or possibly slave) has in recent years been accepted by experts, but this character occurs very seldom in oracle texts.[74] The identification of the character *ch'ieh* 妾 (modern context "concubine") in oracle inscriptions has never been contested. The rare occurrences of the use of *ch'ieh* as human sacrifices in royal burials have led some zealous proponents of ancient Chinese slave society to regard *ch'ieh* as female slaves.[75] But the normal usage of *ch'ieh* in oracle texts is such that it means a female spouse, virtually a synonym of *ch'i* 妻 (wife) during lifetime and of *mu* 母 (mother) when addressed posthumously. A number of female ancestors within

---

[73] Kuo Mo-jo, *Ku-tai ming-k'e hui-k'ao hsü-pien* [Collection of Ancient Inscriptions, with Annotations, Second Series] (Tokyo, 1934), pp. 7a–7b.

[74] The identification of the archaic character *p'u* is now accepted in Li Hsiao-ting, *Chia-ku wen-tzu chi-shih*. Hu Hou-hsüan, in his essay, "The Shang Society Was Not a Slave Society," p. 1a, in his *Chia-ku-hsüeh Shang-shih lun-ts'ung ch'u-chi*, mentions that published oracle texts refer to *p'u* only once.

[75] Li Ya-nung, *Yin-tai she-hui sheng-huo* [Social Life during the Shang Period] (Shanghai, 1955), pp. 68–69.

the late-Shang royal sacrificial network were *ch'ieh*.[76] *Pei* 婢, domestic female servants or slave girls, were rarely used as human sacrifices. More commonly sacrificed at the time of their lord's passing were the *hsi* 奚、羮, males who wore a special hair braid as a social stigma.[77]

Significantly, the largest single category of slaves was the Ch'iang 羌, a non-Chinese people of southwestern Shansi and parts of Shensi. Ch'iang in a narrow sense probably meant proto-Tibetans, but broadly used it meant all the non-Chinese peoples northwest of the Shang kingdom.[78] Large numbers of Ch'iang war captives were used as slaves in royal households, as horse grooms, occasionally as agricultural workers and auxiliary soldiers, and were most consistently sacrificed by decapitation.[79] Human victims, decapitated but with skeletons intact, have been discovered in the royal tombs and temples in Hsiao-t'un near An-yang and in other Shang sites in Honan, although their ethnic origins, obviously, cannot be ascertained.[80]

The matter of human sacrifice in Shang times was considered by Kuo Mo-jo in the early 1950s to be crucial to the formulation of the thesis that the Shang was a slave society. Oracle texts indicate that the largest group of slaves were alien war captives. The voluntary suicide or forcible sacrifice of some favorite consorts, servants, or even ministers at the death of their lord was not exclusively a Shang

---

[76] Hu Hou-hsüan, "The Shang Society Was Not a Slave Society" (see note 74 above), p. 1a; also Ch'en Meng-chia, *Yin-hsü pu-tz'u tsung-shu,* pp. 486–489.

[77] For *pei,* see Li Hsiao-ting, *Chia-ku wen-tzu chi-shih,* XII, pp. 3631–3633; for *hsi,* see Hu Hou-hsüan, "The Shang Society Was Not a Slave Society," p. 8a.

[78] Li Hsüeh-ch'in, *Yin-tai ti-li chien-lun,* p. 80.

[79] Yü Hsing-wu, "Ts'ung chia-ku-wen k'an Shang-tai she-hui hsing-chih," p. 116; Hu Hou-hsüan, "The Shang Society Was Not a Slave Society," pp. 5b–7b.

[80] For human victims at the important Hsiao-t'un site near An-yang, see Shih Chang-ju, *Yin-hsü chien-chu i-ts'un,* preface, pp. 7–9 and ch. 6. For a summary of human victims at other Shang and Chou sites in Honan, see Kuo Mo-jo, *Nu-li-chih shih-tai,* pp. 105–108.

custom. At the burial of Lord Wu 武公 of Ch'in 秦 in 678 B.C., sixty-six persons were sacrificed; and for the burial of Lord Mu 穆公 of Ch'in in 621 B.C. the number was as high as 177, including some able ministers.[81] When China's first emperor, Ch'in-shih-huang-ti, died in 210 B.C., all the women in his harem who had not given birth to sons were ordered to be buried along with their master.[82] It is clear, therefore, that the use of human sacrifice is not a sure indication of a slave society.

During the dynastic Shang period, large urban centers arose. Ancient literary records mention that the Shang capital had been changed five times before P'an-keng moved it to the vicinity of An-yang in 1300 B.C. Yen-shih in western Honan is now believed to have been the capital of the Shang founder, Ta-i. An unusually large house floor measuring about 100 meters square at the center of the Yan-shih site is believed to have been a palace foundation, though the whole site has been explored only preliminarily. More is known about the large Shang cities near Cheng-chou in central Honan and near An-yang in northernmost Honan.

Whether any of the Shang settlements near Cheng-chou were pre-1300 B.C. Shang capital remains to be verified. Here, the relics of ancient city walls, which enclosed most though not all of the Shang settlements, have a perimeter of 7,195 meters, with maximum height of 9.1 meters and maximum width at the base of 36 meters. Experiments carried out by mainland Chinese archaeologists have shown that to build a city wall of this dimension, including all the preliminary work of digging, transporting, and compressing earth, would have required the mobilization of 10,000 workers for a period of eighteen years.[83] It has been a matter of debate whether such a

[81] *Shih-chi,* ch. 5, p. 8b, pp. 16b–17a.

[82] *Shih-chi,* ch. 5, p. 29b.

[83] For systematic summaries of the Shang sites in Cheng-chou, see K. C. Chang, *The Archaeology of Ancient China* (1968), pp. 201–209, and Wheatley, *The Pivot of the Four Quarters,* pp. 31–36.

gigantic city wall actually was built in Shang times.[84] But there can be little doubt that the Shang settlements near Cheng-chou were considerably larger than the enclosed area of 3.2 square kilometers (1.24 square miles), for many residential sites and handicraft workshops were outside the enclosure.[85] Considering that the area within the walls of late-Roman and medieval London was only 330 acres (half a square mile plus 10 acres), the Shang settlements near Cheng-chou certainly constituted a large conurbation. Of special interest to students of Shang society is the fact that "the bronzesmiths of the Shang dynasty lived in stamped-earth houses and thus seem to have enjoyed a higher privilege than the common folk, who had to be satisfied with semi-subterranean houses."[86]

The best known Shang sites are those near An-yang. Thanks to systematic excavations carried out by the Institute of History and Philology of Academia Sinica from 1928 to 1937 and to smaller excavations resumed by the Institute of Archaeology of Peking since 1949, it is now clear that the seventeen attested Shang sites altogether cover an area of approximately 24 square kilometers or roughly 9.26 square miles. The core of this late-Shang capital area was near the modern village of Hsiao-t'un, and consisted of an ensemble of royal temples, ceremonial halls, dwellings, and underground drainage ditches. Radiating from the central core were a main service area with bronze foundries and bone factories, various cemeteries for kings, nobles, and commoners (including thousands of sacrificial burials), and various residential districts. While no city wall has been discovered and the settlements do not form a continuous area, the distribution of settlements was fairly dense. The whole settlement pattern of the late-Shang capital area seems

---

[84] An Chih-min, "Kuan-yü Cheng-chou 'Shang-ch'eng' ti chi-ke wen-t'i" [Some Queries about the "Shang City" near Cheng-chou], *KK*, 1961, No. 8, pp. 448–450.

[85] Hsia Nai, "Workshops at the Dawn of History," *China Reconstructs,* VI, No. 12 (December 1957), pp. 18–21.

[86] K. C. Chang, *The Archaeology of Ancient China,* pp. 206–207.

to have been one of sprawling conurbation, by ancient standards at least.[87]

Something should be said now about the extent of the Shang kingdom and its chief means of political control. The Shang kingdom comprised the modern province of Honan, the southern two-thirds of Hopei, much of Shantung, and those areas of Anhwei and Kiangsu north of the Huai River. Southern Shansi, with its rich copper and tin ores, was a much contested area and was under Shang domination during most of the last two hundred years of the dynastic period. At times Shang military campaigns were carried even into Shensi. Beginning with the reign of Wu-ting, Shang forces occasionally penetrated southward into the lower Han River area in central Yangtze. The last years of the Shang dynasty were actually a period of military expansion toward the east and southeast, with the I 夷 peoples of southwestern Shantung and the Huai River area as a main target. The central districts of the kingdom were governed by various officials, and the outlying areas were entrusted to various *hou* and *po* lords and to supervisors of agricultural colonization holding the *nan* or *t'ien*. Many smaller tribal states paid tribute to the Shang kings.[88] There can be little doubt as to the ability of the Shang royal house to mobilize its masses for large-scale construction work, which is well attested to archaeologically, and for warfare. It was out of this dynastic Shang period, when state and society became sufficiently advanced, that Chinese civilization eventually emerged.

So much for the complex, multiclass nature of Shang society. We now turn our attention to the religious beliefs of the Shang

---

[87] Of the sizable literature on excavations near An-yang, we need to mention only the most detailed reports: Shih Chang-ju, *Yin-hsü chien-chu i-ts'un* and Kao Ch'ü-hsün, *Hou-chia-chuang*, 3 Vols. (Academia Sinica, 1962–67). A good summary of the physical layout is in Wheatley, *The Pivot of the Four Quarters*, pp. 36–47.

[88] My discussion of the geographical extent of the Shang kingdom is based on Li Hsüeh-ch'in, *Yin-tai ti-li chien-lun*; Ch'en Meng-chia, *Yin-hsü pu-tz'u tsung-shu*, chs. 8 and 9; and Kuo Mo-jo, *Pu-tz'u t'ung-ts'uan k'ao-shih*, pp. 103b–149a.

people who ushered China into the first verified historical period. In reconstructing Shang religion, two technical questions concerning methodology and sources should be briefly discussed.

First, it is true that the aggregate of published oracle-bone inscriptions yield very rich information on the ancestral cult and thus enable modern scholars to confirm the general accuracy of the lists of Shang kings and their predynastic ancestors preserved in the *Shih-chi* and the *Bamboo Annals*. But oracle bones deal only with specific auguries, sacrifices, and isolated events and were never intended to be systematic theological treatises. Beyond the specific names of royal ancestors and of certain natural deities, oracle texts neither tell stories of creation nor provide variant names for the identification of the supreme deity *Ti* or *Shang Ti* 上帝 (God on High). Thus none of the attempts by the late Wang Kuo-wei and his followers to identify *Ti* with a legendary progenitor of the Shang tribe exclusively through oracle texts are sufficiently convincing.[89]

---

[89] The late Wang Kuo-wei, a leading and most imaginative sinologist and paleographer of the early Republican period, first interpreted the character 夋、夒 and its variant forms in the oracle texts as archaic versions of Chün 夋、俊. He then used some authentic Chou texts to prove that Chün was the tribal god and God on High of the Shang. His disciple, the late Wu Ch'i-ch'ang, pointed out that pictographically the most striking feature of this perplexing character in its archaic forms is a bird's head and a man's body, features which may conceivably have had something to do with the special significance of the black bird in legends pertaining to the beginnings of the Shang tribe. However, Wang later interpreted the same character phonetically as Ngao 爽 and as a near-synonym of K'u 嚳, which according to other authentic Chou texts is a variant name of Chün. If the character K'u was pronounced by the Shang and early-Chou peoples as it is in modern times, then K'u obviously does not rhyme with Ngao and cannot be regarded as a synonym or near-synonym of Ngao. If the archaic pronunciation of the character K'u was determined by "kao" 告, the phonetic which forms the lower part of the complex character K'u, then Wang's phonetic identification of Ngao and K'u would be valid. But the difficulty is that no one can be sure of the archaic pronunciation of K'u in Shang or early-Chou times. In spite of Wang's subjective and tortuous phonetic identification, his views are accepted by many Chinese paleographers, though rejected by some.

My own view is that Wang's philological identifications are not sufficiently convincing but that his identification of the Shang tribal god and God on High

To regard as definitely nonexistent certain aspects of Shang religion because they were not explicitly mentioned in oracle inscriptions even though they can be reconstructed from important Chou texts is methodologically untenable. As students of historical method well know, the *argumentum ex silentio,* especially when applied to the ancient past, has to be used with extreme caution. Indeed, the failure to realize the limits of that argument has been the fundamental methodological mistake of leading iconoclastic historians of twentieth-century China and of a few of their Western admirers.

Second, the best available sources for filling some vital lacunae in Shang religion are what Bernhard Karlgren calls "free" Chou texts. He is referring to those Chou texts in which ancient legends and myths were preserved as they were handed down and which had not been tampered with by the late-Chou and Han Confucianist school in the course of their reconstruction of remote antiquity according to their own moral ideals. "The free pre-Han texts," concludes Karlgren in his methodological study of ancient Chinese legends, "present a system of legends and beliefs which, on the whole, is remarkably consistent and identical in all the texts of the

---

through authentic Chou texts is methodologically valid. In my opinion, much of the scholarly controversy on the Shang tribal god and God on High could have been avoided had Wang and his followers been willing to concede, as I do, that in this case the Shang oracle-bone inscriptions are a blind alley and that methodologically the only valid identification must be through a study of various fragments of ancient mythology preserved in authentic Chou texts. The more important findings of the Wang Kuo-wei school, which are so useful for the identification of the Shang tribal god and God on High by means of authentic Chou literature, includes the following: Wang Kuo-wei, *Kuan-t'ang chi-lin,* ch. 9, pp. 2a–3b; Wang Kuo-wei, *Wang Kuan-t'ang hsien-sheng ch'üan-chi* (Taipei reprint), VI, pp. 2080–2082; Wu Ch'i-ch'ang, "Pu-tz'u so-chien Yin-hsien-kung hsien-wang san-hsü k'ao" [Third Continual Study of Shang Kings and Their Predynastic Ancestors], *Yen-ching hsüeh-pao,* XIV (December 1933), pp. 1–58, esp. pp. 5–15; Kuo Mo-jo, *Ch'ing-t'ung shih-tai,* pp. 7–13, and his *Chung-kuo ku-tai she-hui yen-chiu* (1964 ed.), pp. 196–201; and Yang K'uan, "Chung-kuo shang-ku-shih tao-lun" [An Introduction to the Ancient History of China], reprinted in *Ku-shih pien,* VII, Book I, pp. 65–421, esp. pp. 223–246.

most varying schools."[90] The remarkable consistency and relative paucity of the various legends preserved in such free Chou texts, in sharp contrast to the inconsistency, abundance, and systematization of the legends given in Han and post-Han texts, suggest the superiority and reliability of free Chou texts as sources for the reconstruction of Shang-Chou religion.

With these basic methodological principles in mind, I shall appraise and present only the most crucial data concerning the tribal god and God on High of the Shang culled from the best free Chou texts, without duplicating the detailed studies of the late Wang Kuo-wei and his followers. It needs scarcely be said that of all Chou works *The Book of Odes* is unsurpassed for its authenticity and general textual excellence. Somewhat like the oracle texts, however, its odes pertaining to ancient religious beliefs and practices yield only valuable fragments of facts and do not give the name or variant names of God on High. For tracing the supreme Shang deity, the most important source is the collection of the songs of the people of the great southern state of Ch'u in the Yangtze valley, known as *Ch'u-tz'u* 楚辭. A recent study of the culture of Ch'u based on Shang oracle texts, Western Chou bronze inscriptions, and Chou literary works has established that the Ch'u state, which had been on good terms with the Shang kingdom and was originally located in North China, was forced to migrate to the south some time after the Chou conquest of Shang and was at odds with the Chou royal house during much of the Western Chou period.[91] Because of the northern origin of the Ch'u ruling class and the prolonged semi-isolation of the Ch'u state in the south, the Ch'u culture preserved some Shang lore and legends not found in Chou

---

[90] Bernhard Karlgren, "Legends and Cults in Ancient China," *BMFEA*, No. 18 (1946), pp. 199–366, esp. p. 344.

[91] Jao Tsung-i, "Ching-Ch'u wen-hua" [The Culture of Ch'u], a draft chapter for the Project on the History of Ancient China of the Institute of History and Philology of Academia Sinica, Taiwan, *BIHP*, XXXXI, No. 2 (June 1969), pp. 273–310, esp. pp. 274–275.

works. Especially valuable among the songs of Ch'u are "Li Sao" 離騷 (On Encountering Sorrow) by the great Ch'u patriot-poet Ch'ü Yüan 屈原 of the fourth century B.C., and "T'ien Wen" 天問 (The Heavenly Questions), which consists of a series of queries into problems of cosmogony and China's remote antiquity and is textually likely to be a century or so earlier than "Li Sao."[92]

Another very important source is the *Shan-hai ching* 山海經 (The Classic on Mountains and Seas), by far the richest depository of ancient Chinese mythology. A few Han place-names in the extant text were obviously added by Han scholars, but these minor Han additions do not in any way affect the value of this work as a free Chou text.[93]

---

[92] David Hawkes, *Ch'u Tz'u: The Song of the South* (London, 1959), "General Introduction" and p. 45.

[93] Bernhard Karlgren, in his "Legends and Cults of Ancient China," pp. 204–205, regards the *Shan-hai ching* as a free Han text because of its inclusion of a few Han place names. The views of some traditional and modern Chinese scholars on the subject seem more balanced. The erudite and unusually observant Yen Chih-t'ui 顏之推 (A.D. 531–591) was the first to point out that the addition of a few Han place names by some Han transmitters of the text is not definitive evidence that the text of *Shan-hai ching* on the whole had not been written and compiled much earlier. See Chou Fa-kao, ed., *Yen-shih chia-hsün hui-chu* [Syncretic Commentaries on Yen (Chih-t'ui's) Family Instructions] (Academia Sinica, Taiwan, 1960), 2d *ts'e*, pp. 109a–110a. Yen's view has been greatly amplified by Meng Wen-t'ung, who points out that the *Shan-hai ching* is referred to not only in such Former Han works as the *Shih-chi* and the *Huai-nan-tzu* but also in the late-Chou work *Lü-shih ch'un-ch'iu*. He further argues that the complete lack of systematization of the San-huang 三皇 (The Three August Ones) and the Wu-ti 五帝 (The Five Gods) indicates that the bulk of the text of *Shan-hai ching* was written and compiled some time before the middle of the fourth century B.C., when these legendary figures had already formed an important part of an all-embracing Pantheon. Meng is also of the opinion that parts of the extant *Shan-hai ching* text may have been written considerably earlier than the fourth century B.C. See Meng Wen-t'ung, "Lüeh-lun *Shan-hai ching* ti hsieh-tso shih-tai chi ch'i ch'an-sheng ti-yü" [*Shan-hai ching*: A Brief Inquiry into the Period in which it was Compiled and the Geographic Regions which Contributed to its Contents], in *Chung-hua wen-shih lun-ts'ung*, First Series (Shanghai, 1962), pp. 43–70. Also of interest to textual critics is Hsü Hsü-sheng, *Chung-kuo ku-shih ti ch'uan-shuo shih-tai*, Appendix III, "Notes on the *Shan-hai ching*," pp. 291–301.

In sharp contrast to Confucian texts of Han times, which offer a vast cohesive pantheon genealogically headed by the Yellow Emperor, the *Shan-hai ching* retains much of ancient mythological tales in crude and fragmented form. Through these indisputably authentic and unsystematized texts and some recent paleographic identifications of inscriptions on Shang artifacts, the Shang tribal god and God on High will be traced and identified.

The relevant parts of *The Book of Odes,* "T'ien Wen," and "Li Sao" enable us to reconstruct the following. The Shang tribe's legendary male ancestor, whom the odes simply call *T'ien* 天 (Heaven) and *Ti* (God on High), was K'u 嚳 or Ti K'u 帝嚳 (God K'u). The earliest biological ancestress of the Shang tribe was Chieh Ti 簡狄, whose clan name was Sung 宋 or Yu Sung 有娀, Yu being a particle often attached to an ancient clan name. It was K'u who dispatched to Chieh Ti a black bird, by which she became pregnant and gave birth to the Shang tribe. K'u was therefore at once the tribal god and God on High of the Shang.[94] The uncompromising skeptic may still say that the relevant odes were composed during the seventh century B.C. by people of the Sung state, the official successor to the defunct Shang kingdom, and that "T'ien Wen" and "Lai Sao" were composed during the fifth and fourth centuries B.C., too late to be considered definitive evidence. But one piece of late-Shang oracle bone proves beyond doubt the historicity of the Sung or Yu Sung clan, which even toward the end of the Shang dynasty still supplied the king with a wife; and a late-Shang aristocratic lady, instead of inscribing her bronze vessel with her formal name, indicated her status with an archaic compound character *Hsüan-niao-fu* 玄鳥婦 ("Black-Bird-Wife," see Figure

---

[94] Odes 303 and 304, for Chinese and English texts, see Karlgren, tr., *The Book of Odes*, pp. 262–265; *Ch'u-tz'u pu-chu* (SPPY ed.), ch. 1, p. 25b, ch. 3, p. 16b, and ch. 4, p. 23a; for English translation and annotations, see Hawkes, *Ch'u Tz'u*, p. 30, p. 52, and p. 72.

FIGURE 27. A late-Shang bronze vessel bearing the inscription of a compound pictographic character "Black-Bird-Wife," with a symbol of bird engraved on each of its two "ears." From Yü Hsing-wu, "Lüeh-lun t'u-t'eng," *Li-shih yen-chiu*, 1959, No. 11, p. 66.

27).[95] These recent paleographic identifications of inscriptions on Shang artifacts not only enhance our confidence in the reliability of free Chou texts but also indicate that the legends about the Shang tribal origin which focused on the black bird must have been very old in late-Shang times.

The *Shan-hai ching* mentions a number of gods, some with prolific offspring consisting of legendary and early historic figures.

[95] The identification both of the text of the oracle bone and of the compound pictographic character on the bronze vessel were both done by Yü Hsing-wu in his "Lüeh-lun t'u-t'eng yü tsung-chiao ch'i-yüan ho Hsia Shang t'u-t'eng" [On Totemism and Origins of Religions, with Special Reference to Hsia and Shang Totems], *Li-shih yen-chiu*, 1959, No. 11, pp. 60–69. See also Hu Hou-hsüan, "Chia-ku-wen Shang-tsu niao-t'u-t'eng ti i-chi" [On the Vestiges of Bird-Totem in Shang Oracle Inscriptions], *Li-shih lun-ts'ung*, First Series (Peking, 1964), pp. 131–160.

The presence of many gods no doubt reflects diverse tribal origins. One of the most important gods is Ti Chün 帝俊 (God Chün); thanks to the meticulous analyses by Wang Kuo-wei and his followers of Chün's genealogical relations with some legendary and early historic figures, his name has been established as a variant of K'u. Since Shun 舜, a legendary sage-king, rhymes with Chün, it can be legitimately regarded as a synonym of Chün. The identity of K'u and Chün can be further established through their legendary spouses and descendants.[96] That Chün was at once the tribal god and God on High of the Shang is best shown by passages in the *Shan-hai ching* telling how Chün's wives gave birth to ten suns and twelve moons.[97] These accounts cannot have been interpolations of Han Confucianists, because the famous Ch'u silk manuscript of late-Chou times contains the important sentence: "Suns and moons were created by Chün."[98]

Like most ancient peoples, the Shang worshiped various natural forces, such as the sun, the moon, stars, wind, rain, clouds, thunder, earth, mountains, rivers, forests, and marshes. In addition to all these natural deities, they also worshiped deities representing the four directions—east, west, north, and south. But God on High reigned supreme over all the natural deities. Since oracle texts are available only for the post-1300 B.C. period, it is impossible to trace the evolution of K'u from the Shang tribal god to God on High, if indeed there was such an evolution. All we know is that God as a supreme moral ruler was so awe-inspiring that the Shang king dared to ask for his favor only through the medium of his ancestral spirits. Crop failures, natural calamities, and invasions of the Shang

---

[96] For detailed studies in which K'u, Chün, and Shun are identified through free Chou texts as the same god, see the works by Wang Kuo-wei, Wu Ch'i-ch'ang, Kuo Mo-jo, and Yang K'uan listed in note 89.

[97] *Shan-hai ching* (SPTK ed.), Book II, pp. 71b and 76a.

[98] Jao Tsung-i, "Ch'u-tseng-shu shu-cheng" [Annotations on the Ch'u Silk Manuscript], *BIHP*, XXXX, Part I (1969), pp. 1–32, esp. p. 8.

domain by alien tribesmen were all viewed as God's punishment for men's wrongdoings on earth. But close ties between God and the spirits of Shang kings continued. It was the belief of the Shang people that when their kings died their spirits served in the heavenly court of God. Since deceased kings were also regarded as *ti* (gods), oracle texts occasionally refer to them as *wang-ti* 王帝 (literally "king-gods") so as to be distinguished from God on High. The relationship between God on High and king-gods was therefore just as hierarchical as that between father and sons or between the ruler and his ministers.[99]

Although, in theory, God on High remained the ultimate ancestor of the Shang people, his most exalted status made him aloof. So it was to the spirits of his own biological ancestors, both male and female, that the Shang king offered sacrifices cyclically. By late-Shang times there were but few days in the year when the king was not occupied with one sacrifice or another that he had to offer to his ancestral spirits according to fixed schedules. It was from the spirits of his ancestors that the king expected the answers which would guide him in practically everything, from intimate personal and family matters to vital state affairs. There was therefore a constant spiritual communion, through sacrifices and divinations, between the living and the dead. The use of ordinals for royal ceremonial names, the performance of five kinds of sacrifice according to fixed cycles, the use of animal scapulae and tortoiseshells for augury, and much else, were all uniquely Sinitic. Since the ritualistic aspects of Shang ancestor worship have been briefly described in chapter 6, they will not be further discussed here. My special concern is to explain why the social and cultural ramifications of ancestor worship, just as much as the self-sustaining agriculture that began in Yang-shao times, contributed to making Chinese civilization the most enduring in the annals of man.

[99] Hu Hou-hsüan, "Yin pu-tz'u chung ti shang-ti ho wang-ti" [The God on High and the King-gods in Shang Oracle Inscriptions], *Li-shih yen-chiu,* 1959, No. 9–10.

In ancient China there were three prerequisites to ancestor worship. First, a kinship group had to be able to perpetuate, if not to multiply, itself biologically, for without descendants there could be no ancestor worship.

Second, since in Shang-Chou times ancestor worship was a cult mainly for the high ruling class, it was an absolute requisite for descendants of royal and of various noble lineages to maintain forever, if not further to improve, their status. For the political hierarchy determined the ritualistic hierarchy of ancestor worship. The one concrete symbol of the ritualistic hierarchy in ancestor worship was that the specific kinds and numbers of animals to be sacrificed were determined by the political status of the one who offered the sacrifice. In other words, it was necessary for a royal lineage perpetually to produce kings so as to enable the royal ancestral spirits to enjoy the kind of sacrificial ritual to which they were accustomed. This ritualistic symbol was important because of the belief, then held, which was very likely of prehistoric origin, that ancestral spirits needed and relished freshly sacrificed animals. This was called *hsüeh-shih* 血食 (literally to "eat blood"). In Shang-Chou times, the inability of ancestral spirits to "eat blood" because of their descendants' political downfall was considered to be a most serious matter. This was why, after the Shang conquest of Hsia, the Ch'i and Tseng states, whose heads were descended from the Hsia royal clan, were reinstated; and why, after the Chou conquest of Shang, the Sung state was created with a member of the Shang royal lineage as its head. The purpose was to enable the spirits of Hsia and Shang kings to continue to receive sacrifices offered by their blood descendants. But since by early-Chou times the Hsia and Shang dynasties were both defunct and their legal heirs no longer kings but only lords of states, the rituals for the worship of Hsia and Shang kings had to be revised a grade downward to befit the status of lords of states.

Third, since the sacrificial rituals had to be performed by the king's, or a noble's, legal heir and that heir had to be a male, ancestor worship required the breeding of sons and grandsons. Oracle texts reveal that Shang kings frequently asked their female ancestral spirits about the pregnancies of royal wives and consorts and about the sex of infants yet to be born. In asking about the sex of a forthcoming royal infant, the word "good" (*chia* 好、嘉) was used to denote a boy and the phrase "not good" (*pu-chia* 不嘉) to denote a girl.[100] The Shang people's wishes for male descendants are further reflected in the etymology of the character *sun* 孫 (literally "grandson" but actually remoter male descendants as well). Its archaic form 孫 consists of the character *tzu* (son) on the left and a simplified pictographic representation of a silk thread on the lower right, symbolizing a long unbroken line. Oracle texts also yield such sayings as "to have plenty of sons and grandsons."[101] Contrary to Kuo Mo-jo's premature generalization that the desirability of male descendants was a hazy concept to the Shang people because of the survival of matrilineal descent characteristics in their kinship system,[102] existing evidence clearly shows a strong desire for male heirs.

As Chinese literary works in the orthodox sense began to appear in early-Chou times, we are struck by the pivotal idea of a perpetual line of male descent in the entire religious and social outlook. This idea is exemplified in parts of ode 247 of *The Book of Odes*:

> Your reverent demeanor was altogether what the occasion required,
> And not yours alone, but that also of your filial sons;
> Such filial sons will never be lacking,
> There will ever be conferred blessings on you.
> What will the blessings be?
> That along the passages of your mansion

---

[100] Hu Hou-hsüan, "Yin-tai hun-yin chia-tsu tsung-fa sheng-yü chih-tu k'ao," pp. 18b–23a.

[101] Li Hsiao-ting, *Chia-ku wen-tzu chi-shih*, XII, pp. 3865–3866.

[102] Kuo Mo-jo, *Yin-Chou ch'ing-t'ung-ch'i ming-wen yen-chiu* [Studies of the Inscriptions of Shang and Chou Bronzes] (Shanghai, 1931), *ts'e* 1, p. 2b.

> You shall move for myriad years,
> And forever there will be granted to your posterity.
> What will be your posterity?
> Heaven will cover you with rewards,
> Yea for myriad years,
> The bright appointment and followers.
> What will be your followers?
> Heaven will give you young ladies and young gentlemen [*i.e.,* children],
> Young ladies and young gentlemen,
> And from them shall come ever more sons and grandsons.[103]

Ode 249 clearly says that of the hundred blessings one can hope for, none is greater than to have sons and grandsons who will multiply themselves to "a thousand, a hundred thousand."[104] This basic desire for male heirs is fully reflected in Chou bronze inscriptions. An inscription often concludes with the earnest wish: "May my sons and grandsons forever cherish [this vessel]." Or the wish is expressed even more emphatically: "May my sons and grandsons, for all generations and over myriad years, eternally cherish [this vessel]." It is no exaggeration to say that the core of the ancient Chinese religion is ancestor worship, and, from the standpoint of the living, the crux of ancestor worship is to have male descendants.

It is beyond the scope of this section fully to discuss the metamorphosis of ancestor worship since Confucius (551–479 B.C.), but two important changes should be explained. First, Confucius seems, on the surface, to have weakened ancestor worship as a religion. His skeptical and agnostic attitude toward afterlife and the spirits is summarized in the following terse statements. "He sacrificed [to the ancestors]," he said, "*as if* they were present." On another occasion, Confucius said: "To devote oneself earnestly to one's duty to humanity, and while respecting the spirits to keep

---

[103] To make this ode both readable and faithful in translation, I have freely mixed the translations by Legge and Karlgren with small modifications of my own. See Legge, tr., *The Chinese Classics,* IV, *The She King,* pp. 477–478, and Karlgren, tr., *The Book of Odes,* pp. 203–204.

[104] Karlgren, tr., *The Book of Odes,* p. 205.

away from them, may be called wisdom."[105] The subsequent rationalization of sacrificial rites by Confucian thinkers of the third and second centuries B.C. has been interpreted by a leading historian of Chinese philosophy as a necessary and useful expression of man's affectionate longing for and gratitude to the dear departed, hence as a catharsis of emotions.[106] But the social value of ancestor worship was actually more critical to the self-conscious Confucianist than its personal, psychological value. Hsün K'uang, commonly known as Hsün-tzu, the great synthesist of Confucian thought of the third century B.C., offered by far the most balanced view on sacrificial rites:

Sacrificial rites are the expressions of man's will, emotion, remembrance and love .... With sorrow and reverence, one serves the dead as he serves the living. ... What is served has neither appearance nor shadow, and yet the social order is completed in this way.[107]

Using Hsün-tzu as a point of departure, G. William Skinner analyzed the nature of post-Confucian ancestor worship and assessed its long-range effect on the elite religion of China:

This [Hsün-tzu's] statement called attention to the agnosticism of the elite religion, to the central place of rites within it, to its this-worldly orientation, and to its social purpose. The elite religion excluded any belief in personal immortality; it gave the concept of life after death a social and ethical interpretation: whereas the individual self is subject to death and decay, the sum total of his achievements lives on in the immortality of the social body. But the rites were no less important for this agnosticism. The emphasis was on the rites themselves, not on their object. The importance of ritual lay in its effect on the living. Rites integrated collectivities from the family to the nation, reinforcing their unity through joint participation and the manipulation of symbols of a common origin; they reinforced those relationships (father-son, ruler-ruled, etc.) which were the key to the social order; they celebrated models for behavior. A sophisticated sociology of religion was in effect built into religious belief.[108]

---

[105] The sayings are in *The Analects*. These versions are taken from Fung Yu-lan, *A History of Chinese Philosophy*, Vol. I, translated by Derk Bodde (Peiping, 1937), p. 58.

[106] Fung, *A History of Chinese Philosophy*, I, pp. 350-352.

[107] *Hsün-tzu* (SPPY ed.), ch. 13, pp. 14b-16a.

[108] Skinner's Stanford University lecture on Chinese religion, mimeographed.

While diluting the original religious tenets of Shang-Chou ancestor worship, the Confucianists made such worship all the more viable by their full realization of its social purpose.

Second, with the passing of feudalism in 221 B.C., ancestor worship was no longer a cult mainly for the ruling aristocracy; it gradually permeated all social strata. The long historical process of the universalization of an ancient focal value—the emphasis on the continuity of patrilineal descent—was facilitated by the efforts of the elite since Later Han times to strengthen family and kinship ties and by the efforts of both the elite and commoners since A.D. 1050 to organize themselves into common descent groups.[109] Consequently, the famous saying of Mencius (371–289? B.C.), that of all unfilial deeds none is more serious than the failure to produce male descendants, has exerted abiding and ever-increasing influence on the social behavior of the Chinese. While man's desire to reproduce his own species is certainly universal, never in world history has a large nation been more subjected to powerful and sustained ethical and cultural pressures for biological perpetuation than the Chinese.

In further analysis, however, what is perpetuated is a line of descent, which can be continued even when a man biologically fails to produce a son. The line of descent goes from father to son in the ideal case, to be sure, but there are many other ways to keep the line going in the absence of a biological son—notably, adoption of a son or bringing in a son-in-law. The continuum of kin is a cultural and social creation; it is expressed in virilocal residence, corporate kin groups, ancestor worship, etc. It is social perpetuation, achieved whenever possible biologically.

The cumulative influence of the post-Confucian, metamorphosed ancestor worship on the social values, behaviors, and goals

---

[109] For changes in the family and kinship system in China during the entire imperial age, see Ping-ti Ho, "An Historian's View of the Chinese Family System," in Seymour M. Farber, Piero Mustacchi, and Roger H. J. Wilson, eds., *Man and Civilization: The Family's Search for Survival* (New York, 1965), pp. 15–30.

of Chinese peasants in Thailand, which William Skinner has observed and assessed with deep insight, applies equally well to the average adult Chinese in modern China.

> The Chinese peasant [in Thailand] had a definite place in the temporal continuum of kin. Within the extended kin group—dead, living, and yet to be born—he looked to the past as well as to the future: he was not only grateful to his ancestors for what his immediate family had, but was responsible to them for what he did to further the fortune of his family and lineage. His world view was, therefore, historical and kin-centered, and in this context his industriousness and thrift served ends transcending his individual life. His primary goal was not individual salvation, but lineage survival and advancement. Protracted labor and extreme thrift were the means to these strongly sanctioned ends.[110]

The present mainland Chinese government has certainly made systematic efforts to modernize the family system and to shake off the burden of the past. But there is little in its repeated exhortations to the nation that is not in keeping with a long series of traditional didactic sayings to the effect that the individual, the family, and the nation should work hard, live frugally, and make sacrifices, if necessary, for posterity. For over three millennia, therefore, there has been no weakening of the overriding concern of the Chinese for posterity, which offers a striking contrast to the current American way of "living on credit."

In retrospect, the uniquely Chinese concern for biological and social perpetuation—which originated from a prehistoric and early historic religious focus on ancestor worship and which, in the course of time, became the most primary of all human and social considerations—contributed probably as much to making Chinese civilization enduring as did China's self-sustaining agriculture.

In comparison with other ancient religions, the early Sinitic religion was much more worldly and man-centered. It is not surprising, therefore, that humanist and rationalist thought emerged

---

[110] G. William Skinner, *Chinese Society in Thailand: An Analytical History* (Ithaca, N.Y., 1957), p. 92.

in China considerably earlier than elsewhere in the ancient world. The germinal humanist and rational ideas have generally been attributed to the Duke of Chou, who played a key role in the Chou conquest of Shang. Since there is no extant literature in the orthodox sense that can be definitely dated to the Shang period, and oracle texts deal mostly with divinations, the humanist and rationalist kernel of the Duke of Chou's political theory is commonly regarded as so strikingly fresh as to constitute a real break with the past. Insofar as is traceable, the Duke of Chou was undoubtedly the first Chinese to formulate a coherent political theory. But because early philosophical ideas, in ancient China as in the ancient West, were usually born of religious thought, our discussion of the Duke of Chou's political philosophy will be prefaced by a brief review of Chou religious thought, which, as will be shown, was borrowed almost *in toto* from the Shang. Such a procedure will enable us to distinguish between the old and new elements in the system of thought of this remarkable early-Chou statesman.

The Chou people's "borrowing" of Shang religion is nowhere better shown than in their adoption of the original Shang tribal god, K'u, as their own legendary ultimate ancestor, hence also their God on High.[111] Precisely because of its adopted origin, the Chou people

---

[111] The *Kuo-yü* [Discourses of the States], ch. 4, pp. 6b–7a, mentions that the legendary ancestor of the Chou tribe was Shun. The *Li-chi* [Records of Rites] (SPPY ed.), ch. 46, p. 1a, mentions that the legendary ancestor of the Chou tribe was K'u. Since Shun and K'u were variant names of the same god, it can be seen that the Chou tribe adopted the tribal god of the Shang as its own ultimate legendary ancestor. Although the general authenticity of the *Kuo-yü* cannot be doubted, this specific passage on ancient tribal gods already reveals a gigantic genealogical tree with the Yellow Emperor at the apex. The *Li-chi* definitely represents, at least in part, the Confucian idealization and systematization that went on from late-Chou to Han times. Fortunately, "T'ien Wen" and the *Shan-hai ching* concur in stating that the Lord of Millet (Hou Chi) was a "son" of K'u or Chün, thus indicating that the accounts of the Chou tribal god given in the *Kuo-yü* and the *Li-chi* are correct. See *Ch'u-tz'u pu-chu*, ch. 3, pp. 21b–22a; Hawkes, *Ch'u Tz'u*, p. 54; *Shan-hai ching*, Book II, p. 73b.

A different view of the Chou tribal god and God on High has been expounded by Herrlee G. Creel, *The Birth of China: A Study of the Formative Period of Chinese Civilization* (New York, 1937), p. 342: "But we find Shang Ti also called by another name—Heaven. There is no question that in the Chou period these are commonly used for the same deity. On the other hand, we find that on early Chou bronzes Heaven is mentioned very commonly, while Shang Ti occurs but rarely. But Heaven, as the same deity, does not occur once in all of the thousands of Shang oracle inscriptions that are known. What apparently happened is that the Chou people had a chief deity, called Heaven, before they came into close contact with the Shangs." This opinion has been maintained by him for thirty-three years and is expressed in more detail in his recent book, *The Origins of Statecraft in China*, I, *The Western Chou Empire* (Chicago, 1970), Appendix C. Creel's mistakes are manifold. First, his failure to grasp the basic fact that the Chou tribal god was borrowed from the Shang. Second, his failure to understand that K'u, or under the variant names Chün and Shun, after due metamorphosis in Shang times, was in fact Shang Ti or Heaven. Third, the reason why the term "Heaven" as a deity has yet to be found in Shang oracle inscriptions is that Ti was a time-honored term and late-Shang kings standardized the names of deities by prohibiting the use of alternative names in divination.

These errors in Creel's studies of Chou deities are understandable because of his unwillingness to accept the limited validity of "the argument from silence" in Shang oracle inscriptions and early-Chou literature. But what is not easily understandable is that, in spite of the disproportionate emphasis which he has always placed on Chou bronze inscriptions, nowhere in his discussions of Chou deities in his two chronologically widely separated books has he ever cited the inscription on the famous Ta-feng-kuei 大豐段, the earliest Chou bronze vessel extant. In the text inscribed on this most important vessel commemorating the conferring of noble titles by the first Chou ruler, King Wu, sacrifice was offered to Shang Ti, not to Heaven. The character *t'ien* (heaven) appears twice in this text, once as a surname of the official who assisted King Wu in performing the ceremony and hence also cast this vessel, and once in the noun phrase *t'ien-shih* 天室, which literally means "the Hall of Heaven." According to Huang Sheng-chang, "Ta-feng-kuei-ming chih-tso ti nien-tai ti-tien yü shih-shih" [The Date and History of the Bronze Vessel Ta-feng-kuei], *Li-shih yen-chiu*, 1960, No. 6, pp. 81–95, the term *t'ien-shih* was actually *ta-shih* 大室 (the Great Hall), which was a part of the architectural ensemble for august religious ceremonies. Heaven as the name for the supreme deity is therefore conspicuously missing from the engraved text of this earliest Chou bronze vessel.

Lastly, as will be cited and discussed later in the present text, the former Shang kings "in their conduct stood in awe of Heaven's clear laws and of the small people." Had Heaven been exclusively a Chou deity and alien to the Shang, as Creel postulates, then the Duke of Chou's theory of the mandate of Heaven would have further antagonized the Shang people rather than facilitated their submission. In any

had to make their God even more omnipotent, impartial, and universalistic than he had been during Shang times. A rationale for doing this was belatedly provided in an early-Chou ode:

> God on High in sovereign might
> Looked down majestically,
> Gazed down upon the four quarters,
> Examining the ills of the people.
> Already in two kingdoms [*i.e.*, Hsia and Shang]
> The government had been all awry;
> Then every land
> He tested and surveyed.
> God on High examined them
> And hated the laxity of their rule.
> So he turned his gaze to the west [*i.e.*, the Chou domain]
> And here he made his dwelling-place.[112]

The introduced origin of Chou religion was thus explained away by the ingenious theory that God had voluntarily elected to reside with the Chou people because of their moral superiority. Not only did God thus become completely indigenous, but the Chou people also became his chosen children. The Shang religion was therefore thoroughly adapted to Chou needs with the one necessary revision that King Wen, during whose lifetime the Chou state became strong enough to prepare for an eastern expansion, replace the Shang kings in serving in the heavenly court, "to the left and right of God."[113]

But the exigencies of the Chou wars of conquest over the

---

case, during the thirty-three years since the appearance of his *The Birth of China*, neither Creel nor anybody else has been able to find any evidence to substantiate his conjecture that "the Chou people had a chief deity, called Heaven, before they came into close contact with the Shangs." I have taken pains to prepare this long note because Creel's erroneous view has been the only one known for a generation to Western scholars who do not know the Chinese language.

[112] Waley, tr., *The Book of Songs*, p. 255.

[113] Karlgren, tr., *The Book of Odes*, p. 185.

Shang[114] compelled the Chou leaders to formulate a coherent political theory by which to legitimize the Chou replacement of Shang. Although the brilliant Chou strategy resulted in the capture of the Shang capital area in 1027 B.C., there was urgent need to use moral and political suasion to soften the resistance of the rest of the Shang subjects, especially the main Shang forces stationed in southwestern Shantung and the Huai River area. It was from the repeated pronouncements of the Duke of Chou and other Chou leaders that the theory of the mandate of Heaven emerged.

The total lack of reference in oracle inscriptions to the thought and ideas of the Shang people, other than aspects of their religious beliefs, should not prevent us from tracing the intellectual sources of the Duke of Chou's theory of the mandate of Heaven from authentic early-Chou works. It is true that half a century of relentless intellectual iconoclasm in China has made all students of ancient Chinese history extremely cautious in using early-Chou sources for reconstructing Shang thought, and parts of what early-Chou rulers and statesmen said about the Shang may have been biased. But some of the old sayings explicitly quoted by early-Chou leaders and preserved in *The Book of Documents* cannot but have been sayings of Shang times. The very purpose of early-Chou leaders in quoting old Shang sayings was to make their own political propaganda more persuasive and convincing to the newly subjugated Shang people, many of whom were certainly familiar with the words, deeds, and beliefs of their own former illustrious kings and statesmen.

We may begin with the secular wisdom of a pre-1300 B.C. Shang statesman, Ch'ih Jen, whose historicity is proved by oracle bone inscriptions. He said: "In men one seeks such of old standing;

---

[114] The best studies of the exigencies and strategy of the Chou conquest of Shang are Fu Ssu-nien, "Ta-tung hsiao-tung shuo" [On the Two Phases of the Eastward Expansion of the Chou], *BIHP*, II, No. 1 (1930), and his "Chou tung-feng yü Yin-i-min" [The Eastward Expansion of the Chou and the Descendants of the Subjugated Shang People], *BIHP*, IV, No. 3 (1934).

in utensils one does not seek old ones, but new."[115] The seemingly conservative attitude reflected in the first half of this saying was apparently dictated by contemporary social realities, for in an age when education was available almost exclusively to high-status families it was natural for the royal Shang government to recruit men from families of established reputation and integrity. The latter half of Ch'ih's saying reflected the strong desire of Shang kings for incessant technological innovation, which is well attested to by the constant changes and improvements in Shang art and artifacts.[116] The whole saying suggests that in formulating policies early Shang leaders were not guided by hard and fast principles but by pragmatic reactions to specific circumstances, needs, and reasons.

In "The Announcement about Drunkenness" in *The Book of Documents,* King Ch'eng of Chou said: "The ancients had a saying: 'Men should not mirror themselves in water but should mirror themselves in the people.'" This famous saying quoted by King Ch'eng should be compared with a similar one preserved in the *Shih-chi*: "T'ang [the founder of the Shang dynasty] said: 'I have remarked that when a man looks at water he sees his own image, when he looks at the people he knows whether the government is viable.'"[117] There can be little doubt that the "ancients" cited by King Ch'eng were the exemplary kings and wise men of the Shang. In the same announcement King Ch'eng further said: "I have heard it said that anciently Yin's [Shang's] former wise kings in their conduct stood in awe of Heaven's clear laws and of the small people. They practised virtue and held on to wisdom."[118]

---

[115] Karlgren, tr., *The Book of Documents,* p. 21.

[116] This is the overall impression of Dr. Li Chi of Academia Sinica, Taiwan, a leading authority on Shang decorative art and artifacts, expressed in his various articles and monographs on the Shang material culture.

[117] The two similar sayings are in Karlgren, tr., *The Book of Documents,* p. 55, and in *Shih-chi,* ch. 3, p. 2b.

[118] Karlgren, tr., *The Book of Documents,* p. 45.

These indisputably Shang sayings reveal three things of interest to students of ancient Chinese religious and political thought. First, since "anciently Yin's former wise kings in their conduct stood in awe of Heaven's clear laws and of the small people," it is obvious that *T'ien* (Heaven) as an alternative expression of *Ti* (God on High) must have existed in Shang times, although Shang oracle texts used only the formal *Ti* for God.[119] In fact, in almost all early-Chou literature *T'ien* and *Ti* are completely identical and interchangeable; but nowhere is such identity and interchangeability more firmly established than in the Duke of Chou's speech addressed exclusively to Shang officials, which is preserved in the chapter entitled "Numerous Officers" in *The Book of Documents*. Since the Duke's strategy was to evoke the authority of the judicious Shang supreme deity to help soften the resistance and induce the adherence of Shang officials, at the very least he had to be correct about the deity's formal and alternative names. He would have defeated his own purpose if the term *T'ien* that he used throughout his address were indeed an exclusive Chou god alien to the Shang people, as Herrlee Creel would have us believe. Second, the belief in an all-ruling Heaven and the notion that laws were derived from Heaven were basic elements in the Duke of Chou's theory of the mandate of Heaven. Third, from the few gems of down-to-earth Shang wisdom cited above, there is reason to believe that, at least during the reigns of some wise Shang kings, public policies were rationally formulated and their effects empirically assessed so as to secure the general acquiescence if not the active support of the Shang people.

In spite of the inseparability of policy making and religious ritualism, therefore, there was some germinal rationalist thinking in Shang times; the welfare of the king, the state, and society were

---

[119] This may have been because of the efforts of late-Shang kings to standardize royal ancestral ceremonial names and names of deities. See Tung Tso-pin, *Yin-li p'u*, ch. 1, pp. 4a–4b.

deemed to depend primarily on the application of human reason to public policies rather than on the blessing of Heaven or of God. All this, and much else about Shang history and thought that was known to the Duke of Chou but has since been lost, must have been the sources of his famous theory of the mandate of Heaven.

This theory, which can be reconstructed from authentic early-Chou chapters of *The Book of Documents,* from many early-Chou odes, and from some early-Chou bronze inscriptions, was used as political propaganda aimed at winning the adherence of recalcitrant Shang subjects but also as a serious moral exhortation to the Chou people. When applied to Shang subjects, the theory boils down to the following. First, each of the previous dynasties, Hsia and Shang, came into existence because its founder, being a leader of ability and virtue, had received a mandate from Heaven. Second, the mandate of Heaven must be justified by continued good government by succeeding rulers. Third, the Hsia and Shang dynasties fell because of Heaven's revocation of its mandate, which resulted from the repeated negligence and abuses of the late rulers of these two dynasties. Fourth, how the Chou, in turn, received the mandate of Heaven is best explained by the Duke of Chou:

You, Yin's remaining many officers! The merciless and severe Heaven has greatly sent down destruction of the Yin. We Chou have assisted the decree, and taking Heaven's bright majesty we effected the royal punishment and rightly disposed the mandate of Yin; it was terminated by God. Now, then, you many officers, it was not that our small state dared aspire to Yin's mandate. Heaven's not giving favor to Yin was definite; without our taking advantage of the disorder [of Yin], it helped us. How should we have dared to seek the throne?[120]

The Chou's superseding the Shang dynasty was therefore preordained by God or Heaven because of the Chou leaders' superior virtue.

What is of special interest to students of ancient Chinese thought is that the tone and emphasis of the theory of the mandate of Heaven drastically changed when the theory was set forth for the

---

[120] Karlgren, tr., *The Book of Documents,* p. 55.

Chou people. While holding to the view that Chou's mandate was preordained by God, Chou leaders did their utmost to drive home to their own people that "Heaven's mandate is not easy [to preserve]"; that "Heaven is difficult to rely on"; and that "the appointment of Heaven is not constant."[121] On one occasion, the Duke of Chou went so far as to say that "Heaven cannot be trusted."[122] Accompanying this deep skepticism about Heaven was an endless series of harangues that the Chou rise to power resulted from the industry and toil of both its rulers and its people and that political success depended primarily on sustained human endeavor. A most dramatic admonition to the Chou people never to soften was the proclamation that anyone, from the prince on down to the commoners, found addicted to wine was to be put to death.[123] Early-Chou leaders' apprehensiveness about their political future and their realization of the importance of unrelenting human effort are well reflected in the following ode:

> Mighty is God on High
> Ruler of his people below;
> Swift and terrible is God on High,
> His charge has many statutes.
> Heaven gives birth to the multitudes of the people,
> But its charge cannot be counted upon.
> To begin well is common;
> To end well is rare indeed.[124]

In fact, so much emphasis is placed on human effort that in the last analysis the theory of the mandate of Heaven becomes essentially a rationalist and humanist doctrine. The ultimate determining factor is no longer the will of Heaven but the will of the people. This basically humanist approach is further illustrated by various early-Chou sayings:

---

[121] *Ibid.*, p. 59.
[122] Legge, tr., *The Chinese Classics*, III, *The Shoo King*, p. 477.
[123] Legge, tr., *The Shoo King*, pp. 399–412.
[124] Waley, tr., *The Book of Songs*, p. 252.

What the people desire, heaven will be found to give effect to.[125]

Heaven sees as my people see; Heaven hears according as my people hear.[126]

Great Heaven has no affection;—it helps only the virtuous.[127]

All these early-Chou sayings are quite in keeping with the more ancient Shang saying quoted earlier: "Men should not mirror themselves in water but should mirror themselves in the people."

Interesting as the budding humanist thought is, however, it was born of religious thought and was not yet completely divorced from it. It would be an exaggeration to say that early-Chou leaders were already so daringly skeptical as to have abandoned God entirely. On the contrary, it was their religious faith that provided them with much of the motivation and confidence needed to complete the difficult task of conquering and pacifying the entire Shang world and many adjacent areas. In terms of political theory, therefore, a belief in heaven's mandate and a reliance on human reason and effort appear to be not strictly compatible logically. But if one begins by believing, as the Duke of Chou did, that Chou's rise to power was a God-approved act based on a moral principle, one will feel better assured of the maintenance of God's favor if his people will respond positively to his repeated exhortations for good

---

[125] This sentence is in the very first Chou document, "The Great Declaration," in *The Book of Documents*. In its present form it contains Han interpolations. But since the revealing sentence herein cited is quoted in the *Tso-chuan*, a work which was compiled long before the Han interpolations in *The Book of Documents*, the saying is unquestionably based on an early-Chou text. The Chinese text of the sentence cited in the *Tso-chuan* is in Legge, tr., *The Ch'un Ts'ew with the Tso Chuen*, p. 288.

[126] This sentence is also in "The Great Declaration," but is cited in *The Works of Mencius*, tr. Legge, p. 357, hence is based on an early-Chou text.

[127] This sentence is in the document "The Charge to Chung of Ts'ai" in *The Book of Documents*. In its present form it contains Han interpolations, but the sentence is cited in the *Tso-chuan*, hence is based on a Chou text. See Legge, tr., *The Ch'un Ts'ew with the Tso Chuen*, p. 146.

government and moral excellence. In this sense, a belief in the mandate of Heaven and a reliance on human reason and effort are, at least psychologically, compatible.[128]

For historical perspective, we need to make two long-range observations which are relevant to the evolution of Chinese thought. First, the theory of the mandate of Heaven, first formulated by the Duke of Chou, was to remain the one theory by which the Chinese interpreted and assessed the fundamental morals underlying all subsequent dynastic changes. During the past three millennia the only addition to this theory was made in the latter half of the second century B.C. by the Han scholar Tung Chung-shu 董仲舒, who put the theory into a cosmological framework by treating natural anomalies as warnings against possible misgovernment in the human world. There was no change in the net rationalist and humanist kernel of the original theory of the mandate of Heaven, which did not become obsolete until China was systematically exposed to Western thought in modern times.

Second, the germinal rationalist and humanist ideas in the early-Chou theory of the mandate of Heaven came increasingly to the fore during the half-millennium separating the Duke of Chou from Confucius. It is beyond the scope of this section to trace and

---

[128] Karl Marx's economic determinism offers an interesting analogy to the theory of the mandate of Heaven. A. D. Lindsay, *Karl Marx's Capital* (London, 1925), p. 34: "[Marx's economic determinism] is not scientific, but religious. The devoted, passionate fighter for an ideal easily achieves an assurance that victory is bound to come, whatever may be the success or failure of his individual efforts. Just because he loses himself in an ideal, it assumes a form and a might independent of himself or of his fellows; it becomes something for which the stars in their courses are fighting. A belief in thoroughgoing determinism and a vigorous call to action are logically incompatible, but, if the call to action comes first, they are psychologically compatible. If you begin by believing in the inevitableness of economic laws, as some of the individualist economists did, you will preach inaction; but if you begin, like Marx, with a passionate sense of the need to act, you will be easily persuaded that the economic laws are inevitably working on your side."

analyze the widening streams of moral, ethical, humanist, and rationalist thought and ideas reflected in pre-Confucian bronze inscriptions,[129] odes and songs, and the sayings of a long series of aristocrats, statesmen, and learned men preserved in the *Tso-chuan* and the *Kuo-yü*. There is valid reason to agree with Confucius' conscientious though not unduly modest self-appraisal that he was more a "transmitter" than a "creator" of philosophical thought and with his repeated insistence that the Duke of Chou was one of his most important intellectual predecessors. It can justly be claimed, therefore, that although humanism and rationalism did not become a system of philosophy until Confucius made it into one, incipient humanist and rationalist thought dawned five centuries before Confucius, if not still earlier—even before the Chou conquest of the Shang.

Throughout world prehistory and history the types of society have been rather limited in number. Some of the traceable characteristics of prehistoric Chinese and Shang society may well have been shared in part by other human societies. But there can be no doubt that prehistoric and early historic Chinese religion and thought are uniquely Sinitic in character. No other major religious system, ancient or modern, is earlier and more focused on man's concern for biological and social perpetuation than the Chinese cult of ancestor worship. No other ancient civilization ever produced a system of divination, with all its religious, institutional, and cultural ramifications, quite like that of prehistoric and Shang-Chou China. Although civilization emerged in China considerably later than in Mesopotamia and Egypt, germinal thought and notions that deserve the epithet "philosophical" appeared in China about half

---

[129] For the growth of moral and ethical ideas reflected in Chou bronze inscriptions, see Kuo Mo-jo, *Chin-wen ts'ung-k'ao* [Essays Based on Bronze Inscriptions] (Tokyo, 1932), ch. 1.

a millennium earlier than in the ancient West; for it was not until the sixth century B.C. that philosophical thought occurred in Greece.[130] Early Chinese ideas, much like early Chinese techniques, fully betoken their indigenous origins.

[130] The absence of philosophical thought and ideas in ancient Mesopotamia and Egypt is nowhere more strikingly told than in the title of a very learned book, *Before Philosophy: The Intellectual Adventure of Ancient Man* (Baltimore, 1949). The original and fuller version is Henri and H. A. Frankfort, eds., *The Intellectual Adventure of Ancient Man: An Essay on Speculative Thought in the Ancient Near East* (Chicago, 1946), which contains a chapter on ancient Hebrew thought omitted from *Before Philosophy*. It is clear from this learned symposium that the ancient West prior to the rise of the Greeks failed to produce thought and ideas that deserve to be called philosophical. For a good distilled discussion of the emergence of philosophical thought in Greece from the sixth century B.C. onward, see William H. McNeill, *The Rise of the West*, pp. 212-217.

VIII
The Birth of China: A Résumé

THE PREVIOUS chapters have analyzed the typically Sinitic characteristics of some major technological elements—field agriculture, animal husbandry, pottery, and bronze metallurgy including a review of available evidence on the existence of a prior stage of copper metallurgy—and some even more uniquely Sinitic ideas that underlay Chinese numerals, ordinals, script, language, religion (focused on ancestor worship), divination by scapulimancy and plastromancy, and embryonic rationalist and humanist thought. There is reason to believe that, up to the late second century B.C., Chinese astronomy, too, was devoid of ancient Western influence (see Appendix III). We have seen that the pattern of geographic spread of both the major technological elements and of the basic ideas was invariably centrifugal. A necessary, though minimal, comparison with the ancient West has shown that the trait complex of each of the major Chinese cultural elements, whether belonging to the realm of technology or of ideas, is marked at once by a regionally distinctive Sinitic character and a pattern of centrifugal geographic spread. I therefore conclude that the totality of the trait complexes of the major cultural elements that belatedly coalesced and became articulated in the Shang civilization must have been indigenous.

In this final chapter I first show that the birth of China was the outcome of long processes of intermingling and acculturation of the various ancient peoples who lived mostly within the area of present-day China proper. I then inventory all detectable ancient cultural imports and assess their net significance to the birth of China.

First, it is necessary to redefine the term "proto-Chinese." From the standpoint of physical anthropology, all those ancient peoples with distinctive Mongoloid physical characteristics, especially the presence of the shovel-shaped upper incisor teeth, should be regarded as "proto-Chinese." Davidson Black, who first studied the skulls unearthed from some prehistoric sites in Honan and Kansu, has arrived at the following conclusion:

As a result of the foregoing investigations into the group measurements and form relations of the Honan and Kansu prehistoric crania in comparison with recent North China material, it would seem to be established beyond any reasonable doubt that the prehistoric populations represented were essentially oriental in physical character. Further, the resemblances between these prehistoric and recent North China populations would appear to be such that the term "proto-Chinese" may with some propriety be applied to the former.[1]

Throughout this study of the origins of Chinese civilization, however, I have regarded the Yang-shao people of the southeastern portion of the loess highlands as the "proto-Chinese" for physical-anthropological as well as for cultural reasons. A significant amount of recent data clearly indicates close physical resemblances between the Yang-shao people and the modern Chinese of the southern half of China. That the Yang-shao people were physically more akin to the southern rather than the northern Chinese of modern times is easily explainable. Without going back to prehistory, it is fairly safe to say that during the long imperial age North China was several times conquered by alien peoples of the northern steppe, and ethnic and racial commingling took place on a significant scale. Although the southern half of China was under the domination of the

---

[1] Davidson Black, "A Study of Kansu and Honan Aeneolithic Skulls and Specimens from Later Kansu Prehistoric Sites in Comparison with North China and Other Recent Crania," *Paleontologia Sinica,* Series D, VI, Fascicle 1 (1928), p. 81.

Mongols from 1279 to 1368 and of the Manchus from 1644 to 1911, it has never been a true melting pot as compared with North China. It seems more than coincidental that the southern Chinese of modern times should bear very close physical resemblance to the Yang-shao people.

Culturally, recently discovered paleographic evidence, discussed in chapter 6 and further supplemented in Appendix IV, shows that the Yang-shao numerals (if not also many other simple word-signs which disappeared without a trace or which conceivably may still be discovered) are definitely archetypal Chinese logographs. Throughout China's long history no cultural element has played a more important role than the Chinese script in making the Chinese aware of their common heritage. Judging from the view already prevalent in early-Chou times that there had been a cultural continuum since at least the Hsia era, there is reason to believe that the incipient script played a similarly important role in fostering the sense of being "Sinitic" and in enlarging the Sinitic world.

Furthermore, the Yang-shao people deserve to be called proto-Chinese because their self-sustaining agriculture exerted a permanent influence over all those later peoples of North China who, after a prolonged process of acculturation, regarded themselves as members of the enlarged Hua-Hsia or Sinitic world.

From the rise of various regional and local Lungshanoid cultures to the founding of the Shang dynasty, potsherds and other artifacts are almost completely mute about the ethnic origins of the peoples who created them. All that we are reasonably sure of is that the peoples of the various Lungshanoid cultures east, southeast, and south of the Neolithic nuclear area belonged, like the Yang-shao Chinese, to the large "Southern Mongoloid" racial group. It is difficult to know whether, as compared with the Yang-shao proto-Chinese, these Lungshanoid peoples spoke different languages or merely different dialects, although I suspect that the latter was probably the case. Since the early Lungshanoid period, the expansion of the Sinitic world seems to have been the expansion of a peculiarly Sinitic way of life based essentially on the development of a script system originating from the Yang-shao archetypal word-signs and numerals, and on the Yang-shao pattern of self-sustaining cereal agriculture. From early Lungshanoid times onward this Sinitic way of life acquired an important new attribute—a religion focused on ancestor worship, with all its social and institutional ramifications.

By Chou times, when literary works became relatively plentiful, it had become abundantly clear that the criteria by which the various peoples were differentiated into Sinitic and non-Sinitic groups were cultural rather than racial or ethnic. Whether the criteria had been more or less the same during the preceding millennia cannot be definitely known. But a startlingly iconoclastic saying of Mencius gives us some clue: "Shun was . . . a man of the Eastern I [barbarians]; King Wen [of Chou] was . . . a man of the Western I [barbarians]."[2] As we saw in chapter 7, Shun was a legendary sage-king and a synonym for K'u, the Shang tribal god; King Wen, the most illustrious Chou ruler, laid the foundation for the Chou conquest of Shang. What Mencius really meant to say is that the original "Sinitic" group was relatively small and that any subsequent leaders of non-Sinitic tribes who adopted the original Sinitic way of life and contributed to its enrichment were retrospectively to be regarded as sage-kings of the progressively enlarging Sinitic world. This saying of Mencius, providing us with a long-range historical perspective, suggests that long before the rise of Chou the fundamental criterion for defining membership in the Sinitic world was the awareness of a common cultural heritage rather than of true racial or ethnic affinity; for in all likelihood the

---

[2] This saying of Mencius, which is no doubt based on very old oral traditions, is so iconoclastic that for ages it has baffled Chinese classical commentators and also a modern Western translator. Legge, tr., *The Chinese Classics,* II, *The Works of Mencius,* p. 316, rendered the sentences as follows: "Shun was . . . a man near the wild tribes of the east. . . . King Wen was . . . a man near the wild tribes of the west."

majority of the ancient peoples of North China took their ethnic affinity for granted.

The Chou people regarded those of the two preceding dynasties of Hsia and Shang and themselves as the standard-bearers of the Hua-Hsia or Sinitic cultural tradition. While the Hsia has not yet been identified with a specific late prehistoric culture, Shang oracle inscriptions and Chou literary records make it possible for us broadly to define the Sinitic world in Shang-Chou times and the various non-Sinitic peoples around it.[3]

The Shang kingdom had its headquarters in the present Honan province. Mineral-rich southern Shansi, which was originally within the Yang-shao nuclear area, was frequently invaded by the proto-Tibetan Ch'iang people and sometimes by the Kuei-fang 鬼方 people, whom two generations of cumulative research have firmly established as proto-Turcic.[4] By Chou times, the Ch'iang people were relatively quiet and had probably been driven west by various tribes belonging to two ethnic groups generically referred to as the Jung 戎 and the Ti 狄. The Jung and Ti peoples were generally proto-Turcic, occupying much of northern Shansi and Shensi and areas further north and northeast. Some of the Jung and Ti tribes formed small enclaves within the Chou domain. The only Jung group which was not proto-Turcic was the Shan Jung or Mountain Jung, a proto-Tungusic people who by the Chou era had expanded from southern Manchuria and eastern Inner Mongolia to northeasternmost Hopei. Thus, broadly speaking, the immediate

---

[3] My generalization of the ethogeography of Shang times is based on the following works: Li Hsüeh-ch'in, *Yin-tai ti-li chien-lun, passim.*; Ch'en Meng-chia, *Yin-hsü pu-tz'u tsung-shu*, ch. 8; and Kuo Mo-jo, *Pu-tz'u t'ung-ts'uan k'ao-shih*, pp. 103b–149a.

[4] The first modern study of the proto-Turcic peoples in the North China of ancient times is by Wang Kuo-wei, *Kuan-t'ang chi-lin*, ch. 13, pp. 1a–14b. The best recent study with detailed philological and ethnic identifications is Ma Ch'ang-shou, *Pei-Ti yü Hsiung-nu* [The Northern Ti Peoples and the Huns] (Peking, 1962), esp. pp. 1–20.

northern neighbors of the Chou Chinese were peoples belonging to the agglutinative Altaic language family. Because of the linguistic and cultural differences, the process of sinicization of these proto-Turcic and proto-Tungusic peoples in North China proper was so protracted that it was far from complete even by late-Chou times.

East of the main Shang domain in Honan were the I 夷 peoples, numerically a very large group. In Shang-Chou times, the various I tribes inhabited southwestern Shantung and the area further south to the Huai River region. Some subgroups of the I peoples were probably descendants of those who had created a number of Lungshanoid and Lung-shan cultures, including the Ta-wen-k'ou Lungshanoid culture in western Shantung and the important Ch'ing-lien-kang Lungshanoid culture in parts of Anhwei and Kiangsu. The famous classical "black-pottery" Lung-shan culture discovered at Ch'eng-tzu-yai in western Shantung was probably also an early I culture.

From prehistoric times to the late-Chou period, the central and lower Yangtze had been inhabited by various peoples who were collectively referred to in Chou times as the Man 蠻 or Ching-Man 荊蠻. The Ching-Man were probably descendants of those who had given rise to the Lungshanoid Ch'ü-chia-ling culture in Hupei and the late prehistoric Hu-shu 湖熟 culture in southern Kiangsu.[5] West of the Ching-Man group were the Yung 庸 and Pa 巴 peoples, who inhabited western Hupei and eastern Szechwan.[6] The inhabitants of the three modern southern coastal provinces of Chekiang,

---

[5] The best studies of the prehistoric and early historic cultures of the proto-Ching-Man peoples are Tseng Chao-yü and Yin Huan-chang, "Shih-lun Hu-shu wen-hua" [On the Hu-shu Culture], *KKHP*, 1959, No. 4, pp. 47–58; and their introduction to *Chiang-su-sheng ch'u-t'u wen-wu hsüan-chi*. The integration of archaeological data with ancient literary records seems to have been the work by Tseng Chao-yü, a leading female archaeologist in mainland China who died in 1970.

[6] Ch'en P'an, *Ch'un-ch'iu-ta-shih-piao lieh-kuo chüeh-hsing chi ts'un-mieh-piao hsün-i*, III, pp. 218b–223b, and IV, pp. 375b–377a. Much of my generalization about the ethnogeography of Chou times is based on this seven-volume work.

Fukien, and Kwangtung were lumped together in Chou times as the Yüeh 越 or Po-Yüah 百越 (literally the "hundred Yüeh"). We are least clear about the prehistoric and early historic ethnogeography of Kansu. According to post-Chou sources, the Kansu area was inhabited mainly by two proto-Tibetan peoples, the Ch'iang and the Ti 氐,[7] but we are far from certain that prehistoric Kansu had been stocked with the same peoples.

From our necessarily oversimplified discussion of ethnography, it is quite clear that even prehistoric and early historic China was a cultural mosaic. Although the major cultural elements originated mostly from the Yang-shao proto-Chinese and from those who regarded themselves as members of the expanding Sinitic family, the contributions made by various ancient peoples who were originally non-Sinitic merit a systematic review.

First, the earliest evidences of rice culture have all been found outside the Yang-shao nuclear area. Rice remains found in a number of Ch'ing-lien-kang cultural sites in the Huai River area and parts of the lower Yangtze can now be dated around 4000 B.C. (bristlecone-pine dates). Rice was cultivated about 3300 B.C. by people belonging to the Liang-shu culture in northern Chekiang. And around 2700 B.C., rice culture spread to the lower Han River valley in Hupei, which was within the Ch'ü-chia-ling cultural sphere.[8] If my identifications are right, the peoples belonging to the Ch'ing-lien-kang and Ch'ü-chia-ling cultures were the proto-Ching-Man, and those of the Liang-chu culture were the proto-Yüeh. Thus the one food crop destined to overshadow all others in the future Chinese agricultural system was a contribution by peoples that were not originally Sinitic.

---

[7] The earliest systematic historical account of the extreme northwest of China proper and its peoples is *Hou-Han-shu,* ch. 87, "The Western Ch'iang." Its narrative goes back to Shang-Chou times, but it throws no light on the ethnogeography of the Kansu area in remote antiquity.

[8] See note 39 of chapter 2.

Second, the soybean, another important agricultural crop, was said by Chou works to have been domesticated by the Mountain Jung, a proto-Turcic people. While Chou works mention that soybeans were first brought to the early-Chou royal court as a tribute from the Mountain Jung people and that quantities of soybeans were procured from them in 664 B.C. for wider dissemination in North China, one cannot rule out the possibility that soybeans might have been domesticated considerably earlier than 1000 B.C. in the Manchurian plains by some unspecified proto-Tungusic tribesmen. Thanks to this northeastern contribution, the ancient Chinese cropping system became more balanced.

Third, the first knowledge of metal within the area of present-day China proper was acquired, insofar as is traceable, by the people of the Ch'i-chia culture in ancient Kansu. In the light of Davidson Black's study, the Ch'i-chia people are likely to have been Mongoloid, but it is fairly clear that they were outside the pale of ancient Chinese civilization. Available data is too meager to confirm that Ch'i-chia copper indeed represents the earliest phase of metallurgy in China. As some Chinese archaeologists have conjectured, evidence of even earlier metal may someday be found in sites belonging to the K'e-hsing-chuang II culture in the Wei River basin in Shensi, an area which was once the headquarters of the western group of the Yang-shao people and had close cultural contacts with pre-Shang Honan. Certain antecedent factors in the Ch'i-chia area, however, conform in the main to those which historians of technology generally believe to have been essential to the discovery of metal. It might have been just a happy coincidence that the most important raw material for the local lithic industry turned out to be green stones, which led Ch'i-chia potters to experiment with unusually beautiful green or blue stones for ceramic decoration, which in turn led them to the discovery of copper. For the time being, educated conjecture seems to point to areas west and northwest of the Shang domain for the first knowledge of metal, areas outside what was then the center of the Sinitic world.

Though not as fundamental as the introduction of rice and soybean, and the beginnings of metallurgy, many contributions to the birth of China by various peoples, within and beyond the Neolithic nuclear area after the Yang-shao culture had run its course, are nevertheless very remarkable. Not to duplicate the detailed typological descriptions of the artifacts of post-Yang-shao cultures given elsewhere,[9] I will give only two examples.

The first concerns post-Yang-shao ceramics and decorative art. New pottery forms and new motifs and techniques in ceramic decoration were developed by various peoples from Lungshanoid times onward, from the Kansu area far in the landlocked northwest to the Pacific coast. We need mention only such achievements as the superbly beautiful polychrome wares of Ta-tun-tzu in northern Kiangsu,[10] which belonged to the Lungshanoid Ch'ing-lien-kang culture, and the lustrous eggshell black pottery which has made the classical Lung-shan culture of Shantung famous. We know that the peoples who perfected these wares are very likely to have belonged to the numerically large proto-I group. Many new pottery forms of diverse origins were eventually perpetuated, with some adjustments, in Shang-Chou bronze vessel shapes. Since Lungshanoid times, the cumulative experience of mold-making to form many pottery shapes, especially the complicated *li* tripod, accounted for at least one-half of the complex technology of Shang piece-mold bronze casting. There can be little doubt that Shang decorative art was highly composite in character, with many regional and local Neolithic roots, not all of which can be ethnically identified. Suffice it to say that the ancient Chinese ceramic industry and decorative

---

[9] The best preliminary syntheses of the archaeology of prehistoric China are: *Hsin-Chung-kuo ti k'ao-ku shou-huo*, pp. 1–43; Cheng Te-k'un, *Archaeology in China*, I, *Prehistoric China* (Cambridge, England, 1959); and K. C. Chang, *The Archaeology of Ancient China*, pp. 1–184.

[10] "Chiang-su P'ei-hsien Ssu-hu-chen Ta-tun-tzu i-chih t'an-chüeh pao-kao" [Report on the Exploratory Excavations at Ta-tun-tzu, Ssu-hu Borough, P'ei-hsien, Kiangsu], *KKHP*, 1964, No. 2, pp. 9–56, esp. Plates I and II.

art would have been considerably poorer without the variegated contributions by technologically ingenious and artistically gifted peoples who were not originally regarded as Sinitic.

Second, although the failure of the ancient Chinese to make use of clay resulted in an extreme scarcity of durable writing materials in China prior to 1300 B.C., the development of the Chinese script since the invention of numerals and simple word-signs in Yang-shao times was almost inevitably the outcome of cumulative contributions by more than one group of people. As was implied in our discussion of Chinese ordinals and their complex religious and institutional contexts, the ruling class of the Hsia people is very likely to have been literate to some degree. The sphere of activities of the Hsia people is generally believed to have been southern Shansi or western Honan,[11] within the Yang-shao nuclear area. But the time interval between Yang-shao and Hsia times is about three thousand years; it is very difficult to know whether the Hsia people—the first standard-bearers of the Sinitic tradition that the Chou people could identify—were biologically descended from the Yang-shao proto-Chinese. The predynastic Shang people are believed to have originated from the northeastern part of North China, probably in the Gulf of Pohai area. Their tribal origin legends focusing on the black bird were shared by a number of northeastern peoples of proto-Tungusic stock and by the Koreans.[12] The curious saying of Mencius that Shun, the Shang tribal god, was "a man of the Eastern I people" suggests that the predynastic Shang people may have been ethnically, dialectally, or even linguistically more heterogeneous than early-Chou works would have us believe. This saying also suggests that sinicization of some I subgroups had begun very early—so early, as a matter of fact, that leaders of some prehistoric I subgroups had long since become

---

[11] *Hsin-Chung-kuo ti k'ao-ku shou-huo*, pp. 43-45.

[12] Fu Ssu-nien, *Tung-pei-shih kang* [An Outline of the History of the Northeast] (Peiping, 1932), ch. 1.

sage-kings and important contributors to the later enriched Sinitic cultural tradition.[13] In the course of their migration and expansion southward to Honan, the Shang people both before and during the dynastic period must have undergone a prolonged process of intermingling and acculturation with some I subgroups of Shantung, who were also known in ancient times as the "squatting barbarians."[14] The important role played by the I people in the growth of pre-historic and early historic China as an ethnocultural entity is best attested to by an early-Chou document, "The Great Declaration," which says that among the subjects of the last Shang king were "tens of thousands" or even "millions" of the I people.[15] The contribution by men of genius of some sinicized I groups to the accelerated development of the Chinese script before and during the Shang dynasty may have been not inconsiderable.

Even from our necessarily brief review, it becomes clear that prehistoric and early historic China was always a cultural mosaic and that the birth of China was the outcome of the coalescence of various cultures created by the men of genius of many peoples. According to present knowledge, these peoples lived mostly within the area of present-day China proper. With the exceptions of the proto-Turcic Jung and Ti and the proto-Tungusic Mountain Jung, all the rest belonged to the "Southern Mongoloid" racial family.

---

[13] For the importance of the large I ethnic group in ancient Chinese legends, see Yang K'uan, "Chung-kuo shang-ku-shih tao-lun," in *Ku-shih pien,* VII, Book I, pp. 65–246.

[14] For a brief discussion of the acculturation of the predynastic Shang people with the Eastern I people and the I influence on Shang decorative art, see Li Chi, *The Beginnings of Chinese Civilization,* pp. 20–21.

[15] The present text of "The Great Declaration" in *The Book of Documents* is a forgery by Han scholars. But this important passage on the I population within the Shang domain is quoted in *Tso-chuan,* hence authentic. For Chinese text, see Legge, tr., *The Ch'un Ts'ew with the Tso Chuen,* p. 701. For a general discussion of the significance of the I ethnic groups in the formation of the Chinese nation, see Lin Hui-hsiang, *Chung-kuo min-tsu shih* [History of the Chinese Nation], 2 Vols. (Taiwan, 1965 reprint), I, ch. 4, pp. 73–93.

It is highly probable that from time immemorial the differences among these peoples, who by Chou times were all regarded as members of the Sinitic family, were dialectal rather than linguistic.

In the last analysis, it was the proto-Chinese of the Yang-shao nuclear area who laid the foundation of the Sinitic culture. Its two foundation stones were self-sustaining agriculture based on millet and dry-land farming and the archetypal Chinese script. These were subsequently to serve as the two primary criteria for classifying various ancient peoples as members of the Sinitic or the non-Sinitic conglomerates.

The following inventory of ancient cultural imports is as full as archaeologic and paleographic evidence will allow. I shall review separately those objects of foreign origin that were introduced into the low plain area of North China and those that were brought into Kansu, the extreme northwest of the loess highlands.

The major imports into the low plain area of North China were wheat and barley. Up to the present, as we saw in chapter 2, there has been no verified find of prehistoric wheat in China, and the character for wheat first appeared in the oracle inscriptions belonging to the reign period of Wu-ting, the fourth king after the Shang capital was moved permanently to An-yang in 1300 B.C. Wu-ting's reign probably did not begin until about 1250 B.C. The absence of the character for barley in late-Shang oracle inscriptions is no sure indication that barley was not introduced along with wheat, for barley was a commoner's food which would hardly attract the attention of the Shang court as wheat did. Although one cannot rule out the possibility of their introduction into the Shang domain shortly after 1300 B.C., especially in the light of our aggregate evidence on late-Shang cultural imports, it is safer to say that they were introduced into China some time during the second millennium B.C. That these two ancient Near Eastern crops were introduced into North China so late, together with the equally significant fact that they were adapted to the typically Sinitic system of dry-land farming and completely dissociated from primitive irrigation on flood plains, testifies convincingly that they had nothing whatever to do with the beginnings of field agriculture in China.

Another striking example of a cultural import was the presence, among the vast number of An-yang bronze artifacts, of a very few types of weapons and tools which bear unmistakable Seima motifs. The metal-rich Seima culture flourished between 1600 B.C. and 1300 B.C. and has been instrumental in enabling modern archaeologists to reconstruct the ancient trade routes between the West and the East (see Map 3, in chapter 5). The trade route thus reconstructed shows that this remarkable phase of cultural diffusion took place north of the 50th parallel in Eurasia in an area that includes both the true steppe and the southern fringe of the forest-steppe zone. With the use of Russian archaeological data, this trade route has been traced to the Lake Baikal area, and we may safely assume that from there the Seima types of weapons and tools reached the Shang headquarters in Honan more or less via the present Ulan Bator-Peking route. The absence of Seima motifs in the bronze assemblage of Cheng-chou, a major pre-1300 B.C. Shang city, enables us to date these cultural imports reasonably precisely: they must have been brought in after 1300 B.C. Late-Shang China, as S. V. Kissélev, the leading archaeologist of southern Siberia, has observed, was by no means a passive recipient culturally, for its rich bronze designs and pottery forms exerted a powerful influence over the various Karasuk cultures (ca. 1300–1000 B.C.) east and west of Lake Baikal, and over the Ordos area, which Kissélev regards as a joint Shang-Karasuk cultural sphere.

Kissélev has further postulated that the proto-Turcic Ting-ling 丁零 people was probably the main agent in this cultural transmission. Ting-ling, being one of the most northerly of the proto-Turcic peoples, appeared in Chinese historical treatises rather late, but the *Wei-shu* 魏書 [History of the Northern Wei Dynasty, A.D. 386–534] did say retrospectively that the Ting-ling had lived for a long time in the Lake Baikal area.¹⁶ Whether they occupied the same territory between 1300 B.C. and 1000 B.C. cannot be, or at least has not been, ascertained. What is reasonably sure is that from Lake Baikal southward to the northern fringe of the Shang-Chou domain there were a number of proto-Turcic groups and that east of Lake Baikal the ancient populations were mostly proto-Tungusic.[17]

Our chronology for the inception of the Shang dynasty is, we repeat, conservative, and our comparative chronologies for the beginnings of the bronze age in southern Siberia and in China are so perilously close as to make any hypothesis of diffusion of bronze metallurgy from the former to the latter untenable. According to A. P. Okladnikov, the authority on Siberian archaeology, the first bronze age culture in Siberia, the Andronovo, flourished between 1500 B.C. and 1200 B.C.; and even the conservative *Bamboo Annals'* date for the inception of the Shang dynasty is 1523 B.C. Further, judging from the discovery of bronze articles and a bronze foundry site at Yen-shih (probably the capital city of the founder of the Shang dynasty), the beginnings of bronze metallurgy must have occurred sometime in the predynastic period. In any case, we can be reasonably sure that southern Siberia cannot have been responsible for the beginning of bronze metallurgy in China, for the Andronovo culture was in general very weak in metallurgy, and the Shang Chinese knew nothing about the ancient Western cire-perdue process and developed instead their unique piece-mold casting system. The Seima motifs only indicate, therefore, that late-Shang China did have indirect cultural contacts with the West through the medium of some proto-Turcic peoples.

A third important cultural import missing from the early-Shang Cheng-chou artifactual assemblage but present in the

---

[16] *Wei-shu* (Taipei reprint of Ch'ing palace ed.), ch. 103, pp. 20b–28a. Also, Ma Ch'ang-shou, *Pei-Ti yü Hsiung-nu*, pp. 1–21.

[17] For occasional references to the presence of proto-Tungusic peoples in the Lake Baikal area, see Karl Jettmar, "The Altai before the Turks," p. 142.

post-1300 B.C. An-yang artifactual complex is the horse chariot (see Figure 28).[18] The horse chariot in Eurasia is sometimes dated around 1700 B.C.,[19] but a Finnish orientalist is more cautious:

The importance of the war chariot, as is well known, is connected with that of the horse, which became really familiar to the Babylonians relatively late. While it is true that the horse was already known in Mesopotamia in the first half of the third millennium, it did not become popular until much later, in about the middle of the second millennium. The code of Hammurabi, for example, does not mention the horse or even the chariot. It mentions, however, the draught wagon, *eriqqum*, which was drawn by other draught animals and used in Mesopotamia before the horse was popular.... *Narkabtu* was the two-wheeled chariot and the royal hunting chariot of the king. The oldest occurrences of this word are to be found in the Cappadocian tablets (dating after 2100 B.C.).... The word, however, begins to occur with greater frequency at the time the horse began to be used in war, *i.e.*, after 1500 B.C.[20]

Yet only about two and a half centuries after the horse chariot was used in war in Mesopotamia, the oracle inscriptions of the Wu-ting reign-period often refer to horse chariots, especially for royal hunting. The frequent association of chariots with hunting, of course, does not mean that they were not used in war. For the term *ma* ("horses") or *to-ma* ("the many horses") definitely meant the officers of the horse chariotry; and cavalry did not begin to replace chariots in China until the fourth century B.C.

The similarity between ancient Western and Shang chariots is so striking and their comparative chronologies are so close that we are reasonably certain that the horse chariot was introduced into Shang China from the north. Unlike the centrifugal geographic spread of major Chinese cultural elements, the spread of the chariot was centripetal. A badly decayed piece of oracle bone of the Wu-ting

---

[18] Shih Chang-ju, *Yin-hsü chien-chu i-ts'un*, introduction, pp. 8–9, gives by far the best study, based on archaeological evidence, of Shang horse chariotry as a part of the Shang army system. A more comprehensive study of chariots in ancient China is M. von Dewall, *Pferd und Wagen im frühen China* (Bonn, 1964).

[19] McNeill, *The Rise of the West*, p. 104.

[20] Armas Salonen, "Notes on Wagons and Chariots in Ancient Mesopotamia," *Studia Orientalia* (Societas Orientalis Fennica, Helsinki), VIII (1950), pp. 1–6.

FIGURE 28. An early-Chou grave containing horse chariots. From *Hsin-Chung-kuo ti k'ao-ku shou-huo,* Plate XLVII.

period fortunately preserves the key phrase Kung-chü 舌車 ("chariots of the Kung people"), Kung being the name of a proto-Turcic tribe.[21] The surviving text of a large but damaged piece of oracle bone belonging to the reign of Ling-hsin, Wu-ting's

[21] The text is given in Shima Kunio, *Inkyo bokuji sōrui,* p. 465.

grandson, clearly records the capture by the Shang army of several chiefs of the proto-Turcic Wei-fang 危方 people, their chariots, armors, and arrows.[22] The impact of the techniques of war, as revolutionized by the Indo-Europeans on the great Eurasian steppe, was felt as far away as Shang China. Fortunately, Shang China was protected by immense distances from the Indo-European strongholds and was shielded on the north by various proto-Turcic tribes, which were as yet too loosely organized to be a really formidable foe to China. Although the violent waves generated by the "high barbarism" of the Eurasian steppe had become mere ripples by the time they reached the borders of Shang China, oracle texts reveal that the Wu-ting period had an unusually high frequency of wars and campaigns. There can be little doubt that the thirteenth century B.C. was one of accelerated contacts between the Chinese and their northern neighbors.

Fourth, among the rich artifacts of An-yang are certain art motifs which Dr. Li Chi of Academia Sinica, Taipei, a leading authority on Shang decorative art, has regarded as being of "obvious Western affiliation." An outstanding example is a disintegrated wooden article, unearthed from a royal tomb of Hou-chia-chuang near An-yang, in the form of the *fei-i* 肥遺 monster. It consists of a head, now split and partially disintegrated, and two intertwining snake bodies, a pattern which reappeared many times in later Chinese art (see Figure 29). Having compared it with illustrations in standard works on ancient Near Eastern archaeology, Li believes that the *fei-i* was a Shang adaptation of a motif of ultimate Sumerian origin.[23]

Another famous ancient Mesopotamian motif, the "hero and beast," is clearly discernible in Shang and Chou bronzes, in spite

---

[22] The text is given in and discussed by Li Hsüeh-ch'in, *Yin-tai ti-li chien-lun*, pp. 72–73.

[23] Li Chi, *The Beginnings of Chinese Civilization*, pp. 26–27.

FIGURE 29. The *Fei-i* monster on Shang wood-carving. From Kao Ch'ü-hsun, *Hou-chia-chuang*, II, Part I, Figure on p. 57.

of significant modifications by ancient Chinese craftsmen (see Figure 30).

Li Chi has also generalized on Western influence on Shang pottery forms:

> The most interesting proof of China's contact with the West in the second millennium B.C. or even earlier comes from pottery forms. The example I have for illustration is a jar cover, in the shape of a flower pot, with a phallic-shaped handle standing upright in the center inside the pot [see Figure 31]. This type of cover, as made known by McKay and publicized by Gordon Childe, was also found in Jemdet Nasr and Mohenjo-daro. Comparing the pottery forms of the Shang period with those of the Middle East and the Near East regions, one may find a number of instances that exhibit close resemblances; but I take this one as the most indisputable example indicating cultural contact, as no imaginable reason could be conceived for the independent invention of covers so similar in structure in two different and widely separated parts of the world.[24]

While Li Chi's generalization is in fact disputable, I need only supplement it by pointing out that, insofar as I have been able to check through the massive post-1949 mainland Chinese archaeological reports, all the art motifs just discussed are absent from the artifactual assemblages of the two important early-Shang cities near Yen-shih and Cheng-chou and from those of earlier Chinese Neolithic cultures. Always a careful scholar, however, Li Chi cautions his readers by saying that the cultural contact between late-Shang China and the West "may have been a very remote one resulting in partial imitations, such as most of the instances cited actually were."[25]

Indeed, the aggregate evidence presented and scrutinized in all previous chapters of this book supports the view that cultural contacts between the ancient West and the ancient East most probably did not begin on any detectable scale until the thirteenth century B.C., and then only through the medium of many ethnic groups of southern Siberia and of Outer and Inner Mongolia.

[24] *Ibid.*, p. 29.
[25] *Ibid.*

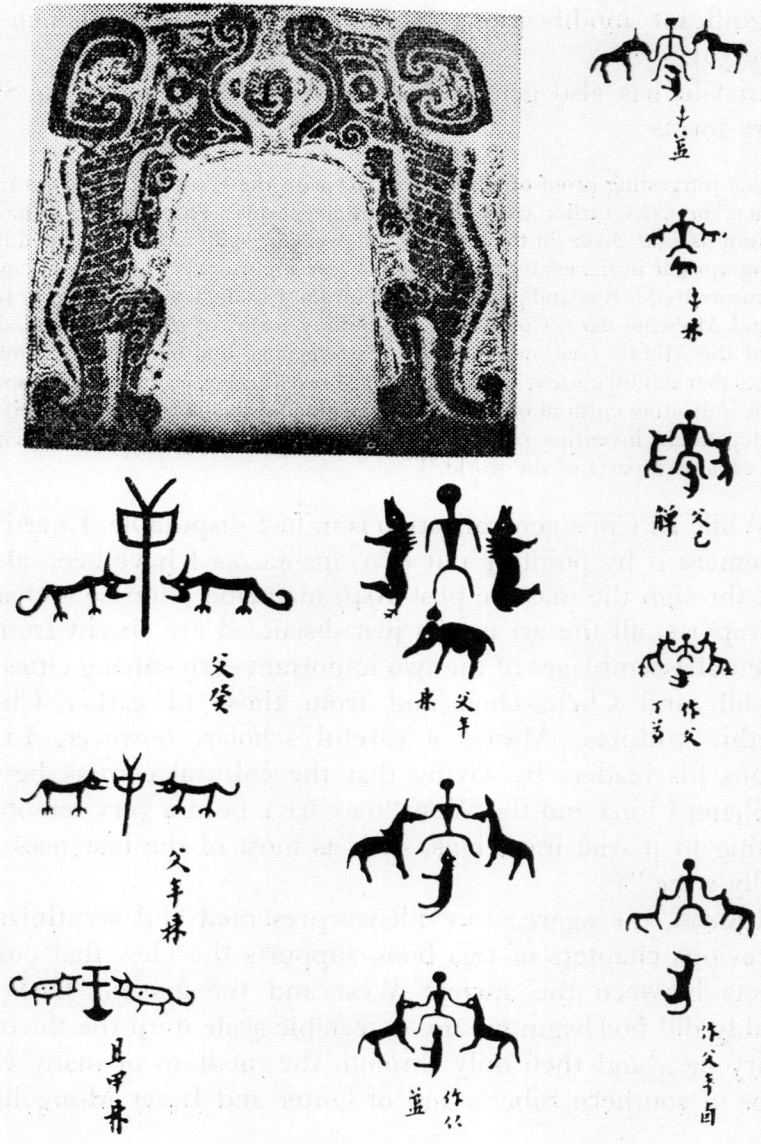

FIGURE 30. Ancient Chinese adaptation of the "hero and beast." From Li Chi, *The Beginnings of Chinese Civilization*, Plate I.

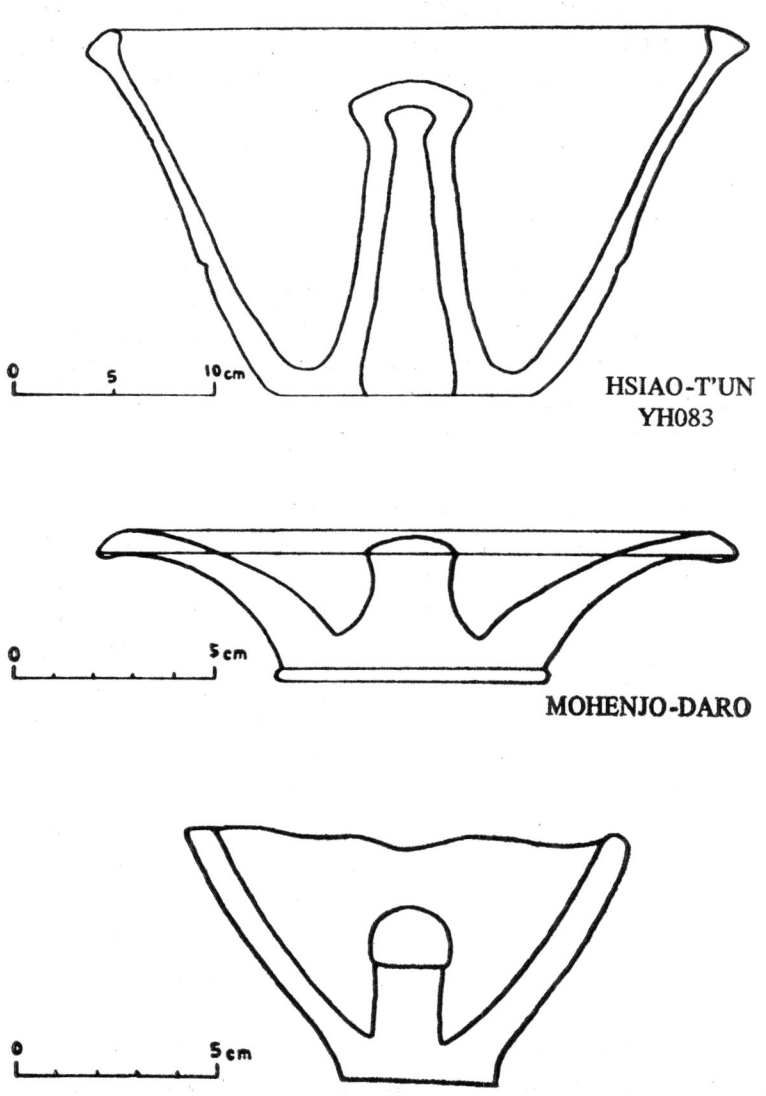

FIGURE 31. A peculiar Shang and ancient Western pottery form. From Li Chi, *The Beginnings of Chinese Civilization*, p. 28.

Turning from the low plains of North China to the dry northwest, our evidence has shown that the "silk route," which played so important a role in cultural transmission from Han times onward, simply did not perform the same function in prehistoric times. The counterclockwise spiral motif of prehistoric Kansu pottery, which J. G. Andersson believes to have originated in Tripolje in the Ukraine, is shown to have been the outcome of long processes of stylistic evolution from the Yang-shao zoomorphic bird. The existence of local variations of this motif, both on Neolithic ceramics in the low plains of North China and in Shang stone and jade carving, further indicates its native origins. So well documented archaeologically is the native origin and artistic evolution of the counterclockwise spiral motif that Andersson's postulation of its Ukrainian origin, first made in the 1920s and reaffirmed in 1943, must now be declared completely invalid.

All that we have found so far in prehistoric Kansu that is of indisputable Near Eastern origin is the domesticated goat in the osteological remains of some Ch'i-chia cultural sites. The lack of detailed stratigraphical reports with respect to the Ch'i-chia goat makes precise dating impossible. The goat could have arrived some time after 2000 B.C. or as late as the end of the second millennium B.C. In any case, it took more than five thousand years for the domesticated goat of the Near East finally to reach Kansu through many intermediary herdsmen of the dry belt of Central Asia—most unlikely agents for transmitting eastward the higher elements of the ancient Near Eastern civilization. Obviously, the goat arrived in Kansu too late to have anything to do with the origins of animal domestication in China. (See Appendix V for further data on the Kansu "goat.")

Thus the full inventory of cultural imports into ancient China is not only meager in quantity, but qualitatively and chronologically such as to have had no bearing whatever either on the beginnings of any of the major Chinese cultural elements or on the birth of China as a whole.

Our discussion of ancient China's cultural imports may be useful in refining the theory of cultural diffusion. "When something new has been evolved in a culture," generalized the late Alfred L. Kroeber, "whether a tool or an idea or a custom, there is a tendency for it to be passed to the culture of other societies."[26] This generalization is borne out by much of human history, from Paleolithic times to the present. The use of fire and the crudest lithic tools, to name two of the most fundamental ingredients that differentiated men from animals, in due course of time became the common cultural heritage of Paleolithic men over wide areas of the globe. Instances of cultural diffusion during the historical period can usually, though not always, be documented with more accuracy. Yet the aggregate evidence on the birth of China, particularly that pertaining to cultural imports, argues strongly against the diffusion to China of prehistoric and early historic Near Eastern cultural elements—at least until the Chinese civilization had definitely emerged. What made ancient China a major exception to the general rule that culture has a natural tendency to diffuse?

To answer this question, we have to consider three factors basic to early cultural diffusion. First, the time scale. The diffusion of the use of fire and the first lithic tools, for example, required tens, if not hundreds, of thousands of years at a time when human populations were sparse and widely separated, and when distances could be conquered only painfully and slowly on foot. But gifted Neolithic men in separate parts of the world did not have tens of thousands of years for tools, ideas, and customs to diffuse to the maximum geographical extent; they had but very few millennia in which to lay the foundations of higher civilizations.

Second, compelling needs. Within the few postglacial millennia Neolithic men of ability in widely separated parts of the world had a great deal more than their Paleolithic ancestors had with which to occupy themselves gainfully. There was a manifold increase during

[26] Kroeber, *Anthropology,* p. 411.

Neolithic times in the sources of human sustenance, consequent upon the domestication and exploitation of plants and animals. Field agriculture entailed a sedentary life and created a food surplus, which in turn released Neolithic manpower for nonagricultural pursuits. In fact, in times of peace and for reasons of trade and conquest, basic techniques and ideas did diffuse remarkably widely both in the ancient Near East and way beyond to the Indus Valley. This Near Eastern and Middle Eastern world was large, varied, and resourceful enough to satisfy the basic and even the more sophisticated needs of early men. Not until the rise of "high barbarism" based on extensive but well-knit nomadism on the Eurasian steppe some time in the second millennium B.C. did the Indo-Europeans begin to show signs of restlessness and to feel a compelling need to venture beyond the Near and Middle Eastern world, which had hitherto provided them with all their wants. Even then they showed no great desire to penetrate farther to the east, where climatic and natural conditions were less hospitable. From the best available history of the art of the steppes based on extensive Russian archaeological data, we know that, with the exception of possibly earlier turmoil in Turkmanistan and further south to northwestern India, the vast Eurasian steppe had remained relatively peaceful until about 1250 or 1200 B.C.[27] The beginnings of unrest on the Eurasian steppe thus coincide remarkably well with the earliest traceable cultural imports into Shang China.

Third, the means of conquering immense distances and natural barriers, especially in the dry belt of Eurasia. The distance between Mesopotamia and Shang China is more than 4,000 miles. The tortuous land route could easily have exceeded 5,000 miles, mostly through the Eurasian steppe north of the 50th parallel, occasionally through dry plateaus and deserts and over mountain passes. Difficult

---

[27] Karl Jettmar, *Art of the Steppes: The Eurasian Animal Style* (London, 1964), pp. 208–210. For the origins of the Indo-Europeans, see Marija Gimbutas, "The Indo-Europeans: Archaeological Problems," *American Anthropologist*, LXV, No. 4 (August 1963), pp. 815–836.

as this route was, it was preferred in prehistoric times to a more direct one leading from the Aral Sea through the vast expanse of Central Asian deserts and semideserts, south of the 50th parallel, through the Dzungarian gate, and then over more mountains and deserts to the Kansu corridor. If the relatively small Sinai desert served as an effective barrier between Egypt and the Fertile Crescent and accounted partly for the isolated and so-called "African" character of the ancient Egyptian civilization, how much more formidable a natural barrier must have been the immense arid areas of Central Asia, which stretch 2,500 miles from the Aral Sea to the Kansu corridor.

It is easy for jet-age diffusionists to take for granted that "ideas have wings." But the "wings" that carried early ideas had to be men, who were intelligent enough not to venture into seemingly endless deserts and cross other natural barriers for no compelling reason. Systematic Soviet archaeological data show that the ancient Near Eastern culture first diffused to Transcaucasia and then farther north to the southern Russian steppe; that from southern Russia certain cultural elements were gradually transmitted through the steppe zone to southwestern Siberia; that there was a somewhat accelerated west-east cultural diffusion consequent upon the rise of the metal-rich and expansive Seima culture between 1600 and 1300 B.C.; and that the bronze age did not begin in Soviet Central Asia and southwestern Siberia until about 1500 B.C.[28] The fact that it took so long for bronze to spread within Eurasia indicates how slowly the "wings" flew over the vast distances involved.

It seems more than coincidental that the earliest verifiable phase of long-range west-east cultural contact, necessarily through many intermediary ethnic groups of the Eurasian steppe, can be synchronized in the main with the invention and dissemination of

---

[28] The data in this paragraph are based on Alexander Mongait, *Archaeology in the U.S.S.R.;* see also last section of chapter 5 above, and Grégoire Frumkin, *Archaeology in Soviet Central Asia,* esp. synopsis of metallurgy on p. 132.

horse chariotry, and that the conquest of the immense dry belt of Central Asia eastward to the Kansu corridor had to wait until the nomads of Eurasia had begun to master the art of horse riding, which can be traced back only to the ninth century B.C.[29] As a matter of fact, the silk route could not begin to serve its historic function as the thoroughfare for east-west cultural exchange until the domestication and utilization of the Bactrian camel, which Chinese historical texts can trace back only to the late fourth century B.C.[30]

These three factors not only explain why the cultural contact between the ancient West and the ancient East was so long delayed, but also serve as a reminder that cultural diffusion on a hemispherical scale during prehistoric and early historic times cannot always be taken for granted. Indeed, even well into the historical age, when means of long-range transportation by land and by sea were continually being improved, there were occasions when new technology and new ideas simply did not diffuse interculturally for unbelievably long periods of time. Outstanding examples are Chinese cast iron, which antedated European cast iron by nearly two thousand years, and the Chinese crossbow, which was unknown in Europe for more than a millennium after its invention in China. Because of the drastically shrunken time scale of Neolithic and early historic times and the important fact that early men first had to find means of conquering vast distances and formidable natural barriers, one must exercise special caution in formulating a theory of cultural diffusion for the postglacial millennia immediately preceding the births of civilizations.

In closing, a word should be said about the special significance of China to the general theory of the origins of civilizations. Remark-

[29] Franz Hančar, *Das Pferd in prähistorischer und früher historischer Zeit* (Wiener Beiträge zur Kulturgeschichte und Linguistik), XI (1955), pp. 551–563.

[30] Edward H. Schafer, "The Camel in China down to the Mongol Dynasty," *Sinologica,* II (1950), esp. pp. 174–177.

able progress in archaeology, anthropology, and some other closely related sciences has, in the past decades, given rise to the polygenetic view. The various early civilizations—such as the Mesopotamian, Egyptian, Indus, European, Chinese, and Meso-American—are now regarded not as having sprung from a single ancestral hearth but as having evolved, in a multilinear fashion, from their respective prior native cultures.[31] The recent intensive multidisciplinary study of prehistoric Meso-America has proved beyond doubt that agriculture even in that comparatively limited geographic area had multiple origins, a scientific finding so solid that it will surely have an important bearing on future theories of the origins of civilizations.[32]

While there is no doubt that the current views on the origins of civilizations are much closer to historical truth than the once seemingly invulnerable theory of monogenesis, I cannot refrain from pointing out that the births of the New World and the Chinese civilizations were qualitatively different from the births of Old World civilizations other than the Mesopotamian. The independent origins of New World civilizations have long been conceded; it is hoped that the data and reasoning offered in the present study are sufficiently comprehensive and valid to persuade the learned world that the birth of China had nothing to do with Mesopotamia and was an entirely independent occurrence.

Although the Egyptian and Indus civilizations had their distinctly regional characters which must be largely accounted for by an evolution from their respective native prior cultures, Mesopotamian influence on some vital cultural elements of these two civilizations is undeniable. Take the agricultural systems of Mesopotamia, Egypt, and the Indus area as an example. Science and archaeology have definitely established that wild wheats and barley were not native either to Egypt or to the Indus valley, and that field

---

[31] The most articulate expression of this new view is Glyn Daniel, *The First Civilizations: The Archaeology of Their Origins* (New York, 1968).

[32] See note 57 of chapter 3.

agriculture began in these two areas considerably later than it did in Mesopotamia. Yet the earliest field agriculture of Egypt and of the Indus valley was based on flood plains, primitive irrigation, and a cropping system with wheat and barley as the core—exactly the same triad that characterized the Mesopotamian agriculture from the fifth millennium B.C. onward. Although the Egyptian hieroglyphics and the Indus script were totally different from those of the Sumerians and Akkadians, there is artifactual evidence showing stimulus diffusion from Mesopotamia. The recent discovery of an ancient urban culture at Tepe Yahya in southeastern Iran further confirms the overland contacts between ancient Mesopotamia and the Indus valley and seems to point to the former as a source of knowledge of urbanism in the Indus valley, even though the technicalities of the planning of Harappan cities and towns bore distinctly regional characteristics.[33]

No evidence of primary or stimulus diffusion, however, is revealed by our analysis of each of the major cultural elements that eventually coalesced in the Shang civilization. The Chinese civilization was just as pristine as the Mesopotamian and in terms of originality could claim equal primacy. It can no longer be treated as one of the several "peripheral" civilizations of the Old World. As Mesopotamia is rightly known as the cradle of the West, so the loess area of North China deserves to be called the cradle of the East. The Chinese may well be judged the more remarkable of the two pristine civilizations because of its unique longevity, the richness of its later contents, and its dominant influence over all of East Asia, whose inhabitants now account for more than one-third of humanity.

[33] Robert Reinhold, "New Link to Dawn of Urban Culture Is Found in Iran," *New York Times,* 20 December 1970, p. 53.

APPENDIXES

APPENDIX I

CHINA AND SOUTHEAST ASIAN "AGRICULTURE" AND BRONZE

DURING THE past few years anthropologists of the University of Hawaii have published some preliminary reports on evidence of "domestication" of plants discovered at the Spirit Cave, sixty kilometers north of Mae Hongson in northwestern Thailand near the Burmese border. Although the radiocarbon datings for the so-called domesticated plant material given in two such preliminary reports do not agree with each other, being respectively 7000 and 8000 B.C., even the later dating is as early as the beginnings of wheat and barley culture on the hilly flanks of the Fertile Crescent of Mesopotamia. Chester F. Gorman, the discoverer of the Spirit Cave site, reports:

In addition to the lithic and faunal material a number of botanical macro-fossils have been tentatively identified from Cultural Level I. Layer 4: Species of *Prunus* (almond), *Terminalia*, *Areca* (betal), *Vicia* (bean) or *Phaseolus* (bean), *Pisum* (pea) or *Raphia*, *Lagenaria* (bottle gourd), and *Trapa* (Chinese water chestnut). Layer 4/3 interface: *Piper* (pepper tree), *Madhuca* (butternut), *Canarium*, *Aleurites* (candlenut), and *Areca*. Layer 3: *Canarium*, *Lagenaria*, and *Cucumis* (cucumber). Layer 2: *Piper*, *Areca*, and *Canarium*.

The pattern of plant consumption indicated by these remains and the ethnographic information on use of such plants in modern indigenous contexts for the area is one of exploitation of wild or tended nuts for food, butternut *(Madhuca)*, *Canarium*, and *Terminalia;* for lighting and possibly consumption, candlenut *(Aleurites);* pepper *(Piper)* as a condiment; and the betel nut *(Areca)* as a stimulant. The use of the bottle gourd *(Legenaria)* and *Cucumis*, a cucumber type, with Chinese water chestnut *(Trapa)*, the leguminous beans *(Phaseolus, Vicia)*, and possibly the pea *(Pisum)*, however, form a group of food plants which suggests economic development beyond simple food-gathering. The leguminous plants in particular point to a very early use of domesticated plants.[1]

---

[1] Chester F. Gorman, "Hoabinhian: A Pebble-Tool Complex with Early Plant Associations in Southeast Asia," *Science*, CLXIII (14 February 1969). See also his "Excavations at Spirit Cave, North Thailand: Some Interim Interpretations," in

Wilhelm G. Solheim, II, director of the University of Hawaii's archaeological program in Thailand, is reported to have made the following remark: "This points to Southeast Asia as the area for the origin of agriculture and shows it to be very much more important than anyone has thought. This will change history and may embarrass China by indicating [that] she was not the first to develop agriculture in the Far East."[2] Recently Solheim is reported to have said that "these discoveries [at Spirit Cave] contradicted theories that the Near East's 'Fertile Crescent' gave birth to agriculture."[3]

The above reports and claims, however, cannot be fully accepted without further inquiry. Jack R. Harlan, professor of plant genetics and director of the Crop Evolution Laboratory of the University of Illinois, has kindly allowed me to use the following, as yet unpublished comments:

From the point of view of the plant specialists there are two points that need to be answered. First the identification, in some cases, appears suspect. If the material was really well preserved one could surely tell a pea from a palm and *Vicia* from *Phaseolus*. The other problem is a strange association of tropical plants with cool-temperature plants adapted to Mediterranean climates (*Pisum* and *Vicia*). The almond also seems out of place along with very tropical species such as *Areca* and *Aleurites*. I do not know of a large-seeded *Phaseolus* in that part of the world, but the material might have been *Dolichos* (?). The pea-palm suggests the material was an unidentified round seed, but perhaps not much more could be said than that.

The case of cultivated plants is based primarily on the leguminous grains, and these are the most suspect of the identifications.

For a proper understanding of the problem of agricultural origins in the entire Far East, one has to define the key word

---

Asian Perspectives, XIII (1970), pp. 79–108. Wilhelm G. Solheim II, in his "Northern Thailand, Southeast Asia, and World History," *Asian Perspectives*, XIII, p. 145, has revised the date of plant "domestication" further upward to 9700 B.C.

[2] "Origins of Agriculture Seen in Southeast Asia," *Asian Student*, XVII (29 March 1969).

[3] "First Agrarians Said to be Thais," *New York Times*, 12 January 1970.

agriculture so that it will be acceptable to the entire learned world. At the beginning of chapter 2, I adopted the standard definition for agriculture, that is, field agriculture based on cereal grains. Although anthropologists can name a few minor sophisticated cultures in which cereal agriculture has played little part, virtually all of what historians consider to be the major early civilizations, such as those of Mesopotamia, Egypt, the Indus valley, and North China, were based on cereal agriculture. If scholarly discourses on agricultural origins are based on this standard definition, then the evidence from the Spirit Cave indicates no trace of agriculture, especially when the identifications of the legumes are most suspect. What an unbiased scholar can deduce from the reported plant material is intelligent plant-food gathering—a far cry from agriculture.

For a proper understanding of the problem of agricultural origins in the entire Far East, one has to differentiate agriculture from protohorticulture and horticulture, and to grasp the fundamental difference in natural environment between China's loess area and monsoon East Asia. The loess area of China, where Chinese cereal agriculture began, is characterized by a harsh and semiarid climate and a sparsity of natural vegetation. Monsoon East Asia, which includes China south of the Yangtze and the Southeast Asian mainland and archipelagoes, is an area with a year-round warm climate and extremely rich plant resources. That monsoon East Asia may have given rise to an early phase of intensive plant-food collecting or even of protohorticulture, based mainly on fruits, nuts, and root crops, is indeed to be expected. The implications of a recent palynological study of Taiwan sponsored by Yale University indicate the possibility of rather early protohorticultural activities on this subtropical island.[4]

But protohorticulture and horticulture cannot be equated with agriculture. As far as the grain-centered agriculture of the Far East

---

[4] K. C. Chang, *The Archaeology of Ancient China,* pp. 82–83.

is concerned, the aggregate evidence still clearly indicates that it made its debut in the southeastern portion of the loess highlands of China. While in early times protohorticulture and horticulture in the southern half of China may have been mainly developed *in situ* and partially enriched by cultural influx from Southeast Asia, what is truly instructive is that monsoon China remained economically and culturally much more backward than North China down to Former Han times. The Grand Historian Ssu-ma Ch'ien described the region south of the Yangtze and the Huai River—monsoon China—as of the late second century B.C.:

> [People there] are able to gather all the fruit, berries, univalve and bivalve shellfish they want without waiting for merchants to come around selling them. Since the land is so rich in edible products, there is no fear of famine, and therefore the people are content to live along day to day; they do not lay away stores of goods, and many of them are poor. As a result, in the region south of the Yangtze and Huai rivers no one ever freezes or starves to death, but on the other hand there are no very wealthy families.[5]

The Grand Historian's description no longer holds for present-day southern China, but to a certain extent it may still apply to parts of contemporary Southeast Asia.

During the past twenty years no one has been more responsible than the geographer Carl O. Sauer for shaping the provocative view that Southeast Asia was the oldest "hearth" of agriculture and for confounding the nonexperts with an extremely loose definition for agriculture. A systematic criticism of his general view and lack of factual evidence is beyond the scope of this appendix. But it is necessary to reexamine here one of his more specific opinions that "rice, pigs and chickens all originated in Southeast Asia,"[6] which is still taken for granted by many Southeast Asian experts today.[7]

---

[5] *Records of the Grand Historian of China, Translated from the Shih Chi of Ssu-ma Ch'ien* by Burton Watson (New York, 1961), II, p. 490.

[6] Carl O. Sauer, *Agricultural Origins and Dispersals* (New York, 1952).

[7] For example, by Froelich Rainey, director of the University Museum of the University of Pennsylvania, in "First Agrarians Said to be Thais."

Manifold evidence regarding rice culture in China from 4000 B.C. onward was presented in detail in chapter 2, including the possibility that some of the rice finds from the cultural stratum of certain sites belonging to the Ma-chia-pin phase of the southern type of the Ch'ing-lien-kang culture may yield radiocarbon dates within the range of 3395 ± 105 B.C. and 3835 ± 105 B.C. (3995 ± 105 B.C. and 4435 ± 105 B.C., according to bristlecone-pine dendrochronology). The quantity, quality, and chronology of the Chinese rice finds compare favorably with the scanty indirect evidence from northern Thailand, which has led to a tentative beginning of wet rice farming in northern Thailand from ca. 3500 B.C. onward.[8] The accuracy of the thermoluminescence method of age determination, from which the date for prehistoric Thai rice is derived, is a matter for scientists to decide; but a comparison of the date of the beginning of rice culture in northern Thailand should be made against the Chinese dates based on bristlecone-pine dendrochronology. It is worth mentioning in passing that recent finds of rice in eastern India show a radiocarbon date of around 3000 B.C., although a leading Indian paleobotanist is not sure whether the rice was domesticated or wild.[9]

We should further remind Sauer's followers that, while the rice remains unearthed from the Ch'ing-lien-kang cultural site of Sung-tse were morphologically of the *indica* subspecies and those from the Liang-chu cultural site of Ch'ien-shan-yang contained both the *indica* and *japonica* subspecies, the enormous amounts of rice husks in the baked red clay of several prehistoric Ch'ü-chia-ling cultural sites in central Yangtze were of the *japonica* subspecies.

---

[8] Chester Gorman, "*A Priori* Models and Thai Prehistory: A Reconsideration of the Beginnings of Agriculture in Southeastern Asia," prepared for The Conference on the Origins of Agriculture, IXth International Congress of Anthropological and Ethnological Sciences, 28th August to 2nd September, 1973. This paper, together with other papers presented at the Conference, will be published in 1974.

[9] Vishnu-Mittre, "Changing Economy in Ancient India," prepared for the Conference on the Origins of Agriculture, IXth ICAES.

The abundance of prehistoric Chinese rice finds, their greater antiquity, the predominance of the *japonica* varieties in ancient Chinese literary records and local histories, and the strong paleographic and historical records of the occurrences of wild varieties of rice during the past three thousand years make it extremely difficult for data-minded scientists to believe that rice, whether of the *indica* or of the *japonica* subspecies, could only have originated in tropical Southeast and South Asia. Interpreting the available evidence on early rice in China, Thailand, and India, I am inclined to believe in multiple, independent occurrences of rice culture in these three regions.

The detailed osteological data presented in chapter 3 show that one of the more common wild ancestors of pigs, *Sus scrofa vittatis*, was native to late Pleistocene and Yang-shao China. Even during the initial phase of animal domestication in Yang-shao times, pigs were already so ubiquitous that it is very hard to imagine they had all come from Southeast Asia. The semiwild pig from the late prehistoric site of Hung-shan-hou in Eastern Inner Mongolia has been studied by a Japanese zoologist who is of the opinion that it is definitely different from *Sus scrofa vittatis*. It is clear that the pigs of China and of East Asia are descended from more than one subspecies. In addition, there is recent evidence that pigs may have been domesticated in the Crimea as early as 10,000 B.C. All this clearly militates against a view that pigs originated only in Southeast Asia and were descended from only one Southeast Asian subspecies.

Wild fowl and domesticated chickens have been found in many prehistoric sites in China in recent decades. The distribution has by no means been confined to the warmer parts of China. Chicken bones unearthed from a Lungshanoid site at Miao-ti-kou and from a Ma-chia-yao site in Kansu probably fall between the late years of the fourth and the early part of the third millennium B.C. All these and the clay chicken figurines unearthed from a Ch'ü-chia-ling cultural site in Hupei should antedate those of Mohenjo-dara by many centuries. Even as late as the period after 1300 B.C. there was a place along the T'ai-hang Mountain foothill, the favorite hunting ground of late-Shang kings, which was named Chi 雞 (literally "chicken"). The quantitatively significant evidence from China again argues against the lingering belief of some scholars that chickens originated only in Southeast Asia.

The triad of rice, pigs, and chickens, the special pride of Southeast Asianists, was far from a Southeast Asian monopoly.

It will take much more than the Spirit Cave finds to convince the learned world that plant "domestication" or "agriculture" occurred first in Southeast Asia. For the time being, a far more balanced view on the question of agricultural origins has resulted from many years of painstaking integration of all the available sources of information. In his recent article "Agricultural Origins: Centers and Noncenters," Jack R. Harlan defines a center as a "nuclear area that is definable . . . in terms of time and space." He summarizes his view as follows:

> I propose the theory that agriculture originated independently in three different areas and that, in each case, there was a system composed of a center of origin and a noncenter, in which activities of domestication were dispersed over a span of 5,000 to 10,000 kilometers. One system includes a definable Near East center and a noncenter in Africa; another system includes a North Chinese center and a noncenter in Southeast Asia and the South Pacific; the third system includes a Mesoamerican center and a South American noncenter. There are suggestions that, in each case, the center and noncenter interact with each other.[10]

Such questions as when, where, and how did the North Chinese center and the Southeast Asian noncenter agriculturally interact throughout the ages, can only be answered by the future combined research of scholars of various correlated disciplines.

Unlike the opinions of some Southeast Asianists on agricultural origins, the views of Donn T. Bayard on the early evidence of copper

---

[10] Jack R. Harlan, "Agricultural Origins: Centers and Noncenters," *Science*, CLXXIV (29 October 1971). See also his latest evaluation of the Spirit Cave finds in his "On the Quality of Evidence for Origin and Dispersal of Cultivated Plants," to appear shortly in *Current Anthropology*.

and bronze found at the Non Nok Tha site in northeastern Thailand are remarkably balanced. Although the copper and bronze indicate "a minimum age of about 2700 B.C." and are considerably earlier than metal objects so far found in China and slightly earlier than those of the Indus valley, he has methodically reached the following conclusion:

> [The Non Nok Tha metal technology] seems to bear little or no resemblance to the Chinese material (Noël Barnard, personal communication). Moreover, the Non Nok Tha technology also seems completely unrelated to that of the Indus Valley civilizations in that it totally lacks flat-mold casting and any sign of tanged or shaft-hole hafting. . . . In short, at present it appears to be quite possible that a separate invention of metalworking based on a socketed hafting technology and the use of double molds may have developed in Southeast Asia independently of stimulus from either China or the Indus and earlier than both areas.[11]

This conclusion, coupled with the multifarious evidence regarding the indigenous origins of metallurgy in China and in the Balkans,[12] lends further support to the belief in multiple independent occurrences of metallurgy in the Old World.

In speculating about the possibly wider significance of the new archaeological finds in northern Thailand, one should not lose sight of basic geographic and historical facts. It is a fact that "mountains close off Thailand on the west, north, and northeast"[13] and that much of the political, cultural, linguistical, and ethnic segmentation of the Southeast Asian mainland has been accounted for by geography. It is also a fact that, in spite of recent archaeological finds which reveal the existence of a more sophisticated early material culture than had previously been believed, the ancient

---

[11] Donn T. Bayard, "Excavation at Non Nok Tha, Northeastern Thailand, 1968: An Interim Report," *Asian Perspectives*, XIII (1970), p. 139. Also an earlier report by W. G. Solheim, "Early Bronze in Northeastern Thailand," *Current Anthropology*, IX, No. 1 (February 1968), pp. 59–62.

[12] See note 88 of chapter 5.

[13] George B. Cressey, *Asia's Lands and Peoples* (New York, 1944), p. 507.

Southeast Asian mainland suffered from such a low level of political organization that its various local cultures did not coalesce into larger entities until after the introduction of Indian political and religious concepts, which occurred close to the beginnings of the Christian era. The basic geographic and historical facts weigh heavily against a presumption of maximal and fairly rapid diffusion of Southeast Asian cultural elements in prehistoric times.

Appendix II
THE PUZZLE OF THE CHINESE SORGHUM

UNFORTUNATELY FOR archaeologists, botanical scientists, and historians there has never been a systematic report on the natural remains of the important Yang-shao site at Ching-ts'un, southern Shansi, discovered in 1931. Not until years after the outbreak of the Sino-Japanese War in 1937 were the natural remains of Ching-ts'un studied by a Japanese botanist. Of the cereal plants identified, one is *Andropogon sorghum* var. *vulgaris,* or common sorghum.[1] There is no way for scholars outside of mainland China, decades after the Ching-ts'un finds were made, to know whether the circumstances under which the excavation was carried out and the stratigraphical level ascertained were beyond reproach.

In 1955 some carbonized stems, leaves, and roots of sorghum were discovered at San-li-tun in northern Kiangsu in a cultural layer which is believed to belong to late-Shang or early-Chou times.[2] The botanical identification was made by a well-qualified scientist. In the 1950s traces of sorghum were also found in southern Manchuria, Hopei, and Lo-yang in western Honan. Chronologically these finds fell within the period 400 B.C. and the time of Christ.[3]

---

[1] An Chih-min, "Chung-kuo shih-ch'ien-shih-ch'i chih nung-yeh" [Prehistoric Chinese Agriculture], *Yen-ching she-hui-k'e-hsüeh* [Yenching University Journal of Social Sciences], II (October 1949), p. 39.

[2] Nanking Museum, "Chiang-su Hsin-i-hsien San-li-tun ku-wen-hua i-chih ti-erh-tz'u fa-chüeh chien-pao" [A Brief Report of the Second Excavation of the Ancient Cultural Site at San-li-tun, Hsin-i county, Kiangsu], *KK,* 1960, No. 7, pp. 21–22.

[3] Yü Hsing-wu, "Shang-tai ti ku-lei tso-wu," pp. 81–82; Ho Kuan-pao, "Lo-yang lao-ch'eng hsi-pei-chiao 81-hao Han-mu" [The No. 81 Han Grave in the Northwestern Suburb of the Ancient City of Lo-yang], *KK,* 1964, No. 8, p. 406.

Chinese sorghum presents a twofold puzzle. First, the cumulative scientific evidence points to Africa as the original homeland of sorghum. Second, a review of Chinese historical texts strengthens my earlier belief that sorghum was introduced into China from abroad.[4] Since the scientific literature on the original habitat of sorghum is fairly voluminous and will be summarized by Dr. Jack R. Harlan later in this appendix, let us first review the highlights of Chinese historical texts about sorghum.

Unlike other ancient cereal plants, sorghum did not acquire a name in Chinese until about A.D. 300. The earliest reference to sorghum is found in *Po-wu chih,* a work on natural history, attributed to Chuang Hua, a famous scholar and statesman of the late third century A.D. While this work may be problematical in terms of authorship, its contents are generally believed to be authentic. In it sorghum is called *shu-shu* 蜀黍, literally "the millet of Szechwan." Its earliest Chinese name of *shu-shu,* which remained its standard-Chinese botanical name until very late, is highly significant. Being new to China, it was at first regarded as akin to millet but had to be differentiated from indigenous millet by the prefix *Shu* (Szechwan), which indicates its introduction from the southwest. The value of this etymological evidence is enhanced by that of the parallel case of maize, which was introduced into China in the first half of the sixteenth century. Since maize was first brought to the Ming court as a tribute by southwestern tribesmen, it was called *yü-mai* 御麥 (literally "imperial wheat") or *yü-shu-shu* 御蜀黍 (literally "imperial sorghum"). Soon the character *yü* (imperial) was replaced, by the common people, by its homonym *yü* (jade). Hence maize's standard botanical name in Chinese, *yü-shu-shu* (jade sorghum).[5] The

---

[4] My early view on the subject of Chinese sorghum was given in my *Studies on the Population of China, 1368–1953* (Cambridge, Mass., 1959), ch. 8, section 2, and again in my "Some Problems of Shang Culture and Institutions: A Review Article," *Pacific Affairs,* XXXIV, No. 3 (Fall, 1961), esp. pp. 295–296.

[5] Ping-ti Ho, "The Introduction of American Food Plants into China," *American Anthropologist,* LVII, No. 2, Part I (April 1955).

etymological sequence of millet-sorghum-maize, therefore, accords exactly with our knowledge of these crops derived from ancient texts and from later voluminous agricultural, botanical and other local records.

That sorghum is very unlikely to have been an indigenous crop of North China in ancient times is further borne out by *Ch'i-min yao-shu,* the earliest systematic agricultural treatise extant, compiled during the first half of the sixth century A.D. by Chia Ssu-hsieh 賈思勰. There can be no doubt about Chia's authority and familiarity with northern dry-land crops, yet significantly he listed *shu-shu* (sorghum) in the appendix as an uncommon exotic food plant of the southwest.[6]

To my knowledge, the first unmistakable botanical description of sorghum, both black and red, glutinous and nonglutinous, is given in the 1175 edition of the history of Hui-chou 徽州 prefecture in southern Anhwei by the famous natural historian Lo Yüan 羅願.[7] Hsü Kuang-ch'i 徐光啟 (1562–1633), the famous cabinet minister, scientist, and disciple of Matteo Ricci, pointed out in his agricultural encyclopedia that sorghum cultivation became extensive only since Mongol times.[8] Hsü's remark is unquestionably correct, because it was permitted to use sorghum for tax payment in kind only from the early fifteenth century onward.[9]

Chinese historical texts indicate, therefore, a first introduction of sorghum some time before A.D. 300 as well as some much later "introductions" consequent upon the development in Sung times

---

[6] *Ch'i-min yao-shu chin-shih* [*Chi-min yao-shu*: With Textual Criticism, Annotations, and Translation into Modern Chinese], by Shih Sheng-han, 4 Vols. (Peking, 1957–58), IV, pp. 723–724.

[7] Lo Yüan, *Hsin-an chih* (1175 ed., 1888 reprint), ch. 2.

[8] Hsü Kuang-ch'i, *Nung-cheng ch'üan-shu* [A Cyclopedia of Agriculture] (1843 ed.), ch. 25, p. 15b.

[9] *Ming-shih* [History of the Ming Dynasty] (Taipei reprint of Ch'ing palace ed.), ch. 77, pp. 8b–9a, and ch. 150, pp. 1a–1b.

of overseas trade with the lands of the South China Sea and the Indian Ocean, and with Africa.[10] For unknown reasons, the varieties of sorghum first introduced into China did not do well for a long time, but the more recently introduced varieties have gained permanent importance in the Chinese agrarian economy.

I shall conclude this appendix with Dr. Harlan's comments:

All the evidence we have at the present time indicates that cultivated sorghum is an African domesticate. There is, as yet, no primary evidence from archaeology or other sources to indicate the time or place of domestication, but the enormous diversity and the advanced stage of evolution of the more specialized cultivars indicate a substantial antiquity for the crop.

At some time, also unknown, sorghum was introduced into India, where it became the basic cereal food for many millions of people. The earliest archaeological evidence so far in India dates to about the beginning of the Christian era, but sorghum had, no doubt, been in India long before that. The Sanskritized name for sorghum, however, does suggest that sorghum was introduced well after agricultural settlers came from the Near East. The Hindi name *Jowar* is a derivative from *Jo* or *yuva,* meaning barley, which was for some millennia the basic cereal food of the Near East.

Reports of sorghum appearing in archaeological sites in China as early as 1000 B.C. may shed light on the time of introduction of sorghum into Asia and at the same time tell us something of the time of domestication in Africa. These reports need to be confirmed, however, before one could reconstruct the history of sorghum in Asia with any reliability. Archaeobotanical materials are often very difficult to identify; dating is often uncertain even with C14 determinations, of which there are none in China at present, and archaeological techniques often leave much to be desired, especially in sites dug some decades ago. All of this means that one should accept these finds with extreme caution until more evidence becomes available.

If these reports should prove to be genuine, and sorghum had, indeed, found its way to China by 1000 B.C. or earlier, some reassessments of early contacts between Africa and Asia might be in order. Historically, it is clear that sorghum was not an important crop in China until as late as the Mongol conquest. Between that time and the twentieth century sorghum had become an absolutely basic crop for considerable areas of Manchuria and other parts of North China. Western observers found it difficult to conceive of farming in these areas without sorghum.[11]

---

[10] W. W. Hirth and W. W. Rockhill, *Chau Ju-kua: His Work on the Chinese and Arab Trade in the Twelfth and Thirteenth Centuries, Entitled Chu-fan-chi* (St. Petersburg, 1912).

[11] C. R. Ball, "The Kaoliangs: A New Group of Grain Sorghums," *United States Department of Agriculture, Bureau of Plant Industry, Bulletin* No. 253 (1913).

APPENDIX II

Botanically, the Chinese sorghums or kaoliangs are said to be rather distinct from other sorghums. Our examination of the small sample available to us did not reveal any unique morphological features. Many of them do show certain features in common concerning growth habits. The Chinese have probably made more use of the stalks than other sorghum growers. Kaoliang stems are commonly used in house and fence construction; in the manufacture of baskets, storage bins, and containers of many sorts; and for fuel. As a result, Chinese growers have selected for hard, fibrous, and woody stems, which may explain the rather distinctive appearance of many of the kaoliangs. Other than this we find it rather difficult to characterize the kaoliangs as a group.

Appendix III
A NOTE ON ANCIENT CHINESE ASTRONOMY

OF ALL the ancient peoples who succeeded in creating a civilization, few, if any, had a greater need than the proto-Chinese for at least a rudimentary knowledge of astronomy. In comparison with the homelands of other major ancient civilizations of the Old World, the loess area of China suffered from a harsher climate and more meager plant resources. In an area noted for severe winters, killing frosts in autumn, frequent spring sandstorms, and a limited annual rainfall concentrated in the very hot summer months, farming was undoubtedly more difficult than in milder areas where the rain falls in the cooler months. Ancient Egypt was, it is true, even more arid than North China; but the usually gentle and rhythmic rise and fall of the flood waters of the Nile made wheat cultivation a relatively simple and safe matter and made Egypt a much-envied granary of the ancient Orient. By contrast, the lower course of the Yellow River has remained to the present day the world's most ungovernable river. The proto-Chinese were therefore forced to move from the great Yellow River flood plain, to settle on numerous loess terraces along smaller rivers and tiny streams, and to wrest a livelihood from what a niggardly nature allowed. Since the choice of cereal plants, and the range of temperature and rainfall within which such cereal plants could be successfully grown, were both very narrow, it was imperative for the prehistoric Chinese farmers carefully to observe seasonal changes and thus follow the movements of the moon and the sun and the changing positions of the stars.

Although the long protoliterate phase of China's prehistory has so far yielded no direct information on the beginnings of Chinese astronomy, there is reason to believe that it is of much greater antiquity than is usually imagined. Certainly the calendrical system and other fragmentary information about astronomy revealed in Shang oracle inscriptions by no means reflect the earliest stages of Chinese astronomy.[1] Legends preserved in ancient Chinese literary works must be used with caution, but the effort must be made to sift from them some historical facts about the beginnings of astronomy.

An entry for the year 564 B.C. in the *Tso-chuan* mentions a very early practice of observing the *huo* 火, Fire Star, which has been identified with Antares (Scorpii):

O-po 閼伯, who served as *huo-cheng* 火正 (Director of the Office for the Observation of the Fire Star) under T'ao-t'ang-shih 陶唐氏 (*i.e.*, the sage-king Yao 堯, 2357–2256 B.C. according to traditional chronology), took Shang-ch'iu 商丘 as his official residence and was charged with the worship of the Fire Star. By observing the changing positions of the Fire Star, he regulated the seasons. Hsiang-t'u 相土 came after him and henceforth the people of Shang paid special regard to the Fire Star.[2]

---

[1] In chapter 7 I discussed the historicity of the Hsia period, which in Chou times was best remembered for its calendar. The Hsia calendar began the new year two months later than the Chou calendar. A succinct discussion of the use of the Hsia calendar by the Chin state in southern Shansi was made by the great early-Ch'ing scholar, Ku Yen-wu (1613–82), in his research notes entitled *Jih-chih lu* (Commercial Press ed.), Part II, pp. 30–32. As many as eight entries proving the adoption of the Hsia calendar by the Chin state were culled from the *Tso-chuan* and the *Bamboo Annals* by another early-Ch'ing scholar, Wan Ssu-t'ung (1638–1702), in his research notes entitled *Ch'ün-shu i-pien* (1816 ed.), ch. 5, pp. 10a–11a. There is further evidence that the Hsia calendar was popular among Chou farmers and that it definitely coexisted with the Chou calendar in the Chou domain. The best evidence is found in the famous agricultural song "Ch'i-yüeh" 七月, ode no. 154 in *The Book of Odes*. Upon being asked how the government of a state should be administered, Confucius said that he regarded the adoption of the Hsia calendar as a most important thing. See Legge, tr., *The Chinese Classics*, I, *Confucian Analects*, pp. 297–298. Legge's translation of the key sentence 行夏之時 as: "Follow the seasons of Hsia" may well be put in another way: "Adopt the calendar of Hsia." All these establish beyond doubt the historicity of both the Hsia period and the Hsia calendar. There is no question that the Hsia calendar preceded that of the Shang.

[2] Chinese text in Legge, tr., *The Chinese Classics*, V, *The Ch'un Ts'ew with the Tso Chuen*, pp. 436–437. I have retranslated this passage, in order to make its meaning clearer.

While it is not yet possible to prove the existence or the chronology of the legendary sage-king Yao with archaeological data, several aspects of the above *Tso-chuan* entry can be correlated with Shang oracle-bone inscriptions. O-po, for instance, is referred to three times in oracle inscriptions under the name O 夭 (modern pronunciation Yao), to whom late-Shang kings offered sacrifices. The additional prefix *wang* (king) would indicate that he was a remote lineal ancestor of the Shang kings far back in the predynastic period.[3] The identification from Shang oracle texts of Hsiang-t'u by the late Wang Kuo-wei[4] has been challenged in recent years,[5] but there can be little doubt that Hsiang-t'u was more recent than O-po and was a real historical personage. Since the late-Shang kings did not offer sacrifices to all their remote ancestors because sheer numbers required an arbitrary cut-off point, the names of some of the remote ancestors are missing from oracle texts. Hsiang-t'u is mentioned in the *Shih-chi* as the eleventh-generation ancestor of the founder of the Shang dynasty and is also immortalized in *The Book of Odes* as one of the illustrious remote ancestors of the Shang kings.[6] Oracle inscriptions also indicate that Shang-ch'iu, in eastern Honan, was one of the important headquarters of the Shang people both before and during the dynastic period. The key personages and the locality mentioned in the *Tso-chuan,* no doubt based on old oral traditions, both tally well with oracle texts. In ancient times diviners, scribes, and "astronomers" were necessarily learned men close to the tribal chiefs, so that the *Tso-chuan's* reference to the

---

[3] Jao Tsung-i, *Yin-tai chen-pu jen-wu t'ung-k'ao* [A Comprehensive Study of the Royal Diviners of Shang Times], 2 Vols. (Hongkong, 1958-59), I, p. 123.

[4] Wang Kuo-wei, *Kuan-t'ang chi-lin,* ch. 9, pp. 3b-4a.

[5] Wang's identification of Hsiang-t'u from oracle texts has been challenged by, among others, Ch'en Meng-chia, *Yin-hsü pu-tz'u tsung-shu,* p. 340, Jao Tsung-i, *Yin-tai chen-pu jen-wu t'ung-k'ao,* I, pp. 120-121, and by Chou Hung-hsiang, *Shang-Yin ti-wang pen-chi* [The Annals of Shang Kings] (Hongkong, 1958), pp. 3-6.

[6] *Shih-chi,* ch. 3, pp. 1b-2a; and Karlgren, tr., *The Book of Odes,* pp. 263-266.

office for the observation of the fire star in remote antiquity may contain grains of historic truth. Since the Yang-shao proto-Chinese had already invented an ingenious system of numerals before 4000 B.C., it is likely that Chinese astronomy—long before the rise of the Shang as a dominant power in North China, that is, prior to 1500 B.C.—had already become "official" in character and that "official" astronomers had numerals, ordinals, and other signs and symbols with which to do simple astronomical computations.

The amount of modern literature on ancient Chinese astronomy is considerable and cannot be systematically assessed here. Beyond supplying a historical footnote on the likely prehistoric origins of Chinese astronomy, we are mainly concerned here with whether ancient Chinese astronomy was developed indigenously. We cannot settle this question without comparing its major characteristics with those of ancient Western astronomy. Here, fortunately, we have at our disposal the methodical and comprehensive study of the subject by Joseph Needham, with the able collaboration of Wang Ling, which also contains a great deal of useful information on the astronomy of other ancient civilizations of the Old World.

Needham explains the first major difference between ancient Chinese and ancient Western astronomy thus:

It is now established beyond question that ancient (and medieval) Chinese astronomy was based upon a system quite different from that of the Egyptians, Greeks and later Europeans, though in no way less logical or useful. . . . Early astronomers faced the great difficulty that the star which determines the seasons (the sun) dims the other stars to invisibility by its brilliance, so that its position among them, unlike that of the moon, cannot easily be obtained. Simultaneity of observation being thus impossible, there remained only the methods of contiguity and opposability. The method of contiguity was that adopted by the Egyptians and the Greeks; it involved the observation of heliacal risings and settings, i.e., the risings and settings of stars near the ecliptic just before sunrise and just after sunset. . . . Such observations required no knowledge of pole, meridian or equator, nor any system of horary measurements; but naturally led to the recognition of ecliptic (zodiacal) constellations, and to stars appearing and disappearing simultaneously with them near or farther away from the ecliptic (their paranatellons). Attention was concentrated on the horizon and ecliptic.

The method of opposability, on the contrary, was that adopted by the ancient

Chinese. They concentrated attention, not on heliacal risings and settings, not on the horizon, but on the pole star and on the circumpolar stars which never rise and never set. Their astronomical system was thus closely associated with the concept of the meridian (the great circle of the celestial sphere passing through the pole star and the observer's zenith), and they determined systematically the culminations and lower transits (meridian passages) of these circumpolar stars. . . . The pole was thus the fundamental basis of Chinese astronomy.[7]

An equally fundamental difference between ancient Chinese and ancient Western astronomy is star nomenclature.

The next question that arises is to what extent there was any similarity between Chinese and European recognition of asterisms and constellations. As will appear, the answer is that there was very little. The number of cases in which parallelism of symbolic nomenclature can be made out is remarkably small, and the same groups of stars were not seen in the same pattern. Frequently a single European constellation appears on the Chinese planisphere as several different asterisms. . . .

[From 89 constellations recognized internationally in modern astronomy], only three zodiacal and seven extra-zodiacal constellations show any similarity of symbolism as between Chinese and European nomenclature. . . . The list is not at all impressive, and strongly suggests that the nomenclature of the Chinese constellations grew up in almost complete independence of the West.[8]

All this, together with the uniquely Sinitic sexagenary cycle of day count, the division of the month into ten-day *hsün* periods instead of weeks, the graduation of the circle in $365\frac{1}{4}°$ instead of $360°$, and a vast body of ancient records of celestial phenomena which rank high among those of the ancient civilizations,[9] should all point in the direction of indigenous origins and independent development. Yet Needham has repeatedly mentioned the possibility that early Babylonian astronomical knowledge was transmitted to ancient China, a tentative conclusion not entirely congruent with the strikingly Sinitic character or ancient Chinese astronomy, which he has so painstakingly and masterfully presented.

There is a general reason as well as a particular reason why the

---

[7] Joseph Needham, *Science and Civilization in China,* III, *Mathematics and the Sciences of the Heaven and the Earth* (Cambridge, England, 1959), pp. 229–230.

[8] *Ibid.,* pp. 271–273.

[9] *Ibid.,* pp. 409–436.

best historian of Chinese science and technology finally leaned toward the belief of possible diffusion of astronomical knowledge from Babylonia to Shang-Chou China. It was hardly Needham's fault that so little was known about the origins of the Chinese cultural elements and of Chinese civilization when he first launched his monumental *Science and Civilization in China*. Before 1949, when scholars discussed the "birth" of China, they usually began with a summation of the results of the excavations at An-yang, as if anything worthy of the name of Chinese culture or civilization could be dated only as far back as 1300 B.C. The intellectual atmosphere of those days was such that even the most chauvinistic Chinese scholars took it almost for granted that certain elements of ancient Chinese culture had been transmitted directly or indirectly from Mesopotamia.

The particular reason for Needham's tentative conclusion as to Babylonian influence on ancient Chinese astronomy lay in two pieces of unmistakable documentary evidence, the significance of which deserves to be reexamined. The first consists of a number of astral omina made in cuneiform tablets, most of which came from the library of King Ashurbanipal of the seventh century B.C., and some similar astral omina in chapter 27 of the *Shih-chi* of Ssu-ma Ch'ien.[10] The second is found in the *Chou-pei suan-ching* 周髀算經 (The Arithmetical Classic of the Snomon and the Circular Paths of Heaven), a work compiled around A.D. 300, which contains a diagram closely resembling the Babylonian planisphere.[11]

In all objectivity, however, by far the most direct and reasonable explanation of the first piece of documentary evidence is that, because of the intensive and frequent diplomatic missions to, and wars with, the Greco-Bactrian states of Central Asia during the last two decades of the second century B.C., Babylonian astral omina

---

[10] Needham, *Science and Civilization in China*, II, *History of Scientific Thought* (Cambridge, England, 1956), p. 353.

[11] *Ibid.*, III, pp. 256–257.

were belatedly introduced into China and immediately incorporated into the *Shih-chi,* since astronomy had traditionally been a function of the Grand Historian. What the second piece of evidence truly indicates is the continual transmission of Babylonian-Hellenistic astronomy throughout the remainder of Han times until parts of such knowledge were embodied in the *Chou-pei suan-ching*.

Astronomy is so specialized a subject that I have asked Professor David E. Pingree, of Brown University, who has the requisite philological and mathematical tools, to comment on Needham's view of possible Babylonian influence on pre-Han Chinese astronomy. The following is Pingree's comment:

Joseph Needham in his monumental *Science and Civilization in China* at several points hypothesizes a Babylonian influence on Chinese astronomy. Though it is certainly true that elements of the Babylonian linear astronomy of the Seleucid and Parthian periods became known in China at about the beginning of the Christian era (presumably through some Iranian intermediary), the early contacts assumed by Needham do not seem to be plausible. The earliest contribution of Babylonian astronomy to the Chinese envisaged by Needham is the list of 28 *hsiu* 宿.[12] Such a list of 28 "lunar stations" has never been found on a cuneiform tablet, however, and there is no reason to assume that any was ever written on one.

The other early influence hypothesized by Needham[13] is that of the planetary omina in cuneiform texts of the seventh century B.C. upon the source of some similar material in the history of Ssu-ma Ch'ien, which he completed after 100 B.C. This influence seems indeed to have been real, but was probably indirect. The most likely route appears to be through the Indian omina-series imitated from the cuneiform series in the fifth or fourth century B.C., and perhaps carried by the Buddhists (under Asoka, and later the Indo-Greeks) into the parts of Central Asia visited by Han envoys and generals.

A final connection between Babylonian and early Chinese astronomy that has been suggested is the "Metonic" cycle of seven intercalations of a synodic month in nineteen solar years. There is indeed evidence of an attempt to make the lunar and solar years coincide empirically by intercalations in China from about 600 B.C.; but the "Metonic" cycle implies a mathematical computation of the times of intercalation, and a resulting regular pattern within successive nineteen-year cycles. As the intercalations in the Chinese calendar are not regular, there is no evidence that they knew of the basic period-relations used to construct the "Metonic" cycle. Since the

---

[12] *Ibid.,* III, pp. 252–259.

[13] *Ibid.,* II, pp. 153–154.

"Metonic" cycle is fairly accurate, empirical observation of new moons and solstices or equinoxes and the desire to make the solstice or equinox fall in a particular month will lead to an irregular intercalation of seven months in nineteen years such as is found in the Chinese calendar. A regular pattern of intercalation within successive nineteen-year periods is not found in Babylon until the fourth century B.C.

There remains, therefore, no solid evidence for any connection between Mesopotamian and Chinese astronomy before Ssu-ma Ch'ien.

APPENDIX IV

A FURTHER NOTE ON ANCIENT CHINESE SCRIPT AND LANGUAGE

TWENTY-SIX MONTHS have elapsed since I completed the draft of the chapter on numerals, ordinals, script and language. It was not until 7 August 1972 that I received the journal *K'ao-ku* (1972, No. 3), which contains a leading article on the origins of Chinese script by Kuo Mo-jo, President of Academia Sinica, Peking, and

---

Approximately six months after I had finished a manuscript (in Chinese) entitled *The Loess and the Origin of Chinese Agriculture,* in the late summer of 1968, I began an extensive examination of archaeological data relating to other major Chinese cultural elements. To my utter disbelief, the numerals on Pan-p'o potsherds, which had been available to the learned world since 1965 and which are so obviously numerals even to a nonpaleographer like me, had not been discussed at all by paleographers and archaeologists. In the late spring of 1969, therefore, I wrote to Professor Li Hsiao-ting of Nanyang University in Singapore to call his attention to the Pan-p'o material and to ask him to correct me if my layman's identifications were wrong. As a result, he wrote a long article, "Ts'ung chi-chung shih-ch'ien ho yu-shih-tsao-ch'i t'ao-wen ti kuan-ch'a li-ts'e Chung-kuo wen-tzu ti ch'i-yüan" [A Survey of the Origin of Chinese Writing on the Basis of Some Prehistoric and Early Pottery Inscriptions]. This article is now in *Nan-yang-ta-hsüeh hsüeh-pao,* III (1969); it was not actually printed until the spring of 1971 and did not reach me until after I had completed the first draft of chapter 6.

Not until late January 1973 did Dr. Cheng Te-k'un of Cambridge University send me a carbon copy of his article, "Chung-kuo shang-ku shu-ming ti yen-pien chi ch'i ying-yung" [The Evolution of Ancient Chinese Numerals and their Applications], which is scheduled to appear in *Hsiang-kang-Chung-wen-ta-hsüeh hsüeh-pao* [The Journal of The Chinese University of Hong Kong], I (1973). Dr. Cheng reviews various types of artifacts that were directly and indirectly related to numerals and to counting, including the efforts on the part of the "Upper Cave Men" of Chou-k'ou-tien 周口店 of Paleolithic times to "count."

Readers are advised to consult the articles by Li and Cheng, both of which confirm the numerals on the Pan-p'o potsherds.

dean of Chinese paleography.[1] Just as his introductory remark on the four carbon-14 determinations for the Yang-shao culture constitutes a landmark in Chinese archaeology, the main conclusions and observations of the corpus of his article stand out as a milestone in the seventy-year history of modern research on Chinese paleography. It is a broad-gauged article, ranging from the earliest forms of Chinese writing and ancient Chinese writing materials to the geneses of various styles of Chinese calligraphy and epigraphy from Yang-shao times to the Ch'in unification of China in 221 B.C. Most of his conclusions, and even some of his hypotheses, speak with authority and will find wide acceptance by the learned world. In this appendix we shall examine only those points made by Kuo which are directly relevant to chapter 6 above.

1. Kuo believes that the Chinese script began with the stage exemplified by the twenty-two word-signs incised on Pan-p'o pottery shown in Figure 26 in chapter 6. Since four carbon-14 determinations indicate the birth of the Yang-shao culture represented by the Pan-p'o site at about 4000 B.C., Chinese script has had a living history of at least six thousand years. (The four Pan-p'o radiocarbon dates range from 4115 ± 110 B.C. to 3635 ± 105 B.C., which correspond to 4865 ± 110 B.C. to 4235 ± 105 B.C. in bristlecone-pine dates, so that Kuo's statement is conservative by a few centuries.)

2. Although Kuo thinks that the meanings of those Pan-p'o word-signs are not yet clear, he believes that "they are unquestionably signs and symbols of the nature of archetypal logographs," which are likely to have been "signatures or clan insignias." In his opinion, some Pan-p'o word-signs bear close resemblance to or are even identical with some clan insignias he has culled from Shang-Chou bronze inscriptions, as shown in Figure 32. Thus the Pan-p'o word-signs ↑ 、 ↑ 、 ∧ 、 ∧ , which I thought might have been the archetypal forms of the character *jen* (man), on the basis of my

---

[1] "Ku-tai wen-tzu chih pien-cheng ti fa-ch'an," *KK*, 1972, No. 3, pp. 2–13.

comparison with incised characters on Chou pottery, may have more probably been the first and simplest clan insignia in Figure 32. Likewise, the Pan-p'o word-sign ↑, which I did not try to interpret, may well have been the second clan insignia in Figure 32.

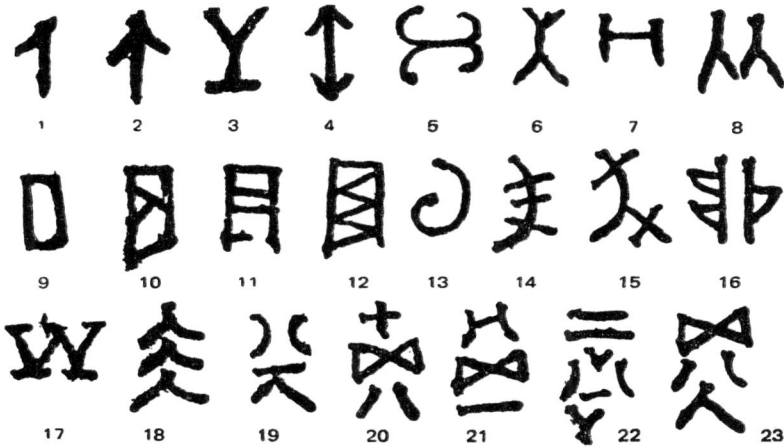

FIGURE 32. Ancient Chinese clan insignias chosen from Shang-Chou bronze inscriptions. From Kuo Mo-jo, "Ku-tai wen-tzu chih pien-cheng ti fa-ch'an," Figure 2 on p. 13 (numbers added). Nos. 18, 19, 20, 22, and 23 seem to be composed exclusively of basic numerals.

3. With his intimate knowledge of archaic Chinese script, Kuo divides ancient clan insignias into two styles: the simpler ones reminiscent of the Pan-p'o incised word-signs (see Figure 32), and the complex pictographic ones found in Shang-Chou bronze inscriptions, which are formal and artistic (see Figure 33). According to him, the former may have evolved from some primitive attempts at recording, such as tying knots in ropes and cutting notches on wood as described in ancient legends, and is likely to have been the creation of the common people; the latter began to appear only from late-Shang times onward and is likely to have been a creation of the elite. There is no question in Kuo's mind that the former preceded the latter by a considerable margin. He generalizes: "Casual incising

396 APPENDIX IV

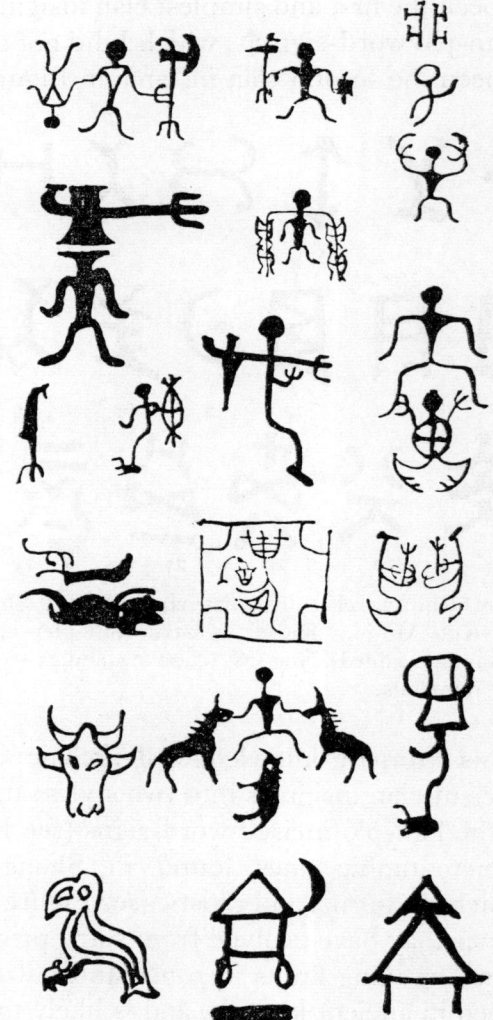

FIGURE 33. Pictographic ancient clan insignias chosen from Shang-Chou bronze inscriptions. From Kuo Mo-jo, "Ku-tai wen-tzu chih pien-cheng ti fa-ch'an," Figure 3 on p. 13.

is relatively easy. The fact that those [simple] incised clan insignias are much fewer in number [as compared with the complex pictographic ones] indicates that they were earlier, appearing early and also disappearing early. The incipient stage of this kind of script had already appeared on Yang-shao painted pottery but its vestiges were still present in Shang oracle and Chou bronze inscriptions."[2]

4. Kuo's comprehensive discussion of the nonpictographic ancient clan insignias leads us to a reexamination of the crucial problem of whether some of the Pan-p'o word-signs are numerals. In addition to the six samples given in Figure 32 (nos. 18-23), Kuo has culled from various sources twelve more samples of ancient clan insignias which are nonpictographic and which he regards as "indexical." I have rearranged them as follows:

Writing in 1957 without the benefit of the Pan-p'o data, the well-known paleographer T'ang Lan regarded these unusual characters as ancient clan insignias, an opinion with which Kuo fully concurs. With the benefit of the Pan-p'o data, Kuo goes a step further by saying that "these incised characters obviously belong to the same system of incised word-signs on [the Pan-p'o] painted pottery." Whereas I concur with T'ang that the components of these nonpictographic but unusually complex characters are invariably numerals, Kuo disagrees with T'ang for no other reason than

---

[2] A central point in Kuo's article is that at any major stage in the evolution of the Chinese script and calligraphy the casual, cursive style preceded the formal, artistic style. This point is bound to be discussed by epigraphers for some time to come. But even as a lay student of Chinese paleography, I was immediately struck by the fact that incised characters on Shang-Chou pottery are simpler, cruder, more casual, and somewhat different in style from those in oracle-bone and bronze inscriptions. There does seem to have been a "people's" style and an "elite" style in ancient Chinese script and calligraphy. The latest knowledge derived from the Pan-p'o finds also seems to lend support to Kuo's contention that the casual and simple style was earlier than the complex and artistic style.

his long-cherished belief that early man's sense of number was too weak for him to have created all the basic numerals from 1 to 9. As early as 1931, in his long study of the etymologies of the two series of Chinese ordinals, Kuo said that early man could not comprehend any number beyond 4.[3] In his present article, he still maintains that some early men had difficulty in comprehending any number beyond 7.

It is a relatively simple matter to show that Kuo's belief is not supported by historical and anthropological facts. It is well known that the Sumerians displayed a remarkable sense of number in their sexagesimal system, supplemented by a decimal system. There are special symbols for 60, 3,600, and so on.[4] And a leading expert of Maya hieroglyphics confirms that "all Maya dialects and languages made use of vegesimal system for general purpose of counting."[5] Twentieth-century aborigines have little difficulty in counting up to 10, 20, or more with their fingers, toes, and counting sticks. I have been told by my distinguished anthropologist colleague, Professor Fred Eggan, that most primitive peoples have multipliers for large numbers, whether their basic counting system is based on 5, 10, 20, or more. The hypothesis that of all the ancient peoples who laid foundations for higher civilizations the proto-Chinese alone should have been unable to comprehend any number beyond 4 or 7 is certainly at variance with empirical knowledge. Indeed, the strikingly consistent phenomenon is that not only do all early scripts contain basic numerals but numerals are among the earliest written signs created by men.

Since Kuo's refusal to identify some Pan-p'o word-signs as numerals is made in the midst of his discussion of archaic Chinese

---

[3] Kuo Mo-jo, *Chia-ku wen-tzu yen-chiu*, the long article on the etymologies of the two series of ordinals, pp. 1a–93b.

[4] A. Falkenstein, *Archaische Texte aus Uruk*, "Zahlen."

[5] J. Eric Thompson, *Maya Hieroglyphic Writing* (Washington, D.C., 1950), p. 51 and also the whole section on counting, pp. 51–54.

clan insignias, it is pertinent to discuss briefly the ancient Chinese practice of adopting numerals and ordinals as surnames and personal names. Owing to the fact that Chinese characters have individual meanings, all except a very few formal personal names of the later highly literate dynastic periods were chosen from words with auspicious, didactic, or commemorative meanings, with the result that numerals and ordinals as formal personal names became increasingly uncommon. As we saw in chapter 6, some Hsia rulers and all Shang kings were given series A ordinals as ceremonial names. The first three ordinals of series A, Chia, I, and Ping, are known to have been surnames at least until Han times.[6] The fourth ordinal of the same series, Ting, has remained today one of the common surnames.[7]

An excellent example of the use of ordinals as surnames is found in the biography of a Later-Han official, Ti-wu Lun 第五倫. The surname Ti-wu literally means "the fifth." The biography says: "Ti-wu Lun . . . was a native of the Ch'ang 長 imperial mausoleum township. His ancestors were members of the T'ien 田 ruling clan of the Ch'i 齊 state. [At the inception of the Former Han dynasty] members of the various lineages of the T'ien clan were required to take up residence in imperial mausoleum townships, hence they adopted surnames in the order of seniority."[8] We learn further from the commentaries that there were eight lineages with surnames from

---

[6] *Yüan-ho hsing-ts'uan* (1880 ed.), a compendium of the origins of various surnames compiled in A.D. 812, ch. 7, pp. 17b–18a, ch. 8, p. 47b, and ch. 10, pp. 15b–16a.

[7] It should be noted once more that the etymologies of the twenty-two characters that form the ordinals of series A and B are still uncertain and that they are not, strictly speaking, ordinals in the sense of first, second, third, and so on. But the important point is that, as far as is traceable, these twenty-two characters have been used mainly as ordinals for various purposes at least since Shang times. Although the origins of certain surnames given in the above-mentioned T'ang work are not always accurate, there can be little doubt that the earliest traceable uses of Chia, I, Ping, and Ting are as ordinals.

[8] *Hou-Han-shu*, ch. 14, p. 1a.

Ti-i 第一 ("the first") to Ti-pa 第八 ("the eighth"). The accuracy of this account is proven by the fact that an academic official of the Wang Mang period (A.D. 9–23) was named Ti-pa Chiao 矯.

Of the basic numerals that were adopted as surnames, Wu 伍、五 is almost certain to have been ultimately derived from the numeral 5. San 三 (3) and Ch'i 七 (7) as surnames were recorded in Ming times.[9] In spite of the fact that the use of numerals as personal names was increasingly considered to be vulgar, some bannermen in Ch'ing times had personal names, such as Ch'i-shih 七十 (70) and Liu-shih-ch'i 六十七 (67).[10]

Aside from vestiges of using numerals and ordinals as surnames and personal names, it is common knowledge that in traditional China the various lineages of a kinship group, the various branches of a lineage, brothers and male first cousins, and unmarried daughters were usually intimately referred to by kin as the eldest, the second, the third, and so forth, although each individual had his formal personal name. Indeed, numbers in the broad sense, that is, cardinals and ordinals together, had so much to do with the denoting of kinship relations that they were indispensable. Moreover, as far as we can trace, ever since Shang or even earlier times, cardinals were used in a variety of ways as ordinals so that the difference between these two kinds of numbers can only be detected contextually. As compared with other ancient peoples, the early Chinese probably had a greater need for numbers, in the broad sense, to indicate orders of seniority and various lines of descent because of

---

[9] Wang Su-ts'un, *Hsing-lu* (Taipei, 1960), p. 1.

[10] In the 1950s I went through wide-ranging Ch'ing sources and was struck by the relative frequency with which Manchu and Mongol bannermen took numerals for personal names. Unfortunately, it would take more time than I can now afford to sort them out from old notes. The case of Ch'i-shih is found in *Wen-hsien ts'ung-pien* (Palace Museum), 1937, No. 1, in a memorial submitted by the Imperial Household Department dated 1733. Ch'i-shih was a Mongol captain. The case of Liu-shih-ch'i is cited in Wang Su-ts'un, *Hsing-lu,* p. 20. He was a Manchu censor. Wang errs by treating Liu as a surname, for Liu-shih-ch'i is a personal name and Manchu customs usually did not give polysyllabic clan or surname.

the highly developed ancestral cult which has now been traced back to Lungshanoid times. It stands to reason, therefore, that some clans of remote antiquity should have used specific combinations of numbers as their insignias.

Indeed, following the logic of Kuo's article, one would expect him to have been the first to identify some of the Pan-p'o word-signs as numerals. For, as has been discussed in chapter 6, the striking consistency in form of the numerals from Yang-shao to late-Shang times rules out the possibility of coincidence. With his mastery of archaic Chinese, Kuo might also have been the first to confirm T'ang Lan's observation that the components of those complex nonpictographic ancient clan insignias are basic numerals. Thanks to Kuo's otherwise highly judicious and affirmative remarks, I can now restate with even greater assurance that the Pan-p'o numerals, according to our present knowledge, were the earliest ever created by man, and the most intelligent numerals until the Hindu-Arabic numerals came into use; that the Pan-p'o word-signs represent the earliest effort by man to create a script; and that the interval separating Pan-p'o and An-yang—some three millennia—should be regarded as a prolonged proto-literate period.

The lack of textual evidence before 1300 B.C. makes speculation about the character of the pre-Shang Chinese language extremely difficult. It has been suggested in chapter 6 that pre-Shang Chinese is extremely unlikely to have been of a nature drastically different from what it was in 1300 B.C., namely, a positional language in which the grammatical functions of words are determined by their positions in the sentence. While the history of Chinese script has been pushed back to the fifth millennium B.C., the evolution of the Chinese language from Yang-shao to late-Shang times is still unrecorded. Having received wise counsel from some linguist friends to steer away from the problem of the pre-Shang Chinese language, I fully realize the high risks involved in such speculation, especially when the speculator is a historian of insatiable curiosity but with no competence in linguistics. Since the problem of the pre-Shang language is so challenging precisely because of its impregnability, I cannot resist the temptation of supplying the learned world with a note which amplifies an observation made by Professor Wang Li 王力 of Peking University, a leading historian of Chinese language.[11]

The *Confucian Analects* contains an extremely important entry, the true meaning of which, because of the "orthodox" commentaries of the great Sung Neo-Confucian philosopher Chu Hsi (1130-1200), has escaped the notice of scholars until recently. This entry, when textually emended and properly interpreted, is: "The Master sometimes spoke the standard language [*i.e.*, dialect]; when discussing *The Book of Odes, The Book of Documents,* arts and rituals, he spoke the standard language."[12] The key phrase in this entry is "*ya-yen* 雅言," which means the "standard language." Two leading Ch'ing etymologists, Wang Yin-chih 王引之 (1766-1834) and Chu Chün-sheng 朱駿聲 (1788-1858), firmly established through the text of *Hsün-tzu* that *ya* is a synonym of *Hsia* 夏—the name of the state or "dynasty" which preceded the Shang.[13] In other words,

---

[11] Wang Li, *Han-yü-shih kao* [A Draft History of the Chinese Language], 3 Vols. (Peking, 1957-58), I, p. 36.

[12] The entry is: 子所雅言，詩書執禮，皆雅言也。 That the character 執 should be 藝 was convincingly shown by Fang I-chih 方以智 (1611-71) in his *Tung-hsi chün* (Shanghai, 1962), p. 82. My translation is based on Wang Li's interpretation and also on Yang Po-chün, *Lun-yu i-chu* [Confucian Analects: Translations and Commentaries] (Shanghai, 1965), p. 76.

[13] Wang Yin-chih, *Tu-shu tsa-chih* (*Kao-yu Wang-shih ssu-chung* ed.), Part VIII, "*Hsün-tzu*," ch. 1, pp. 35b-36a; Chu Chün-sheng, *Shuo-wen t'ung-hsün ting-sheng* (1851 ed.), ch. 9, pp. 112b-113a. It should be noted that Miao Yüeh, in his article "Chou-tai chih 'ya-yen'" [The 'Standard Language' of the Chou Dynasty], *Che-chiang-ta-hsüeh wen-hsüeh-yüan chi-k'an* [Bulletin of the Faculty of Arts and Letters of Chekiang University], I (1941), pp. 13-24, preceded Bernhard Karlgren by a few years in establishing the existence of a "standard" or "elite" language or dialect in Chou times by studying the strict rhyming systems of a large majority of songs and odes in *The Book of Odes*. He also preceded Wang Li in using the findings of Wang Yin-chih and Chu Chün-sheng. Whereas Miao conjectured that the

what was regarded by Confucius and members of the Chou elite before him as the standard dialect was the one generally believed to have been that spoken by the Hsia people. This entry is therefore powerful evidence that there must have been linguistic continuity from the Hsia, through the Shang, to the Chou, and that this linguistic continuity may have been one of the most important factors, if not the single most important one, accounting for the deep-seated Chou belief in an overall cultural continuity of the Hsia, Shang, and Chou.[14]

A conservative chronology would put the beginnings of the Hsia "dynasty" before 2000 B.C. Since the Hsia language must have

---

"standard" dialect of the Chou might have been that adopted by the Shang elite, Wang is the first scholar explicitly to interpret the "standard" Chou dialect as that of the Hsia people. Since it is almost certain that the word *ya* (standard or elite) is derived from Hsia, I endorse Wang's interpretation.

[14] For Confucius and subsequent research scholars, a knowledge of archaic elite pronunciations was scholastically important. For, in spite of the fact that the Chinese character usually contains a "phonetic" to indicate sound and a signific to indicate meaning, the "phonetic" is often only an approximation of the sound. The existence of various local dialects, and inevitable changing pronunciations through the course of time, made it necessary for the ancient Chinese to have a standard elite spoken language. The existence, from at least the beginnings of the Chou, of such an elite language is definitely shown by the uniformity of the rhyming systems of a large majority of the 305 odes in *The Book of Odes* gathered from various feudal states, which must have been composed in different dialects and later edited by the royal court according to the elite pronunciations. It is also obvious that the texts of most of the philosophical schools were written in the standard elite language. Imperial governments of later periods had the same need. An outstanding example was the compilation of the rhyming dictionary *Ch'ieh-yün* 切韻, consequent upon the reunification of China in A.D. 589, after North China had been ruled by various alien conquerors for nearly three centuries. Although the phonetic system upon which this dictionary was based was necessarily a composite one, among the essential components were the old elite dialect of Lo-yang, the imperial capital from A.D. 25 to its fall in 317, and the elite dialect of the Southern Dynasties. See Ch'en Yin-k'o, "Ts'ung shih-shih lun *Ch'ien-yün*" [The *Ch'ien-yün*: A Historical Study], *Liang-nan hsüeh-pao* [Journal of Ling-nan University], IX, No. 2 (June 1949), pp. 1–19; and Kun Chang and Betty Shefts Chang, *The Proto-Chinese Final System and the Ch'ieh-yün* (Academia Sinica, Taiwan, 1972), pp. 2–3.

been considerably older than the emergence of the Hsia as a dominant tribal state in North China, one may infer from the evidence provided by the *Confucian Analects* that during much of the third millennium B.C. the proto-Sinitic language which has now been linked with that of the Chou was already essentially a noninflectional, positional, and mainly monosyllabic language. For otherwise it would have been impossible for the Chou elite to "standardize" the spoken language according to what it believed to have been the Hsia dialect. In the light of our discussion on the use of ordinals for ceremonial names of some Hsia rulers and of the implications of the use throughout the Chou period of such expressions as "chu-Hsia," "yu-Hsia," "ch'ü-Hsia," "shih-Hsia," and "Hua-Hsia" for all the lands, peoples, and states that had shared a common Sinitic tradition, the Hsia people must have made significant contributions to the development of the Chinese script, aside from speaking essentially the same language as did the Chou.

The homeland of the Hsia people is generally believed to have been southern Shansi and western Honan. From late-Chou sources, one can be reasonably sure that the southern Shansi area was one of the headquarters of the Hsia tribal state. For an entry of the year 506 B.C. in the *Tso-chuan* recalls that the first lord of the Chin state in southern Shansi was to have "the old capital of Hsia" as the heart of his domain and that he "was to commence his government according to the principles of Hsia."[15] The lingering Hsia cultural influence over this area may best be indicated by the adoption by the Chin state of the old Hsia calendar.[16] Archaeologically, the southern Shansi and western Honan area was well within the orbit of the Miao-ti-kou I type of the Yang-shao culture (radiocarbon dates: 3280 ± 100 B.C.; bristlecone-pine dates: 3880 ± 100 B.C.) and of the subsequent Lungshanoid Miao-ti-kou II culture (radiocarbon dates: 2310 ± 95 B.C.; bristlecone-pine dates: 2760 ± 95 B.C.). The chrono-

---

[15] Legge, tr., *The Chinese Classics*, V, *The Ch'un Ts'ew with the Tso Chuen*, p. 754.
[16] See Appendix III, note 1.

logical gap between the "predynastic" Hsia and the Miao-ti-kou II Lungshanoid offshoot of the late Yang-shao Miao-ti-kou I culture is therefore only a few centuries at most.

All this does not mean that a linguistic link can be established in the same western Honan and southern Shansi area between Yang-shao and "predynastic" Hsia times. For artifacts are as a rule mute, and much more excavating and research will be needed for the identification of the Hsia and of "predynastic" Hsia culture. One can only infer from available physical anthropological evidence that the Yang-shao people were true proto-Sinids, bearing close physical resemblances to the people of present-day southern China and having rather different physical features from those various proto-Turcic and proto-Tungusic peoples who constituted the group of northern Mongoloids. Since evidence from physical anthropology, though suggestive, cannot be equated with linguistic evidence, no one can say definitely whether the Yang-shao language was substantially different from that of the Hsia, Shang, and Chou times. It is my opinion that future research on this subject should take the following factors into account. First, if the Chinese language has not changed basically during the past thirty-three textually documented centuries, it would be very risky to assume that the language must have undergone drastic changes in the same relatively small geographic area in those few centuries during which the Lungshanoid Miao-ti-kou II culture—undoubtedly an offshoot of the late Yang-shao Miao-ti-kou I culture—ran its course and the "predynastic" Hsia culture arose. Second, there is no longer any intellectually valid basis for assuming that all languages evolve in the same way, that is, in the way the Indo-European languages did: from a simple to a complex morphology and back again. This popular nineteenth-century view formulated by Indo-Europeanists may not apply to the Chinese language.

Appendix V

THE GOAT AND THE EARLY
EAST-WEST TRADE ROUTE

IN JULY 1974 I had an opportunity to present the main findings of this book to the faculty and students of the Department of History of National Peking University and some members of the Institute of Archaeology and the Institute of History of Academia Sinica. One of the questions I brought up during my presentation was whether the mention of the remains of the goat in the Miao-ti-kou II cultural stratum might not be due to a typological error in the report on the important twin sites of Miao-ti-kou and San-li-ch'iao. Professor An Chih-min, a senior member of the Institute of Archaeology and also a leader of the team that had excavated the twin sites, clarified my query by affirming the presence of the goat in the Miao-ti-kou II cultural stratum. Remains of the goat from that stratum were subsequently identified by paleontologists. I am grateful to Professor An not only for this technical clarification but also for affording me an additional opportunity to pursue the question of early east-west trade route.

The Miao-ti-kou II stratum has been radiocarbon-dated at 2310 ± 95 B.C., which corresponds to 2760 ± 95 B.C. of bristle-cone-pine dendrochronology. The remains of goat unearthed from this stratum represent by far the earliest evidence of intercultural exchange between China and the Eurasian steppe. They also rule out the possibility that the goat arrived first in some Ch'i-chia cultural sites in the northwestern province of Kansu, which are at least 700 years later than the Miao-ti-kou II culture. Since the Miao-ti-kou II goat arrived two thousand years later than the pig husbandry in the Pan-p'o nuclear area, it could not have had anything to do with the origins of animal domestication in China.

But the arrival of the goat in Honan during the first half of the third millennium B.C. does serve as a reminder that wheat and barley might have been brought into the low plains of North China centuries before they were recorded in Shang oracle texts and Western-Chou literary works and bronze inscriptions.

Like bronze weapons and tools of Seima motif and the horse chariot, the goat, wheat, and barley must have been brought into the low plains area of North China through the intermediary of a number of Neolithic, proto-Turcic, and possibly also some proto-Tungusic, peoples who inhabited the area south and east of Lake Baikal. I have pointed out, in chapters VI and VIII, that from Lake Baikal westward to Soviet Europe prehistoric trade took place in the steppe zone, north of the 50th parallel, where water supply was not a serious problem. The location of the earliest goat finds in China further strengthens the belief that the "silk route," which traverses the world's largest dry belt between the Kansu corridor and the Aral and Caspian Seas, cannot have been a thoroughfare for intercultural exchange in prehistoric times, at least not until man had mastered the art of horse-riding and succeeded in using camels for caravan trade.

CHINESE CHARACTERS FOR ARCHAEOLOGICAL SITES MENTIONED IN THE TEXT

An-ning 安寧
Ch'an (River) 滻
Ch'ang-an 長安
Cheng-chou 鄭州
Ch'eng-tzu-yai 城子崖
Ch'i-chia 齊家
Ch'i-chia-p'ing 齊家坪
Ch'ih-feng 赤峯
Ch'ih-k'ou-chai 池口寨
Chin-ning 晉寧
Ch'in-wei-chia 秦魏家
Ch'ing-kang-ch'a 青崗岔
Ch'ing-lien-kang 青蓮崗
Ching-shan 京山
Ching-ts'un 荆村
Ch'ü-chia-ling 屈家嶺
Chu-chia-tsui 朱家嘴
Ch'ü-fu 曲阜
Chuan-lung-tsang 轉龍藏
Ch'üan-hu-ts'un 泉護村
Chung-chou-lu 中州路
Erh-li-kang 二里岡
Erh-li-t'ou 二里頭
Feng-hsiang 鳳翔
Feng-pi-t'ou 鳳鼻頭
Ho-yang 邰陽
Hou-ma 侯馬
Hsi-hsiang 西鄉
Hsi-p'o-wo 西坡崡
Hsi-wang-ts'un 西王村
Hsi-yin-ts'un 西陰村
Hsia-chia-tien 夏家店

Hsia-meng-ts'un 下孟村
Hsien-li-tun 仙蠡墩
Hsin-i 新沂
Hsin-tien 辛店
Hsin-yeh-ts'un 莘野村
Hsien-jen-tung 仙人洞
Hsing-p'ing 興平
Hu-hsien 鄠縣
Hua-hsien 華縣
Huang-niang-niang-t'ai 皇娘娘台
Hung-shan-hou 紅山後
Jih-chao 日照
Jui-ch'eng 芮城
Kang-shang-ts'un 岡上村
Kao-tui 高堆
K'e-hsing-chuang 客省莊
Lan-chou 蘭州
Li-chia-ts'un 李家村
Lin-hsi 林西
Lin-hsia 臨夏
Ling-t'ai 靈台
Liu-lin 劉林
Liu-tzu-chen 柳子鎮
Lo-han-t'ang 羅漢堂
Lung-shan 龍山
Ma-ch'ang 馬廠
Ma-chia-pin 馬家濱
Ma-chia-yao 馬家窰
Mei-yen 梅堰
Miao-ti-kou 廟底溝
Ning-yang 寧陽

Niu-ts'un 牛村
Pan-p'o 半坡
Pan-shan 半山
Pao-chi 寶雞
Pao-t'ou 包頭 (Inner Mongolia)
Pao-t'ou 堡頭 (Shantung)
P'ei-hsien 邳縣
Pei-shou-ling 北首嶺
San-li-ch'iao 三里橋
San-li-tun 三里墩
Sha-wo-tzu 沙窩子
Shan-hsien 陝縣
Shih-chai-shan 石寨山
So-chin-ts'un 鎖金村
Ssu-hu-cheng 四戶鎮
Ta-ch'eng-shan 大城山
Ta-ho-chuang 大何莊
Ta-pei-kou 大北溝
Ta-wen-k'ou 大汶口
Teng-hsien 滕縣
Ts'ao-hsieh-shan 草鞋山
Tung-kou 洞溝
Wan-nien 萬年
Wu-chiang 吳江
Wu-hsi 無錫
Wu-wei 武威
Yang-shao 仰韶
Yen-shih 偃師
Yo-wang-miao 藥王廟
Yün-ch'eng 運城
Yung-ching 永靖

ABBREVIATIONS USED IN NOTES AND BIBLIOGRAPHY

BIHP	*Chung-yang-yen-chiu-yüan li-shih-yü-yen-yen-chiu-so chi-k'an* 中央研究院歷史語言研究所集刊 [Bulletin of the Institute of History and Philology, Academia Sinica]
BMFEA	*Bulletin of the Museum of Far Eastern Antiquities* (Stockholm)
KK	*K'ao-ku* 考古 [Archaeology]
KKHP	*K'ao-ku hsüeh-pao* 考古學報 [Archaeological Review]
SPPY	*Ssu-pu pei-yao* 四部備要 edition
SPTK	*Ssu-pu ts'ung-k'an* 四部叢刊 edition
WW	*Wen-wu* 文物 [Objects of Cultural Interest]
WWTKTL	*Wen-wu ts'an-k'ao tzu-liao* 文物參考資料 [Materials for Reference to Objects of Cultural Interest]

BIBLIOGRAPHY

Note: The part of this bibliography dealing with ancient Chinese agriculture is not intended to be exhaustive. Scientists and sinologists interested in a fuller listing of ancient and recent Chinese literature on paleoenvironment and agricultural origins are advised to consult the bibliography of my *Huang-t'u yü Chung-kuo nung-yeh ti ch'i-yüan* 黃土與中國農業的起源 [The Loess and the Origins of Chinese Agriculture] (The Chinese University of Hong Kong, 1969).

CHINESE AND JAPANESE SOURCES

AN CHIH-MIN 安志敏, "Chung-kuo shih-ch'ien-shih-ch'i chih nung-yeh" 中國史前時期之農業, *Yen-ching she-hui-k'e-hsüeh* 燕京社會科學, II (1949).

—, "Kuan-yü Cheng-chou 'Shang-ch'eng' ti chi-ke wen-t'i" 關於鄭州「商城」的幾個問題, *KK*, 1961, No. 8.

—, "Kuan-yü wo-kuo jo-kan yüan-shih-wen-hua nien-tai ti t'ao-lun" 關於我國若干原始文化年代的討論, *KK*, 1972, No. 2.

—, "Lüeh-lun wo-kuo hsin-shih-ch'i-shih-tai wen-hua ti nien-tai wen-t'i" 略論我國新石器時代文化的年代問題, *KK*, 1972, No. 6.

—, and Ch'en Ts'un-hsi 陳存洗, "Shan-hsi Yün-ch'eng Tung-kou ti Tung-Han t'ung-k'uang ho t'i-chi" 山西運城洞溝的東漢銅礦和題記, *KK*, 1962, No. 10.

"Ch'ang-an Chang-chia-p'o-ts'un Hsi-chou i-chih ti chung-yao fa-hsien" 長安張家坡村西周遺址的重要發現, *WWTKTL*, 1956, No. 3.

CHANG HUA 張華, *Po-wu chih* 博物志. SPPY ed.

CHANG PING-CH'ÜAN 張秉權, "Chia-ku-wen chung so-chien jen ti t'ung-ming k'ao" 甲骨文中所見人地同名考, *Ch'ing-chu Li Chi hsien-sheng ch'i-shih-sui lun-wen-chi* 慶祝李濟先生七十歲論文集. Taipei, 1967, Part II.

—, "Chia-ku-wen ti fa-hsien yü ku-pu hsi-kuan ti k'ao-cheng" 甲骨文的發現與骨卜習慣的考証, *BIHP*, XXXVII (1967), Part II.

—, "Wu-ting shih-tai ti i-pan fu-yüan kuei-chia" 武丁時代的一版復原龜甲, *Ta-lu tsa-chih* 大陸雜誌, XXIX, Nos. 10-11 (1964).

—, *Yin-hsü wen-tzu ping-pien* 殷墟文字丙編. 5 Vols. (to date). Academia Sinica, Taiwan, 1957-67.

CHANG TZU-KAO 張子高, *Chung-kuo hua-hsüeh-shih kao* 中國化學史稿. Peking, 1964.

CHAO HSI-YÜAN 趙錫元, "Shih-lun Yin-tai chu-yao sheng-ch'an-che 'chung' ho 'chung-jen' ti she-hui shen-fen" 試論殷代主要生產者「眾」和「眾人」的社會身分. *Tung-pei-jen-min-ta-hsüeh jen-wen-k'e-hsüeh hsüeh-pao* 東北人民大學人文科學學報, 1956, No. 4.

"Che-chiang Chia-hsing Ma-chia-pin hsin-shih-ch'i-shih-tai i-chih ti fa-chüeh" 浙江嘉興馬家濱新石器時代遺址的發掘, *KK*, 1961, No. 7.

CH'EN CH'ENG-HUI 陳承惠, CH'EN SHIH-MIN 陳碩民, and CHOU K'UN-SHU 周崑叔, "Liao-tung-pan-tao P'u-lan-tien fu-chin han ku-lien-tzu ti ch'üan-hsin-shih ch'en-chi-wu ti p'ao-fen fen-hsi" 遼東半島普蘭店附近含古蓮子的全新世沉積物的孢粉分析, *Chung-kuo ti-ssu-chi yen-chiu* 中國第四紀研究 *(Quaternaria Sinica)*, IV, No. 1 (1965).

CH'EN MENG-CHIA 陳夢家, *Yin-hsü pu-tz'u tsung-shu* 殷墟卜辭綜述. Peking, 1956.

CH'EN P'AN 陳槃, *Ch'un-ch'iu-ta-shih-piao lieh-kuo-chüeh-hsing chi ts'un-mieh-piao hsün-i* 春秋大事表列國爵姓及存滅表譔異. Academia Sinica, Taiwan, 1970. 7 ts'e.

———, "Hou yü she-hou" 侯與射侯 and Lao Kan's 勞榦 comment, *BIHP*, XXII (1950).

CH'EN PANG-HUAI 陳邦懷, *Yin-tai she-hui shih-liao ch'eng-ts'un* 殷代社會史料徵存. Tientsin, 1959.

CH'EN YIN-K'O 陳寅恪, "Ts'ung shih-shih lun *Ch'ieh-yün*" 從史實論切韻, *Ling-nan hsüeh-pao* 嶺南學報, IX, No. 2 (June 1949).

Cheng-chou Erh-li-kang 鄭州二里岡. Peking, 1959.

CHENG TE-K'UN 鄭德坤, "Chung-kuo shang-ku shu-ming ti yen-pien chi ch'i ying-yung" 中國上古數名的演變及其應用, *Hsiang-kang-Chung-wen-ta-hsüeh hsüeh-pao* 香港中文大學學報 *(Journal of The Chinese University of Hong Kong)*, I (March 1973).

Ch'eng-tzu-yai 城子崖. Academia Sinica, 1934.

"Chiang-hsi Wan-nien Ta-yüan Hsien-jen-tung tung-hsüeh i-chih shih-chüeh" 江西萬年大源仙人洞洞穴遺址試掘, *KKHP*, 1963, No. 1.

"Chiang-su P'ei-hsien Liu-lin hsin-shih-ch'i-shih-tai i-chih ti-erh-tz'u fa-chüeh" 江蘇邳縣劉林新石器時代遺址第二次發掘, *KK*, 1965, No. 2.

"Chiang-su P'ei-hsien Ta-tun-tzu i-chih t'an-chüeh pao-kao" 江蘇邳縣大墩子遺址探掘報告, *KKHP*, 1964, No. 2.

Chiang-su-sheng ch'u-t'u wen-wu hsüan-chi 江蘇省出土文物選集. Peking, 1963.

CHIANG TSUAN-CH'U 蔣纘初, "Kuan-yü Chiang-su ti yüan-shih wen-hua" 關於江蘇的原始文化, *KKHP,* 1959, No. 4.

"Chin-nan wu-hsien ku-tai jen-lei wen-hua i-chih ch'u-pu tiao-ch'a" 晉南五縣古代人類文化遺址初步調查, *WW,* 1956, No. 4.

CHIN HSIANG-HENG 金祥恒, *T'ao-wen pien* 陶文編. Taipei, 1964.

Chin-shu 晉書. Taipei, I-wen 藝文 reprint of Ch'ing palace edition.

Ching-shan Ch'ü-chia-ling 京山屈家嶺. Peking, 1965.

CHOU CH'Ü-FEI 周去非, *Ling-wai tai-ta* 嶺外代答. *Ts'ung-shu chi-ch'eng* 叢書集成 ed.

CHOU FA-KAO 周法高, *Chung-kuo yü-wen lun-ts'ung* 中國語文論叢. Taipei, 1963.

—, ed., *Yen-shih chia-hsün hui-chu* 顏氏家訓彙注. Academia Sinica, Taiwan, 1960.

CHOU HUNG-HSIANG 周鴻翔, *Shang-Yin ti-wang pen-chi* 商殷帝王本紀. Hong Kong, 1958.

CHOU JEN 周仁, CHANG FU-K'ANG 張福康, and CHENG YUNG-P'U 鄭永圃, "Wo-kuo Huang-ho-liu-yü hsin-shih-ch'i-shih-tai ho Yin-Chou shih-tai chih t'ao kung-i ti k'e-hsüeh tsung-chieh" 我國黃河流域新石器時代和殷周時代製陶工藝的科學總結, *KKHP,* 1964, No. 1.

CHOU K'UN-SHU 周昆叔, "Hsi-an Pan-p'o hsin-shih-ch'i-shih-tai i-chih ti p'ao-fen fen-hsi" 西安半坡新石器時代遺址的孢粉分析, *KK,* 1963, No. 9.

—, "Tui Pei-ching-shih fu-chin liang-ke mai-ts'ang ni-t'an-chao ti tiao-ch'a chi ch'i p'ao-fen fen-hsi" 對北京市附近兩個埋藏泥炭沼的調查及其孢粉分析, *Quaternaria Sinica,* IV, No. 1 (1965).

—, LIANG HSIU-LUNG 梁秀龍, YEH YUNG-YING 葉永英, and WANG WEN-LIN 王文琳, "Shan-hsi Li-shih Wang-chia-kou Ch'en-chia-yai lao-huang-t'u mai-ts'ang-t'u-jang chung ti p'ao-fen chi ch'i chih-wu ts'an-t'i" 山西離石王家溝陳家崖老黃土埋藏土壤中的孢粉及其植物殘體, *Quaternaria Sinica,* III, No. 1-2 (1960).

Chou-li chu-shu 周禮注疏. SPPY ed.

CHOU T'ING-JU 周廷儒 and LIU P'EI-T'UNG 劉培同, *Chung-kuo ti ti-hsing ho t'u-jang kai-shu* 中國的地形和土壤概述. Peking, 1956.

CHU CHÜN-SHENG 朱駿聲, *Shuo-wen t'ung-hsün ting-sheng* 說文通訓定聲. 1851 ed.

CHU K'E-CHEN 竺可楨, "Lun wo-kuo ch'i-hou ti chi-ke t'e-tien yü liang-shih-tso-wu sheng-ch'an ti kuan-hsi" 論我國氣候的幾個特點與糧食作物生產的關係, *Ti-li hsüeh-pao* 地理學報 *(Acta Geographica Sinica),* XXX, No. 1 (1964).

Ch'u-tz'u pu-chu 楚辭補注. SPPY ed.

Ch'u-tz'u yen-chiu lun-wen-chi 楚辭研究論文集. Peking, 1957.

CH'Ü WAN-LI 屈萬里, *Yin-hsü wen-tzu chia-pien k'ao-shih* 殷墟文字甲編考釋. Academia Sinica, Taiwan, 1961.

Chung-kuo k'e-hsüeh-yüan k'ao-ku-yen-chiu-so shih-yen-shih 中國科學院考古研究所試驗室, "Fang-she-hsing-t'an-su ts'e-ting nien-tai pao-kao" 放射性碳素測定年代報告, Part I, *KK,* 1972, No. 1; Part II, *KK,* 1972, No. 5.

FAN HSIANG-JUNG 范祥雍, *Ku-pen Chu-shu-chi-nien chi-chiao ting-pu* 古本竹書紀年輯校訂補. Shanghai, 1956.

FANG I-CHIH 方以智, *Tung-hsi chün* 東西均. Shanghai, 1962 reprint.

FANG YANG 方楊, "Yang-shao-wen-hua ho-tsang hsi-su ti chi-tien pu-ch'ung chieh-shih" 仰韶文化合葬習俗的幾點補充解釋, *KK,* 1962, No. 3.

FANG YU-SHENG 方酉生, "Ho-nan Yen-shih Erh-li-tou i-chih fa-chüeh chien-pao" 河南偃師二里頭遺址發掘簡報, *KK,* 1965, No. 5.

Feng-hsi fa-chüeh pao-kao 灃西發掘報告. Peking, 1962.

FU SSU-NIEN 傅斯年, "Chou tung-feng yü Yin-i-min" 周東封與殷遺民, *BIHP,* IV, No. 3 (1934).

—, *Hsing-ming ku-hsün pien-cheng* 性命古訓辨証. Academia Sinica, 1940.

—, "Lun so-wei wu-teng-chüeh" 論所謂五等爵, *BIHP,* II, No. 1 (1930).

—, *Tung-pei-shih kang* 東北史綱. Peiping, 1932.

HAMADA SOSAKU 濱田耕作, and MIZUNO SEIICHI 水野清一, *Ch'ih-feng: Hung-shan-hou* 赤峯:紅山後. Tokyo, 1938.

Han-shu 漢書. Taipei, I-wen reprint.

HAO I-HSING 郝懿行, *Erh-ya i-shu* 爾雅義疏. SPPY ed.

—, *Shan-hai-ching chien-shu* 山海經箋疏. SPPY ed.

HO KUAN-PAO 賀官保, "Lo-yang lao-ch'eng hsi-pei chiao 81-hao Han-mu" 洛陽老城西北角81號漢墓, *KK,* 1964, No. 8.

"Ho-pei T'ang-shan-shih Ta-ch'eng-shan i-chih fa-chüeh pao-kao" 河北唐山市大城山遺址發掘報告, *KKHP,* 1959, No. 3.

HO PING-TI 何炳棣, *Huang-t'u yü Chung-kuo nung-yeh ti ch'i-yüan* 黄土與中國農業的起源. Hong Kong, 1969.

—, "Chou-ch'u nien-tai p'ing-i" 周初年代平議, *Journal of The Chinese University of Hong Kong,* I (1973).

Hou-Han-shu 後漢書. Taipei, I-wen reprint.

"Hou-ma Niu-ts'un ku-ch'eng Tung-Chou i-chih fa-chüeh chien-pao" 侯馬牛村古城東周遺址發掘簡報, *KK,* 1962, No. 2.

Hsi-an Pan-p'o 西安半坡. Peking, 1963.

Hsi-an Pan-p'o-po-wu-kuan 西安半坡博物館, "1972-nien ch'un Lin-t'ung Chiang-chai i-chih fa-chüeh chien-pao" 1972年春臨潼姜寨遺址發掘簡報, *KK*, 1973, No. 3.

HSIA NAI 夏鼐, "Ch'ang-chiang-liu-yü k'ao-ku wen-t'i" 長江流域考古問題, *KK*, 1962, No. 2.

——, "Lin-t'ao Ssu-wa-shan fa-chüeh chi" 臨洮寺窪山發掘記, *Chung-kuo k'ao-ku hsüeh-pao* 中國考古學報, No. 4 (December 1949).

——, "Wo-kuo chin-wu-nien ti k'ao-ku shou-huo" 我國近五年的考古收穫, *KK*, 1964, No. 10.

——, "Wo-kuo ku-tai ts'an-sang ssu-ch'ou ti li-shih" 我國古代蠶桑絲綢的歷史, *KK*, 1972, No. 2.

HSIA WEI-YING 夏緯瑛, *Lü-shih-ch'un-ch'iu shang-nung teng ssu-p'ien chiao-shih* 呂氏春秋上農等四篇校釋. Shanghai, 1956.

Hsin-Chung-kuo ti k'ao-ku shou-kuo 新中國的考古收穫. Peking, 1962.

Hsin T'ang-shu 新唐書. Taipei, I-wen reprint.

HSÜ CHUNG-SHU 徐中舒, "Lei-ssu k'ao" 耒耜考, *BIHP*, II, No. 1 (1930).

HSÜ HSÜ-SHENG 徐旭生, *Chung-kuo ku-shih ti ch'uan-shuo shih-tai* 中國古史的傳說時代. Peking, 1962.

HSÜ JEN 徐仁, "Chung-kuo yüan-jen shih-tai ti Pei-ching ch'i-hou huan-ching" 中國猿人時代的北京氣候環境, *Quaternaria Sinica*, IV, No. 1 (1965).

HSÜ KUANG-CH'I 徐光啟, *Nung-cheng ch'üan-shu* 農政全書. 1843 ed.

HSÜ WEI-YÜ 許維遹, *Lü-shih-ch'un-ch'iu chi-shih* 呂氏春秋集釋. Peiping, 1935.

Hsün-tzu 荀子. SPPY ed.

HU HOU-HSÜAN 胡厚宣, *Chia-ku-hsüeh-Shang-shih lun-ts'ung ch'u-chi* 甲骨學商史論叢初集. Ch'eng-tu, 1944.

——, "Chia-ku-wen Shang-tsu niao-t'u-t'eng ti i-chi" 甲骨文商族鳥圖騰的遺蹟, *Li-shih lun-ts'ung* 歷史論叢, 1st Series, Peking University, 1964.

——, "Yin pu-tz'u chung ti shang-ti ho wang-ti" 殷卜辭中的上帝和王帝, *Li-shih yen-chiu* 歷史研究, 1959, No. 9-10.

——, "Yin-tai nung-tso shih-fei shuo" 殷代農作施肥說, *Li-shih yen-chiu*, 1955, No. 1.

"Hu-pei Ching-shan Chu-chia-tsui hsin-shih-ch'i i-chih ti-i-tz'u fa-chüeh" 湖北京山朱家嘴新石器遺址第一次發掘, *KK*, 1964, No. 5.

HU TAO-CHING 胡道靜, "Shih-shu p'ien" 釋菽篇, *Chung-hua wen-shih lun-ts'ung* 中華文史論叢, 3d Series, Peking, 1963.

"Hua-hsien Liu-tzu-chen ti-erh-tz'u fa-chüeh ti chu-yao shou-huo" 華縣柳子鎮第二次發掘的主要收穫, *KK*, 1959, No. 11.

Huai-nan-tzu 淮南子. SPPY ed.

HUANG SHENG-CHANG 黃盛璋, "Ta-feng-kuei-ming chih-tso ti nien-tai ti-tien yü shih-shih" 大豐殷銘製作的年代地點與史實, *Li-shih yen-chiu*, 1960, No. 6.

——, "Shih ch'u-chi" 釋初吉, *Li-shih yen-chiu*, 1958, No. 4.

Hui-hsien fa-chüeh pao-kao 輝縣發掘報告. Peking, 1956.

"1971-nien An-yang Hou-kang fa-chüeh chien-pao" 1971年安陽后崗發掘簡報, *KK*, 1972, No. 3.

"1972-nien ch'un An-yang Hou-kang fa-chüeh chien-pao" 1972年春安陽后崗發掘簡報, *KK*, 1972, No. 5.

I Chou-shu 逸周書. SPPY ed.

JAO TSUNG-I 饒宗頤, "Ching-Ch'u wen-hua" 荊楚文化, *BIHP*, XXXI, No. 2 (June 1969).

——, "Ch'u-tseng-shu shu-cheng" 楚繒書疏証, *BIHP*, XXX, Part I (1969).

——, *Yin-tai chen-pu jen-wu t'ung-k'ao* 殷代貞卜人物通考, 2 Vols. Hong Kong, 1958–59.

JUNG KENG 容庚, *Chin-wen pien* 金文編. Academia Sinica, 1938.

——, and CHANG WEI-CH'IH 張維持, *Yin-Chou ch'ing-t'ung-ch'i t'ung-lun* 殷周青銅器通論. Peking, 1958.

"Kan-su Lan-chou Hsi-p'o-wa i-chih fa-chüeh pao-kao" 甘肅蘭州西坡岇遺址發掘報告, *KK*, 1960, No. 9.

"Kan-su Wu-wei Huang-niang-niang-t'ai i-chih fa-chüeh pao-kao" 甘肅武威皇娘娘台遺址發掘報告, *KKHP*, 1960, No. 2.

K'ANG CHIEH 康捷, "Kuan-yü T'ang-shan Ta-ch'eng-shan i-chih wen-hua hsing-chih ti t'ao-lun" 關於唐山大城山遺址文化性質的討論, *KK*, 1960, No. 6.

KAO CH'Ü-HSÜN 高去尋, *Hou-chia-chuang* 侯家莊. 3 Vols. Academia Sinica, Taiwan, 1962–67.

KISSÉLEV, C. V., "Su-lien ching-nei ch'ing-t'ung wen-hua yü Chung-kuo Shang-wen-hua ti kuan-hsi" 蘇聯境內青銅文化與中國商文化的關係, *KK*, 1962 No. 2.

Ku-shih pien 古史辨.
    I. ed. Ku Chieh-kang 顧頡剛. Peking, 1926.
    II. ed. Ku Chieh-kang. Peiping, 1930.
    VII. ed. Lü Ssu-mien 呂思勉 and T'ung Shu-yeh 童書業. Shanghai, 1941.

KU TUNG-KAO 顧棟高, *Ch'un-ch'iu ta-shih-piao* 春秋大事表. 1748 ed.

Ku Yen-wu 顧炎武, *Jih-chih lu* 日知錄. Commercial Press ed.

Kuan En-wei 關恩威, "Wei-ho ku-ti ti-mao fa-yü-shih chi ch'i yu-kuan wen-t'i ti t'ao-lun" 渭河谷地地貌發育史及其有關問題的討論, *Quaternaria Sinica*, IV, No. 1 (1965).

Kuan Hsieh-ch'u 管燮初, *Yin-hsü chia-ku k'e-tz'u ti yü-fa yen-chiu* 殷墟甲骨刻辭的語法研究. Peking, 1953.

Kuan-tzu 管子. SPPY ed.

Kuo Mo-jo 郭沫若, *Chia-ku wen-tzu yen-chiu* 甲骨文字研究. Shanghai, 1933.

——, *Chin-wen ts'ung-k'ao* 金文叢考. Tokyo, 1932.

——, *Ch'ing-t'ung shih-tai* 青銅時代. Peking, 1957.

——, *Chung-kuo ku-tai she-hui yen-chiu* 中國古代社會研究. Peking, 1964.

——, ed., *Chung-kuo-shih kang* 中國史綱. I. Peking, 1962.

——, *Ku-tai ming-k'e hui-k'ao hsü-pien* 古代銘刻彙考續編. Tokyo, 1934.

——, "Ku-tai wen-tzu chih pien-cheng ti fa-chan" 古代文字之辨証的發展, *KK*, 1972, No. 3.

——, *Liang-Chou chin-wen-tz'u ta-hsi t'u-lu k'ao-shih* 兩周金文辭大系圖錄考釋. Peking, 1958.

——, *Nu-li-chih shih-tai* 奴隸制時代. Peking, 1966.

——, *Pu-tz'u t'ung-ts'uan k'ao-shih* 卜辭通纂考釋. Tokyo, 1933.

——, *Yin-ch'i ts'ui-pien* 殷契粹編. Peking, 1965.

——, *Yin-Chou ch'ing-t'ung-ch'i ming-wen yen-chiu* 殷周青銅器銘文研究. Shanghai, 1931.

Kuo Pao-chün 郭寶鈞, *Chung-kuo ch'ing-t'ung-ch'i shih-tai* 中國青銅器時代. Peking, 1963.

——, "I-chiu-wu-ling-nien ch'un Yin-hsü fa-chüeh pao-kao" 一九五〇年春殷墟發掘報告, *Chung-kuo k'ao-ku hsüeh-pao*, V, No. 1-2 (December 1951).

Kuo-yü 國語. SPPY ed.

Lei Hai-tsung 雷海宗, "Yin-Chou nien-tai k'ao" 殷周年代考, *Wen-che chi-k'an* 文哲季刊 (Wu-han-ta-hsüeh 武漢大學), II, No. 1 (1931).

Li Ch'ang-nien 李長年, *Tou-lei* 豆類. I. Shanghai, 1958.

Li-chi cheng-i 禮記正義. SPPY ed.

Li Chi 李濟, "An-yang tsui-chin fa-chüeh pao-kao chi liu-tz'u kung-tso chih tsung-ku-chi" 安陽最近發掘報告及六次工作之總估計, *An-yang fa-chüeh pao-kao* (Academia Sinica), No. 4 (1933).

—, "Chi Hsiao-t'un ch'u-t'u chih ch'ing-t'ung-ch'i" 記小屯出土之青銅器, *Chung-kuo k'ao-ku hsüeh-pao,* No. 3 (1948).

—, "Chung-kuo shang-ku-shih chih ch'ung-chien-kung-tso chi ch'i wen-t'i" 中國上古史之重建工作及其問題, *Min-chu p'ing-lun* 民主評論, V, No. 4 (16 February 1954).

—, *Hsi-yin-ts'un shih-ch'ien ti i-ts'un* 西陰村史前的遺存. Peiping, 1929.

—, *Hsiao-t'un* 小屯, III: *T'ao-ch'i* 陶器, Part I. Academia Sinica, Taiwan, 1956.

—, and WAN CHIA-PAO 萬家寶, *Yin-hsü ch'u-t'u ch'ing-t'ung chüeh-hsing-ch'i chih yen-chiu* 殷墟出土青銅爵形器之研究. Academia Sinica, Taiwan, 1966.

—, and WAN CHIA-PAO, *Yin-hsü ch'u-t'u ch'ing-t'ung ku-hsing-ch'i chih yen-chiu* 殷墟出土青銅觚形器之研究. Academia Sinica, Taiwan, 1964.

LI HSIAO-TING 李孝定, *Chia-ku wen-tzu chi-shih* 甲骨文字集釋. 16 ts'e. Academia Sinica, Taiwan, 1965.

—, "Ts'ung chi-chung shih-ch'ien ho yu-shih-tsao-ch'i t'ao-wen ti kuan-ch'a li-ts'e Chung-kuo wen-tzu ti ch'i-yüan" 從幾種史前和有史早期陶文的觀察蠡測中國文字的起源, *Nan-yang-ta-hsüeh hsüeh-pao* 南洋大學學報, III (1969).

—, "Ts'ung liu-shu ti kuan-tien k'an chia-ku-wen-tzu" 從六書的觀點看甲骨文字, *Nan-yang-ta-hsüeh hsüeh-pao,* II (1968).

LI HSÜEH-CH'IN 李學勤, "T'an An-yang Hsiao-t'un i-wai ch'u-t'u ti yu-tzu chia-ku" 談安陽小屯以外出土的有字甲骨, *WWTKTL,* 1956, No. 11.

—, *Yin-tai ti-li chien-lun* 殷代地理簡論. Peking, 1958.

LI YA-NUNG 李亞農, *Li Ya-nung shih-lun chi* 李亞農史論集. Shanghai, 1962.

—, *Yin-tai she-hui sheng-huo* 殷代社會生活. Shanghai, 1955.

Liang-shu 梁書. Taipei, I-wen reprint.

"Lin-hsia Ta-ho-chung Ch'in-wei-chia liang-ch'u Ch'i-chia-wen-hua i-chih fa-chüeh pao-kao" 臨夏大何莊秦魏家兩處齊家文化遺址發掘報告, *KK,* 1960, No. 3.

LIN HUI-HSIANG 林惠祥, *Chung-kuo min-tsu shih* 中國民族史. Taipei, 1965 reprint.

LIU I-CH'ING 劉義慶, *Shih-shuo hsin-yü* 世說新語. SPTK ed.

LIU PAO-NAN 劉寶楠, "Shih-ku" 釋穀 in *Huang-Ch'ing ching-chieh hsü-pien* 皇清經解續編.

LIU TUNG-SHENG 劉東生, and CHANG TSUNG-YU 張宗祐, "Chung-kuo ti huang-t'u" 中國的黃土 in *Ti-chih hsüeh-pao* 地質學報 *(Acta Geologia Sinica),* XLII (March 1962).

—, *Chung-kuo ti huang-t'u tui-chi* 中國的黃土堆積. Peking, 1965.

—, YANG LI-HUA 楊理華, and CH'EN CH'ENG-HUI, "Chung-kuo ti-ssu-chi ch'en-chi-wu ch'ü-yü fen-pu t'e-cheng ti t'an-t'ao" 中國第四紀沉積物區域分佈特徵的探討, *Chung-kuo ti-ssu-chi wen-t'i* 中國第四紀問題. Peking, 1964.

LIU YÜ-HSIA 劉嶼霞, "Yin-tai yeh-t'ung-shu chih yen-chiu" 殷代冶銅術之研究, *An-yang fa-chüeh pao-kao*, No. 4 (June 1933).

LO CHEN-YÜ 羅振玉, *Yin-hsü shu-ch'i ch'ien-pien* 殷墟書契前編. 1931 reprint.

—, *Yin-hsü shu-ch'i hou-pien* 殷墟書契後編. Tokyo, 1916.

Lo-yang Chung-chou-lu 洛陽中州路. Peking, 1959.

LO YÜAN 羅願, *Hsin-an chih* 新安志. 1175 ed., 1888 reprint.

LÜ TSUN-EH 呂遵諤, "Nei-Meng Ch'ih-feng Hung-shan-hou k'ao-ku tiao-ch'a pao-kao" 內蒙赤峯紅山後考古調查報告, *KKHP*, 1958, No. 3.

—, "Nei-Meng Lin-hsi k'ao-ku tiao-ch'a" 內蒙林西考古調查, *KKHP*, 1960, No. 1.

MA CH'ANG-SHOU 馬長壽, *Pei-Ti yü Hsiung-nu* 北狄與匈奴. Peking, 1962.

MA CH'ENG-YÜAN 馬承源, *Yang-shao-wen-hua ti ts'ai-t'ao* 仰韶文化的彩陶. Shanghai, 1957.

MA TUAN-LIN 馬端臨, *Wen-hsien t'ung-k'ao* 文獻通考. Commercial Press ed.

MENG WEN-T'UNG 蒙文通, "Lüeh-lun *Shan-hai-ching* ti hsieh-tso shih-tai chi ch'i ch'an-sheng ti-yü" 略論山海經的寫作時代及其產生地域, *Chung-hua wen-shih lun-ts'ung*, 1st Series, 1962.

Miao-ti-kou yü San-li-ch'iao 廟底溝與三里橋. Peking, 1959.

Ming-shih 明史. Taipei, I-wen reprint.

MIU YÜEH 繆鉞, "Chou-tai chih ya-yen" 周代之雅言, *Che-chiang-ta-hsüeh wen-hsüeh-yüan chi-k'an* 浙江大學文學院集刊, I (1941).

Nanking Museum, "Chiang-su Hsin-i-hsien San-li-tun ku-wen-hua i-chih ti-erh-tz'u fa-chüeh chien-pao" 江蘇新沂縣三里墩古文化遺址第二次發掘簡報, *KK*, 1960, No. 7.

"Nei-Meng-ku Ch'ih-feng Yao-wang-miao Hsia-chia-tien i-chih shih-chüeh pao-kao" 內蒙古赤峯藥王廟夏家店遺址試掘報告, *KK*, 1961, No. 2.

P'AN HUNG-SHENG 潘鴻聲, and YANG CH'AO-PO 楊超伯 "Chan-kuo-shih-tai ti liu-kuo nung-yeh sheng-ch'an" 戰國時代的六國農業生產, *Nung-shih yen-chiu chi-k'an* 農史研究集刊, Vol. II, Peking, 1960.

San-kuo-chih chi-chieh 三國志集解. Taipei, I-wen reprint.

Shan-hai-ching 山海經. SPTK ed.

"Shan-hsi Feng-hsiang Hsing-p'ing liang-hsien k'ao-ku tiao-ch'a chien-pao" 陝西鳳翔興平兩縣考古調查簡報, *KK*, 1960, No. 3.

"Shan-hsi Hsi-hsiang Li-chia-ts'un hsin-shih-ch'i-shih-tai i-chih" 陝西西鄉李家村新石器時代遺址, *KK*, 1961, No. 7.

"Shan-hsi Hsi-hsiang Li-chia-ts'un hsin-shih-ch'i-shih-tai i-chih i-chiu-liu-i-nien fa-chüeh pao-kao" 陝西西鄉李家村新石器時代遺址一九六一年發掘報告, *KK*, 1962, No. 6.

"Shan-hsi Pin-hsien Hsia-meng-ts'un Yang-shao-wen-hua i-chih hsü-chüeh chien-pao" 陝西邠縣下孟村仰韶文化遺址續掘簡報, *KK*, 1962, No. 6.

"Shan-hsi-sheng shih-nien-lai ti wen-wu k'ao-ku hsin-shou-huo" 山西省十年來的文物考古新收穫, *WW*, 1972, No. 4.

"Shan-hsi shih-nien-lai k'ao-ku yü wen-wu kung-tao ti kai-k'uang" 山西十年來考古與文物工作的概況, *KK*, 1959, No. 2.

"Shan-tung Ch'ü-fu hsin-shih-ch'i-shih-tai i-chih tiao-ch'a" 山東曲阜新石器時代遺址調查, *KK*, 1963, No. 7.

"Shan-tung Ning-yang-hsien Pao-t'ou i-chih ch'ing-li chien-pao" 山東寧陽縣堡頭遺址清理簡報, *WW*, 1959, No. 10.

"Shan-tung P'eng-lai Tzu-ching-shan i-chih shih-chüeh chien-pao" 山東蓬萊紫荊山遺址試掘簡報, *KK*, 1973, No. 1.

"Shan-tung T'eng-hsien Kang-shang-ts'un hsin-shih-ch'i-shih-tai mu-tsang shih-chüeh pao-kao" 山東滕縣崗上村新石器時代墓葬試掘報告, *KK*, 1963, No. 7.

SHANG CH'ENG-TSO 商承祚, *Yin-ch'i i-ts'un* 殷契佚存. Nanking, 1933.

Shang-chün-shu 商君書. SPPY ed.

SHIH CHANG-JU 石璋如, *Hsiao-t'un* 小屯, I: *Yin-hsü chien-chu i-ts'un* 殷墟建築遺存. Academia Sinica, Taiwan, 1959.

—, "Ku-pu yü kuei-pu t'an-yüan" 骨卜與龜卜探源, *Ta-lu tsa-chih*, VIII, No. 9 (May 1954).

—, "Yin-tai chu-t'ung kung-i" 殷代鑄銅工藝, *BIHP*, XXVI (1955).

Shih-chi 史記. Taipei, I-wen reprint.

SHIH HSING-PANG 石興邦, "Yu-kuan Ma-chia-yao-wen-hua ti i-hsieh wen-t'i" 有關馬家窰文化的一些問題, *KK*, 1962, No. 6.

SHIH SHENG-HAN 石聲漢, *Ch'i-min yao-shu chin-shih* 齊民要術今釋. 4 Vols. Peking, 1957–58.

—, *Fan-Sheng-chih-shu chin-shih* 氾勝之書今釋. Peking, 1956.

—, *Ssu-min yüeh-ling chiao-chu* 四民月令校注. Peking, 1965.

SHIH T'AO 石陶, "Huang-ho-shang-yu fu-hsi-shih-tsu-she-hui—Ch'i-chia-wen-hua she-hui ching-chi hsing-t'ai ti t'an-t'ao" 黃河上游父系氏族社會——齊家文化社會經濟形態的探討, *KK*, 1961, No. 1.

SHIMA KUNIO 島邦男, *Inkyo bokuji kenkyu* 殷墟卜辭研究. Tokyo, 1958.

—, *Inkyo bokuji sōrui* 殷墟卜辭綜述. Tokyo, 1967.

SHINJO SHINZO 新城新藏, *Tōyō temmongaku shi kenkyu* 東洋天文學史研究. Tokyo, 1928.

SU PING-CH'I 蘇秉琦, "Kuan-yü Yang-shao-wen-hua ti jo-kan wen-t'i" 關於仰韶文化的若干問題, *KKHP*, 1965, No. 1.

SUN HAI-P'O 孫海波, *Chia-ku-wen lu* 甲骨文錄. K'ai-feng, 1937.

—, *Chia-ku-wen pien* 甲骨文編. Taipei, I-wen reprint.

SUN HSING-TUNG 孫醒東, and KENG CH'ING-HAN 耿慶漢, "Ta-tou p'in-chung ti fen-lei" 大豆品種的分類, *Chih-wu-fen-lei hsüeh-pao* 植物分類學報 (*Acta Phytotaxonomica Sinica*), II, No. 1 (1959).

SUN I-JANG 孫詒讓, *Mo-tzu chien-ku* 墨子閒詁. Taipei, I-wen reprint.

SUN MENG-JUNG 孫孟蓉, "Chou-k'ou-tien Chung-kuo yüan-jen hua-shih-ts'eng ti p'ao-tzu hua-fen tsu-ho" 周口店中國猿人化石層的孢子花粉組合, *Quaternaria Sinica*, IV, No. 1 (1965).

SUN TIEN-CH'ING 孫殿卿, and YANG HUAI-JEN 楊懷仁, "Ta-ping-ch'uan shih-ch'i Chung-kuo ti ping-ch'uan i-chih" 大冰川時期中國的冰川遺址, *Acta Geologia Sinica*, XXXXI, No. 3–4 (December 1961).

SUNG CHIH-CH'EN 宋之琛, "San-men-hsi chih-wu-hua-shih ho p'ao-tzu-hua-fen-tsu-ho ti yen-chiu" 三門系植物化石和孢子花粉組合的研究, *Quaternaria Sinica*, I, No. 1 (1958).

Sung-shu 宋書. Taipei, I-wen reprint.

Ta-Ming hui-tien 大明會典. 1587 ed. Taipei, Tung-nan-shu-pao-she 東南書報社 reprint.

T'ang hui-yao 唐會要. Taipei, Shih-chieh-shu-chü 世界書局 reprint.

T'ANG LAN 唐蘭, "Pu-tz'u shih-tai ti wen-hsüeh ho pu-tz'u-wen-hsüeh" 卜辭時代的文學和卜辭文學, *Ch'ing-hua hsüeh-pao* 清華學報, XI, No. 3 (July 1936).

—, "Ts'ung chia-ku chin-wen chung so-chien ti i-chung i-ching i-shih ti Chung-kuo ku-tai wen-tzu" 從甲骨金文中所見的一種已經遺失的中國古代文字, *KKHP*, 1957, No. 2.

TING FU-PAO 丁福保, *Shuo-wen chieh-tzu ku-lin* 說文解字詁林. Shanghai, 1931.

TING SHAN 丁山, *Chia-ku so-chien shih-tsu chi ch'i chih-tu* 甲骨所見氏族及其制度. Peking, 1956.

TING YING 丁穎, "Chiang-Han-p'ing-yüan hsin-shih-ch'i-shih-tai hung-shao-t'u chung ti tao-ku-k'e k'ao-ch'a" 江漢平原新石器時代紅燒土中的稻穀殼考查, *KKHP*, 1959, No. 4.

TSENG CHAO-YÜ 曾昭燏, and YIN HUAN-CHANG 尹煥章, "Shih-lun Hu-shu wen-hua" 試論湖熟文化, *KKHP,* 1959, No. 4.

TSOU PAO-CHÜN 鄒豹君, "Chung-kuo wen-hua ch'i-yüan-ti" 中國文化起源地, *Ch'ing-hua hsüeh-pao,* New Series (Taipei), VI (December 1967).

TUAN YÜ-TS'AI 段玉裁, *Shuo-wen chieh-tzu chu* 說文解字注. Commercial Press ed.

WAN SSU-T'UNG 萬斯同, *Ch'ün-shu i-pien* 群書疑辨. 1816 ed.

WANG CHIA-YIN 王嘉蔭, "Li-shih shang ti huang-t'u wen-t'i" 歷史上的黃土問題, *Quaternaria Sinica,* IV, No. 1 (1965).

WANG CH'UNG 王充, *Lun-heng* 論衡. SPPY ed.

WANG KUO-WEI 王國維, *Kuan-t'ang chi-lin* 觀堂集林. Taipei reprint.

—, *Wang Kuan-t'ang hsien-sheng ch'üan-chi* 王觀堂先生全集. Taipei reprint.

WANG LI 王力, "Chung-kuo wen-fa-hsüeh ch'u-t'an" 中國文法學初探, *Ch'ing-hua hsüeh-pao,* IX, No. 1 (January 1936).

—, *Han-yü-shih kao* 漢語史稿. 3 Vols. Peking, 1957-58.

WANG SU-TS'UN 王素存, *Hsing-lu* 姓錄. Taipei, 1960.

WANG TA 王達, "Shih-p'ing *Chung-kuo tu-liang-heng shih* chung Chou Ch'in Han liang-heng mou-chih chih k'ao-cheng" 試評中國度量衡史中周秦漢量衡畝制之考証, *Nung-shih yen-chiu chi-k'an,* I, Shanghai, 1957.

WANG YIN-CHIH 王引之, *Tu-shu tsa-chih* 讀書雜志. *Kao-yu Wang-shih ssu-chung* 高郵王氏四種 ed.

WANG YÜ-HU 王毓瑚, *Chung-kuo hsü-mu-shih tzu-liao* 中國畜牧史資料. Peking, 1958.

Wei-shu 魏書. Taipei, I-wen reprint.

WU CH'ENG-LO 吳承洛, *Chung-kuo tu-liang-heng shih* 中國度量衡史. Shanghai, 1937.

WU CH'I-CH'ANG 吳其昌, "Pu-tz'u so-chien Yin-hsien-kung hsien-wang san-hsü-k'ao" 卜辭所見殷先公先王三續考, *Yen-ching hsüeh-pao* 燕京學報, XIV (December 1933).

WU SHAN-CHING 吳山菁, "Lüeh-lun Ch'ing-lien-kang wen-hua" 略論青蓮崗文化, *WW,* 1973, No. 6.

YABUUCHI KIYOSHI 藪內清, "Kuan-yü Yin-li ti liang-san-ke wen-t'i" 關於殷曆的兩三個問題, Chinese translation in *Hsien-Ch'in-shih yen-chiu lun-chi* 先秦史研究論集 *(Ta-lu tsa-chih),* 1960.

YANG CHÜN-SHIH 楊君實, "K'ang keng yü Hsia-hui" 康庚與夏諱, *Ta-lu tsa-chih,* XX (March 1967).

YANG CHUNG-CHIEN 楊鍾健, "K'ao-ku-kung-tso ho jen-ku shou-ku teng i-ts'un wen-t'i" 考古工作和人骨獸骨等遺存問題, *WW*, 1956, No. 3.

—, and LIU TUNG-SHENG, "An-yang Yin-hsü chih p'u-ju-tung-wu-ch'ün pu-i" 安陽殷墟之哺乳動物群補遺, *Chung-kuo k'ao-ku hsüeh-pao*, No. 4 (1949).

YANG HSIUNG 楊雄, *Fang-yen* 方言. SPTK ed.

YANG K'UAN 楊寬, "Chung-kuo shang-ku-shih tao-lun" 中國上古史導論, in *Ku-shih pien*, VII, Book I.

—, *Ku-shih hsin-t'an* 古史新探. Peking, 1965.

YANG PO-CHÜN 楊伯峻, *Lun-yü i-chu* 論語譯注. Shanghai, 1965.

YEN YIN 顏誾, et al., "Hsi-an Pan-p'o jen-ku ti yen-chiu" 西安半坡人骨的研究, *KK*, 1960, No. 9.

—, "Hua-hsien hsin-shih-ch'i-shih-tai jen-ku ti yen-chiu" 華縣新石器時代人骨的研究, *KKHP*, 1962, No. 2.

—, et al., "Pao-chi hsin-shih-ch'i-shih-tai jen-ku ti yen-chiu pao-kao" 寶雞新石器時代人骨的研究報告, *Ku-chi-tsui-tung-wu yü ku-jen-lei* 古脊椎動物與古人類 (*Paleovertebrata et Paleoanthropologia*), II, No. 1 (March 1960).

YIN HUAN-CHANG 尹煥章, and CHANG CHENG-HSIANG 張正祥, "Tui Chiang-su T'ai-hu ti-ch'ü shin-shih-ch'i-wen-hua ti i-hsieh jen-shih" 對江蘇太湖地區新石器文化的一些認識, *KK*, 1962, No. 3.

YOSHIDA MITSUKUNI 吉田光邦, "Chugaku kodai kinzoku gijutsu" 中國古代金屬技術, *Tōhōgakuhō* 東方學報, XXXIV (1959).

YU YÜ 友于, "Kuan-tzu tu-ti-p'ien t'an-yüan" 管子度地篇探源, in *Nung-shih yen-chiu chi-k'an*, I (1957).

YÜ HSING-WU 于省吾, "Lüeh-lun t'u-t'eng yü tsung-chiao ch'i-yüan ho Hsia-Shang t'u-t'eng" 略論圖騰與宗教起源和夏商圖騰, *Li-shih yen-chiu*, 1959, No. 11.

—, "Shang-tai ti ku-lei tso-wu" 商代的穀類作物, *Tung-pei-jen-min-ta-hsüeh jen-wen-k'e-hsüeh hsüeh-pao*, 1957, No. 1.

—, "Ts'ung chia-ku-wen k'an Shang-tai she-hui hsing-chih" 從甲骨文看商代社會性質, *Ibid.*, 1957, No. 2–3.

Yüan-ho hsing-ts'uan 元和姓纂. 1880 ed.

Yün-nan Chin-ning Shih-chai-shan ku-mu-ch'ün fa-chüeh pao-kao 雲南晉寧石寨山古墓群發掘報告. Peking, 1959.

WORKS IN WESTERN LANGUAGES

A. Engler's *Syllabus der Pflanzenfamilien*. 11th ed., Berlin, 1936.

ALLCHIN, BRIDGET and RAYMOND, *The Birth of Indian Civilization*. Baltimore, 1968.

ANDERSSON, J. G., "An Early Chinese Culture," *Bulletin of the Geological Survey of China*, No. 5, Part I (October 1923).

—, *Children of the Yellow Earth*. London, 1934.

—, "Researches into the Prehistory of the Chinese," *BMFEA*, No. 15 (1943).

ANGRESS, SHIMON, and CHARLES A. REED, *An Annotated Bibliography on the Origin and Descent of Domestic Mammals, 1900–1955*. Chicago, 1962.

BALL, C. R., "The Kaoliangs: A New Group of Grain Sorghums," *Bureau of Plant Industry Bulletin* (United States Department of Agriculture, 1913), No. 253.

BARNARD, NOEL, *Bronze Casting and Bronze Alloys in Ancient China*. Australian National University, Canberra, 1961.

—, "The Special Character of Metallurgy in Ancient China," in *Application of Science in Examination of Works of Art*. Boston Museum of Art, 1965.

BAYARD, DOON T., "Excavation at Non Nok Tha, Northeastern Thailand, 1968: An Interim Report," *Asian Perspectives*, XIII (1970).

BENDIX, REINHARD, *Max Weber: An Intellectual Portrait*. New York, 1960.

BISHOP, CARL W., "Beginnings of Civilization in Eastern Asia," *Antiquity*, XIV (1940).

—, "Origin and Early Diffusion of the Traction Plow," *The Smithsonian Report for 1937*.

—, "The Neolithic Age in Northern China," *Antiquity*, VII (December 1938).

BLACK, DAVIDSON, "A Study of Kansu and Honan Aeneolithic Skulls and Specimens from Later Kansu Prehistoric Sites in Comparison with North China and Other Recent Crania," *Paleontologia Sinica*, Series D, VI, Fascicle 1 (1928).

BOODBERG, PETER, "Some Proleptical Remarks on the Evolution of Archaic Chinese," *Harvard Journal of Asiatic Studies*, II (1937).

BRAIDWOOD, R. J., "The Agricultural Revolution," *Scientific American*, CCIII (September 1960).

—, and CHARLES A. REED, "The Achievement and Early Consequences of Food Production: A Consideration of Archaeological and Natural-Historical Evidence," *Cold Spring Harbor Symposia on Quantitative Biology*, XXII (1957).

BURKILL, I. H., *A Dictionary of the Economic Products of the Malay Peninsula*. 2 Vols. London, 1935.

BYLIN-ALTHIN, MARGIT, "The Sites of Ch'i Chia P'ing and Lo Han T'ang in Kansu," *BMFEA*, No. 18 (1946).

CAJORI, FLORIAN, *A History of Mathematical Notations*. 2 Vols. Chicago, 1928.

CALLEN, E. O., "The First New World Cereal," *American Antiquity*, XXXII, No. 4 (1967).

CAMBEL, HALET, and R. J. BRAIDWOOD, "An Early Farming Village in Turkey," *Scientific American*, CCXXII, No. 3 (March 1970).

CHANG K'UN, "Sino-Tibetan Words for 'Needle,'" *Monumenta Serica*, XXVII (1968).

—, and BETTY SHEFTS CHANG, *The Proto-Chinese Final System and the Ch'ieh-yün*. Academia Sinica, Taiwan, 1972.

CHANG KWANG-CHIH, *The Archaeology of Ancient China*. New Haven, Conn., 1968.

—, *Fengpitou, Tapenkeng, and the Prehistory of Taiwan*. New Haven, Conn., 1969.

—, "The Yale Expedition to Taiwan and the Southeast Asian Horticultural Evolution," *Discovery*, I (Spring 1967).

—, and Minze Stuiver, "Recent Advances in the Prehistoric Archaeology of Taiwan," *Proceedings of the National Academy of Sciences*, LV (March 1966).

CHAO, LIN, *Marriage, Inheritance and Lineage Organization in Shang-Chou China*. Taipei, 1971.

CHAPLINE, W. R., and C. K. COOPERRIDER, "Climate and Grazing," in *Climate and Man*. U. S. D. A., Washington, D. C., 1941.

CHENG TE-K'UN, *Archaeology in China*, Vol. I, *Prehistoric China*. Cambridge, England, 1959.

—, *Archaeology in China*, Vol. II, *Shang China*. Cambridge, England, 1960.

—, *Archaeological Studies in Szechwan*. Cambridge, England, 1957.

Chicago Assyrian Dictionary. 10 Vols., not yet completed, Chicago, 1956—.

CHOU FA-KAO, "Certain Dates of the Shang Period," *Harvard Journal of Asiatic Studies*, XXIII (1960–61).

—, "Chronology of the Western Chou Dynasty," *Journal of the Institute of Chinese Studies of The Chinese University of Hong Kong*, IV, No. 1 (1971).

CLARK, GRAHAME, *World Prehistory: A New Outline*. Cambridge, England, 1969.

CLARK, J. DESMOND, "Africa South of the Sahara," in R. J. Braidwood and G. R. Willey, eds., *Courses Toward Urban Life*. Chicago, 1962.

COGHLAN, H. H., *Notes on the Prehistoric Metallurgy of Copper and Bronze in the Old World*. Occasional Paper on Technology, No. 4, Pitts Rivers Museum, Oxford University, 1951.

CREEL, HERRLEE G., *The Birth of China: A Study of the Formative Period of Chinese Civilization.* New York, 1937.

—, "On the Nature of Chinese Ideography," *T'oung-pao,* 2d Series, XXXII (1936).

—, *The Origins of Statecraft in China,* Vol. I, *The Western Chou Empire.* Chicago, 1970.

CRESSEY, GEORGE B., *Asia's Lands and Peoples.* New York, 1944.

DANIELS, GLYN, *The First Civilizations: The Archaeology of Their Origins.* New York, 1968.

DEMIÉVILLE, PAUL, "Le chinois," in the *Cent-cinquantenaire de l'École des Langues Orientales.* Paris, 1948.

DEWALL, M. VON, *Pferd und Wagen im frühen China.* Bonn, 1964.

DIXON, ROLAND B., *The Building of Culture.* New York, 1928.

DOBSON, W. A. C. H., *Early Archaic Chinese: A Descriptive Grammar.* Toronto, 1962.

—, *Late Archaic Chinese: A Grammatical Study.* Toronto, 1959.

EDMAN, G., and E. SÖDERBERG, "Auffindung von Reis in einer Tonscherte aus einer etwa funftausendjährigen chinesischen Siedlung," *Bulletin of Geological Society of China,* VIII, No. 4 (1929).

EMENEAU, MURRAY B., "Numerals in Comparative Linguistics, with Special Reference to Dravidian," *BIHP,* XXIX, Part I (1957).

FAIRBANK, WILMA, "Piece-mold Craftsmanship and Shang Bronze Design," *Archives of the Chinese Art Society of America,* XIV (1962).

FAIRSERVIS, WALTER A., JR., *The Origin, Character, and Decline of an Early Civilization.* American Museum Novitates, No. 2303, 20 October 1967.

FALKENSTEIN, A., *Archaische Texte aus Uruk.* Berlin, 1936.

"First Agrarians Said to be Thais," *New York Times,* 12 January 1970.

FORBES, R. J., *Metallurgy in Antiquity: A Notebook for Archaeologists and Technologists.* Leiden, 1950.

FRANKFURT, HENRI and H. A., eds., *Before Philosophy: The Intellectual Adventure of Ancient Man.* Baltimore, 1949.

FRUMKIN, GRÉGOIRE, *Archaeology in Soviet Central Asia.* Leiden, 1970.

FUNG YU-LAN, *A History of Chinese Philosophy,* I, translated by Derk Bodde. Peiping, 1937.

GAUL, JAMES H., "Observations on the Bronze Age in the Yenisei Valley, Siberia," in Carleton S. Coon and James M. Andrews, eds., *Studies in the Anthropology of Oceania and Asia.* Peabody Museum Papers, XX, Cambridge, Mass.

GELB, IGNACE J., *A Study of Writing.* Chicago, 1963.

GIMBUTAS, MARIJA, "Norodino, Seima and Their Contemporaries: Key Sites for the Bronze Age Chronology of Eastern Europe," *Proceedings of the Prehistoric Society for 1956,* XXII.

—, "The Indo-Europeans: Archaeological Problems," *American Anthropologist,* LXV, No. 4 (August 1963).

—, "The Kurgan Culture," *Actes du VIIe Congrès International des Sciences Préhistoriques et Protohistoriques,* I. Prague, 1966.

GORMAN, CHESTER F., "*A Priori* Models and Thai Prehistory: A Reconsideration of the Beginnings of Agriculture in Southeastern Asia," to be published by the Conference on the Origins of Agriculture, IXth International Congress of Anthropological and Ethnological Sciences, Chicago, 1973.

—, Excavations at Spirit Cave, North Thailand: Some Interim Interpretations," *Asian Perspectives,* XIII (1970).

—, "Hoabinhian: A Pebble-Tool Complex with Early Plant Associations in Southeast Asia," *Science,* CLXIII, No. 3868 (14 February 1969).

HANČAR, FRANZ, *Das Pferd in prähistorischer und früher historischer Zeit.* Wiener Beiträge zur Kulturgeschichte und Linguistik, XI. 1955.

HARLAN, JACK R., "Agricultural Origins: Centers and Noncenters," *Science,* CLXXIV (October 1971).

—, "On the Quality of Evidence for Origin and Dispersal of Cultivated Plants," *Current Anthropology,* forthcoming.

—, and DANIEL ZOHARY, "Distribution of Wild Wheats and Barleys," *Science,* CLIII (1966).

HAWKES, DAVID, *Ch'u Tz'u: The Song of the South.* London, 1959.

HERMANN, F. J., *A Revision of the Genus Glycine and Its Immediate Allies.* U.S.D.A. Technical Bulletin, No. 1268. 1962.

HIGGS, E. S., and M. R. JARMAN, "The Origins of Agriculture: A Reconsideration," *Antiquity,* XLIII (1969).

HIRTH, W. W., and W. W. ROCKHILL, *Chau Ju-kua: His Work on the Chinese and Arab Trade in the Twelfth and Thirteenth Centuries, Entitled Chu-fan-chi.* St. Petersburg, 1912.

HO, PING-TI, "An Historian's View of the Chinese Family System," in Seymour M. Farber, Piero Mustacchi, and Roger H. J. Wilson, eds., *Man and Civilization: The Family's Search for Survival.* New York, 1965.

—, "Early-Ripening Rice in Chinese History," *Economic History Review,* 2d Series, IX (December 1956).

—, "Some Problems of Shang Culture and Institutions: A Review Article," *Pacific Affairs*, XXXIV, No. 3 (Fall 1961).

—, *Studies on the Population of China, 1368–1953*. Cambridge, Mass., 1959.

—, "The Indigenous Origins of Chinese Agriculture," to be published by the Conference on the Origins of Agriculture, IXth International Congress of Anthropological and Ethnological Sciences, Chicago, 1973.

—, "The Introduction of American Food Plants into China," *American Anthropologist*, LVII, No. 2, Part I (April 1955).

—, "The Loess and the Origin of Chinese Agriculture," *American Historical Review*, LXXV, No. 1 (October 1969).

HOLE, FRANK, KENT V. FLANNERY, and JAMES A. NEELEY, *Prehistory and Human Ecology of the Deh Luran Plain: An Early Village Sequence from Khuzistan, Iran*. Memoirs of the Museum of the University of Michigan, No. 1, 1969.

HSIA NAI, "Workshops at the Dawn of History," *China Reconstructs*, IV, No. 12 (December 1957).

HYMOWITZ, THEODORE, "On the Domestication of the Soybean," *Economic Botany*, XXIV, No. 4 (October–December 1970).

JACOBSON, THORKILD, and ROBERT M. ADAMS, "Salt and Silt in Ancient Mesopotamian Agriculture," *Science*, CXXVIII, No. 3334 (21 November 1958).

JASNY, NAUM, *The Wheat of Classical Antiquity*. Baltimore, 1944.

JASPERSEN, OTTO, *Language: Its Nature, Development and Origin*. London, 1922.

JETTMAR, KARL, *Art of the Steppes: The Eurasian Animal Style*. London, 1964.

—, "The Altai before the Turks," *BMFEA*, No. 23 (1951).

JONES, A. H. M., "Slavery in the Ancient World," *Economic History Review*, 2d Series, IX, No. 2 (December 1956).

KANNGIESSER, F., "Die Flora des Herodot," *Archiv für die Geschichte der Naturwissenschaften und der Technik*, III (1912).

KARLBECK, O., "Anyang Moulds," *BMFEA*, No. 7 (1935).

KARLGREN, BERNHARD, tr., *The Book of Documents*. Stockholm, 1950.

—, tr., *The Book of Odes*. Stockholm, 1950.

—, *The Chinese Language: An Essay on Its Nature and History*. New York, 1949.

—, "Glosses on The Book of Documents," *BMFEA*, No. 20 (1948).

—, "Grammata Serica: Script and Phonetics in Chinese and Sino-Japanese," *BMFEA*, No. 12 (1940).

—, "Legends and Cults of Ancient China," *BMFEA*, No. 18 (1946).

—, "Loan Characters in Pre-Han Texts," *BMFEA,* No. 35 (1963).

—, "Le proto-chinois, langue flexionnelle," *Journal Asiatique,* 2d Series, XV (1920).

—, "Some Weapons and Tools of the Yin Dynasty," *BMFEA,* No. 17 (1945).

—, *Sound and Symbol in Chinese.* London, 1923.

KING, LAWRENCE J., *Weeds of the World: Biology and Control.* London, 1966.

KINGERY, W. D., and others, "Progress Report on a Cursory Technical Examination of Some Near-Eastern Ceramic Sherds," manuscript.

KOMAROVA, M. N., "Otnositelnaya Khronologiya Pamyatnikov Andronovskoi Kultury," *Arkheologicheskiy Sbornik Ermitazha,* 1962, No. 5.

KRAMER, SAMUEL, *The Sumerians: Their History, Culture, and Character.* Chicago, 1963.

KRISHNASWAMY, N., "Origin and Distribution of Cultivated Plants of South Asia: Millets," *Indian Journal of Genetics and Plant Breeding,* XI (June 1951).

KROEBER, ALFRED L., *Anthropology: Race, Language, Psychology, Prehistory.* New York, 1948.

LANDSBERGER, BENNO, "Tin and Lead: The Adventure of Two Vocables," *Journal of Near Eastern Studies,* XXIV (1965).

LARICHEV, V. Y., "Ancient Cultures of North China," in Henry N. Michael, ed., *The Archaeology and Geomorphology of Northern Asia: Selected Works.* Toronto, 1964.

LARSEN, MOGENS T., *Old Assyrian Caravan Procedures.* Istanbul, 1967.

LAUFER, BERTHOLD, *Sino-Iranica: Chinese Contributions to the History of Civilization in Ancient Iran with Special Reference to the History of Cultivated Plants and Products.* Chicago, 1919.

—, "Some Fundamental Ideas of Chinese Culture," *Journal of Race Development,* V (1914).

LEE, J. S., *The Geology of China.* London, 1939.

LEGGE, JAMES, tr., *The Chinese Classics.* Taipei reprint of original Hong Kong ed.
    I. *Confucian Analects,* etc.
    II. *The Works of Mencius.*
    III. *The Shoo King.*
    IV. *The She King.*
    V. *The Ch'un Ts'ew with the Tso Chuen.*

LI CHI, *The Beginnings of Chinese Civilization: Three Lectures Illustrated with Finds at Anyang.* Seattle, 1957.

—, "Diverse Backgrounds of the Decorative Art of the Yin Dynasty," *Proceedings of the Fourth Far-Eastern Prehistory and the Anthropology Division of the Eighth Pacific Science Congress Combined.* Quezon City, 1956.

LI, HUI-LIN, "Endemism in the Ligneous Flora of Eastern Asia," *Proceedings of the Seventh Pacific Science Congress,* V (1953).

—, "Floristic Significance and Problems of Eastern Asia," *Taiwania,* I (1948).

—, "Metasequoia, a Living Fossil," *American Scientist,* LII, No. 1 (March 1964).

LINDSAY, A. D., *Karl Marx's Capital.* London, 1925.

LINES, JOAN L., "The Al 'Ubaid Period in Mesopotamia and Its Persian Affinities." Cambridge University dissertation, unpublished. 1953.

LLOYD, SETON, and FUAD SAFAR, "Tell Hassuna: Excavations by the Iraq Government Directorate General of Antiquities in 1943 and 1944," *Journal of Near Eastern Studies,* IV, No. 4 (October 1945).

LOEHR, MAX, *Chinese Bronze Age Weapons.* Ann Arbor, Mich., 1956.

—, "Weapons and Tools from Anyang, and Siberian Analogies," *American Journal of Archaeology,* LIII (1949).

MACDONNELL, A. A., and A. B. KEITH, *Vedic Index of Names and Subjects.* London, 1912.

MACNEISH, RICHARD S., "Mesoamerican Archaeology," in Bernard J. Siegel and Alan R. Beals, eds., *Biennial Review of Anthropology.* Stanford, Calif., 1967.

MANGELSDORF, PAUL C., "Wheat," *Scientific American,* CLXXXIX (July 1953).

MASPERO, HENRI, *La Chine antique.* Paris, 1927.

MCCOWN, DONALD E., *The Comparative Stratigraphy of Early Iran.* Chicago, 1957.

MCNEILL, WILLIAM H., *The Rise of the West: A History of the Human Community.* Chicago, 1963.

MEI, YI-PAO, tr., *The Ethical and Political Works of Motse.* London, 1929.

MERRILL, E. D., "Plants and Civilizations," *Scientific Monthly,* XLIII (November 1936).

—, "The Phytogeography of Cultivated Plants in relation to the Assumed Pre-Columbian Eurasian-American Contacts," *American Anthropologist,* XXXIII (1931).

MONGAIT, ALEXANDER, *Archaeology in the U.S.S.R.* Moscow, 1959.

MONIER-WILLIAMS, SIR MONIER, *A Sanskrit-English Dictionary.* London, 1956.

MORGAN, LEWIS H., *Ancient Society.* New York, 1878.

NEEDHAM, JOSEPH, *Science and Civilization in China,* II, *History of Scientific Thought.* Cambridge, England, 1956.

III, *Mathematics and the Sciences of the Heavens and the Earth.* Cambridge, England, 1959.

OKLADNIKOV, A. P., *Ancient Population of Siberia and Its Cultures.* Russian Translation Series of the Peabody Museum of Archaeology and Ethnology, Harvard University, I, No. 1 (1959).

OLSSON, INGRID U., ed., *Radiocarbon Variations and Absolute Chronology: Proceedings of the Twelfth Nobel Symposium Held at the Institute of Physics at Uppsala University.* Stockholm and New York, 1970.

OPPENHEIM, LEO, *Ancient Mesopotamia: Portrait of A Dead Civilization.* Chicago, 1964.

OPPENHEIM, MAX VON, *Tell Halaf: A New Culture in Oldest Mesopotamia.* London, 1933.

—, *Tell Halaf,* I, *Die prähistorischen Funde.* Berlin, 1943.

"Origins of Agriculture Seen in Southeast Asia," *Asian Student,* XVII (29 March 1969).

PALMGREN, NILS, *Kansu Mortuary Urns of the Pan-shan and Ma-ch'ang Group.* Paleontologia Sinica, Series C, III, Fascicle 1. Peiping, 1934.

PASSEK, T., "Relations entre l'Europe Occidentale et l'Europe Orientale à l'époque néolithique," *Atti del VI Congresso Internazionale delle Scienze Preistoriche e Protoistoriche.* Union Internationale des Sciences Préhistoriques et Protohistoriques, Rome, 1962, I.

PEARSON, HELGA S., *Chinese Fossil Suidae.* Paleontologia Sinica, Series C, V, Fascicle 5. Peiping, 1928.

POLUNIN, NICHOLAS, *Introduction to Plant Geography and Some Related Sciences.* London, 1960.

PUMPELLY, RAPHAEL, ed., *Explorations in Turkestan: Prehistoric Civilizations of Anau.* 2 Vols. Washington, D. C., 1908.

QUITTA, HANS, "The C14 Chronology of the Central and SE European Neolithic," *Antiquity,* XLI (1967).

Records of the Grand Historian of China, Translated from the Shih Chi of Ssu-ma Ch'ien by Burton Watson. 2 Vols. New York, 1961.

REED, CHARLES A., "Animal Domestication in the Prehistoric Near East," *Science,* CXXX, No. 3389 (11 December 1959).

—, "Osteo-Archaeology," in Don Brothwell and Eric Higgs, eds., *Science in Archaeology.* New York, 1963.

—, "The Pattern of Animal Domestication in the Prehistoric Near East," in Peter J. Ucko and G. W. Dimbleby, eds., *The Domestication and Exploitation of Plants and Animals*. Chicago, 1969.

REINHOLD, ROBERT, "New Link to Dawn of Urban Culture Is Found in Iran," *New York Times*, 20 December 1970.

RENFREW, COLIN, "The Autonomy of the South-east European Copper Age," *Proceedings of the Prehistoric Society for 1969*, New Series, XXXV.

RENFREW, J. M., "The Archaeological Evidence for the Domestication of Plants: Methods and Problems," in Ucko and Dimbleby, eds., *The Domestication and Exploitation of Plants and Animals*. Chicago, 1969.

RODE, A. A., *Soil Science*. Washington, D. C., 1962.

ROXBY, P. M., "The Terrain of Early Chinese Civilization," *Geography*, XXIII (1938).

SALONEN, ARMAS, "Notes on Wagons and Chariots in Ancient Mesopotamia," *Studia Orientalia* (Societas Orientalis Fennica, Helsinki), VIII (1950).

SAUER, CARL O., *Agricultural Origins and Dispersals*. New York, 1952.

SCHAFER, EDWARD, "The Camel in China down to the Mongol Dynasty," *Sinologia*, II (1950).

SCHAFER, ROBERT, Review of Bernhard Karlgren's *The Chinese Language* in *Journal of the American Oriental Society*, LXX, No. 2 (1950).

SCHNEIDER, DAVID, and KATHLEEN GOUGH, eds., *Matrilineal Kinship*. Berkeley, Calif., 1961.

SHEPARD, ANN O., *Ceramics for the Archaeologist*. Washington, D. C., 1965.

SKINNER, G. WILLIAM, *Chinese Society in Thailand: An Analytical History*. Ithaca, N. Y., 1957.

SKVORTZOW, B. V., "The Soybean—Wild and Cultivated in Eastern Asia," *Manchurian Research Society Publication*. Natural History Section, Series A, No. 2. 1927.

SMALLEY, IAN J., "The Loess Deposits and Neolithic Culture of North China," *Man*, III, No. 2 (June 1968).

SMITH, CYRIL S., "Materials and the Development of Civilization and Science," *Science*, CXLVIII (1965).

SOLHEIM II, WILHELM G., "Early Bronze in Northeastern Thailand," *Current Anthropology*, IX, No. 1 (February 1968).

—, Northern Thailand, Southeast Asia, and World History," *Asian Perspectives*, XIII (1970).

STREU, O. VAN, "Zur Technik der altorientalischen Keramik," *Zeitschrift der Deutschen Morgenländischen Gesellschaft*. Leipzig, 1943.

SWANN, NANCY LEE, tr., *Food and Money in Ancient China*. Princeton, N. J., 1950.

SYLWAN, VIVI, "Silk from the Yin Dynasty," *BMFEA*, No. 9 (1937).

TEILHARD DE CHARDIN, P., and C. C. YOUNG, *On the Mammalian Remains from the Archaeological Site of Anyang*. Paleontologia Sinica, Series C, XII, Fascicle 1. Nanking, 1936.

THOMPSON, J. ERIC, *Maya Hieroglyphic Writing*. Washington, D. C., 1950.

TING, V. K., "Professor Granet's *La civilisation chinoise*," *Chinese Social and Political Science Review*, XV (1931).

TOYNBEE, ARNOLD J., *A Study of History*. I, London, 1934.

TSIEN, T. H., *Written on Bamboo and Silk: The Beginnings of Chinese Books and Inscriptions*. Chicago, 1962.

VAVILOV, N. I., *The Origin, Variation, Immunity, and Breeding of Cultivated Plants*. Chronica Botanica, XIII, No. 1–6, 1949–50.

VISHNU-MITTRE, "Changing Economy in Ancient India," to be published by the Conference on the Origins of Agriculture, IXth International Congress of Anthropological and Ethnological Sciences, Chicago, 1973.

WALEY, ARTHUR, tr., *The Book of Songs*. New York, 1937.

WARD, LAURISTON, "The Relative Chronology of China through the Han Period," in Robert Ehrlich, ed., *Relative Chronologies in Old World Archaeology*. Chicago, 1954.

WHEATLEY, PAUL, *The Pivot of the Four Quarters: A Preliminary Enquiry into the Origins and Character of the Ancient Chinese City*. Chicago, 1971.

WHEELER, SIR MORTIMER, *Civilizations of the Indus Valley and Beyond*. London, 1966.

WICHIZER, V. D., and M. K. BENNETT, *The Rice Economy of Monsoon Asia*. Stanford, Calif., 1941.

WISSMANN, HERMANN VON, "On the Role of Nature and Man in Changing the Face of the Dry Belt of Asia," in William L. Thomas, ed., *Man's Role in Changing the Face of the Earth*. Chicago, 1956.

WITTFOGEL, KARL A., *Oriental Despotism: A Comparative Study of Total Power*. New Haven, Conn., 1957.

WU, G. D., *Prehistoric Pottery in China*. London, 1938.

YOSHINOBU KOTANI, "Upper Pleistocene and Holocene Environmental Conditions in Japan," *Arctic Anthropology*, V, No. 2 (1969).

ZEUNER, FREDERICK E., *A History of Domesticated Animals*. New York, 1963.

INDEX

Afanasievo culture, 216–217
Agriculture: definition of, 43–44; in Southeast Asia, 43, 371–377; in Mesopotamia, 43; in Meso-America, 43; early Chinese agricultural settlements, 45, 48; northern Chinese agriculture since Yang-shao, 48–56; southern Chinese agriculture, 55–56; Chinese and ancient Western agriculture, 116–120; regional traits, 116–120.
An Ch'ih-min, 189n, 312n, 380n, 406
Anau, 122, 168–169
Ancestor worship: in Shang-Chou times, 238–326; in Lungshanoid times, 281–283; etymology of *tsu* (ancestor), 282; in Hsia times, 286; in rationalization by Confucius and Hsün-tzu, 324–326; in post-feudal times, 326
Andersson, J. G., 13, 61, 81, 122, 168–169, 171, 175, 362
Andronovo culture, 171, 174–175, 354
Animal husbandry: osteoarchaeology in China, 91–92; in Yang-shao, 92–95; in Lungshanoid and Lung-shan times, 96–101; in Inner Mongolia and Kansu, 101–105, 110–111. *See also* Cattle; Chicken; Dog; Goat; Horse; Sheep; Water Buffalo
An-yang, 3, 11–12, 46, 176, 179, 186, 190, 198–199, 211–215, 283, 312–313, 353, 355
Artemisia, predominance of, in loess areas, 25, 28–30
Astronomy, 385–392

Balkans, and copper metallurgy, 221
Bamboo Annals, 2–7, 10–12, 240, 245, 286
Barley, 73–76, 352; etymology, 74; yields, 86–87

Barnard, N., 183, 190, 192, 196–198, 203, 208, 210–211
Beeswax, 204–208
Book of Documents, 7, 51, 287, 296–297, 305, 333–336, 351n
Book of Odes, botanical data of, 30–33, 52, 76, 81–82, 87n, 188, 275–276, 287, 323–324
Braidwood, R. J., 120
Brassica, 87n, 108
Bronze: Shang foundry sites, 176, 178; geographic spread in China, 178, 210–211; technology, 189–200; and ceramic technology, 192–200. *See also* Andronovo culture; Karasuk culture; Mesopotamia; Southeast Asia
Burial patterns, Yang-shao and Lungshanoid, 274–275

Camel, Bactrian, 366
Cast-iron metallurgy, 219–220
Cattle, 93–97, 99–100, 103, 107; in lower Yangtze, 99; underutilization, 114–116
Ch'ang-an, 271, 279
Chang, K. C., 13–14, 95, 112–113n, 115n, 272–273, 311n, 312n, 373n
Chariot, 355–357
Ch'en Meng-chia, 242n, 244n, 263n, 278n, 297n, 301n
Ch'eng (King of Chou), 4–5, 287, 332
Cheng-chou, 176, 186, 190, 195, 211, 214, 311–312, 353
Cheng Te-k'un, 199–200, 203
Ch'eng-tzu-yai, 13, 95–96, 284, 346
Chenopodiaceae, 28–29, 33
Chi. See *Panicum miliaceum*
Ch'i-chia culture, 17, 21, 58, 109–111, 215, 217, 348, 362, 406
Ch'i-chia-p'ing, 95, 104

Ch'i state, 78, 399
Chiang-chai, 93
Ch'iang people, 310, 345
Chicken, 96, 98, 105, 376–377
Ch'ien-shan-yang, 16
Ch'ih Jen, 220, 331–332
Ch'ih-k'ou-chai, 93, 95
Ch'in empire, 2–3, 311, 404
Chin state, 2, 286–287, 386, 404
Ch'in state, 2, 275, 286–287, 311, 386n
Ch'in-ling Mountain, 18, 40–41, 112, 125, 270–271, 279
Chin-ning, 208
Ch'in-wei-chia, 179–180
Chinese language, 258–265, 401–405
Chinese script: Pan-p'o word-signs, 223–226; Shang oracle script, 226, 228–235; logographic principles, 254–258
Ch'ing-lien-kang culture, 13, 16, 20–21, 99–100, 346–347
Ching-ts'un, 93–95, 380
Chou: chronology, 1–11; tribal origins, 276; religion, 322–330; rationalist and humanist thought, 331–338
Chou Ch'ü-fei, on primitive rice culture, 72
Chou Fa-kao, 10–11
Chou-li, on short fallow system, 52–54
Ch'ü-chia-ling culture, 17, 63, 96–98, 347, 376
Ch'ü-fu, 96–97
Ch'u state, 47, 204, 316–317
Ch'u-tz'u, 316–317
Ch'ü Yüan, 317
Chuan-lung-tsang, 101
Chün, 314, 320
Chung, 296, 306–308
Chung-chou-lu, 93, 95
Clan insignias, archaic, 231–232, 394–397
Clan names, archaic forms of, 276–277
Confucius, 4, 324–325, 337–338
Copper deposits, geographic distribution of, 183–188
Copper metallurgy: in Kansu, 180–181; in Siberia and Soviet Central Asia, 216; in Balkans, 221
Copper mines, vestiges of, 188–189

Cord-marked pottery, 18, 39–40, 122, 124–126
Creel, H. G., 329n, 333
Cultural diffusion, 216–217, 363–366

Dairy products, Chinese avoidance of, 113–114
Demiéville, P., and Karlgren, 261n
Dobson, W. A. C. H., 261–262n, 263
Dog, 93–97, 99, 101, 103, 108
Double cropping, early records of, 84
Duke of Chou, 328, 331, 333, 336–338

East-West trade route, 215–217, 406–407
Egypt, 44, 367–368
Erh-li-kang, 176, 228
Erh-li-t'ou, 176, 228
Exogamy, 275

Fairbank, W., 198, 200–201
Fallow system, 50–54
Fan-sheng-chih-shu, 75
Fauna, of the loess area, 25–26
Fei-i monster, 357–358
Feng-hsiang, 271
Feng-pi-t'ou, 14
Fu Ssu-nien, 305n, 331n
Fuel, for bronze foundry, 192

Glaciation, in China, 35–37
Goat, 96, 100–101, 104–105, 108, 111, 215, 362, 406–407
Granet, M., 32
Greco-Bactrian states, 75, 390

Hai, 244
Harlan, J. R., 51n, 74n, 372, 381–383
Hemp, 81
Honan Lung-shan culture, 17, 182
Honey, 204–206
Horse, 93–94, 96, 101, 107, 355–357, 366
Horse chariot, 355–357
Hou Chi, 61
Ho-yang, 225, 279
Hsi-tin-ts'un, 81

INDEX

Hsia: chronology, 12; list of kings, 240–241, 288–289; ancestor worship, 286; as an expression of Sinitic tradition, 287–288, 350, 402–404
Hsia calendar, 386n
Hsia-chia-tien, 101, 104
Hsia Nai, 42n, 81n, 104, 126n, 312n
Hsiao-t'un, 46, 226, 228, 312
Hsien. See *Oryza sativa,* indica subspecies
Hsien-jen-tung, 124–125
Hsien-li-tun, 62
Hsin, 51–52
Hsin-yeh-ts'un, 225, 279
Hsing-p'ing, 271
Hsün-tzu: on double cropping, 84; on bees, 204; rationalization of ancestor worship, 325
Hu Hou-hsüan, 83n, 293n, 304n, 310n, 319n, 321n, 323n
Hu-hsien, 271
Hu-shu culture, 282–283, 346
Huai-nan-tzu, on wild rice, 66
Huang-niang-niang-t'ai, 179–180
Huang Sheng-chang, 8–9, 329n
Hung-shan-hou, 101, 103–104

I-Chou-shu, on origins of soybeans, 77–78
I peoples, 313, 344, 346
Indo-European languages, 260–261, 264, 405
Indo-Europeans, 357, 364
Indus valley, 44, 367–368
Irrigation, 46–48

Jao Tsung-i, 316n, 320n, 387n
Jesperson, O., 260
Jettmar, K., 217–218, 364
Jih-chao, counter-clockwise ceramic design, 171, 173
Jomon, 122–123

Kang-shang, 96–97
Karasuk culture, 214
Karlgren, B., 5n, 30n, 257, 260–264, 266, 315–316

Keng. See *Oryza sativa,* japonica subspecies
K'e-sheng-chuang II culture, 96–97, 182, 284
Kissélev, S. V., on Shang and Seima bronzes, 214, 353
Kroeber, A. L., 259–260, 285
K'u, 314, 318, 320, 344
Ku Chieh-kang, 288n
Kung Ho, regency of, 1
Kuo Mo-jo, 257 n, 299n, 300n, 306, 309, 310n, 313n, 323, 393–398
Kuo-yü, 276, 328n, 338

Lai, as weeds or Chenopodiaceae, 33; as fallow land, 53–54
Lei Hai-tsung, 3–4
Li (king of Chou), 1
Li Chi, 195, 198, 201–203, 359
Li-chi, 328n
Li-chia-ts'un, 18–19
Li K'uei, estimate of millet yields, 82–84
Li Sao, 317–318
Liang-chu culture, 16, 21, 62, 347
Liu-lin, 96, 98–99, 167
Liu Yü-hsia, 189–190, 201
Loehr, M., 176, 212–213
Loess highlands: paleoenvironment, 21–35; climate, 22; soil, 22–30, 49–51; pollen profiles, 23–30; vegetation recorded in *Book of Odes,* 30–34
Lo-han-t'ang, 95, 104
Lü-shih ch'un-ch'iu, on use of manure, 83–84
Lu state, chronology of, 4–5
Lung-shan culture, 13, 17, 73, 96, 101, 280, 284
Lungshanoid cultures, 13, 55, 280. *See also* Ch'ing-lien-kang culture; Ch'ü-chia-ling culture; Liang-chu culture; Ma-chia-yao culture; Miao-ti-kou II culture

Ma-chia-pin, 20
Ma-chia-yao culture, 17, 104, 109–110, 168–169, 172
Male heir, importance of, 323–324
Ma Tuan lin, on wild rice, 68

Mandate of Heaven, 333–338
Manure, early use of, 83–84
Matrilineal kinship: Yang-shao, 274–279
McNeill, W. H., 34n, 339n
Mei-yen, 96, 99
Mencius, 4, 326, 344, 350
Meso-America, agricultural origins, 120
Mesopotamia: agriculture, 44; pottery, 138–153; metallurgy, 191; divination, 285
Miao-ti-kou I culture, 16, 19, 160–167
Miao-ti-kou II culture, 13, 93, 100–101, 406
Millets, 18, 50; ancient nomenclature, 57. See also *Panicum miliaceum*; *Setaria italica*
Mo-tzu, on writing materials, 227
Mountain Jung people, 77–79, 348
Mulberry, 81–82

Needham, J., 234–235, 388–391
Ni (Oryza sativa perennis), 65
Numerals, 228–235

Okladnikov, A. P., 216–217, 354
O-po, 386
Ordinals, 235–246: for sexagenary cycle of day-count, 238–239; for ten-day *hsün* cycles, 238–239; for posthumous royal ceremonial names, 239–246
Ordos, style of bronze, 212n
Oryza sativa: japonica subspecies, 61–63, 70; indica subspecies, 61–63, 70
Oryza sativa perennis, 65

P'an-keng, 294, 307–308
Pan-p'o: chronology, 16, 18–19; village layouts, 272–274. *See also* Agriculture; Animal husbandry; Chinese script; Pottery; Stone implements
Panicum miliaceum, 33, 57–61, 95, 117
Pao-t'ou, 96–97
Phallic symbol, 282–283
Pig, 18, 93–107
Plastromancy, 283–285
Pleistocene climate, 21–22, 37
Plow, 114–116

Pottery: in pre-1949 Chinese archaeology, 18–19; and speculation on cultural borrowing, 122; Anau, 122, 168–169; Tripolje, 122, 168–171, 173, 362; Jomon, 122–123; Taiwan Lungshanoid, 123–124; Hsien-jen-tung, 124–125; Pan-p'o, 130–132, 136, 154–160; Miao-ti-kou I, 160–167; Ma-chia-yao, 169, 172; Pan-shan, 168; Ma-ch'ang, 169; Hsin-tien, 169; Hassuna-Halaf, 129–137, 163–164; Mesopotamia and Iran, 138–153, 155; counter-clockwise spiral design, 170–173; Andronovo, 171, 174–175
Pottery kiln: range of firing temperature, 133–135; Pan-p'o, 193–195; Shang, 195; Tepe Sialk, 195–196
Pottery shapes: Hassuna-Halaf, 129–130; Yang-shao and Lungshanoid, 130–132
Primogeniture, 291
Proto-Chinese, physical anthropological features, 38, 342–343
Proto-Ching-Man peoples, 97, 346
Proto-Tungusic peoples, 77, 345, 348, 357
Proto-Turcic peoples, 345, 357
Proto-Yüah peoples, 347
Pumpelly, R., on loess, 49

Rationalist and humanist thought, 335–338
Reed, C. A., 106, 108
Religion. *See* Ancestor worship; *Shang-ti*; *Wang-ti*; Worship of natural forces
Rice, 21, 61–73; radiocarbon dates, 61–64, 375

San-li-ch'iao I, 93, 95, 193
San-li-ch'iao II, 96, 100
Scapulimancy, 283–285
Seima culture, 213–215, 365
Setaria italica, 57, 59, 95, 104, 108–109, 117; yields in ancient China, 82–87
Sexagenary cycle, 238–239
Sha-wa-tzu, 101, 103
Shan-hai-ching, 317–320

INDEX 439

Shang: chronology, 11; system of day-count, 238–239; sacrificial system, 238–239, 289–293; list of kings, 240, 289–291; logographic principles, 246–258; grammar, 258–259; royal succession, 289–293; royal consorts, 293–294; royal sons, 294; patrimonial administration, 295–304; functionaries, 295–301; administration of outer domains, 301–305; major cities, 311–313; commoners, 296, 306–308. *See also* Bronze; Chinese script; Numerals; Ordinals; Rationalist and humanist thought
Shang-ti, 294–295, 314–321
Sheep, 93–94, 96–97, 99–104
Shih-chai-shan, 208
Shih-chi, 4, 240, 245, 286, 289, 291–292n, 374, 390–391
Shih Chang-ju, 180, 201, 300n, 310n, 355n
Shima, K., 293n, 297n, 304n, 356n
Shu. See Panicum miliaceum
Shui-ching-chu, 47–48
Shun, 320, 344, 350
Shuo-wen chieh-tzu, 65, 73, 241, 257
Siberia: pottery, 171, 174; metallurgy, 214–217
Skinner, G. W., 327
Slaves, 308–311
Sorghum, Chinese, 380–384
Southeast Asia: agriculture, 371–377; bronze, 377–378
Soviet Central Asia, 171, 216
Soybean, 76–81. *See also* Mountain Jung people
Spring wheat, 75–76
Ssu-ma Ch'ien, 4–5, 240, 374, 390
Stone implements: Li-chia-ts'un, 40; Yang-shao, 49–50; post-Yang-shao, 81–82
Su. See Setaria italica
Su Ping-ch'i, 160, 166
Sumerian script, 246–253
Sung (part of Shang tribe), 318–319
Sung state, 2
Sung-tze, 16, 20

Ta-ch'eng-shan, 96

Ta-ho-chuang, 101, 179
Ta-i, 187
Ta-pei-kou, 101, 104
Ta-tun-tzu, 16, 20, 96, 98–99, 167, 349
Ta-wen-k'ou, 13, 346
Taiwan Lungshanoid culture, 14
T'ang Lan, 231–232, 259n
T'ien, 329–330
T'ien-wen, 317–318
Tin deposits, geographic distribution of, 183–188
Ting, V. K., on loess highlands, 32
Ting-ling people, 353
Tripolje. *See* Pottery
Ts'ao-hsieh-shan, 62
Tso-chuan, 5, 46–47, 336n, 338, 351n
Tung Chung-shu: on wheat cultivation, 75; on Mandate of Heaven, 337
Tung Tso-pin, 2, 5–11, 291n, 305n, 333n
Tzu, 51–52
Tzu-ching-shan, 96–97

Urban centers, 311–313

Vavilov, N. I., 58–59, 63
Village layouts: Yang-shao, 271–273; Jarmo, 272

Wan Chia-pao, 201–203
Wang Kuo-wei, 8–9, 243n, 298n, 314–315n, 345n
Wang Li: on archaic Chinese grammar, 258; on pre-Shang Chinese language, 402
Wang-ti, 294
Water buffalo, 93, 99
Wen (king of Chou), 330, 344
Wen-hsüan, 31
Wheat: etymology, 73–74; ancient Chinese methods of cultivation, 75–76; yields, 86–87; introduction into China, 352–353
Wild rice, literary records of, 65–69
Worship of natural forces, 320
Writing materials, 226–228
Wu (king of Chou), 4
Wu Shan-ching, 20

Wu-ting, 186–187, 278, 301, 305, 356
Wu-wei, 179

Yabuuchi, K., 9
Yang-shao culture. *See* Pan-p'o; Miao-ti-kou I

Yang-shao people: origins, 35–42; physical features, 38–39
Yen-shih, 176, 186, 190, 211
Yü, 51–52
Yü Hsing-wu, 46n, 65n, 303n, 308n, 319n, 380n